# Organizational Transformation and Learning

# Organizational Transformation and Learning

## A Cybernetic Approach to Management

Raul Espejo[1]
Werner Schuhmann[2]
Markus Schwaninger[3]
Ubaldo Bilello[4]

(1) University of Humberside, Hull, UK and Syncho Ltd, Birmingham, UK
(2) University of Mannheim, Mannheim, Germany
(3) Institute of Management, University of St Gallen, Switzerland
(4) Hoechst A. G. Frankfurt, Germany

## JOHN WILEY & SONS
Chichester · New York · Brisbane · Toronto · Singapore

Copyright © 1996 by John Wiley & Sons Ltd,
              Baffins Lane, Chichester,
              West Sussex PO19 1UD, England

              National     01243 779777
              International (+44) 1243 779777

Reprinted January 1997

*Other Wiley Editorial Offices*

John Wiley & Sons, Inc., 605 Third Avenue,
New York, NY 10158-0012, USA

Jacaranda Wiley Ltd, 33 Park Road, Milton,
Queensland 4064, Australia

John Wiley & Sons (Canada) Ltd, 22 Worcester Road,
Rexdale, Ontario M9W 1L1, Canada

John Wiley & Sons (Asia) Pte Ltd, 2 Clementi Loop #02–01,
Jin Xing, Distripark, Singapore 129809

*Library of Congress Cataloging-in-Publication Data*
Organizational transformation and learning : a cybernetic approach to
    management / Raul Espejo . . . [et al.].
        p.   cm.
    Includes bibliographical references and index.
    ISBN 0-471-96182-5 (cloth)
    1.  Organizational change.   2.   Organizational learning.
    3.   Strategic planning.   I. Espejo, Raul.
    HD58.8.O753   1996
    658.4'06—dc20                                    95–43598
                                                        CIP

*British Library Cataloguing in Publication Data*
A catalogue record for this book is available from the British Library

ISBN 0-471-96182-5

Typeset in 10/12pt Palatino by Dorwyn Ltd, Rowlands Castle, Hants
Printed and bound in Great Britain by Bookcraft (Bath) Ltd
This book is printed on acid-free paper responsibly manufactured from sustainable forestation, for which
at least two trees are planted for each one used for paper production.

# Contents

Contents _____ vii

# Preface

This book is the outcome of collaborative work among the authors over a number of years. It began at the Science Park of Aston University, Birmingham, UK, in May 1988, where two of us agreed to work together. The other two joined the group later that year. Two of us are mainly academics, the other two mainly practitioners, but all share a passion for good theory and good practice; this has been the glue that has kept us together.

The book is both theoretical and practical. We believe that good management and organization requires a good theoretical background. Management is too important to be left to intuition and good common sense. It helps to have both; most certainly they are not enough.

This, indeed has been the dilemma for all of us. We would like to communicate our experiences to as many managers as possible, but we also know that today's managers are increasingly busy and less inclined to cope with difficult theoretical propositions. Yet for these very reasons, the managers to whom this book may be less appealing are the ones we seek to address in order to make their jobs, and the organizations they work for, more satisfying and humane.

This kind of circular causality is at the core of this book. The theory upon which it is based is precisely a theory about how to manage complexity. We are aware we have found neither an easy solution to the problems of management and organization nor an easy way to communicate it. This may disappoint some people. We do not apologize; we can only say that those who make the effort to study it are likely to have a useful and valuable learning experience.

Readers can be assured that the ideas we present have been worked out in practice. Throughout, we have either applied them in our own practice or collaborated with people in several large corporations who have tested them in their own practice. Our work has taken place at the corporate, divisional, business-unit and plant levels. The experience has been very positive. We have, of course, found different reactions but those who have endured the process have recognized the value of the learning process. Overall, we are confident that these ideas add value to people's understanding of their organization and action.

We believe that Part One of the book will resonate with people's current understanding of managerial issues. In fact it was based on interviews with managers. Part Two, the more theoretical part of the book develops and explains systems and cybernetic ideas. Part Three applies these ideas to strategic and information management.

Though stylistically Chapter 4 is out of line with the rest of Part Two and the book in general, we felt the need to keep it as it is. Originally it was intended as a handbook that would explain, with graphical support, basic cybernetic ideas. This intent of the chapter has been kept. Though theoretical in nature it makes few references to other work. The content of this chapter is in the tradition of second order cybernetics, in particular of Humberto Maturana and Francisco Varela's work. We want to acknowledge and thank them for this most significant influence. We were also influenced by Fernando Flores' work in conversation theory and entrepreneurship. More than specific books or papers, their influence was the outcome of personal interactions between them and one of us.

Chapter 5 is an attempt to communicate the viable system model. The basic ideas of this chapter have been presented elsewhere; however, the application of the viable system model (VSM) to a business unit is original and hopefully a contribution to our current understanding of the VSM.

Antonia Gill, of Syncho Ltd, helped in the preparation of these last two chapters. Rob Gilmore, also of Syncho Ltd, helped in discussions and the preparation of the figures of Chapter 4.

Chapter 6 has a similar intent to Chapter 5. However, here the theoretical and practical sides are closely intertwined. The theoretical part is based on a learning model elaborated by Daniel Kim in the article 'The link between individual and organizational learning' that appeared in the *Sloan Management Review*, Fall 1993. The applied side is by and large based on the authors' experiences and research. This model is revisited in Chapter 7 where learning is discussed using the ideas of complexity. This chapter's framework has emerged from much discussion of one of the authors with Dr Nigel Howard.

Chapter 8 in particular owes much to the influence of A. Gaelweiler the German strategic thinker, upon one of the authors.

As with most enterprises, many people have had an influence on the process. Two people we need to mention here. Both had, in very different ways, a fundamental role in the production of this book. One is Stafford Beer. Though he had no direct involvement in its production there is no doubt in our minds that his presence, both as a friend and as chairman of Syncho Ltd, provided us with a strong cohesive force. Indeed, we think this book is an extension of his work—though we accept full responsibility for its content. The other is Nigel Howard who, in fact, had direct involvement in the production of the book. His editorial support, not to mention his insightful contributions and comments, were invaluable in its final production.

Though we do not underestimate the complexity of this book, and accept that it demands much from the reader, we think it is primarily directed toward advanced practitioners of management, in search of continual progress for their organizations. However, scholars, including researchers and students of management science, should also find valuable insights in it.

Raul Espejo
Werner Schuhmann
Markus Schwaninger
Ubaldo Bilello
*July, 1995*

# Introduction

The dazzling rate of change in our age confronts business with challenges of a new order.

Thinkers and 'gurus' see a need for entirely new modes of management in the 'nanosecond nineties' (Peters, 1992)—dominated by the 'three Cs'—customers, competition and change (Hammer and Champy, 1993).

New approaches are recommended under labels such as:

- 'integrated management'
- 'ecological management'
- 'human resources management'
- 'total quality management'
- 'information management'.

Some go further, demanding that the organization be reconceptualized and evolve in entirely new ways. They postulate the need for:

- 'organizational change' or 'corporate transformation'
- 'the learning organization'
- 'organizational architecture'
- 'the virtual corporation'
- 'business process redesign' or 're-engineering the corporation'.

This is not a collection of fads; we shall not try to list the enormous amount of literature that is merely faddish. These are valuable approaches. Important concepts and heuristics are developed under these labels.

Where then is the thread that connects these schools? Is there one? Are these lines of thought in any way commensurable?

We shall argue that, when viewed from a cybernetic stance, they are linked by a common thread. Cybernetics—the science of communication and control—can and should be used to connect these various approaches by presenting them in a common language.

Seen from such a perspective, the common purpose of these approaches boils down to the following issues:

- How can organizations cope with increasing environmental complexity?
- How can they maintain viability and develop further at the same time?
- How can organizational action become more effective?

- How can managers cope with increasing organizational complexity?
- How can their action become more effective?

Complexity is the core issue of organizational concern for the age we have entered: not just for the year 2000, but for the new century we are about to enter. The purpose of this book is showing, both theoretically and practically, how organizational and managerial cybernetics can contribute to this core issue. We believe that the contents of this book provide the thread to relate the above approaches. In a nutshell this book offers a holistic view of both organizations and individual actions; it provides a framework to relate and organize the myriad activities natural to today's businesses.

We think organizational transformation begins with individual transformation and this book is intended as a means for individual transformation. The book offers a rich conceptual framework and also a wealth of practice. Our, perhaps ambitious, expectation is that this framework, intertwined with practice, will change the reader's appreciation of their role in organizations and make their actions more effective. This should be a platform for an enabling contribution to the organization and for achieving more humane and successful organizations.

## STRUCTURE

The book is organized into three parts.

The first will break down the core issue of complexity into a series of sub-issues or issues of organizational concern. As we will explain later the seven issues we develop in Part One emerged from conversations with managers. The issue of identity is critical; what kind of relationships are we developing with our stakeholders? what business are we in? what are our core competencies? This is followed by the issue of adaptation, that is of 'inventing the corporation' in the context of a highly changeable environment. Perhaps a major change of attitude in recent years is managers' increased awareness that they have to, and can, leverage fundamental change. Technological developments and improved communications are seen as enablers, yet managing these change processes remains as a major issue of concern. This issue relates very closely with the third one in our list. Implementing change requires not only resources but also appropriate interactions among the stakeholders. There is fundamental agreement that hierarchical structures are inadequate to get the best out of people, yet even if we espouse non-hierarchical management the chances are that we will behave autocratically. Rather than functional management, today's emphasis is in process management. Managers see the advantage of avoiding bureaucratic constraints and supporting the natural flow of work, yet often the structures they support contradict this view. This is another issue we explore.

The last three issues of concern in Part One are people's issues. They express the increasing realization that it is people that learn and experience the exhilarating rate of change, organizations can only learn through these people. Therefore people and relationship issues are increasing in significance. In Chapter 2 we explore, supported by existing frameworks, human resources management problems, learning difficulties, and interactions with the environment.

As we discuss the above issues we extract a set of postulates for effective management and organization.

Part Two will develop a new language to deal with these issues: a cybernetic framework with particular emphasis on human action in an organizational context. It is in this part that we make our contribution to organization and management theory. Chapter 3 offers an introduction to systemic/cybernetic concepts. We present them in the traditional way they may be encountered in the existing literature. It is only in Chapter 4 that we present these concepts from a different epistemological perspective. The shift we make apparent in this chapter is from the view of social systems as independent entities, external to us, the subjects of our control efforts, to a view in which we appear as the actors producing these very systems. There is a circular causality; we create, invent the organizations that provide the context for the very actions creating, inventing, these organizations. This is a fundamental change in perspective; it brings to the fore our contribution to organizational processes; now we understand that control is by and large intrinsic control. We control as we create organizational processes. This point makes apparent that control is a distributed phenomenon, not something that is exercised by a controller once the task is finished or something that is periodically checked. Control is real time, it is intrinsic to our own actions, and therefore it is the outcome of the myriad activities of all the organizational participants and not of a few managers. Chapter 4 develops the language to understand this epistemology.

An implication of this epistemology is the concept of 'recursive organization'. We argue not only for autonomous units within autonomous units, something that to a larger or lesser degree will always be the case in complex organizations, but for an effective distribution of discretion in order to release people's potentials. Put simply, it is impossible to control everything from the top; control is intrinsic to our actions. However, the cost of autonomy may be unnecessarily high, either in the form of unnecessary games of deception or by the squandering of resources. Chapter 5 offers the viable system model as a heuristic to realize recursive organizations. The model helps to understand the implications of effective autonomous units within effective autonomous units. These ideas are explored with reference to a business unit of a large corporation.

The emphasis on people and their actions creates the need to understand better their learning processes and their co-ordination of actions. We do this in great depth in Chapters 6 and 7. In Chapter 6 we use a model for individual and organizational learning to explore cases of ineffective learning. It is with this understanding that we move into more theoretical grounds and produce a framework for individual and organizational learning based on the management of complexity. The full implications of this framework are seen when we introduce the cybernetic methodology; this methodology allows us to relate each individual learning loop to its structural context, thus making possible a debate of the resources and relations necessary to make more likely the learning process.

Part Three will show how the new language as developed in Part Two can be applied to strategic management. We call this part 'recursive management'. This part makes use of the ideas of complexity, learning and recursive organization. Since the platform for this work was given by large corporations, in this part we apply these ideas to such corporations. However the theoretical framework applies equally to large and small organizations.

Chapter 8 addresses the fundamental issue of performance. It develops a framework for strategic management, which puts organizational development and creation of value potentials as pre-controls to profits. In other words it shows how to relate the long and short term when measuring performance. This chapter offers a comprehensive approach to relate strategy to structure and information management.

It is only in Chapter 9 that we can appreciate the full potentials of the framework created in Chapter 8. Chapter 9 develops the idea of primary business processes. The idea of business processes embedded within business processes becomes clear at the same time that the notion of a subsuming organization is developed. It becomes apparent that to justify an autonomous unit it should add value to the business processes subsumed in its structure, that is, to the business processes of its embedded autonomous units. An important outcome of this discussion is the concept of 'recursive business processes'. In this chapter we offer a recursive template to manage business processes and also an outline of the information requirements for their management.

Chapter 10, the last chapter of Part Three, makes the distinction between management and meta-management. This is a necessary distinction emerging from the ideas of recursive organization and management. Each level of management has to manage on the one hand, the value adding of its total business, in the case of Chapter 10, of the corporation as a whole, and on the other, the value added by its embedded autonomous units. The latter is what we call meta-management; that is, creating the conditions to align the activities of the embedded units with the activities of the total organization. This is the meaning of managing cohesion.

Finally, in the conclusions we go back to the postulates of management, as stated in Part One, and discuss them using the new language, as outlined in Part Two and applied in Part Three.

## METHODOLOGY

The book is grounded both in empirical and in theoretical work. Empirical studies were carried out in five medium- to large-size organizations. Three of these were industrial, two in the services sector. The studies were in the context of long-term efforts to redesign structures and management systems in these organizations.

Several projects were undertaken in these organizations in the period 1988–95. In each of the five organizations these projects ranged over approximately the same time span.

The project teams were typically composed of a core group of line managers and staff from inside the firm, complemented—in the major projects—by two external consultants. This group of persons remained constant over time, but it was completed flexibly by specialists and users, according to the respective project mission. Project activities were typically supervised by a steering committee which consisted of one top manager plus one high level manager and one or two consultants, who were also members of several project teams.

To be more concrete, let us enumerate the main projects developed over a time span of six years, in the largest one of the organizations studied:

1. organizational diagnosis and redesign, including implementation;
2. design and implementation of a new management information system;
3. conception and implementation of a structure for environmental responsibility;
4. re-engineering of primary business processes.

During the projects carried out in three of the five organizations, a certain highly formalized series of contacts was realized. This consisted of the following events:

1. Three seminars for managers and staff specialists, taking place in 1988. The object of these seminars was to teach the conceptual foundations of cybernetic management. About 70 members of the organizations, involving various functions from different locations in two countries, were involved in these three-day events.
2. A series of interviews, involving participants in those seminars as well as a number of extra individuals who had not been available for the seminars but would be involved in the projects as users. These were conducted in 1989. Altogether, 45 persons were interviewed, most of them two or more times, on subjects relevant to organizational diagnosis and MIS design.
3. Working sessions with project teams and steering committees; also workshops involving further personnel.
4. After substantial project work of several years, selected in-depth interviews with seven persons who were key to the organizational transformation processes. These took place in 1992 and 1993 and provided some degree of formal closure.

Contacts with the members of the fourth and fifth organization were less formalized. However, some formal events can be identified in each one of them:

1. A management seminar in 1989.
2. Working sessions with key personnel, taking place in the period 1988–95.
3. In-depth follow-up interviews with one key manager, in 1992 and 1993 respectively.

All these events were thoroughly documented. For each working session and workshop, a protocol was printed. The interviews taking place in 1989 were documented with a detailed protocol of each, including suggestions made by interviewees and addenda including detailed descriptions of the organizational processes in which they were involved. Here are some details of the last round of in-depth interviews during 1992–3.

Interviewees were asked to tell 'stories' about problems they encountered in their day-to-day work. They were then requested to deliberate about issues that seemed to give room for improvement.

The sample of interviewees was not as representative as those in the first round, taken in 1989. However, the interlocutors came from a broad range of different functions:

- director of a multi-billion D-marks division,
- assistant to the director,
- head of an SBU,
- head of production of another SBU,
- co-director of an international joint venture,
- quality manager of a multi-billion D-marks division,
- head of a corporate informatics unit.

The duration of the interviews ranged from 100 to 240 minutes. The average duration was 140 minutes. All interviews were transcribed and then reviewed.

Our empirical data consisted of more than the interview protocols. The task forces also produced various products used in the process of organizational transformation e.g.:

- reports,
- protocols and action plans of task force sessions,
- charts of organization structures and management systems and diagrams of business processes,
- MIS software and documentation.

Such is our empirical data. The cybernetic theory used in carrying out these projects and analysing the data will be explained in the book itself.

The book is the outcome of a reflective process and intellectual interaction between four persons, each of whom belonged to steering committees or task forces in each of the five organizations. The fact that they had these functions to fulfil implied that they viewed what they were doing simultaneously from two perspectives:

- An insider's perspective, that of a member of a firm who is aiming at its progress.
- An outsider's perspective, pertaining to a researcher interested in theoretical aspects of the process.

There is, of course, a high degree of synergy between these perspectives, permitting mutual fertilization.

All four authors maintained their theoretical perspective throughout by continually remaining 'up-to-date' with state-of-the-art management literature and by authoring and editing several books in the period since the beginning of the project. These books are naturally of special interest in relation to this work. They include Espejo and Harnden (1989a); Espejo and Schwaninger (1993); Schuhmann (1991) and Schwaninger (1994a).

# Part One

# Issues for Today's Organizations

# Summary of Part One

This book offers a principled approach to critical issues confronting today's organizations. Part One focuses on identifying these issues.

How do we identify them? Partly from empirical research. We interviewed key people in companies supporting our work. They expressed their concerns and expectations.

However, in Part One our discussion of the issues will be explicitly grounded in current organizational and management theories. Following the methodology described in the introduction, we take into account more than the partial results obtained from project work and empirical investigations in the reference companies. We relate our empirical findings both to experiences gained on projects with other companies and to insights from state-of-the art management literature.

## A PARADIGM SHIFT

From the management literature of the last few years, it is clear that substantial innovations are taking place. We are in the midst of a paradigm shift.

Many authors have carved out specific aspects of this shift. Synoptic tables are drawn up highlighting 'new' values, norms, modes or techniques.

We will adopt a general management stance and try to distil certain 'postulates' as to the nature of management in today's world from this cornucopia of expert recommendations. Our aim: to find postulates that reflect 'state-of-the-art' management—whether or not these are fully embodied in the day-to-day practice of most companies.

In summarizing the advice given to state-of-the-art managers, we shall admittedly be selective. We shall not replicate advice given elsewhere. Inevitably, we will concentrate on the kind of advice we ourselves would give. Some such personal component is unavoidable in any summary. Any arbitrariness will be eliminated in later chapters by laying open our criteria of choice.

For the time being we appeal to the reader's patience. Part One sets the stage for what is to follow. The postulates and issues isolated here are revisited later in Chapter 11 using the conceptual apparatus set out in Part Two.

This order of presentation is inductive. As such, we hope it will be more useful to the reader than a deductive approach. The latter would mean first making our criteria transparent, then finding the management postulates they lead to. Instead, we start from what we observe in state-of-the-art management practice, with the aim of introducing more advanced tools as a way of understanding it better. In this way we begin with material the reader will be relatively familiar with, and offer motivation for a deeper understanding.

## EIGHT KEY ISSUES

Our interview protocols—particularly those from the last round of in-depth interviews—show a condensation of concern around eight general issues:

1. identity
2. adaptation—inventing the corporation
3. implementation—inventing *in* the corporation
4. structure and process
5. understanding organizations better
6. change, transformation and learning
7. human resources management—people in organizations
8. ecological responsibility.

Relative to each issue, the managers we interviewed saw shortcomings in current organizational processes. Of course, any shortcoming represents, at the same time, a potential for improvement—as our managers knew. Hence, while our interviews did not aim at and could not provide full exploration of related possibilities, they did give valuable hints as to where improvements could be found. Our discussion reflects these.

Of the eight issues, five focus most clearly on the structure of the organization. These are:

1. identity
2. adaptation—inventing the corporation
3. implementation—inventing in the corporation
4. structure and process
5. understanding organizations better.

We discuss these in Chapter 1. The other three issues are more to do with people and the problem of organizational transformation:

6. change, transformation and learning
7. human resources management: people in organizations
8. ecological responsibility.

These are discussed in Chapter 2.

# Chapter 1

# Organization Structure

## ISSUE: 'IDENTITY'

One postulate is axiomatic to the practice of contemporary management:

Excellent organizational performance requires delivering high value to all stakeholders.

In practice, not all organizations can be excellent at all times. In principle, all could excel. In order not only to survive but to survive with quality each must be 'world champion in something'. It is the task of every leader to aim at realizing excellence; that is, 'best-in-the-world' (or 'best-in-class' or 'world-class') status for the unit for which he or she is responsible. To do this they must maintain high levels of aspiration and instil them in their units.

Clarity about the specific identity of the organization, of the role it fulfils within the larger whole, is therefore essential:

- What makes it unique? In which activities is it best-in-the-world (or best-in-class)?
- What are its strengths, core competencies or capabilities?
- What are the principles and values underlying its functioning?
- What kind of value can it deliver to its customers?
- What kind of value can it deliver to other stakeholders? These include key constituencies such as employees, stockholders or, in some cases, the general public.

### The Need For Vision

It is, however, dangerous to stick too closely to the actual, current identity of one's firm. Outstanding corporate development has to be fuelled by a strong 'magnet'; that is, a clear vision of the potential, as opposed to the actual identity of the organization:

- What could it be?
- What will it be one day?
- What must it become? and, most important:
- What do we want it to become?

According to Nanus (1992, p. 3):

> There is no more powerful engine driving an organization toward excellence and long-range success than an attractive, worthwhile and achievable vision of the future, widely shared . . . Quite simply, a vision is a realistic, credible, attractive future for your organization.

A good vision is a prod that—if it is really powerful—creates a pull. It attracts commitment and energizes people, creates meaning in workers' lives, establishes a standard of excellence and creates a bridge between present and future.

Note a dilemma related to vision. The more concrete one's vision, the more probable its realization. On the other hand, a vision that is too concrete sooner or later turns out to be a 'straitjacket'.

A good vision has some distinctive features that may be checked by answering the following list of questions—an extension of those given by Nanus (1992, p. 120):

- To what extent is it innovative and future-oriented?
- To what extent is it *utopian*; that is, is it likely to lead to a clearly better future for the organization?
- To what extent is it *appropriate* for the organization; that is, does it fit in with the organization's culture, values and history?
- To what extent does it reach out for new dimensions (*stretch*)? Does it set standards of excellence and reflect high ideals and aspirations?
- To what extent does it *clarify purpose* and direction? Does it include measurable objectives? Is it apt to orientate the operations of the company?
- To what extent will it *inspire enthusiasm* and encourage commitment?
- To what extent does it *reflect the uniqueness* of the organization, its identity and core competencies?
- Does it *change the rules* of the business or industry?
- Is it ambitious and creative enough?

Good vision statements have sharp edges. They contain no platitudes—a point emphasized by Hammer and Champy (1993, p. 156). Usually they require to be concretized further by developing strategies—paths for putting the vision into practice. Each unit of the organization must develop its specific contribution to the realization of the vision.

Indeed, vision is needed at all levels of an organization. Summing up:

> Organizations must develop vision and a strategic management in order to create value potentials. This applies to all structural levels.

## Overlapping Borders

In the age of information technology corporations become 'borderless' in the sense that traditional boundaries become permeable. Boundaries between established industries are falling down. Data integration and networks along the value chain become increasingly a reality. Communication technology makes it possible to overcome traditional limitations.

Thus, increasingly, problems faced by corporations transcend their individual capabilities. Alliances have to be realized to cope with such challenges.

These may include all kinds of connections, co-operations, affiliations, partnerships, associations and joint ventures with suppliers, customers, distributors and other outsourcing partners, institutions and even competitors. The allies, in such cases, 'get in the same boat'. Domains of common interest and responsibility emerge. Effective communication is an imperative for the building of trustworthiness and high performance in these ventures.

**Relationships with stakeholders require effective communications, creating overlapping domains of interest and common responsibility.**

### Deficiencies In Practice

Measured against these theoretical possibilities, organizations often fall short. Many lack awareness of the issues we have discussed.

Few have a clear picture of their identity. Often there are differences in this respect as between the different levels of an organization. In principle, each unit at any level should make transparent the role it fulfils within the more comprehensive system. In practice, one finds nebulous ideas of identity at the corporate level in organizations even when, at lower levels, the strategic business units (SBUs) have developed powerful and lucid identities.

SBUs in one large corporation knew very well, in general, what their customers wanted, what their strengths and weaknesses were, and what were their real missions. But the signals that SBUs got from corporate management were confusing. Basically, corporate management could not decide whether the corporation should be an industrial producer with high backward integration or a highly sophisticated marketing force with an emphasis on knowledge organization. Yet everyone had a vague presentiment that they could not be both.

In other cases, the presentiment 'we can't be both' did not exist; or if it did, it was suppressed. An informatics services unit was established as a profit centre in a particular firm—but was not allowed to offer its services on the external market . . .

Here is a list of some of the problems we came across in our interviews and observations:

- An inflexible 'staff unit mentality' was fostered by internal work regulations. Result: an international videoconference scheduled for 17.30 could not be held because, according to internal regulations, people 'knocked off' at 16.15.
- External consultants were awarded a 'confidence bonus' not given to internal ones, who were thus treated unfairly.
- Experts were 'headhunted' from operations units where they were most needed.
- Corporate accounting principles prohibited an informatics department from generating profits or losses.

These cases are of a very different order, but show the same basic deficiency. In each, visions are too vague!

### The Need For Redefinition

Often the achievement of identity is blocked by a wrong label. A manager from the specialities division of an industrial firm:

The definitions of our business units (BUs) are product-oriented. Therefore potentials not yet present in our product range remain indefinite, or excluded from consideration. We have BUs for product A, product B, product C. As a result, we do not think about other types of specialities. Nobody is in charge of specialities that go beyond our BU-structure . . . We have transposed the operational structure onto our strategy The result is that we exclude from our operations all the things that we don't do today

Units such as these have locked themselves in through a wrong label. They can only be liberated from this lock-in by a redefinition of their identities.

# ISSUE: 'ADAPTATION—INVENTING THE CORPORATION'

Clearly, an organization must adapt in order to survive and prosper, particularly as change continually accelerates. Adaptation, however, may be seen as reactive. 'Adapt when a threat is perceived. Till then, do nothing.'

That is not how we understand adaptation. Adaptation is the process by which an organization improves its fit with its milieu through mutual adjustment. Organizations undergo internal change not only when their existing forms are no longer viable in a given environment, but also when new possibilities are articulated. By their adaptive responses they may modify their environments or procure entirely new ones.

For such proactive adaptation, especially, an organization needs long term goals that establish for it a direction and priorities of action. We come back to a postulate already found necessary for achieving a sustainable identity:

Organizations must develop vision and a strategic management in order to create value potentials. This applies to all structural levels.

Throughout, awareness, foresight and responsiveness are required, as well as management functions that enable the organization to stay on course.

A key to creating new possibilities at the corporate level is the process of strategy-making: creating new opportunities, reshaping modes of doing business, changing the 'rules of the game', discerning core competencies (or core capabilities), and building them up through a long term effort. See Prahalad and Hamel (1990) and Stalk, Evans and Shulman (1992). However, creating potentials is an issue which also concerns the sub-units of an organization.

## Practical Deficiencies Related To Structure

That, in brief, is the concept of adaptation. The practice of many organizations shows serious shortcomings.

Poor adaptation at three levels—corporate, divisional, and SBU—is associated with the following diagnostic signs:

*Signs Of Poor Corporate Adaptation:*

- There is lack of direction. Transparent global goals are missing.
- Investment policies are not focused on the corporate level, but on SBUs.

- Investments are approved more on the basis of the 'watering-can principle' than of strategic considerations; that is, instead of concentrating on priorities, investments are allocated evenly, randomly or in a manner dictated by political opportunism.
- Corporate management is involved in the details of SBU plans.

*Signs Of Poor Divisional Adaptation:*

- There is no clear strategy for the division. 'Strategy' is in effect the sum of SBU plans.
- Adaptation is seen in terms of R&D, lacking a broader concept of innovation, e.g. one that would include organizational requirements.
- The role of the division as intermediary between the corporate and SBU levels is ill-defined.
- There is no strategy that would provide a focus for SBUs' strategic processes.

*Signs Of Poor SBU Adaptation:*

- Strategy is implicitly defined at corporate level. The corporate board approves investment budgets for SBUs two levels below.
- Criteria for investment decisions are operational rather than strategic; for example, poor operational performance is likely to reduce an SBU's chances of receiving investment.
- Emphasis of adaptation is on R&D, with little thought for broader requirements.
- Standards of SBU's strategy formulations are uneven.
- Plans are found that are exclusively oriented toward operations.
- SBUs fall into the 'specialization trap'; that is, overall adaptability is reduced by concentrating on high value products.
- A symptom already noted in our discussion of 'identity': product-oriented definitions of BUs lead to potentials not yet captured in the current product range remaining excluded from consideration. The line manager quoted above expanded on this point: 'There are BUs for NB, NC and NN. That is why we do not think about other types of N. Nobody is in charge of applications, technologies or products going beyond our BU-structure.'
- Lack of direction leads to investments being made that later turn out to be failures.

In each case we see that the structure in place—meaning, the expectations that members of the organization have toward each other—fails to support effective adaptation. As a result, people are overwhelmed by the complexity they have to cope with. We can therefore state the postulate:

Effective structures are a fundamental requirement to manage complexity.
They allow organizations to create opportunities for themselves as well as to respond to disturbances and change.

## Complexity And Customer Orientation

A main theme of this book is that a high degree of appropriate complexity—relevant complexity at each organizational level—is a prerequisite for excellent performance.

One sign of high, appropriate complexity is an organization's orientation to its customers and markets:

**People in organizations need to develop an appreciation of the meaning of customer and market orientation.**

Crosby (1992, p. 16) foresees that in the 21st century

> . . . the only absolutely essential management characteristic will be to acquire the ability to run an organization that deliberately gives its customers exactly what they have been led to expect and does it with pleasant efficiency.

The organization needs to know what its customers want; but this, though necessary, is not sufficient.

Customers' wants change. The organization needs to have profound knowledge of the customer's problems. Such knowledge is future-oriented, leading to a deeper understanding of what customers will need than they themselves could possibly have.

Customer satisfaction must be monitored continuously so that changing expectations are anticipated. The challenge, particularly with consumer goods, is often to go beyond merely satisfying customers—it is to exceed their expectations and attach them emotionally to the firm's product.

Many firms we have contacted were aware of deficiencies in customer service. To quote one line manager: 'We talk a lot about service and customer-supplier-relationships, but often we're quite distant from this orientation'. In his case, the old central sales department had been 'reorganized' to increase customer awareness. However, the structure did not change; there was no decentralization of resources into SBUs. The main result, therefore, was a new name. The sales department was called a 'customer service unit'.

A customer-oriented organization deals with increased complexity. There is no such thing any more as 'the customer'. There are many customers, with specific needs and wishes. New organizational approaches are needed to make customization possible. New systems are required that will feed customer data back into the organization fast, reliably, and in a form enabling sophisticated analysis.

## The Adaptive Significance Of Customer Orientation

Why the stress on customers? How does this make organizations more adaptive?

Customer orientation can be seen as an example of a general truth. It is necessary for adaptation that individuals and organizational units should be able to define their actions in terms of the larger context to which they belong. A 'customer' is not necessarily an external party; it is, in general, the next unit to which one is linked. Those that see their purpose as serving the narrow interests of a functional department will be relatively unwilling or unable to take advantage of opportunities or respond to threats that face the system upon which they depend.

The concept of customer orientation enables individuals and sub-units to define their actions as part of their firm's interaction with its environment.

The most striking recent need for the organization as a whole to consider its environment in order to adapt has been raised by the ecological challenge. The issue is so important that we later devote a separate section to it.

# ISSUE: 'IMPLEMENTATION—INVENTING IN THE CORPORATION'

A vision or strategy is only as good as its implementation.

The ultimate consequence of inadequate implementation is breakdown—a possibility that may not be far away. Particularly in service and knowledge businesses, quite small failures can have disastrous implications. For example, if an information loop between a salesperson and customer is not closed by a secretary, the result may be the crack-up of a long-term business relationship.

Implementation must be adequate at more than one level.

Organizations have to adhere steadfastly to their core values in realizing their visions. This implies going beyond mere efficiency and profit-orientation.

Efficiency—measured by the relation between input and output within a given operation—is an outcome of proper implementation. But implementation is more than efficiency. We must be concerned, in the first place, with implementing the right operation.

A top manager told us:

> We suffer from efficiency paranoia. Our management has good capacity to make processes more efficient. . . . Measured processes are the obvious ones, where rationalization takes place. That's where we are good, but most of our higher managers lack a strategic framework.

The adequacy of implementation must be judged not only in the light of operative, but primarily of strategic and normative orientators. If we plan a rationalization programme we have to consider all three levels.

- Operational level: What will be the gain in cost efficiency?
- Strategic level: How will our core capability be affected? Will there be any impact on our competitiveness in terms, for example, of customer benefit?
- Normative level: Will the value delivered to stakeholders be impaired? Is the programme compatible with our core values, e.g. our principles of environmental responsibility?

Appropriate judgement in relation to all three levels requires profound knowledge of the structures and generative mechanisms underlying daily events. The individuals responsible for implementation have a growing need for appropriate conceptual knowledge. Education is the essential lever for effectiveness!

## Implementation And Quality Management

The management of quality, already discussed under the adaptation issue, is a way of tackling many implementation problems. For adequate implementation:

Organizations need to foster quality ('fitness for purpose') and continual improvement in all their activities; that is, they need to do better what they already do.

Quality management has been a concern of Western firms since the early 1980s—earlier in Japan (Deming, 1986). 'Quality', broadly defined, concerns much more than the immediate properties of products and services. It relates to all functions, each level, and every single person involved in a company. 'Quality' is the delight or benefit experienced by customers in relation to the products they receive from a supplier—the degree to which the attributes of the supplier's product match or exceed the customer's expectations.

Quality, therefore, is a complex property of goods or services that makes them fit for a purpose. The International Standards Organization (1988) defines it as:

> the totality of features and characteristics of a product or service that bear on its ability to satisfy stated or implied needs.

This definition implies aspects such as 'conformance to requirements'—Crosby (1984)—or 'fitness for use'—Juran (1989). Quality emerges or vanishes wherever implementation takes place. Very dangerous instances are where quality erodes slowly and imperceptibly.

Approaches to quality management have evolved from 'quality control' through 'quality assurance' to a comprehensive philosophy of 'Total Quality Management' (TQM). The latter embraces most of the techniques that have been developed as quality management has evolved. Thus state-of-the-art quality management includes feedback-based quality control and proactive quality assurance at the same time, and pervades all sectors of an organization.

The commonly-accepted principles of TQM are summarized in Principles of Total Quality Management.

---

## PRINCIPLES OF TOTAL QUALITY MANAGEMENT

(a) There must be agreed requirements for both internal and external customers.

(b) Customer's requirements must be met first time, every time.

(c) Quality improvement will reduce waste and total costs.

(d) There must be a focus on the prevention of problems, rather than an acceptance of coping in a fire-fighting manner.

(e) Quality improvement can result only from planned management action.

(f) Every job must add value.

(g) Everybody must be involved at all levels and across all functions.

(h) There must be an emphasis on measurement to help assess and meet requirements and objectives.

(i) A culture of continuous improvement must be established.

(j) An emphasis should be placed on promoting creativity.

Source: Flood (1993, p. 147f.)

---

The focus of these principles is on customers and improvement. However, 'continuous improvement', if concerned exclusively with the improvement of existing processes, may not suffice. As we will see under the change issue, progress is needed, be it evolutionary or revolutionary, continuous or discontinuous. The long-range component of quality management may call for a discontinuous approach, if fitness to purpose cannot be realized by the extant process. In such cases, 'second-order' change through process redesign is necessary; this is explored further in Chapter 2.

A comprehensive view of quality management is still rare in practice. To quote an interviewee

> Our quality is high, but there are some defects and complaints. Quality management systems are good, ISO certification is proceeding well. However, we still look at each case of damage individually; it is still difficult to trace patterns of behaviour, accumulations and critical factors for quality. We get accuracy of order fulfilment only once a month.

The symptoms collected across the interviews often suggest that while people intellectually embrace the idea of total quality, in practice they limit their actions to inspection. This impression is corroborated by one of the world leaders in quality management—Crosby (1992):

> People are so busy working on techniques such as 'building teams', and doing statistical process control, that they never get around to actually learning how to build prevention into their organization.

### Customer–Supplier Relationships

In a state-of-the-art approach to 'total quality', all relationships in an organization are seen as customer–supplier relationships. Developing a customer-orientated mentality is seen as necessary not only in the departments that officially deal with marketing. That mentality must be diffused across the company. It must be embodied—and living—in all units at all levels.

The main concern of a quality expert we spoke to was: 'How can we get every person involved in the quality orientation? How can we make everyone customer–supplier-oriented?'

'How can we market our services more effectively?' was the preoccupation of an informatics services associate whose department was in the throes of transition from bureaucratism to dynamism.

Relationships with stakeholders of all kinds—suppliers, allies, regulators, the general public—can be seen as customer–supplier relationships.

### Delegating Responsibility

If quality is demanded wherever implementation takes place, then delegation of responsibility is the core of quality management. Middle managers should delegate responsibility to their personnel. They must learn to energize and trust the capabilities of those reporting to them and see their own task as facilitation, preparing the territory, etc. They should consult their staff.

This, however, is easier said than done. Frequently we observed, in the words of one quality coach, that 'many middle managers have enormous difficulties in adopting this behaviour. The older generation in particular grew up with the mentality: "We know how things have to work. We understand the technique." '

He adds: 'The customer–supplier relationships model is, at the same time, an approach to promoting understanding of the reciprocal processes of delegation.' This kind of advanced thinking is needed in the whole organization. It represents, as we will show in Part Two, good systemic thinking.

**Conflict And Stress**

In our time of fundamental structural change in most industries, implementation at any level requires the implementation of change. The organization must transform itself.

Now the quick and relatively easy part of a change process is often to invent the needed change. Implementing it, however, is difficult and cumbersome. It needs wisdom, strength, and persistence.

Organizations need to be effective in implementing change. Conflict and stress have to be used constructively.

Energy dissipated in conflict often endangers effectuation of strategies. For this reason, conflict is widely seen as something to be avoided. Often the result is that defensive routines take over and lead to impasse.

It is necessary to capitalize on the evolutionary potential of conflict. A culture of dealing constructively with conflict must develop and be cherished. Productive conflict is a property of healthy group and intergroup dynamics.

It can be actively fostered. This is a challenge both to the design of decision processes and to the behaviour of leaders. The key to a conflict-positive organization lies in the simultaneous stimulation of diversity and creation of unity; see the discussion in Tjosvold (1991). The crucial contribution of leaders resides in managing conflict, and getting people to work together productively; see Tjosvold (1993).

Leadership starts where normal consensus ends!

Note, however, that conflict and stress can only become productive if individuals and the units to which they belong are endowed with sufficient autonomy, while respecting

1. the control functions of others
2. others' autonomy.

This is an issue of structure, communication and control.

# ISSUE: 'STRUCTURE AND PROCESS'

We have seen that preservation of identity requires adaptation, and adaptation requires change. Now change requires an organization to have a structure that enables change processes to go on. What is structure, and what is a process?

By 'structure' we mean the set of arrangements by which the resources of an organization, human and others, are connected through relationships 'Process', on the other hand, is the collection of activities that takes one or more kinds of input and creates an output of value to a customer inside or outside the company—as in the discussion by Hammer and Champy (1993, p. 35).

**The Need For Autonomy**

In relation to structure, it is a postulate of modern management that:

Organizations need structures that foster autonomy and local problem solving capacity

We have argued already that responsibility for quality must be distributed through the organization. But 'quality' is to be understood in a general sense. Responsibility for all kinds of issues must be distributed.

This includes such issues as

- designing: shaping a desirable future and ways of bringing it about,
- planning: setting objectives and anticipating action,
- controlling: monitoring and steering execution,
- organizing: setting up effective structures and processes,
- ecology: acting responsibly in relation to the environment,
- marketing: customer-oriented practice,
- leadership: helping ourselves and others to make excellent contributions.

Most of these tasks are specifically management tasks; all involve a managerial component. If they are to be distributed, this implies, as has been claimed, 'that everyone in the company be a manager'.

For many companies this has been no more than a misunderstood catchphrase. In Part Two we show that the concept of distributed responsibility does make sense. We also introduce a 'tool'—cybernetics—that furnishes a solid enough approach to make it really work.

## The Need For Participation

If autonomy is built into each unit and workplace, thereby enhancing local variety, a logical consequence is that participative structural arrangements become imperative. These in turn can only function if the cultural substratum is mature.

Organizations need to develop a capacity for cultural transformation toward more open and participative structures.

Structure and culture are intertwined, since both depend upon relationships between people. The following two ideal types of organization can be distinguished in terms of both structure and culture:

- 'HAT': the hierarchical–authoritarian type;
- 'HPT': heterarchical–participative type.

Hierarchical structures are associated with autocratic modes of behaviour, including monological order-giving that emanates from a centre. In contrast, the heterarchical organization can have many centres and is linked to a highly participative and dialogical culture. Participation and empowerment in this case are so high that any unit in the organization can, in principle, assume a leadership function in relation to the whole. At the same time, it can have a subordinate function in other respects. See the discussion in Hedlund (1993).

The HAT organization is characterized by a high level of determination and control from outside, and little autonomy in the workplace. The emphasis is on permanent structures and on the division of labour. The HPT organization, on the

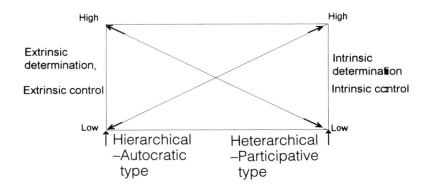

**Figure 1.1** Two ideal types of organization (Schwaninger, 1994b)

other hand, provides high levels of autonomy to units at all levels, thereby fostering self-determination and self-control; see Figure 1.1. The emphasis is on temporary structures, on multiplication and combination. While hierarchies are good at exploiting resources, heterarchies' strength lies in innovation and flexibility. Real-life organizations do not, of course, correspond rigorously to these ideal types.

The strictest hierarchies always exhibit some characteristics of dialogue, even if they operate in placid environments. Alternatively, any heterarchy will show some hierarchical properties, because certain units will have to assume specific overall responsibilities in relation to the encompassing systems. A complete heterarchy would have limited ability to maintain cohesion and identity.

In practice, there is a trend toward fostering autonomy and self-regulation. We applaud this. We maintain that large companies in turbulent environments must show heterarchical traits in order to be viable.

In contrast, there are authors who advocate hierarchy as the necessary solution to coping with complexity. According to Jaques:

> . . . it is the level of responsibility, measured in terms of time span, that tells you how many layers you need in an enterprise . . . As we go higher in a managerial hierarchy, the most difficult problems that arise grow increasingly complex, and as the complexity of the task increases, so does the complexity of the mental work required to handle it.

Jaques (1990, p. 133), suggests that if you structure the company taking care of these aspects you will have a workable hierarchy, which he recommends. 'Hierarchy is the best structure for getting work done in big organizations. . . . We need to stop casting about fruitlessly for organizational Holy Grails and settle down to the hard work of putting our managerial hierarchies in order.'

Jaques' approach assumes that lower hierarchical levels should not deal with long term issues—an assumption that entails operational shortsightedness. His fundamental mistake, however, is to disregard the fact that the complexity of an organization is always orders of magnitude higher than any manager could cope with. A principle of organization must therefore be found by which the cohesion of the organization emerges as a result of mutual interest and not as a result of unilateral control—as pointed out by Espejo (1993b, p. 84). This is the principle of recursion, to be developed in Part Two.

Where does the 'average' organization lie in the continuum between the two types, HAT and HTP? This is impossible to say, if only because there is no such thing as 'the average organization'. We have, however, observed that the HAT model is still commonly used by managers themselves. One interviewee asserted bluntly that in his (large) company '. . . a strong hierarchical orientation is dominant', even though words like 'participation', 'togetherness', 'openness' abounded in the corporate charter.

In this area there are often differences between 'espoused' theories and 'theories-in-use'—in the terminology of Argyris (1993). How people say they behave often has little to do with how they actually behave.

Hierarchical orientation and status thinking are intimately linked. In one firm, many team heads find it difficult to execute their functions if they are not authorized signatories; only those who have such formal insignia of power tend to be esteemed or listened to. This is a typical manifestation of a mentality and culture close to the ideal-type HAT.

At the same time, we have observed and actively supported processes of transition toward more participative modes. We note that the transformation from a hierarchical and authoritarian to a dialogical and participative organization with heterarchical characteristics cannot be imposed by command. Neither are verbal interventions—the mere formulation of new normative principles—sufficient. Structural interventions are a prerequisite for such a transformation.

## Structure In Relation To Process Redesign

If participation and empowerment are necessary to enhance local problem-solving capacity, they are not sufficient to guarantee organizational effectiveness:

> Organizational effectiveness depends upon managing interdependencies so as to move from functional orientation to process orientation; that is, from a tayloristic to a systemic paradigm.

'Process re-engineering' is a major theme of modern management. If carried out well, it can have a dramatic impact on an organization (see box p. 24) . Obsolescent structures are dismantled and redesigned, becoming flatter and less formal. Values, roles, and the nature of work change. Performance improves.

In practice, successful cases of process re-engineering are relatively rare. One manager deeply involved in cross-functional relationships complained:

> Flipover in managers' minds between functional and process orientation has not yet happened. Most people in our organization understand themselves in the first place or exclusively as members of a functional department.

A staff executive demands: 'What we need badly, is a reorientation of personnel from a bureaucratic mentality to a business mentality.'

## Structure, Process And Information Technology

Information technology has made available new ways of implementing participative structures and cross-functional processes. For example:

---

## CHARACTERISTICS FREQUENTLY ENCOUNTERED IN RE-ENGINEERED BUSINESS PROCESSES

- *Several jobs are combined in one.* For example, case workers or case teams take account of a whole process.
- *Workers make decisions.* Thus there is empowerment: workers assume responsibility; decision making becomes part of the work.
- *Steps in a process are performed in a natural order.* Realization that there is no need for linearization. 'Delinearizing'.
- *Processes have multiple versions.* Ending of standardization; multi-version processes can be clean and simple, because each version needs to handle only those cases for which it is appropriate.
- *Work is performed where it makes the most sense.* Often work is relocated across organizational boundaries, eliminating the need for integration of fragmented pieces of processes.
- *Checks and controls are reduced.* Controls are simplified and only applied where they make economic sense.
- *Reconciliation is minimized.* Reduction of the number of points of contact, often through relocation of work across inter-company boundaries. For example, when a customer firm offloads its inventory management function onto its supplier, there is continuous replenishment, with reduction in errors and need for reconciliation.
- *A case manager provides a single point of contact*, thereby acting as a buffer between a still complex process and the customer. The case manager behaves as if he or she were responsible for performing the entire process.
- *Hybrid centralized/decentralized operations are prevalent*, enabling a company to provide high flexibility in virtually autonomous units, while still enjoying the economies of scale that centralization brings. For example, decentralized divisions are linked through corporate-wide databases. (After Hammer and Champy (1993).

---

1. Redesign of processes can enable individuals to control their own activities. This occurs wherever 'acts of execution' and 'acts of control' are united. The same applies to the linking of decision and design processes. It applies, also, when advanced means of communication allow design and control to be carried out in an interactive mode.
2. Process redesign can finally abolish departmental 'fiefdoms', because data and knowledge can be shared and groupware, teleconferencing, can be applied across physical borders (such as walls), over any geographical distances, and even in such a way as to overcome interpersonal fears of contact.

In the longer term it is clear that the structures of most industries and business systems will undergo profound modifications under the impact of advanced information technology. See the discussion of Schwaninger (1994) and Scott-Morton (1991).

## Other Developments Relating To Structure And Process

Other developments are taking place in the structure and process of organizations. Particularly important are:

1. *Outsourcing.* This trend has only just started. Increasingly, companies will contract out to external firms those activities in which they are not 'best-in-the-world', as in Quinn (1980). Drucker (1993, p. 116) even forecasts:

> It is predictable, . . . that ten years from now [1993] a company will outsource all work that does not have a career ladder up to senior management.

2. *Modular corporations.* Ideas of outsourcing and being best-in-the-world are taken further with the 'modular corporation', as in Tully (1993). Here the idea is to nurture those selected core activities in which one is better than anybody else; in the case of a particular company, these might be the design and marketing of computers. Outside experts are then utilized to provide all the other activities necessary along the value chain, e.g. the manufacturing of parts, handling of deliveries, accounting, etc.

In relation to the traditional, vertically integrated corporation, modular corporations may have significant advantages in flexibility, costs and competitiveness. Examples given are Dell Computers, Nike and Chrysler; these have taken market share from their competitors.

In principle, SBUs in large, traditional corporations could also adopt the modular concept; they could act as 'intrapreneurial' units, reaching out for the new dimensions they create.

3. *Strategic networks.* Strategic networks can be defined as long-term arrangements between two or more organizations. Such networks, in the form of alliances between companies, are forming and transforming at an increasing rate. If highly complementary strengths are united, such co-operative arrangements can give competitive strength, as in Jarillo (1988). Partnership between customers and suppliers lead increasingly often to linked information systems and the sharing of data.

Strategic networks may also include customers, competitors, regulators, trade associations and consultants.

4. *Virtual organizations.* This is an emerging concept. The idea is that, by utilizing its core competencies, a virtual organization should be capable of materializing its potential in virtually any form.

We are only starting to put 'virtual organizations' into place. Davidow and Malone (1992) talk more about virtual products, i.e. goods and services that can be made available at any time, in any place, in the size and shape demanded—than about virtual enterprises. The virtual organization will put the principle of flexible networks into practice, enabling it to provide capabilities of almost any size and form almost anywhere and at any time. An application of this principle to project organization has been implemented with Digital; according to Savage (1990, p. 181):

> Virtual enterprises are built upon their ability to define and redefine multiple cross-functional teams as needed. These teams may include not only members of the company, but also persons from vendor and client companies. Virtual enterprises rely more on the knowledge and talents of their people than on the functions. Their managers, professionals, and workers can multiplex their attention to multiple projects with different sets of project members during the course of a day, month, or year.

Instead of defining the enterprise in spatial terms, as is done in the hierarchical organization chart, responsibilities in a virtual organization are allocated using the principle of human time.

Looking at these new forms of organization, it is clear that strategic networks and virtual organizations, in particular, require heterarchical rather than hierarchical structures, and new approaches to knowledge management (See Nonaka/Takeuchi, 1995).

## The Invention Of Change

Though these new forms of organization are still in process of diffusion, enterprises that do not adopt them in some form may in the future suffer from organizational sclerosis.

But how can enterprises discover that they need change and what kind of change they need? This will require a specific capacity to develop innovative approaches:

**Organizations need to provide the conditions for people to develop themselves, i.e. to find and create new possibilities.**

Very often, otherwise excellent organizational models are advocated that do not include structural preconditions for reinventing the corporation. A company must have the prerequisites to reflect continually, what it does: a function of self-reference.

Our interviewees put their fingers precisely on symptoms of a deficit in this respect. They diagnosed:

- inadequate strategic processes,
- lack of checks and balances in strategic decision processes, e.g. inability to question the assumptions and views of powerful directors,
- operational success reducing the chances of thinking strategically, so that in fact 'success stories' become questionable,
- insufficient structural capacity for dealing with strategic issues.

Similar diagnostic points were made under the identity and adaptation issues. This is because we are again considering the same problem—how to reinvent oneself.

The difference is that we are now considering it from the viewpoint of structural prerequisites—the structural requirements for change. In turn, we shall have more to say about these under the issues of human resources management, where we consider how change is made possible at the level of the workplace.

## Control And Communication

Little has been said until now about control and communication. To be viable and reach its objectives, an enterprise must be designed so as to control itself.

This implies coping with complexity successfully. We have seen how important autonomy is for an organization that needs to be a high-variety system, capable of coping with complexity successfully. However design for autonomy is not free of controversy. It gives rise to what is called the 'control-autonomy dilemma'.

Subordinates need freedom to be responsive to the demands of their respective environments. As environmental turbulence increases, managers, in turn, have no option but to accept growing information gaps; but Espejo (1982, p. 15), warns:

If these gaps are interpreted, as they usually are, as lack of control, and more commands are issued, the likely outcome is middle and low level managers perceiving more constraints, less room for autonomous action, less flexibility, etc.

Solving the control–autonomy dilemma requires designing control mechanisms that foster local autonomy while maintaining the cohesion of the organization as a whole.

**Organizations need to develop control mechanisms that foster both autonomy and cohesion.**

The question is, if and how control mechanisms can be designed to fulfil this paradoxical postulate.

In practice, attempts to solve the control–autonomy dilemma mostly result in forcing either centralization or decentralization. Several interviewees discerned too many and too big centralized functions, particularly at corporate level.

In one case, a central group of electronic control specialists (section 'EEE'), served several operational units, all of which were charged for their services, partly on the basis of fixed ratios, without having influence on the design of those services. It took long and cumbersome efforts to obtain a few engineers and craftsmen who would be fully at the disposal of a newly formed unit, consisting of a joint venture with full profit responsibility. Negotiations with central departments were difficult throughout. Even now, the specialists continue to report to EEE.

In a certain large firm, central departments are powerful and have their own service functions. Central accounting has an informatics department of 100 people, considerably more than exist in large divisions.

Centralization often leads to dysfunctionalities. In one multinational, many central staff units attempt to regulate operational units. A manager reported: 'One PPS project has three persons on the project team; thirty-six persons above try to control it.'

If centralization can be excessive, so can decentralization. This question was put by one of our interviewees:

Has our decentralization gone too far? Important functions are not represented at the corporate level or any other higher levels, although it seems necessary to develop concepts and meaningful messages at such levels.

He gave as examples environmental issues, security and overarching rules for information systems.

How can this question be answered? In Part Two we shall see how a methodology for recursive design of viable organizations enables answers to be given in each concrete case.

## ISSUE: UNDERSTANDING ORGANIZATIONS BETTER

Besides the issues of hierarchy, participation, centralization and decentralization, the issue of pluralism plays a crucial role in the discussion of modern organizations and their management.

How are we to understand this issue? Organizations are 'multisystems'; that is, systems of many constituents that represent among themselves a variety of viewpoints. Different constituents ascribe different purposes to the organizations of which they are part, and focus on different modes of action, as in Espejo (1987).

Thus pluralism is not an accidental property. It is a prerequisite for the survival of an organization. However, the fact that an organization is a multisystem that must satisfy the needs of multiple constituents means that it must, in order to maintain its viability and development, manage itself through communication processes between persons holding many different models—models that are necessary to capture the richness of the organization's tasks.

**Effective organization is required for channeling a variety of viewpoints into joint action. This is achieved through the alignment of goals and intents.**

Alignment of goals and intents involves a negotiation of shared meanings—as in Thomas *et al.* (1985). Such negotiation is necessary and fertile, because it is, in the long run, the only way to reach agreement for effective action.

This observation corroborates the need for the dialogical–participative model advocated—despite its shortcomings in practice—in our discussion of structure and process.

## Control And Communication For What?

The problem of designing control processes is thus to a large extent one of enabling effective communication. Therein lies at one and the same time a structural and a behavioural challenge.

**An effective organization is built on ongoing communications, which can be enabled by powerful technology.**

The structural aspect here is the requirement of adequate technical support for reliable, accurate, timely, and constantly accessible information.

The behavioural requirement is for people to have a developed ability for effective interaction. In general, long-term efforts toward fostering high interpersonal competence should be undertaken—particularly in multicultural settings. Effective interaction is a prerequisite for unleashing individuals' potential. It consists of communication processes that, by a self-reinforcing process, enhance motivation, collective productivity, and individual satisfaction. The principles and techniques of effective communication can, to a large extent, be learnt. They are based upon genuine respect for the individual.

In practice, communication processes are often defective or pathological. Typical symptoms we found included:

- People of different functions, such as research and production or marketing and quality assurance, unable to understand one another.
- We found an extreme case in which an information blockade was imposed by a department head.
- In another case, interprocess communications took place but were inadequate due to the functional orientation of actors.
- We found lack of communication between those developing a product and those selling it.

- We found poor communication between those developing an idea and those implementing it.

Three common problems emerge from the evidence gathered:

1. Difficulty in communicating between different disciplines. Attempts at inter-disciplinary communication are made, but often fail due to lack of a common language.
2. The separation of thinking from doing.
3. The mixing-up of dimensions of action (operative, strategic, normative) and of structural levels.

We shall see in Parts Two and Three that management cybernetics, the science of effective organization, can help with all three problems. It can furnish a language for transdisciplinary communication, a concept for re-uniting thinking and doing, and a model for anchoring operative, strategic, and normative management at all levels of recursion of an organization.

### 'Proper' Understanding

What, however, if communication is excellent and the model of management well structured, but the understanding of what the organization is all about is poor?

It is not enough that multiple viewpoints exist. If the dominant viewpoints are enthralled in prejudice or captivated in tunnel vision, organizational pathology will result.

Proper understanding of an organization requires reflection by unorthodox, open minds and team learning.

Here is the second-order challenge to strategy-making: a challenge to the dominant logic that pervades the organization. It can only be successfully met if at least one more postulate is fulfilled.

Creativity must be leveraged by structures that support individual and organizational transformation.

Cybernetics points out that, in a sense, we cannot afford to 'understand' a complex system; no individual can obtain a model representing every detail of what is going on. A 'proper understanding' must, therefore, aim at models of organizational reality that provide insight, not full representation. Such insight must be based on a knowledge of essential variables and interrelationships constituting the system in focus.

We can define essential variables as those that, if maintained within a tolerable bandwidth, assure the viability of 'our' system in focus, i.e. the work unit or organization we are responsible for. Essential relationships can be defined as those needed to hold such variables 'under control'.

How then can leaders achieve 'proper understanding'? One approach is through bringing to the surface orientators such as values and core competencies of the corporation, as well as critical success factors for the business or unit concerned. Substantial theoretical insights are available about these orientators and their interrelationships. To a large extent these are measurable. We deal with them in Part Three.

As far as non-measurable variables are concerned—variables that foster 'rich pictures' of or creative solutions to problems—a complementary approach is necessary. It consists in looking at a company from different angles, in order to grasp its multidimensional nature.

Managers are advised to take one of the following paths when trying to understand better what goes on in their organization:

1. The spotlight approach. This consists of shedding light upon different dimensions of the organization, e.g. from the four perspectives described in detail by Bolman and Deal (1991). These are:
   a. The 'structural' perspective: focuses on goals, tasks, formal roles and rational, techno-instrumental co-ordination and control, as well as on formalized structures and processes.
   b. The human resources perspective: adopts a social systems view, focusing on human behaviour, action, needs and capabilities, and the integration of individual and organization, e.g. through participation.
   c. The political perspective: looks at organizations as political systems, calling attention to issues of power, influence, conflict and coalition-building, with a priority on decisions about scarce resources.
   d. The symbolic perspective: adopts the cultural systems view, which accentuates characteristics such as role-playing, symbols, meanings and interpretations, social interaction and sense-making processes.
2. The metaphor approach. This is built upon conceiving one system in terms of another, using the method of analogy.

Arguably, the metaphor approach is not as special as it seems. All our theories of organization, including the four perspectives of the 'spotlight approach', are built upon metaphors stemming from different sciences. Morgan (1986, p. 12) argues that

> . . . many of our conventional ideas about organization and management build on a small number of taken-for-granted-images, especially mechanical and biological ones . . . The use of metaphor implies a way of thinking and a way of seeing that pervade how we understand our world generally.

Here is a list of widely used organizational metaphors, discussed in detail in Morgan's work:

- organizations as machines
- organizations as organisms
- organizations as brains
- organizations as cultures
- organizations as political systems
- organizations as instruments of domination
- organizations as psychic prisons
- organizations as flux and transformation.

Metaphors can not only illuminate features of a given person, situation, or problem as seen from a certain perspective. From their use one can also draw conclusions about the perspective employed by a metaphor's users, i.e. about the images and models used or preferred by them. Many organizations have dominant metaphors which furnish hints on the assumptions underlying their characteristic patterns of behaviour and interrelationships.

Each of the above two methods can help to visualize or direct the attention to hitherto undiscovered properties of an organization. Thus they can be an effective way of gaining new insights. However, equally 'true', complementary or even paradoxical metaphors or perspectives may lead to a completely different appreciation of a given person, situation or problem. Hence, the use of one and only one metaphor or perspective is liable to predetermine our actions unduly. According to Morgan (1986, p. 13):

> If we frequently talk about organizations as if they were machines to achieve predetermined goals and objectives . . . we often attempt to organize and manage them in a mechanistic way, forcing their human qualities into a background role.

In the same vein, Vickers (1965) has said: 'The nature of the trap is a function of the nature of the trapped.'

A metaphor can be enlightening; it can be of high didactic value when an issue must be illustrated or a situation analysed. It also can be useful in challenging current assumptions and help inventing unorthodox, innovative theories of one's own firm. But in dealing with organizations, one must be aware of the dangers of a mono-perspective. We do not want to add to the number of managers who have foundered on a reductionist view.

Usually, effective leaders are endowed with the ability to look at complex situations from different angles, almost simultaneously, and to synthesize such different perspectives, even when they seem incommensurable to others. No one, however, is immune against one-track-mindedness, and therefore structures must be provided, that foster self-reflection. This applies not only to organizations as a whole, but also to their subsystems. In particular, the issue of team-learning must be raised; we do so in Chapter 2.

In Part Two, we provide a framework for designing and implementing structure for 'intelligent' organizations.

# Chapter 2

# Transformation

## ISSUE: CHANGE, TRANSFORMATION AND LEARNING

The need for change is obvious and ubiquitous. We could postulate 'organizations have to develop continuously'. That, however, would understate the need for change. It would restrict development to being driven by first-order change—breeding 'more of the same'.

It is apparent from some of our earlier examples that 'more of the same' may be closer to suicide than to salvation. Second-order change is equally needed—change that by definition is discontinuous. What can be said is that we need development, both evolutionary and revolutionary, continuous and discontinuous. Moreover, we need it continually.

> Organizations have to discover, articulate and realize potentials all the time and at all structural levels.

Since both types of change are necessary, the capacity for innovation is primary:

> Organizations need to develop capacity for learning new modes of operation; that is, they need to reconfigure themselves.

The capacity for learning new modes is essential. In practice, firms often get caught in patterns that block change. According to Morgan (1993, p. 141): 'People espouse the desire for change but all kinds of factors within the existing situation reinforce the status quo.'

One of our interviewees gave the diagnosis: 'Instead of inventing processes, we keep copying the old ones'. A staff specialist added:

> Large systems are changed incrementally rather than radically. We foster amendments instead of renewal. . . . Some of our operational transaction systems e.g. order processing systems, accounting information systems—have been incrementally changed over the years, but now they have become obsolete—as many of them were already. Many systems have become so complicated, that a breakdown would be disastrous. . . . We need (a) more courage to take decisions on replacing out-of-date systems, (b) to take into account shorter life cycles of software, and to get into systems architectures that are highly open.

The situation thus diagnosed is potentially disastrous, because the c
rises exponentially as they age, while barriers to their replacement
higher and higher. Fortunately, our interlocutor added: 'On the other
have state-of-the-art and even highly advanced systems.'

## Redesign Of Structures And Processes

Where do complication and inefficiency in modern enterprise come from? As re-
engineering specialists assert, tayloristic specialization has led to ever more fragmented structures and processes. People in companies have mostly looked upward
toward their bosses and inward toward their department, but very little outward
toward their customers. This has stifled creativity and innovation, as emphasized by
Hammer and Champy (1993, p. 28).

> To cope with change, organization and business process redesign are
> essential for many corporations. For this the multilevel logic of management
> (operational—strategic—normative) must be understood.

The necessity of reinventing an organization can only be adequately grasped if the
logic of strategic and normative management, set out in Chapter 8, is understood by
those responsible for making redesign happen. Redesign is often more than a matter of
increasing operational efficiency; it is a means of enhancing core competencies or beat-
ing competition on a key success factor such as quality, speed or cost. Beyond that, redesign is often critical to the viability and development of a company or part of a company.

It entails literally reinventing the mode of doing business—and of managing it
also. Established rules have to be broken, if necessary. Assumptions taken for
granted have to be questioned. For example, in several firms we have dealt with the
assumption that firm X or Y was a competitor had to be abandoned. Joint ventures
were formed and once feared competitors transformed into strategic allies.

Furthermore, the boundaries that once separated internal departments from external constituents are increasingly subject to dissolution. External stakeholders go on
internship, as it were. Customers become part of product developing or marketing.
Suppliers are integrated into procurement and product design.

> Organizations need to develop a co-operative culture, breaking boundaries
> and developing synergistic alliances with suppliers, customers, competitors
> and other external stockholders.

When changing processes, there is a tendency to think in categories such as
'hardware' and 'software', rather than to look at the overall potential for redesign.
The box on p. 34 summarizes the changes that occur if business processes are
competently redesigned from scratch.

## The Role Of Information Technology

In the re-engineering of processes, information technology often has a key enabling
role, making possible totally new rules of operation.

Often, the old dichotomy 'flexibility versus efficiency' can be abolished, making
flexible efficiency possible, as in Boynton and Victor (1991). While firms in the past
had to choose between strategies of low cost and strategies of differentiation, they

## THE NATURE OF WORK CHANGES IF BUSINESS PROCESSES ARE DESIGNED IN A SYSTEMIC WAY

- *Work units change* from functional departments to process teams. Bits and pieces that have been artificially separated are rejoined; process or case teams replace the old departmental structure.
- *Jobs change* from simple tasks to multidimensional work. Process team workers share joint responsibility with their team peers; they use a broader range of skills and learn to think systemically. What an individual does is imbued with an appreciation for the process as a whole. Work becomes more rewarding and a vehicle for growth and learning.
- *People's roles change* from controlled to empowered. Employees create their own rules. Interference of supervisors would only disturb the process.
- *Job preparation changes* from training to education. Training teaches the *how* of a job while education teaches the *why*, increasing insight and understanding.
- *Focus of performance measures and compensation shifts* from activity to results. Not execution of an isolated activity, but contribution and performance become the primary basis of compensation.
- *Advancement criteria change* from performance to ability. A job well done is rewarded by a bonus; advancement, by contrast, is a function of ability, not performance. Avoid Peter's Principle by paying for performance and promoting for ability. Review of results is separated from review for development.
- *Values change* from protective to productive. Process redesign entails shifts in structure and in culture. People must believe that they work for their customers, not for their bosses.
- *Managers change* from supervisors to coaches. Managers have to switch from supervisory roles to acting as facilitators, as enablers, and as people whose jobs are the development of people and their skills so that those people will be able to perform value-adding processes themselves.
- *Organizational structures change* from hierarchical to heterarchical. Companies no longer require as much managerial 'glue' as they once did in order to hold work together. Formalized lines of communication become obsolete, because people communicate with whomever they need. Steering becomes a distributed function.
- *Executives change* from scorekeepers to leaders. Senior executives influence and reinforce employees' values and beliefs by their words and deeds, instead of simply running the company by the numbers. (Hammer and Champy (1993, pp. 65f.))

can now achieve both; this is due to the progress of information and production technologies. Boynton (1993, p. 59) points out:

> What used to be competing competitive requirements, where tradeoffs between low-cost and differentiation could be made, are now mutually dependent requirements: competing equally and aggressively on both low cost and differentiation at the same time.

Linked to these innovative approaches is the paradoxical possibility of realizing mass customization, by the use of leading edge technologies; Pine (1993) discusses this.

## Cultural And Structural Resistance To Change

Unfortunately, awareness of these new potentials in many companies is rudimentary, if not absent. One of our interviewees contends:

> Unfortunately, about 80% of the personnel in our firm see informatics only as a cost factor. Only very few consider its constructive use for the design of the organization. . . . At present, many units make up their strategic informatics plans. Some exaggerate, e.g. one division has been planning its strategy for 4 years, without putting anything into practice. Others tend to reduce the problem to a technical one, dealing with compatibility and interfaces between the many extant systems or other matters of detail. But actually few think about an integral design of business processes, cutting across departments . . .

and (we would add) probably making several of the extant systems obsolete.

Frequently, change is actively resisted. An experienced manager says: 'Changing anything in this organization involves cumbersome decision processes, often with too many people involved.'

Resistance to change has both cultural and structural causes. Cultural barriers include:

- Lack of clear identity and vision.
- Functional thinking that hinders the teamwork/business orientation. Instead of joint solutions to problems, there is politics and the defence of functional positions.
- Emotional adherence to past successes and wishful thinking, leading to collective blindness.
- Simple arrogance and complacency.
- Organizational defence patterns (discussed later in this chapter, and in Parts Two and Three as well) prevent learning.

A typical example of cultural barriers to change:

> Growing public resistance to a major commodity product (XTN) has been discernible from about 1985 onwards. Management teams were aware of this. One key leader asserts: 'We were fully conscious that this business was declining and that we had no alternative to offer. There was a strategic option to move into less controversial materials, such as PX and QR. Others have made substitutions in this direction; examples can be cited. Recently, a plant in country N opened a facility for PX. We could have been the first mover; now we are only fifth, sixth or seventh.'

How could this have happened? It is difficult to say exactly. Some of the reasons advanced were:

- Hope that the trend against XTN would reverse.
- Not enough pressure of BU management to move into substitution.
- We did not want to compete against customers who buy our PQ.
- We wanted to avoid cannibalizing our own XTN products.
- Some XTN markets continue to thrive, and we are strong in them.

At the heart of this case we find defensive routines. These, as in Argyris (1993), are policies or actions that prevent someone, or some system, from experiencing embarrassment or threat, while simultaneously preventing anyone from correcting the causes of the embarrassment or threat. In the case illustrated, such defensive routines fostered a non-learning process consisting of lack of awareness of feasible change and counter-productive group dynamics. We shall revert to this subject later in this chapter.

Among structural barriers we find:

- internal monopolies maintained by central services departments,
- inability to detect the need for established management systems to change,
- wrong incentives or lack of incentives to change.

A typical example, taken from our notes, of structural barriers to change:

> Structural inertia was mentioned in several cases. For example: 'If the decision to abandon the services of a central department is taken, the respective BU is charged with 100% of the cost one year after abandonment, with 50% in the second year, with 25% in the third year. So the barrier to change anything is very high, and changes take too long. . . . Central Maintenance, for example, is a department the *raison d'être* of which has been questioned intensively. It seems very difficult to abolish the high fixed cost of such departments.'

These examples document how inadequate learning processes create a gap between current and envisaged situations.

Usually, the disposition to learn, the mood for change, is less developed in profitable BUs than in the ones with difficulties. A quality management consultant, for instance, found the latter much more open to training in quality assurance systems than the former.

We conclude:

**Capacity for learning must be created structurally and fostered culturally.**

The process of change, which links vision, strategy and implementation, is non-linear and non-sequential. It links a present identity of a corporation with a future one, which can only rudimentarily be defined in advance. Many breakdowns of organizations could be avoided if the people working in them learned to understand the nature of this process.

## ISSUE: 'HUMAN RESOURCES MANAGEMENT—PEOPLE IN ORGANIZATIONS'

A central insight has characterized management theory since the 1930s. It is the understanding that the most important resource of a company is neither capital nor land nor information, but people:

- Only the human spirit is qualified to conceive organizations.
- Only creative faculties are able to combine resources inventively.
- Only human activity can generate genuine value.

We argue:

**Organizations are created and shaped by their people. They do not have an existence independent from them.**

The primacy accorded to human has ethical as well as competitive foundations. From an ethical standpoint, it is grounded in the unconditional value of the human being.

The competitive importance of human resources arises from the fact that soft factors such as knowledge, skills and competence are increasingly crucial to obtaining an edge in competitive games and making progress in co-operative ones.

Empirical studies, too, have emphasized the importance of people, culture, values, and capabilities as factors in excellent performance; see, for example, Peters and Waterman (1982) and Clifford and Cavanagh (1985). Quinn (1992, p. 214), sums up his insightful inquiry with the conclusion: 'Ideas and intellect, not physical assets, build great companies.'

As a result, human resources management has gained in importance while enlarging and deepening its perspective.

## Human Needs And Development

If we apply Protagoras' '*Homo mensura rerum est*' ('Man is the measure of things') to organizations, it is clear that they are made to satisfy human needs. If we ask, 'Whose needs?' the answer is 'the needs of various stakeholders, to whom organizations must provide sustained benefits'. Among them we include the people who work in organizations.

Their needs are multifaceted. According to Maslow (1970, pp. 35f.), human beings aim at satisfying a hierarchy of needs, in the following order of urgency:

1. Basic needs: 'physiological drives' such as hunger, sex, and thirst.
2. Safety needs: security, stability, freedom from fear, anxiety and chaos; need for structure, order, law, etc.
3. Belongingness and love needs: need to flock, to join, to belong, to give and receive love.
4. Esteem needs: the need for self-esteem—the desire for individual strength, achievement, adequacy, mastery, competence, confidence in the face of the world, independence and freedom—and for group esteem—the desire for reputation, prestige, status, fame, glory, dominance, recognition, attention, importance, dignity and appreciation.
5. Need for self-actualization: the need to be what one can be, to be true to one's own nature; the desire for self-fulfilment, which is the tendency to become self-actualized in what one potentially is.

The need for self-actualization has also been called the growth motive. The other types of need have been called deficit motives, because tendentially their non-fulfilment leads to disease.

If human needs are important, then organizations must create conditions for people to 'grow'.

> Organizations need to provide the conditions for people to develop themselves—i.e. to find and create new possibilities.

These conditions must open space for individual action, which, at higher system levels—i.e. at the levels of the group, the organization and the inter-organizational domain—should lead to self-organization, self-reference and self-transformation. The conditions referred to can be provided through adequate

- *structures*: providing for autonomy, self-determination, participation, self-reference, and learning;
- *systems*: such as incentives for initiative and information systems that make any information available to anybody at any time;
- *personnel development*: e.g., training programmes that focus on development of personal and interpersonal competence;
- *leadership*: providing strong vision, motivation, coaching, catalysing and help.

However, development is always an activity of the one who develops:

**Individuals and teams need to develop the ability to realize their potentials.**

Individuals in a company strive for happiness and fulfilment. This truth is at the core of learning and development. Happiness is all too often considered as limited to the private domain. It must be understood that happiness can only be a property of the individual as a whole. My happiness is fundamentally a result of my activities. Therefore, individuals must rethink their attitude toward their work: it must have an intrinsic beauty, which they can rediscover every day.

Let us, following Csikszentmihalyi (1992, 1993) call the process of carrying out an activity in happiness 'FLOW'. FLOW can only develop if individual capabilities and the demands or possibilities of the job are in balance. Prerequisites for FLOW and for self-development are, first, a job that 'makes sense'; secondly, sufficient autonomy to carry it out. These prerequisites are neither 'present' nor 'missing' in the initial description of a job. Each person can only co-produce them with his or her 'boss' and collaborators.

Thus the challenge for each member of an organization is in:

- realizing one's potential,
- optimizing one's knowledge about the encompassing whole,
- co-evolving together with that larger whole.

Included in this is the responsibility upon everyone to place themselves and the personnel that report to them in a context appropriate to their individual characteristics and develop them in accordance with their individual potentials.

Commitment of people is the 'raw material' from which organizational effectiveness is made. How can the prerequisites for such commitment be created and cultivated? Motivation theory singles out the following factors as the principal motivators leading to job satisfaction, see Herzberg (1987):

- achievement
- recognition
- the work itself
- responsibility
- advancement
- growth
- salary.

It follows that space for action and self-control, and also interesting work, should be created in the design of the workplace. Jobs should provide possibilities for responsibility, advancement and growth. Salaries should be coupled to performance—individual, group and organizational.

Management systems must provide reliable and relevant feedback information to each member of the organization. In that way, intrinsic motivation is stimulated via experiences of empowerment and self-reinforcement.

Personnel and team development should aim at enhancing individual and group faculties that are among the prerequisites to autonomy and participation. This means that

- the ability to take responsible action and initiative must be fostered;
- to this end, individual and team learning must take place;
- general values such as creativity, quality consciousness, customer orientation, reliability and flexibility must be instilled through training and shown to be relevant in the context of the specific firm;
- firm- and business-specific values, goals, rules and priorities have to be transmitted in such a way that each member understands and applies them in his or her workplace.

To provide self-actualization, it must be possible for each employee to make sense of his or her work environment. Frequently the emphasis is put on 'transmitting sense to employees'. Such approaches often verge on 'manipulative social technology'. Leaders should, however, strive to offer each employee the possibility of 'becoming the one he or she is'. Such an approach is focused on finding sense, not on transmitting sense. It includes the discovery of new potential in the development process.

## Creativity: Reinventing The Organization

The potential most needed is the creative faculty of reinventing the organization:

Individuals and teams need to develop capacity for learning new modes of operation and thinking, as well as learning to do better what they already do.

Learning new modes, a necessity already addressed under the change issue, requires, in the first place, readjustment of mindsets from the hierarchical worldview to a heterarchical perspective. This is explored further in Part Three. It also implies rethinking one's business completely, possibly breaking obsolescent habits. Learning to be more efficient implies benchmarking and continual training in best practices. A long range and conceptually underpinned human resources development effort is at the heart of coping with this challenge.

Training must increasingly become a help for self-development. The view taken by state-of-the-art human resources management is that 'the company develops its personnel'. This view may need to be turned around. 'The company's personnel develop it' is a far more dynamic and adaptive way of seeing things. Under it, people will be less squeezed into rigid structures. A development of customized organizations around people and the core capabilities they embody may take place. Such a development need not be chaotic, as long as higher-level orientation by normative principles is provided.

To foster the creative abilities of individuals or teams, conceptual competence in particular must be cultivated at all levels. This includes the ability to recognize patterns, underlying structures and generative mechanisms, and to invent new modes of doing things. A core aspect of conceptual competence is the awareness of how one's own action affects other units, and particularly the encompassing whole into which one is embedded:

**People and teams in organizations need to develop an awareness of the systemic implications of their actions.**

In this context, a scenario given by Drucker (1992, p. 312) is relevant:

The factory of 1999 will be an information network. Consequently, all the managers in a plant will have to know and understand the entire process, . . . In the factory of 1999, managers will have to think and act as team members, mindful of the performance of the whole. Above all, they will have to ask: What do the people running the other modules need to know about the characteristics, the capacity, the plans, and the performance of my unit? And what, in turn, do we in my module need to know about theirs?

Achieving such an outlook is a challenge for individual learning. At the same time, learning must be fostered at the levels of groups, processes, and the organization as a whole, as well as in the inter-organizational domain, such as that of strategic alliances.

## Obstacles To Learning

Learning is, however, often obstructed by behavioural patterns that can be called pathogenic, i.e. generative of organizational pathologies.

After years of efforts to promote learning in his organization, a high-level manager we interviewed said:

We have many managers who are good chemists or good physicists. Some of them are even nice persons and tough guys at the same time. But they do not understand the principles of systemic effective management. Sometimes I am terribly frustrated, because I don't know how to drive the tayloristic paradigm out of their mindsets and how to instill in them systemic thinking . . .

We have heard similar statements in other contexts, often in more blunt formulations:

- 'We could tell them what their organization needs, but our bosses just don't understand . . . and they don't listen, either . . .'
- 'Everybody in this place talks about change, but nobody wants to burn his fingers . . .'
- 'We are aware of these needs [to adopt new patterns of leadership], but our boss is just a narcissistic autocrat. You cannot discuss these things seriously with him . . .'

Such statements could be condensed into: 'We are great, those above us are chumps.' They reflect mindsets that are widely observable in organizations; they are, however, symptoms of imminent pathology.

Argyris (1990) has called the related patterns of behaviour ODP—for 'organizational defensive pattern'. After decades of studies in organizational behaviour he concludes:

Buried deep in organizations is the capacity to be overprotective and anti-learning and to be unaware that this is the case—and to do all this precisely when organizations need the opposite capacity. That is, when the problems are tough and are also embarrassing or threatening.

Argyris' concept of ODP subsumes:

1. *Organizational malaise.* The pattern of organizational malaise is experienced somewhat as people feel and sense a disease, while feeling helpless to alter it. Symptoms include:

a. Seeking and finding fault with the organization but not accepting responsibility for correcting it. Here, people find fault with the organization but blame others or 'the system' for it. They take no responsibility for creating the faults or for correcting them (op. cit., p. 60).

b. Accentuating the negative and de-emphasizing the positive. Individuals not only see faults in the organization—they magnify them. One reason they do so is that the more powerful and awesome they can make the faults seem, the easier it is for the individuals to explain away their own distancing and feeling of helplessness. Individuals under these conditions often discuss the faults with a sense of pleasure because finding them provides reassurance that their distancing and helplessness are necessary (p. 61).

c. Espousing of values that everyone knows are not implementable (p. 60). In organizations that are genuinely concerned with people, individuals find themselves in a dilemma because they espouse values that are difficult to implement in face of organizational defence routines and fancy footwork (p. 61f.).

2. *Skilled incompetence.* This designates a sense of helplessness that an individual eventually feels as well as the predisposition to live with his or her self-deception in the name of trying to achieve some important objective or vision. Eventually, this sense of helplessness creates a mode of distancing oneself, accompanied by all kinds of excuses for not acting. A sense of hopelessness and even cynicism may emerge that effectively prevents change.

3. *Fancy footwork.* Unintentionally, the individual begins to deceive him or herself, to delude other people, to use defensive reasoning, and to focus on the non-controversial and therefore unimportant issues while suppressing the important ones. The person, in the name of achieving his or her objectives, creates a world similar to the one she or he was actually trying to fight or abolish. Fancy footwork includes actions that permit individuals to be blind to inconsistencies in their actions or to deny that these inconsistencies even exist, or, if they cannot do either, to place the blame on other people. Fancy footwork means to use all the defensive reasoning and actions at their command in order to continue the distancing and blindness without holding themselves responsible for doing so (p. 46).

In this way it happens that highly committed, well-intentioned, safety-oriented players reasoned and acted in ways that violated their own standard while making certain that the violation was covered up—and that the cover-up also was covered up (p. 42).

4. *Defensive routines.* As already mentioned earlier, Argyris and Schon (1978) define defensive routines as policies or actions that prevent someone (or some system) from experiencing embarrassment or threat, while simultaneously preventing anyone

from correcting the causes of the embarrassment or threat. The persons who, infected by skilled incompetence, have distanced themselves often find comfort and protection in the defensive routines and their consequences.

The ODP has a self-reinforcing, positive feedback-driven dynamic that is hard to break. Two strategies can be propounded to reduce ODP activities that create and legitimize error:

1. To design and manage organizations in ways that do not activate the organizational defensive pattern. Examples are the redesign of work (e.g. job enrichment strategies), autonomous groups, and other approaches to getting people involved.
2. To educate individuals and teams in new concepts and skills that tend to reduce the organizational defensive pattern. The strategy is not to bypass and cover up problems, but to engage with them and make them discussible and manageable. As individuals use the new skills, they begin to change the organizational defensive routines and fancy footwork. As that begins to happen, new concepts of control, related especially to budgets, management information systems, and employee rewards, can be introduced (p. 66).

In Part Two, we shall expound a theory of human action and a model of organizational learning that provides a basis for implementing these strategies.

## The Need For Leadership

The need for learning and development makes great demands upon leadership in organizations. An empirical study among Swiss experts in personnel management (Wunderer and Kuhn, 1992) indicates that between the years 1990 and 2000 the following key qualifications of leaders will gain most in importance:

- ability to cooperate
- ability to communicate
- ability to solve problems
- ability to motivate
- creativity
- ability to transfer concepts into practice.

These results lead to the conclusion:

Effective leadership is increasingly based on conceptual and interpersonal rather than technical competencies.

As Crosby (1992) stated recently, new leaders 'will recognize the need to provide a complete concept as a reliable framework for running an organization.' According to Senge (1992, pp. 5f) managers will have to be masters in five disciplines that are essential to build a learning organization:

1. *Personal mastery.* The discipline of continually clarifying and deepening a vision, of focusing energies, of developing patience and of seeing reality objectively.
2. *Mental models.* The construction of assumptions, generalizations, or even pictures or images that influence how we understand the world and how we take action.

3. *Building shared vision.* Unearthing shared images of the future that foster genuine commitment and enrollment rather than mere compliance.
4. *Team learning.* A mode of 'thinking together' that overcomes the following paradox: 'How can a team of committed managers with individual IQs above 120 have a collective IQ of 63?'
5. *Systems thinking.* Seeing connections, patterns, and influences that are usually hidden from view.

These are useful propositions even if they need to be complemental. The coming leaders are, to a large extent, architects of visions and conceptual frameworks, designers of effective structures and systems, and catalysts for powerful action.

Are corporations prepared to breed the effective leaders of the future? A renowned European researcher and management consultant whom we interviewed to supplement our in-company investigations stated: 'Many big corporations have a surplus of managers and a lack of leadership.'

However, the picture from our conversations with managers is mixed. In our interviews we encountered, on the one hand, a lot of advanced management thinking. We also observed that leaders are inclined to the adoption of systemic concepts. On the other hand, statements can be cited that indicate shortages of leadership as well as of systemic thinking. Some examples include:

- '. . . narrow focus of corporate concerns'.
- 'Lower and middle level managers are slowed down by higher level management.'
- 'Cost oriented management is still too punctual and unsystematic. At the lower and middle management levels, not enough people take the trouble to follow in detail their cost patterns and to steer them adequately.'
- 'What is being understood, predominantly, is efficiency. Effectiveness, which is a strategic criterion, is often not considered . . . because it is not so easy to calculate and systems don't furnish the necessary information.'
- '. . . there is not enough conceptual thinking, among our people here.'

Perhaps to ask if corporations are prepared is to put the wrong question. Prepared or not, they have to face the new challenges. There is no choice.

Our contribution is to offer the conceptual building blocks for a new mode of management thinking.

## ISSUE: 'ECOLOGICAL RESPONSIBILITY'

There are few subjects on which our pluralistic society has agreed as much as in this: we face a worldwide crisis of our natural environment.

Ecological issues are on the agenda not only for politicians but for leaders of all organizations, including business firms. The earth itself figured recently on the cover of *Time* magazine as 'Planet of the Year'. For most citizens of the industrialized world, the degradation of the natural environment is a first concern.

A few years ago, ecological concern was widely considered something personal and private; today it is a high-priority public issue.

Environmental associations have grown fast in size and capability. Green parties have emerged: in most national parliaments of Western Europe there are now Green representatives. In Denmark there are more members of environmental organizations than there are Danes—because many belong to more than one group (Burke 1989).

This high level of subjective concern reflects a growing awareness that no one can escape ecological problems. All are somehow affected, the industrial firm in particular.

**Business Versus The Environment?**

There has been a strong feeling among the public of aggravated conflict between business and the environment. A diagnosis put forward at an international conference of leading managers and scientists held at the University of St. Gallen, Switzerland, and reported by Burke (1989) was that industry is not highly regarded by the public. It is seen as monolithic and secretive, as indifferent to the concerns of others, often arrogant, always selfish. Business is thought to be ignorant about the environment and frequently engaged in an all out assault upon it. It is seen as avoiding its responsibilities, cosmeticizing its problems and as being deeply reluctant to act. To many people, industry is powerful and pernicious, dangerous and deceitful.

> This . . . view of industry . . . is certainly not fair. Nevertheless, it is widely held. And it demonstrates clearly the depth of the communications problems industrialists face as the environment climbs inexorably higher on the public agenda.

As a consequence, managers and organizations can no longer refrain from dealing with ecological issues. They must take an active stance; a mere publicity or public relations approach is insufficient.

Organizations need to develop a sustainable ecological balance with their milieu.

The first prerequisite for being ecologically responsible and responsive is to be open to constructive discussion of environmental issues with relevant stakeholders. Here several difficult questions arise:

- Who is 'the public'; which public is involved?
- How can collective opinions be adequately gathered and interpreted?
- Under what circumstances can communication be effective?

Opinions about ecological issues may be highly divergent as between different publics; many opinions are not articulated in a compact form. As a reaction to this, an often pursued approach consists of agreeing opportunistically with one public or the other, for image purposes. This merely exacerbates the long-term problem.

Neither can the 'solution' consist in matching the ecological blindness of certain corporate constituents with the economic blindness of certain politicians. Failure is certain if emotion-laden discussions are conducted while both sides remain ignorant of the actual environmental impact of specific actions.

What has to be done is to make the variety of opinions productive in a fertile dialogue that leads to new and effective approaches. The issue is to design communication processes in which instructive and reflexive interaction with stakeholders can take place.

Some of the ecology-related challenges faced by industrial and service firms can be summarized as follows. On the one hand, environmental issues give rise to certain strains:

1. Image. Firms and products in heavy-emission-industries have suffered from a deterioration of their public image. Products such as PVC and fluorocarbon gases have become subject to attacks from many sides, particularly from single-issue groups, politicians and the media.

2. Product acceptance in the market. As a consequence market acceptance of these products has declined. Further decline threatens in the future. Customers—both consumers and industrial clients—tend to reject products, and even product compo-nents, with a reputation of being hazardous or not 'environment-friendly'.

3. Legal restrictions. There has been a dramatic intensification of legal regulatory activities. An example is the German *Abfallgesetz* (law on waste materials, 1986); this empowers the government to enact decrees to regulate the flows of waste materials. The first resultant regulation is the *Verpackungsverordnung* (decree on packaging materials), enacted in 1991.

4. New obligatory investments. Firms are required to invest in devices for the recov-ery of raw materials, i.e. for recycling, called in the US 'downcycling', and for the reduction of emissions.

5. Cost increases. Political and public institutions strive for internalizing social costs ('costs of environmental damage') via taxes and the imposition of duties.

6. Difficulty in the disposal of waste. The capacity available to receive waste deposits has become scarce, as fewer regions and communities become willing to offer such services. If used products—for example, computers—have to be taken back by their producers, this will pose them many new problems.

7. Wider liability for damage through products sold or used in the working place: the trend in legislation is from liability for guilt to simply causal liability.

8. Due to the higher risks, costs rise not only for liabilities incurred but also for insurance premiums. In several cases, insurance companies have refused to underwrite.

9. It becomes increasingly difficult to acquire new sites for industrial development.

10. The introduction of new products to the market is a process fraught with ever higher hurdles and subject to growing delays. A famous case is that of the American Food and Drug Administration.

11. The recruitment of graduates is getting more difficult for firms considered 'bad environmental performers'.

## From Threat To Opportunity

Until recently, discussion of the consequences of an ecological orientation for busi-ness focused on the above strains, on costs and on feared restrictions. Among man-agers, defensive attitudes were predominant.

This has started to change. The business world has become aware of the oppor-tunities that may arise:

1. *The emergence of new markets.* In countries like Germany and Switzerland, about two thirds of the population consider themselves of high environmental consciousness, even though only 20 to 30% can be considered 'green consumers'; that is, consumers that are ready to choose 'green' products even if they cost more (Source: EMNID and IHA studies, 1990 ff.)

Markets for environmentally friendly and health-relevant products are dynamic. There is ample evidence of a vigorously increasing demand for 'ecologically sound' products.

2. *Potential competitive advantage.* In an increasing number of cases, 'high value for customers' derives directly from making products ecologically compatible.

This applies to consumer goods, such as organic food, but also to investment goods. Industry as well as the public sector have developed new criteria in their procurement strategies that put more weight on the 'cleanness' of technologies.

3. *Spur to innovation.* Numerous examples show that the ecological challenge opens a wide field for innovation, with fascinating prospects for creative solutions. On the one hand, there is a high demand for more economic use of energy and raw-material recovery. New networks and symbiotic relationships between firms will form to meet this demand. On the other hand, there is a need to develop new products to solve customers' ecological problems or substitute products that can fulfil extant needs more 'cleanly'. This gives rise to new opportunities—although for a firm or organizational unit that has conquered a strong position in an established technology or product, the idea of directing its energies to the development of substitutes may be hard to conceive. It may be harder still to accept and implement it.

4. *Cost reduction.* In many cases, the goal of improved environmental performance also supports better economic results. Measures that attain both are, for example, energy savings or investments in closed production systems that minimize losses of inputs; these, by reusing substances like water or chemicals, transform waste into new inputs by a process of recycling.

5. *Reduction of 'strain'.* A firm that switches to non-problematic products is relieved of all the costs we have called 'strains'.

6. *'Soft' factors.* Better ecological performance is something anybody can be proud of. It thus affords relief from the 'cognitive dissonance' between the pursuit of social and private welfare, so enhancing personal satisfaction and sense of achievement.

7. *Motivation and image.* The experience of many companies is that these points relate strongly to the factors of motivation and image. This can also be substantiated on theoretical grounds, for example, by motivation theory. As the diagram in Figure 2.1 shows, several positive feedback loops reinforce each other. Investments in increasing the qualifications of the workforce and the attractiveness of the workplace increase the commitment and capability of the workforce, which are essential ingredients of product quality. Product innovation and quality are generally the strongest levers to improve market position and profitability. We have the following feedback loops:

a. the commitment—earnings—remuneration cycle;

b. the sensation of success (or sense of achievement)—commitment cycles, which operate through quality and image;

c. the sales—experience—qualification cycles, operating through productivity as well as quality.

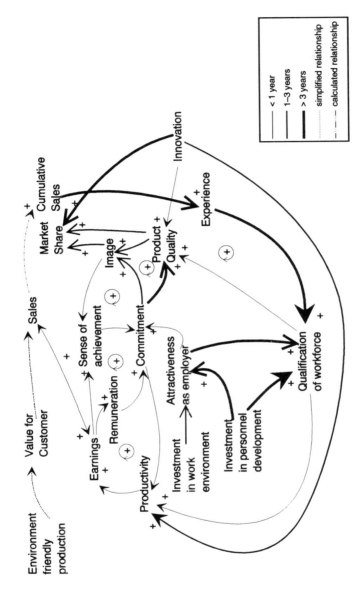

**Figure 2.1**  Positive dynamics in ecologically responsible management: emphasis on the human factors

8. *Recruitment.* There is evidence that companies with a high reputation as 'ecologically progressive' firms are better able to recruit competent manpower. This is important in an era where human resources have become the crucial factor. Better ecological performers come out better in the quest for capable personnel.

9. *'A brighter future altogether'.* This description may seem unscientific. Yet today most business leaders (in Switzerland, for example, 93.5%. Source: Wirt/Preblibest Study, reported in: Index 3/90, p. 13) defend the paradoxical view that social costs must be internalized to a greater extent. In fact, the term 'paradoxical' does not denote a real contradiction so much as a beholder who does not understand. The managers we have mentioned understood very well that reduced external costs meant, in the long run, increased viability for the economy and for their business.

An accumulation of ecological blunders and strategic naiveté can be fatal for corporate health. We shall see, however, that systemic thinking can help to avoid both traps. If organizations are to have a viable future, then:

People in organizations need to develop an appreciation of ecological issues and the capacity to deal with them responsibly.

# Summary of Part One

# Postulates Of Management

At this stage, we can summarize the contemporary postulates of effective management developed in Chapters 1 and 2.

Several of the postulates were discussed under more than one issue. They can be grouped in four domains, according to whether they relate most to:

- the performance of an organization;
- its structural basis;
- the relationships that are at the core of this structure, and transform it into process;
- the individuals and teams that develop these relationships.

## PERFORMANCE

P1. Excellent organizational performance requires delivering high value to all stakeholders.

P2. Organizations must develop vision and a strategic management in order to create value potentials. This applies to all structural levels.

P3. Organizations have to adhere steadfastly to their core values in realizing their visions. This implies going beyond mere efficiency and profit-orientation.

P4. Effective organization is required to channel a variety of viewpoints into joint action. This is achieved through the alignment of goals and intent.

P5. Organizations need to foster quality ('fitness for purpose') and continual improvement in all their activities; that is, they need to do better what they already do.

P6. Organizations need to develop the capacity to learn new modes of operation; that is, they need to learn to reconfigure themselves.

P7. Organizations have to discover, articulate and realize potentials all the time and at all structural levels.

P8. Capacity for learning must be created structurally and fostered culturally.

P9. Organizations need to develop a sustainable ecological balance with their milieu.

# STRUCTURE

S1. Effective structures are a fundamental requirement for the management of complexity. They allow organizations to create opportunities for themselves as well as to respond to disturbances and change.

S2. Organizations need structures that foster autonomy and local problem-solving capacity.

S3. Organizational effectiveness depends on managing interdependencies so as to move from a functional to a process orientation; from a tayloristic to a systemic paradigm.

S4. Organizations need to provide the conditions for people to develop themselves, i.e. to find and create new possibilities.

S5. Organizations need to develop control mechanisms that foster both autonomy and cohesion.

S6. Creativity must be leveraged by structures that support individual and organizational transformation.

# RELATIONSHIPS

R1. People in organizations need to develop an appreciation of the meaning of customer and market orientation.

R2. People in organizations need to develop an appreciation of ecological issues and the capacity to deal with them responsibly.

R3. To cope with change, organization and business process redesign are essential for many corporations. For this, the multilevel logic of management—operational, strategic and normative—must be understood.

R4. Organizations need to develop a co-operative culture, breaking boundaries and developing synergistic alliances with suppliers, customers, competitors and other external stakeholders.

R5. Relationships with stakeholders require effective communications, creating overlapping domains of interest and common responsibility.

R6. An effective organization is built on ongoing communications, which can be enabled by powerful technology.

R7. Organizations need to develop a capacity for cultural transformation towards more open and participative structures.

R8. Organizations need to be effective in implementing change. Conflict and stress have to be used constructively.

# THE INDIVIDUAL AND THE TEAM

I1. Organizations are created and shaped by their people. They do not have an existence independent of them.

I2. Individuals and teams need to develop the ability to realize their potentials.

I3. Individuals and teams need to develop the capacity to learn new modes of operation and thinking, as well as learning to do better what they already do.

I4. Proper understanding of an organization requires reflection by unorthodox, open minds and team learning.

I5. People and teams in organizations need to develop an awareness of the systemic implications of their actions.

I6. Effective leadership is increasingly based on conceptual and interpersonal rather than technical competencies.

At this point, we have summarized a variety of influential, state-of-the-art views on the management of today's organizations and distilled them into a number of postulates which our empirical studies have shown to be relevant.

The language to be developed in Part Two will shed new light on many of these postulates. More important, it will open new paths to their effective realization.

# Part Two

# A Language For Effective Action In Organizations

# Summary of Part Two

In this part of the book we offer a new language through which to understand management action in organizations.

This language has emerged from cybernetics—the 'science of effective organization'—in particular from the works of Ashby (1964), Bateson (1972), Beer (1966, 1975, 1979, 1981, 1985), Maturana and Varela (1980, 1987) and von Foerster (1984). From Ashby we have taken his seminal work on complexity, from Bateson his fundamental insights about learning processes, from Beer his deep insights on the management of complexity—in particular his work on the viable system model—from Maturana and Varela their epistemology and ontology, and from von Foerster the cybernetics of the observer and his insights on circular causality. We will explore the complementarities between these works and produce a synthesis; this will provide a language for action.

## A NEW VIEW WITH WHICH TO SUPPORT EFFECTIVE ACTION

We see a problem with current management trends. In spite of a number of valuable developments, the emphasis is still on information at the expense of communication and action. Consequently, managers still find it difficult to relate the ideas they create and generate as managers to the action capacity of the organizations they manage. It is as if they believed they could do by themselves and through their organizations far more than they can actually do. Their behaviour is like that of a person trying to lift a large load without the use of a fork lift or any other implement to enhance their biological limitations.

While failure in that case would be evident at once, it is not so apparent in organizations. Corporate managers who agree investment plans for their operational divisions unaware of the lack of organizational capacity to support them may precisely be 'trying to lift a load orders of magnitude heavier than their strength'. The opposite may also be the case when they fail to use the organizational potentials. In their case, however, this may not be apparent, perhaps until much later.

There is a general reason for such failures. Managers often lack good means to measure the complexity of organizational tasks and therefore depend on their intuition or good luck for successful decision making.

Current measurement tools in fact lack the capacity needed to capture the complexity of organizational processes. Strategic processes, double-entry book-keeping, management and financial accounting cannot match the actual and potential complexity of organizational interactions.

What is needed is a new way for people in organizations to appreciate the aggregated effects of their actions. Work in organizations is co-operative, sometimes contributed to by many thousands of people; how can managers know the capabilities and potentials of these vast networks of individuals? Perhaps more significantly, how do individuals relate to each other in order to release their potentials and transform individual into organizational capabilities? How, indeed, do they know what these capabilities are?

These are problems of appreciation, measurement and interpretation that people in organizations need to resolve in order to contribute effectively to the global tasks that face them.

Our solution: first, to develop a language for effective action in an organizational context. After that, we will attempt to provide modelling and methodological support to study and improve both such action and the organizational context.

## ORGANIZATION OF PART TWO

Part Two has five chapters:

• Chapter 3 sets out the basic concepts of cybernetics, as understood today by management scientists.
• Chapter 4 offers a theory of action in organizations, leading to a language by which to understand organizational work. It highlights the relevance of communications, conversations, learning and purpose in the management of organizational complexity. It concludes that there is need for 'recursive organizations'; that is, organizations that make it possible for all people to recognize and develop their potentials in an environment of co-operation.
• Chapter 5 discusses how managers can increase their chances of effective performance. The answer: 'by understanding the recursive nature of organizations'. For this purpose Chapter 5 explains a model of recursive organizations; this is the Viable System Model. It defines the communications requirements needed to make the most of organizational resources. It is a model of the organizational structure of any viable system.
• Chapter 6 focuses on individual and organizational learning. It is based on an existing learning model; it is illustrated by many industry-based examples. It concludes with some general principles of effective learning.
• Chapter 7 is methodological in intent. Here we bring together the basic concepts of earlier chapters and revisit the model of organizational learning discussed above. The outcomes are, first, a revised model; second, the 'cybernetic methodology', presented as a heuristic for making individual and organizational learning happen. The cybernetic methodology helps in the discovery of new possibilities and the appreciation of different viewpoints. It also enables virtuous processes to occur by helping people to assess the extent to which the systemic context of their actions is affecting their performance.

# Chapter 3

# Basic Notions

## PRIMARY ACTIVITIES, ENVIRONMENT, THE CORPORATION AND ITS MANAGEMENT

In a certain sense, if we consider those of its activities whose nature seems indisputable, a company is what it does (Beer, 1985).

Its doing defines its primary activities. Consider, for example, the relatively autonomous teams of an organization (Figure 3.1). These are 'primary units'. Other, higher level examples of primary units would be self-contained business processes such as strategic business units or, at a higher level still, divisions or companies.

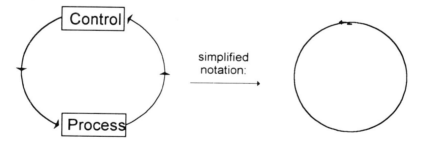

**Figure 3.1**   A primary activity

A primary activity is embedded in a specific environment or milieu. It receives inputs from the environment and feeds back to the environment the outputs it produces (Figure 3.2).

### Aspects Of The Environment

What we call the 'environment' or 'milieu' is a complex totality with a number of different aspects. These include:

- the technological aspect
- the economic aspect

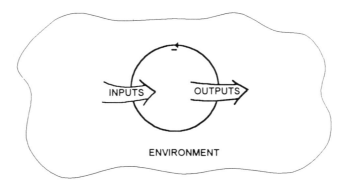

**Figure 3.2** A primary activity in its environment or milieu—containing customers, suppliers, technology, etc.

- the socio-cultural aspect
- the political aspect
- the ecological aspect.

Viewed from each of these aspects, the environment appears different. An institutional analysis would identify different stakeholders in each environment:

- customers
- employees
- suppliers and other strategic allies
- competitors
- financiers
- public institutions
- environmental organizations
- the public in general
- etc.

These are, of course, simple labels for highly complex systems, each of which develops its specific logic. Different inputs derive from and outputs flow to different environmental segments or institutions.

There are usually a number of primary activities in a corporation (Figure 3.3). It is, in fact, a compound of autonomous units with self-contained tasks that are coordinated to form an integrated whole.

### Environmental Complexity And The Need For Management

The pre-eminent characteristic of the environments faced by organizations in our time is their exceeding complexity. To maintain viability and development in a complex environment, a corporation must be managed. In Figure 3.4, corporate management is denoted by a rectangular box. Each primary activity must also be managed—or better, must manage itself. The respective management functions are denoted by the small square boxes.

The corporation and its primary activities with their respective environments are depicted in Figure 3.5.

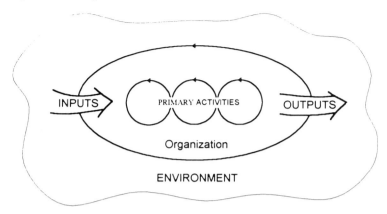

**Figure 3.3** The corporation in its environment

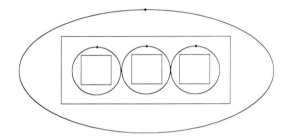

**Figure 3.4** The corporation and its management

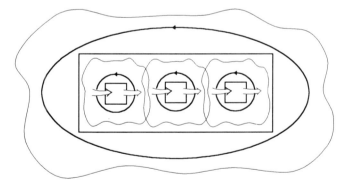

**Figure 3.5** The corporation and it primary activities with their respective environments

## COMPLEXITY AND VARIETY

An organization selects—if not consciously, then by its actions—the environments with which it will interact. Those it does not interact with may nevertheless affect it unilaterally as, for example a corporation may be affected by the weather without affecting it to any significant extent.

Exceeding complexity may emerge from an organization's interactions with the environments it does select. If it wants to survive and perform effectively in these environments, it has to cope with these emergent complexities.

What is complexity? The definition is simple.

> Complexity is the property of a system of being able to adopt a large number of states or behaviours.

It is measured by what we call variety.

> Variety is the number of possible states of a system.

In a figurative sense, variety also stands for terms such as 'behavioural repertory' or 'space to move'.

Mathematically, variety can be expressed by different formulas, of which the two following are most frequently used:

(a) Formula for constellations of relationships ('static picture')

$$V = m \frac{n(n-1)}{2}$$

Where:

V: Variety
$n$: Number of elements
$m$: Number of relations between each pair of elements

For example, a group of five people with reciprocal communication between all members has a variety of 20.

(b) Formula for configurations of states ('dynamic picture')

$$V = z^n$$

Where V and $n$ are as above and:

$z$: Number of possible states of each element

For example, a group of three lightbulbs with two states for each ('on' and 'off') has a variety of eight. Managerial examples will follow shortly.

## Variety Engineering

Generally, managers and the organizations they lead are confronted with situations that do, actually and potentially, overload them. The variety of such situations is much larger than their own. The prime challenge for management in such circumstances is to cope with this variety imbalance.

In principle, a manager or organization can deal with complexity in two kinds of way: these are attenuation and amplification (Figure 3.6).

Balancing the varieties of two interacting systems is what we call 'variety engineering'. Let us illustrate this concept by two examples.

Consider a project manager who is leading a group of people in a problem solving session: What can he do for effective group work? There are, at least, four possibilities:

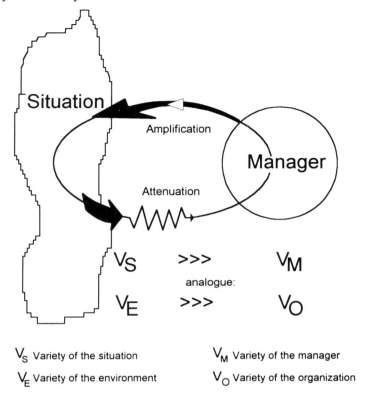

$V_S$ Variety of the situation      $V_M$ Variety of the manager

$V_E$ Variety of the environment     $V_O$ Variety of the organization

**Figure 3.6**   Balancing varieties of management (Espejo and Watt, 1988)

- Amplify variety of group by:
  - ○ stimulating inputs
  - ○ provocation
  - ○ fostering preparation through training
  - ○ etc.
- Attenuate variety of group by:
  - ○ setting goals
  - ○ imposing an order of the day
  - ○ setting 'rules of the game'
  - ○ periodical summaries
  - ○ initiating problem-oriented discussion.
- Amplify own variety by:
  - ○ enhancing own experience and competence
  - ○ good preparation
  - ○ knowledge of the relationships between group members
  - ○ grasping attention.
- Attenuate own variety by:
  - ○ mature behaviour
  - ○ holding him or herself back
  - ○ overcoming narcissism.

In the process of problem solving, the project manager will avoid trying to deal with the 'total' variety of the group. In the first place, the group is endowed with substantial autonomy to cope with the environmental variety it faces; the manager will deal only with the residual variety, for which the group needs his or her help. Second, to be of help the manager needs to consider him or herself as a member of the group, not as an outside controller.

Next, consider a matrix organization. Let the matrix be defined by eight functions and eight product groups. At one extreme, corporate management may be interested in whether any one of the 64 possible intersections is, over time, 'under control' or 'not under control'—two possible states. It may feel the need to respond differently according to which ones are or are not under control.

1. How high is the variety of the system that management is dealing with?

   The answer: $V = 2^{64}$; that is, approximately a one with 20 zeros.

   The exact number is not important; it is evident that the variety is too great. That is why a pure matrix organization does not work.
2. What can be done, in practice, to cope with this problem? It is necessary to conceive the organization in such a way that the complexity faced by corporate management can be handled. This involves the distribution of management functions across the system with enhancement of the self-organization of each unit.

Similar examples could be taken from the domain of strategy, e.g. a business unit (BU) in its market, or a corporation facing a global market.

## Laws Underpinning Variety Engineering

The conceptual basis for variety engineering is Ashby's law—the law of requisite variety (Ashby, 1964, p. 206f). This is:

> Only variety can destroy (i.e. absorb) variety.

From this derives the law of residual variety:

> The behavioural repertory of management must be commensurate to the residual variety of the unit managed; that is, to the variety left unattended by the people in the unit and relevant to its performance.

This principle is as fundamental for managers as the laws of thermodynamics are for engineers.

We must also consider a theorem that derives from Ashby's law—the Conant-Ashby theorem (Conant and Ashby, 1970). It states

> Every good regulator of a system must be a model of that system.

In other words, a management's effectiveness is a function of the model on which it is based. The importance of this lies in the fact that management is always based on some model—whether managers are aware of it or not.

These three theorems are the basis for the rest of this book.

# AUTONOMY

The matrix organization example illustrates the need for devices to break down overwhelming complexity. A whole range of techniques for this are subsumed under the title 'variety engineering'; but one in particular is at the core of any organization's ability to deal with complexity: autonomy.

An organization creates and manages its relevant complexity by means of autonomous units within autonomous units. This is the principle of 'unfolding' complexity. In order to build up sufficient control variety it must differentiate itself into largely self-contained units. These must dispose of a high level of self-determination or freedom to make their own decisions.

The only effective way of coping is to foster responsiveness and adaptation on the many fronts where operations are carried out.

Autonomy is important. However, giving freedom to individual units may not be the most demanding task. Greater difficulty may lie in integrating these autonomous parts to form a cohesive whole.

# CONSTANCY AND CHANGE

As complexity unfolds along the arrow of time, new organizational arrangements become necessary. Therefore change is inevitable; often it is discontinuous. Now as environmental conditions as well as people's concerns, values and interests change, relationships between the organization and its environment have to change as well.

This is, in fact, a requirement if organizational integrity is to be maintained over time. Therefore, in the life of an organization not everything can be subject to change all the time.

Efficiency—'doing things right'—largely consists of getting more out of the resources we have through an ongoing learning process. This is what is involved in amortizing existing equipment, reaping economies of experience, and so on. At a higher logical level, effectiveness—'doing the right things'—may demand changing an orientation or a process e.g. by reinventing a strategy or redesigning an operation using advanced information technology.

These two perspectives have to be balanced; but on the grounds of what criteria? Again, the criteria must remain constant amid all change. They lie in the identity of the organization, in other words the relationships defining its wholeness.

The supreme art of management lies in balancing constancy and change by orchestrating phases of organizational preservation and transformation, thereby maintaining viability and development. That is the maintenance of 'organizational fitness'.

## First- And Second-Order Change

To maintain this balance between preservation and transformation, it must be recognized that not all change is the same. Most 'change' consists of more of the same thing. We call that 'first-order' change. Less frequent is change that produces something new—a new mode or a new quality. This is 'second-order' change.

First-order change is associated with quantitative growth; second-order change, with qualitative development or transformation. Under the former the underlying framework remains the same; the latter results in creating or adopting a new framework.

In business, we are accustomed to demanding 5 or 10% increases in sales, a rationalization of costs in the order of 3 or 4%, or an increase of customer satisfaction of two digits. Such demands can be very little and very much at the same time. Very much, even too much, if we consider what can be achieved by 'pressing a lemon' which has already been squeezed for several years. Maybe still too little, if we consider what has to be accomplished in the market place. Global competition, volatile customers, fragmented markets, shifting market boundaries, technological innovation and new restrictions may dictate another pace, setting challenges that can only be met by reaching entirely new levels of performance.

'Percentage thinking' is, in any case, dangerous. For example, in a railway system a policy of getting rid of the least efficient 5% of routes may, in effect, be a policy of destroying the system by depriving profitable routes of their 'feeder' lines. Another example is from social policy: reducing the working hours by, say, five a week—in Germany, from 37 to 32—in order to 'create' three million jobs may turn out to be a costly illusion. Often qualitative, not quantitative change is needed.

In other words, first-order change is insufficient, second-order change is necessary.

For this, the firm must reinvent itself. It must forget about obsolete practices. It must break established rules when they are outdated. There is no other way to eliminate restrictions, and to transform threats into opportunities.

Reinvention requires both reorientation and redesign. Reorientation must be in relation to values, principles and norms. Redesign must apply to structures and processes.

Can we provide any hints as to where to initiate change? We can describe two critical levers, based upon the keywords 'reorientation' and 'redesign'.

1. 'Redesign'. One key lever is described by the specialists in corporate re-engineering. They point out that today, the principles of mass production and division of labour have lost their importance. The new principles that have emerged are customized production and intelligent labour.

These involve two things:

a. re-unifying work and management,
b. organizing work around processes.

First, the reunification of work and management means abolishing the separation between thinking and doing. On the one hand, management functions such as planning, monitoring and control must be built into tasks. On the other hand, managers must be involved in, not separated from, daily business.

Organizing work around processes is the second requirement.

It is no longer necessary or desirable for companies to organize their work around Adam Smith's division of labour. Task-oriented jobs in today's world of customers, competitors and change are obsolete. Instead, companies must organize work around *process*, as in Hammer and Champy (1993, pp. 27f). Reshaping processes can lead the way to new levels of productivity. According to Hammer and Champy (1993, p. 32):

Reengineering is the fundamental rethinking and radical redesign of business processes to achieve dramatic improvements in critical, contemporary measures of performance, such as cost, quality, service and speed.

2. 'Reorientation'. Redesign, however, requires higher level orientators. Insufficient attention is often paid to these. There is a feeling: 'How can long-range planning or fixed principles be of any value, if everything is changing at an increasing rate?'

The idea of 'constants within change' seems paradoxical. It does not, however, embody a true contradiction. Every member of an enterprise needs to be able to behave intelligently and stay on course; otherwise they cannot continue making a valuable contribution to the larger whole of which they are part. For this they need to hold something crucial constantly in mind. The faster the business context changes, the more important become the constant elements by which people in an organization can verify if they are moving into the right direction.

In a multiperson system, a vision can only be realized if objectives are made clear to everyone involved. It follows that in our age of discontinuity, the importance of normative principles, cast into management concepts, corporate charters or vision statements, is growing.

Last but not least, however, principles have to be continually reexamined to check that they are still adequate orientators.

Summing up, significant organizational change is only possible if:

- there is a vision—a clear idea or image of what has to be changed;
- each organizational unit concerned formulates a specific concept or model of management and realizes it in a stepwise fashion.

## CONTROL AND COMMUNICATION

In order to maintain viability and development, an organization must control itself.

What do we mean by this? Control is simply the process by which a system realizes its vision and goals, in constant adaptation to the milieu into which it is embedded.

The management process can be depicted as a cycle that goes through the three phases: decision, implementation and control (Figure 3.7). Completion of the cycle leads back to the point—in a higher level decision cycle—at which the decision was made.

### Feedback And Feedforward: 'Steering'

Each phase of the management process in Figure 3.7 may itself be considered a cyclic sub-process. Let us look more closely into the structure of the control phase.

In the model of Figure 3.8, management appears first of all as the 'regulator' of a process by which actual data are verified, then fed into a control unit, where they are compared to goals. The comparison of actual and target values may then lead to corrective decisions.

So far, this is a process controlled on the basis of outputs only. We have a self-correcting feedback mechanism based on historical values. In such a regulatory process, the effect of disturbances is not anticipated.

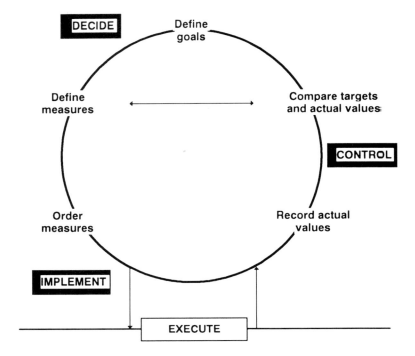

**Figure 3.7**   The management process as a cycle (Ulrich and Krieg, 1974)

A complementary principle must therefore be put into effect, one that is proactive. This is the mechanism of 'feedforward', based upon the detection of possible future disturbances, upon which prospective actions can be taken.

The creation of a desirable future is largely based on what we call 'steering'; that is, on feedforward and on pre-control—concepts that are further discussed below and by Schwaninger (1989).

### Communication

Regulation and steering are the complementary principles of control. As our diagram of the control loop shows, these principles rely on processes of communication.

In its broadest sense, communication means all the processes by which one system may affect another. A more detailed, technical understanding of communication processes is set out in Figure 3.9; it reveals that they convey information, are subject to constraints, and can be described in terms of transformations. The transformations include

● transduction with encoding and decoding,
● transmission,
● distortions due to the characteristics of a channel.

These terms are defined by Krippendorff (1986).

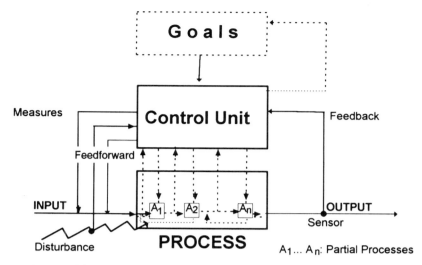

**Figure 3.8** A control loop

Code:   M ... Message
           T ... Transducer

Ideal Case:   $M_1 = M_2 = M_3 = M_4$

Real Case:   $M_1 \approx M_2 \approx M_3 \approx M_4$

**Figure 3.9** Diagrammatic representation of a communication process

Certain important lessons follow from this technical analysis. First, communication should always be designed and handled in such a way that loops are closed i.e. there is adequate confirmation that a signal has been received or acted on. Second, there must be enough redundancy for distortions to be compensated; this means that the channel must have a variety that exceeds the variety of the information to be transmitted.

## FROM FIRST-ORDER CYBERNETICS TO SECOND-ORDER CYBERNETICS

We can now draw upon the concepts of this chapter to make three important points.

1. *Control as a distributed function.* In today's organizations, the functions of management are increasingly decentralized or distributed across the whole system. The

historical separation between the functions of execution and control, characteristic of the age of mass production, is increasingly abolished by uniting these functions in the same hands.

Despite this, it makes sense to separate the management functions analytically, because we must not forget to design them appropriately. Analytical separation of the management function does not affect the principle that managers do and should consider themselves part of the units for which they carry responsibility.

2. *Control as a multilevel function involving pre-control.* The control cycle as we have described it does not take into account different levels of management. In reality, there is not only one type of goal or objective for an organization (or part of one), but goals and objectives are at three logical levels. Each level has its own criteria of 'organizational fitness', see Table 3.1

**Table 3.1**

| Levels of management | Criteria of organizational fitness |
| --- | --- |
| Operational management | Efficiency |
| Strategic management | Effectiveness |
| Normative management | Legitimacy |

Here:

a. Operational management is the management of day-to-day operations. The 'efficiency' criterion is 'to do what one does right' in the unit one is responsible for—the unit in focus.

b. Strategic management is management for the long term. The 'effectiveness' criterion is the creation of competence for better performance by 'doing the right things' in the unit in focus.

c. Normative management is management that balances the needs of the short and the long term by adhering to largely timeless principles, e.g. 'customer orientation', 'ethics' or 'aesthetics'. The 'legitimacy' criterion is the satisfaction of the needs of all relevant stakeholders in the unit in focus.

Being responsible for a unit involves controlling its performance at all three levels simultaneously. This implies knowledge of pre-control mechanisms. Specifically, strategic management has a pre-control function in relation to operative management, normative management in relation to strategic management.

At each one of these levels different orientators must be known and different control variables handled. These will be discussed in detail in Part Three, Chapter 8. For the underlying theory, see Schwaninger (1989).

3. *A new view of management.* We have used the term 'management' as a synonym for 'control'. The latter term, however, can be misunderstood.

Control is often equated with submission, i.e. subjugation to power, authority or influence. To us, this is an antiquated view. It leads to an approach to management that essentially restricts the degrees of freedom of a system. The new view of management we are presenting leads to the contrary: an increase in the number of degrees of freedom of the system in focus—as in von Foerster (1977).

A systemic approach to management, grounded in the new, second-order cybernetics—as in Maturana and Varela (1987), Maturana (1987) and von Foerster (1984)—that will be presented in the next chapter, emphasizes a paradigm expressed, in ordinary language, through attributes such as 'intrinsic' or 'autonomous' and prefixes such as 'self-', 'auto-', and 'eigen-'. We shall use terms such as eigen-behaviour, autonomous action, intrinsic control, self-reference and self-transformation to point to the intrinsic value attributed to individuals in organizations and the concern for the autonomy of decentralized actors—whether persons or organizational units.

What do these terms mean? By self-organization we mean the spontaneous formation of relationships and structural patterns and activities. By self-reference we mean, in this context, a system's reflection upon what it does—be the system an individual, a primary unit of an organization, or the organization as a whole.

By self-transformation we refer to the ability of organizations or organizational units to reorganize and restructure themselves. The term intrinsic control characterizes the activities of autonomous steering or regulation of an actor—whether this be a person in his or her workplace or a larger unit, such as a work group.

These last remarks—and in fact the whole of this last section—point to the need to take a step further the basic notions introduced in this chapter. This is necessary in order to take fully into account the implications of self-reference; that is, (a) of the observer being part of the observed system and (b) of a system observing itself and its interactions. This further step will in fact amount to a reconceptualization of these concepts; they are correct, but need to be seen in a new light. This will yield important new insights into the nature of organization, structure, complexity and communications.

To sum up: the language of this chapter has been largely that of first-order cybernetics. In the next chapter we revisit the concepts introduced here from the perspective of second-order cybernetics.

# Chapter 4

# Effective action in an organizational context

## INTRODUCTION

In this chapter we offer the reader a practical framework for effective action within the company; that is, a framework for managing performance.

We do this by introducing a particular language that will enable people, whether as individuals or members of teams, to adopt a new paradigm for their organizational action. This paradigm will move them away from the boss–subordinate relationship as the cornerstone of the management process, toward a method of effective self-management for individuals and groups within a networked structure of organizational relationships.

We will gradually introduce the reader to this new language. In doing so, we will seek to answer such fundamental questions as:

- What is effective action in an organizational context? How do I define this action? How can I take account of the future in my current actions?
- How can I improve the quality of my interactions in the organization? What is a proper balance between dealing with my local, immediate concerns and responding to distant pressures?
- How can I improve my contribution to the performance of the organization? How can I contribute to an increasingly effective organizational learning?
- How can I decide whether I am spending too much or too little time on a particular activity? How can I prioritize?
- How can group working take into account the wider organizational context by combining empowerment with a broad sense of organizational responsibility?
- How can we take adequate account of the rich interdependencies and different relevant sources of information that must and do exist in our organization, without being overwhelmed by this complexity?

Such questions as these may appear too philosophical to be of practical relevance. We hope, however, that by the end of this chapter the reader will be convinced that they are directly in the path of achieving more effective individual and team action in the organization—and, moreover, that some useful tools exist for resolving them.

# INTERACTIONS, RELATIONSHIPS, ORGANIZATION AND STRUCTURE

In the traditional organization, operating in a relatively stable environment, individual job roles are well defined and complexity is handled by breaking down the tasks of the organization into smaller and smaller divisions. Managers at all levels plan and prioritize the activities under their control, allocate and monitor the performance of resources, and provide a limited amount of liaison with surrounding operational units.

In the restructured workplace of today, this model of management is inadequate: corporate survival depends on less well defined work patterns, supported by better communications and a greater recognition of interdependencies among the organization's members as they collaborate in teams that are often temporary and, to a large degree, self-regulating.

This may sound exciting, stimulating and desirable in theory. However, a new kind of threat is posed if such new-style organizations are not underpinned by sound organizing principles. This is the threat of chaos. The old order and certainty is often replaced by feelings of powerlessness, of operating in a messy and highly stressed environment in which nothing ever appears to get done.

In the face of such feelings, people consciously or unconsciously tend to revert to the old, comfortable forms of authority and structure and the organization pulls back from what was beginning to be seen as a dangerous experiment that was 'getting out of control.' The command-and-control philosophy reasserts itself and the latent capabilities of people remain untapped, often to the detriment of quality and responsiveness to customer needs.

This widely shared experience makes it apparent that unless people develop a deeper understanding of organizational processes and the ways in which they relate to each other, the ideals of flexibility, self-regulation and improved communications will remain disconnected from our everyday experience. An appreciation of organizational processes based on interactions and relationships is an essential prerequisite for effective individual action.

## The Purpose Of Interactions

How are you 'aware' of what is taking place in your environment? How do you 'know' what is happening? A principle way of knowing is through your interactions with other people. I interact with you, you with me and through our reciprocal interaction we co-ordinate and ascribe meaning to our actions. 'No man is an island': if we see no one, talk to no one, listen to no one, our knowledge of the world is limited (Figure 4.1).

'Dance', reciprocal action,
action or influence of persons
or things on each other

**Figure 4.1** Interaction: co-ordination of action

## Conversations And Culture

Our interactions with others take place in two ways: through direct *conversations*, though not necessarily face to face, and through the sharing of common sources of information, in particular by sharing a *culture*.

Conversations are used to share concepts and develop agreements by conveying and receiving meaning through language. Meaning is conveyed not by the words alone, but by their context and a mixture of the words used and the emotions that speaker and listener feel whilst in conversation (Figure 4.2).

Conversation; the braiding of language
and emotions in recurrent interactions.
Action is co-ordinated by direct exchanges

**Figure 4.2** Direct interactions: conversations

Managing conversational moods—meanings and emotions—is vital to creating the space for effective interaction. Awareness of the mood of a conversation is achieved by actively listening to the other person, assessing the motivations revealed by their statements, working out our own expectations and being aware of the cultural context in which the conversation is taking place. These are all conversational skills necessary for effective interaction.

Managing conversational moods is vital to creating the space for effective action. Such awareness makes it more likely that commitments exchanged will be well understood and related actions competently performed. Managing the mood of the conversation in this way helps to create a more positive and open climate for creative problem-solving.

The other form of interaction—through common sources of information and in more general terms through sharing a culture—occurs when two people do not need to converse directly to know something of what the other thinks or believes. They share a common cultural framework for perceiving the world around them that enables them to co-ordinate their actions effectively (Figure 4.3). Examples of such common frameworks are family, local community or organizational culture.

Music

Action is co-ordinated by sharing common source of information

**Figure 4.3**  Indirect interactions: communications without channel capacity

A common framework exerts an influence on individuals' behaviour because the values and expectations of others regarding certain issues are known, e.g. you know whether or not it is acceptable to confront someone directly about a habit that is bothering you. There is no need to find out. We may choose to ignore those values and expectations. That is another matter; we know what they are.

Through our everyday conversations we shape the cultures in which we operate, and vice versa. People who interact strongly together in any group over time begin to have similar ways of perceiving the world, to ascribe a particular importance or significance to certain things and to share similar beliefs and values. Those beliefs and values in turn provide a powerful influence on the tone and nature of individual conversations that take place between group members. Organizational learning is taking place—as we will see in more detail in Chapters 6 and 7.

The stronger the cultural links between people, the greater the 'energy efficiency' of their communications. Given two organizations of a similar size, a few simple words and gestures may convey a wealth of information and subtle shades of meaning in one, whereas a massive investment in corporate communications and sophisticated media may be required to achieve an equivalent effect in the other. In other words, communication 'channels' may have higher capacity in the first organization than in the second, due to a common culture.

A prime function of leadership is to create the necessary conditions for interactions to take place among and between groups of people, i.e. to facilitate the emergence of vibrant cultures that can sustain the organization over time. This deliberate management of culture is everyone's job in the organization. It is supported and encouraged by the example of leaders at all levels.

## Organizational Relationships

As particular norms, values and meanings emerge through people's interactions, *relationships* are formed.

A relationship is the reciprocal outcome of the direct and indirect communications that occur between people over time. Relationships underpin our day-to-day interactions and the culture of organizations.

Therefore, changing the culture of an organization means changing the relationships underpinning people's interactions in that organization. We distinguish between organizational relationships and individual 'relations'. Whereas 'relations' are realized by individual people (those constituting a relationship), relationships are independent of the individuals involved. A particular company's hierarchical manager–workers relationship, for example, is independent of the manager and workers involved; they may change over time while the relationship remains (Figure 4.4).

Relationships are understood to be recurrent forms of interaction in which people ground the attachment of *meanings* (signification) to the symbols they use, establish, tacitly or explicitly, *norms* (legitimation) for their recurrent interactions and accept the *power* of some to allocate the resources implied by their interactions (domination) (see Giddens, 1984).

For as long as the relationship is maintained meanings, norms and power remain even if the particular individuals participating in the relationship, change.

## Definition of an organization: identity and structure

This concept of relationship allows us to offer an important insight concerning the nature of an organization. An organization is a closed network of interrelated people

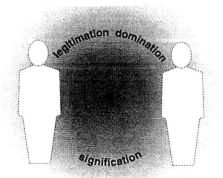

**Figure 4.4**   Relationships: forms of interaction

Organization: A set of relationships
with an identity of its own

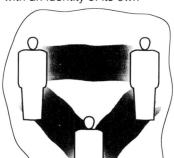

**Figure 4.5** Organization

with an identity of its own (Figure 4.5). It is the relationships between the participants that create a distinct identity for the network or group, giving it a sense of
coherence and wholeness.

An organization is defined as a closed network of relationships with an identity
of its own.

An organization's *identity* does not, therefore, depend on particular individuals:
they can be any, as long as they satisfy the relationships. On the other hand if the
relationships change, even if the people involved are the same, the organization
changes. It has a new identity.

Though identity is an abstract concept, an organization, as we define it, is a
concrete entity; it is realized by particular individuals and resources. Our daily
experience of an organization is the organization's *structure*. Therefore an organization has identity and structure.

Note that a particular organization may share with many others the same class
identity. Its distinctiveness derives from its structure, that is from the specific constitution of its relationships.

Can an organization be regarded as a closed system? Not in the sense of excluding
new members, or information, or communications with other relevant groups and
organizations. It has closure, however, in the sense that its relationships are sufficient to provide identity and cohesion to the organization.

It is apparent that by structure we do not mean the formal, hierarchical and
functionally-based reporting relationships shown on an organization chart. Unfortunately, this is a common meaning given to the word. Using 'structure' in this
sense, people may be tempted by trends toward self-managed teams and horizontal
interactions to conclude that it is no longer a relevant concept.

Our definition of 'structure', based on how we have defined 'organization', is
rather different.

An organization's structure consists of the concrete resources and relations that constitute its relationships; that is, by the interrelation of people, their roles, the units in which they participate and the other resources which they employ.

People's relations may be said to form *mechanisms*. 'Mechanisms', therefore, are formed out of roles, units and other resources that constitute stable forms of interaction—forms that allow the integrated operation of those resources (Figure 4.6).

The network of communication channels between specific people and resources constituting an organization.

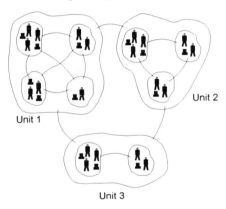

**Figure 4.6** Organizational structure

Understanding the structure of an organization means understanding the different mechanisms of interaction that constitute the organization. The organization chart offers, at best, only a partial view of these rich interdependencies.

**Communication Channels**

The contents of the various channels through which communications flow provides the organization with its structural cohesion: they are like the lifeblood of an organism.

Now our earlier discussion of interactions makes it clear that the capacity of an organization's communication channels will depend on their cultural context. The stronger the culture, the larger the communication capacity of these channels and the leaner the structure can be.

By working out the balance between direct and indirect interaction with other people and groups over time we help to determine not only the structure of the organization but also the cultural requirements for an effective organization.

If within a particular cultural context the channels of communication are inadequate or the conversations taking place between people are full of unresolved misunderstandings, double meanings and misinterpretations, then the structure will not be robust or able to cope with change in the organization's environment. Increasing our ability to identify other relevant people with whom we need to develop interaction and learning how to conduct those interactions to maximum effect is an essential part of making our individual actions consistent with excellent organizational performance.

# ABOUT COMPLEXITY: INVENTING THE WORLD AND INVENTING IN THE WORLD

In Chapter 3 we introduced variety, or the number of possible states of a situation, as a measure of complexity.

In this chapter, while we use the same concept, we emphasize the fact that complexity depends upon the observer; that is, different observers defining a situation will construe different sets of possible states. This section has been influenced by some of the concepts developed by Winograd and Flores (1986), by personal contacts with Flores and by related ideas published in Keen (1991).

Our ability to invent and re-invent the organization depends on our ability to discover and see new possibilities; but creating and seeing possibilities, making distinctions where others see uniformity, is a function of the complexity that we create and see in the world. That, in turn, is grounded in our history and the organizational context of our action.

We all create and see different possibilities. We may say, at the risk of implying that there is a pre-existing pool of possibilities, that we create complexity by *attenuating* differently the infinite space of possibilities; but, of course, there is no pool of predefined possibilities waiting to be discovered.

## Creating Complexity: Conversations For Possibilities

New distinctions and possibilities emerge from the creative braiding of past, present and future. Our understanding of the world is grounded in our histories; in the time and place of our development. These histories contribute to our views of the world; our *Weltanschauungen*. We are sensitive to particular aspects of the world at the expense of not visualizing a whole range of other possible aspects.

This historical structure—the *Weltanschauung*—affects the distinctions we make. If our *Weltanschauung* is one of abundance and large spaces we may be blind to creating and seeing states which depend on sensitivity to frugality and overcrowding. Managers in a company with an uninterrupted history of success may be blind to new management paradigms and therefore unable to see new possibilities by making use of current practices within a new perspective.

Today, inventing the organization is an ongoing process of constituting its identity, based on inventing relationships and, having done so, recognizing practices and behaviours necessary to realize them. Thus inventing the organization implies creating new distinctions and developing related practices. In fact, it is in the interplay between distinctions and practices that complexity is created and managed; that is, putting distinctions into practice necessitates both the making of further distinctions and the delegation of responsibility for them.

For instance, Kaisen—the philosophy of continuous improvement—brought, in recent years, a new *Weltanschauung* to the practice of management and organization in the West, and thereby contributed to the invention of a new kind of enterprise. The technical knowledge necessary for this revolution was available to western managers much earlier, in the 1940s and 1950s. However, their histories and views of the world blinded them, for a long time, to possibilities beyond the view that 'quality products are expensive'. It was Japanese industry that made apparent the possibility of products that were both cheap and of high quality. Today this distinction is commonplace.

Moreover, it can be argued that it has been continuous improvement, in the context of enterprises in decline, that made possible 're-engineering the corporation' as a new distinction. Continuous improvement, while it helped to invent a new corporation, paradoxically made it apparent that its philosophy only supported 'inventing in the corporation' rather than 'inventing the corporation'.

These concepts are based on two different time-spans. The first assumes that the future will be basically a continuation of the past, with only incremental changes in an already defined corporation. The second is based on the view that the future can be invented by people in the organization; it opens the space for revolutionary changes aimed at inventing a new corporation.

Creating complexity is based on conversations for possibilities (Flores, 1982).

These are conversations that invent new distinctions and thereby create altogether new processes, technologies and practices. They may be said to articulate new domains for action. Conversations for possibilities are grounded on appreciative processes, and depend on the awareness people develop about their histories and *Weltanchauungen*. Therefore these conversations, though realized through the resources and relationships of the current organizational structure, are dominated by historical structures.

## Operational Complexity: Conversations For Action

The complexity involved in making things happen, whether by implementing ongoing operations or new commitments, is related to the myriad actions emerging from conversations in which people make offers and commit themselves to perform particular actions. This is the complexity stemming from conversations for action.

Conversations for action are grounded on commitments; their satisfactory completion is dependent upon both people's conversational skills and the structural capacity of the organization to support them. Conversations for action have the following loop structure:

> A makes an offer to B or B a request to A;
> A and B negotiate conditions of satisfaction for offer/request;
> A performs (directly or indirectly) relevant actions;
> B declares satisfaction with A's actions.

Often satisfactory conversations for action depend on the contributions of people who are distant from the conversations themselves. This implies that negotiating adequate conditions of satisfaction for the conversation will depend on an appreciation of a wide range of increasingly distant subsidiary conversations and therefore on the performers' ability to measure the complexity of those distant conversations.

**Braiding The Structure Needed For Change With The Organizational Structure**

In all cases conversations are realized by the people whose relationships constitute the organizational structure. Thus conversations for possibilities and for action are grounded in the organizational structure.

To create possibilities without creating the capacity to make them happen is to be ineffectual. It is ineffectual, also, to negotiate conditions of satisfaction for a conversation without adequate channel capacity for this negotiation. Rushed agreements produced under operational pressures most likely will result in either unexpected costs or unsatisfied customers. These are constraints arising from organizational structure that reduce the possibility of inventing the corporation and inventing in it.

**Breakdowns, Breakthroughs And Issues Of Concern**

Often we appreciate the complexity of business processes because of breakdowns in our conversations.

While everyone is performing according to their commitments, there is nothing to be concerned about; the related processes are well balanced and under control. We experience them as transparent and exhibiting no complexity. Their complexity is in fact being absorbed by previous learning; that is why we do not experience it until we experience breakdowns in these conversations.

Breakdowns may emerge, among other sources, from inadequate communications, unrealistic expectations, poor understanding of others' views and inadequate assessment of the implications of our commitment. It is good to try to understand these experiences and learn from them.

Breakthroughs—new, possibly better ways of doing things—may emerge from breakdowns or independently of them, as a result of discovering new possibilities. Pursuing a breakthrough leads to the making of new distinctions, and so opens the floodgates to new complexity.

In experiencing breakdowns and breakthroughs we are making distinctions in the organizational background. As we do so we are construing issues of our concern.

An issue of concern is construed by a participant in a situation as he observes the situation he is participating in. He perceives issues that must be decided in order to resolve the situation.

All of this is, in a general sense, part of the process of learning. As we and the organization learn, we create distinctions and related practices as a way of reducing the complexity relevant to us—the complexity we experience, that threatens to become overwhelming.

# ON BEING AN OBSERVER: ABOUT MENTAL CONSTRUCTS

As individuals, some people prefer to be thrown into action, others to be observers of it.

While all of us are, by nature, both actors and observers, it is clear that the balance between these two roles may vary from one individual to the next. Observation is not, of course, an end in itself. Effective individuals—those with the ability to learn from their actions—are able to make good use of observation; that is, they are able to use their observations to develop the necessary practices to reduce the operational complexity relevant to them.

By detaching ourselves temporarily from the action of the moment and becoming an observer, we abstract ourselves from the world of experience—the operational domain in which we constitute our realities—and move into the informational domain of ideas and *mental constructs*. The habit of observation is critical for developing not only self-awareness but also awareness of the actions of other people. Observation enables us to create in our minds *mental models* about situations (Figure 4.7).

**Figure 4.7**   Observers construing a situation from their experience

Moreover, when we begin to share our observations, or mental models, with others with whom we are in conversation and try to understand their way of viewing a situation, new, creative possibilities may emerge. For although two or more people can never have identical experiences, since experience is personal to the individual, they can open up new worlds of future potential by sharing understanding as participant observers of a situation.

It is in conversational processes that people ground their ideas and relate their realities. Individual realities are bridged by constructs, i.e. shared mental models, created from grounding experiences on a shared model (Figure 4.8).

**Balancing Experience And Observation**

Every individual, regardless of their organizational role, must strike a balance between experience (being thrown into action) and observation (being a participant observer of this action). However, whether we are managers, supervisors, or anything else, our interaction preferences will affect the roles that we can successfully perform in an organization.

**Figure 4.8**   A shared construct

Consider the case of Mr Knop who is proud of his reputation as a goal oriented man; a man of action and infinite pragmatism. He believes wholeheartedly in quick responses and has no time to get involved in lengthy reflections about his experiences. He 'knows' what each situation is and likes to be close to the action. If he is not busy doing something all the time and witnessing those around him similarly occupied, he becomes uncomfortable and impatient. He involves himself in everything and anything, and is so busy reacting to events on the ground that he is unable to recognize new possibilities in them, let alone to create new possibilities in conversations with others. Using the terms we shall develop in Chapters 6 and 7, we would say that he is good at 'single loop' learning.

In his role as manager, Mr Knop is likely to be a failure. Because of his unwillingness to make use of observation and reflection to get the most out of his experiences, he tends to limit the organization relevant to him to that currently in place. If he had access to changes and innovations he would be unlikely to recognize in them new possibilities or be able to integrate them into new organizational practices. If he were responsible for a large organization, his emphasis on already established practices at the expense of creating new possibilities would have potentially serious consequences for its survival.

Whatever his various roles in life may be—whatever the organizations of his concern—Mr Knop will need to develop his personal capability to detach himself from current pressures in order to open himself up to new possibilities and become effective in those roles.

By contrast, Ms Lessing prefers to spend her time reflecting about situations. She will irritate others in their conversations and meetings by questioning the meaning of every action, delaying decisions. She will avoid action meetings—which are never initiated by her in the first place—in order to provide more time for reflecting about the current situation.

Ms Lessing suffers from lack of operational commitment; she has an extremely rich and creative understanding about organizational situations but is slow in developing new practices and improving existing ones and remains totally oblivious to pressures 'to make things happen'. She is operationally 'out of touch' with the other members of her immediate work group.

Ms Lessing's fine theories, reflections and far-flung connections do not compensate for her failure to support the essentials of her immediate surroundings, making her as ineffective as Mr Knop in handling change in her various life roles.

### Ideas 'Of' And 'About' A Situation

In one form or another we are constantly constructing views about the situations of our concern. Both Mr Knop and Ms Lessing are developing and evolving mental constructs based on their experiences and assumptions of the world. Those who are like Mr Knop tend to develop ideas *of* the situation rather than *about* the situation. The opposite is the case with those like Ms Lessing.

Mr Knop is more likely to think that there is a well defined, uncontroversial, world. Since he spends so little time reflecting on the situation, everything he experiences is the case as he sees it; the world is objective. Ms Lessing, on the other hand, is more likely to procrastinate as she questions everything and feels unsure as to whether her views are shared by the others. Her constant questioning of established views about everything makes it difficult for people to work with her. She is constantly stopping the normal flow of conversations, creating ill feelings and the sense that nothing is well defined. Her inability to work out the consensual domain of people's actions makes it more difficult for them to work in the same direction as her, with a common platform.

Mr Knop is lacking in subtlety; Ms Lessing lacks common sense. Neither of these two extremes offers a model for effective action. While the distinctions of Mr Knop's world may be relatively few, those of Ms Lessing's are too many. On the other hand, while Mr Knop may have solid practices with which to support his distinctions, Ms Lessing may lack practices of the most elementary kind. Neither of the two is producing enough complexity; Mr Knop is not producing enough new distinctions, while Ms Lessing does not create practices to support her wealth of distinctions. A proper balance would require, on the one hand, for Mr Knop to question his 'objective' world. He has to realize that his world is created as he shares views with others, and that it is through conversations that he grounds, jointly with others, his and *others'* views in a shared but not common reality. He may be tempted to disregard the complexity of others by behaving as if there were no other reality than his. On the other hand, Ms Lessing needs to accept that there is an already shared common platform for action; this is a shared reality grounded in the organization's culture. It provides the necessary objectivity to make possible people's co-ordinated actions.

Mr Knop needs to free his mind from predefined blinkers and be ready to produce unconstrained ideas. Ms Lessing needs to develop skills to make things happen; she needs to appreciate the learning responsible for the existing constraints and operate within those constraints.

## MANAGEMENT OF COMPLEXITY

Managing complexity implies on the one hand focusing attention on those tasks that are relevant to us, and on the other, achieving an adequate performance as we carry them out. Though managing complexity is something we do all the time, whether or

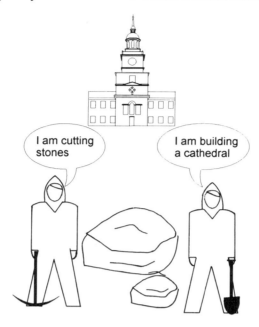

**Figure 4.9**   Ascribing purpose to an action

not we are aware of the 'implicit tasks' we are managing, the idea is applied in what follows to individual action in an organizational context.

### Individual Purpose

It is as observers that we may explicitly ascribe purpose to our action and to the actions of other people, thus construing these actions as activities. Hence, how we construe them will vary from observer to observer; the same action may be construed as 'cutting stones' or 'building a cathedral' (Figure 4.9).

Even if we do not explicitly ascribe purposes to our actions, another observer may infer our purposes by observing our actions and their outcomes. In their eyes we are implicitly ascribing a purpose to our actions.

Ascribing purpose is necessary in order to focus our management of complexity. It helps us to work out the interactions consistent with the ascribed purpose. Having worked these out, it is necessary to define performance criteria; these help us to establish needed response capacity.

If I am clear about the priorities that really matter to me as an individual and keep these few overriding priorities firmly in mind as I go about my day-to-day activities, this is perhaps the most effective 'complexity-reducer' I can employ. It means exercising the self-discipline required to continually hold my organizing priorities in view and refresh or update them regularly.

It also means using this sense of purpose to:

1.  deal first with those things that are important to me and urgently need to be done;
2.  decline, under most circumstances, to commit myself to things that may appear

urgent to myself or to other people, but upon reflection are not important in terms of the priorities, values and long term goals I have established for myself;
3.  avoid altogether time-wasting activities that are neither important for or urgent to me;
4.  use the time freed by 2 and 3 above to spend as long as I possibly can on activities that are important to me but not urgent.

Exercising this personal discipline enables us to integrate long term with short term thinking, and local relations management with the more distant networking that is essential to an accurate understanding of our environment and its potentials.

## Situational Purpose: Tasks

The same discipline applies to a group of people or an organization. Organizational situations do not have inherent purposes of their own: it is only people, as observers in interaction with one another, who ascribe purposes to such situations.

By reaching agreement about their purposes, they can focus their efforts more accurately on the activities that contribute to or are consistent with those purposes (Figure 4.9). These are the tasks of their concern.

Purposes are ascribed in different modes in an organizational context:

1.  as a declaration of current purpose by a person, group or organization in doing what they are doing (their 'espoused purpose');
2.  as a declaration of intent used by an individual or group to state what they believe is a worthwhile future purpose (their 'strategic intent' or 'future' purpose);
3.  as an ascription of tacit purpose as perceived by some observers. For them 'the purpose of an organization is what it does'. For the observers this is the organization's 'purpose in use'.

An example may illustrate these distinctions. Suppose you are in a meeting at which for two hours the conversation has dwelt exclusively on the issue of whether a unit would hit its sales target at the coming year end and whose fault it would be if it did not. It gradually dawns on you that the meeting was originally called to discuss how the unit would position itself in the future, taking into account new market potentials and other environmental factors. What would you then do?

You might decide to offer to the group the observation that it has in fact changed its remit from the original purpose of the meeting; in other words, that its 'purpose in use' now appears significantly different from its 'espoused purpose'. It could be that the group members are happy with this change of purpose, in which case the 'espoused purpose' needs to be changed in line with the 'purpose in use'; whatever the outcome, the observing role is a useful check-point to validate declared purposes and a valuable aid to the study of organizations in action.

The focus throughout is on how people relate their experiences to an informational domain. People do not have direct access to the experiences of other people. Yet they share common domains of experience. It is by observing these experiences and ascribing meaning, i.e. purpose, to them that they reduce them to something they can talk about and share with others.

## Declaring An Organization's Purpose: The Organization As A Task

Whenever we ascribe a purpose to an organization, we reduce the autonomous, purposeless nature of the organization; it becomes a functional, purposeful *primary activity* or *task* (see Chapter 3 and Figures 4.10 and 4.11).

From the viewpoint of an observer, the purpose
of the organization is what it does

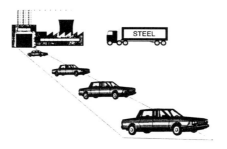

This factory <u>transforms</u> raw materials into cars

T: producing cars is the 'primary process'

Purposes of T • Solve individual transportation
problem
• Create economic activity... etc.

**Figure 4.10**   Ascribing purpose to an organization

Organizational identity
Defines what the organization is

The identity does not necessarily need
purposes or products

## Task Identity

However we recognize an organization
by ascribing purpose to it

Ascribing purpose to the organization
- Do 'T' for the purpose 'Z'

**Figure 4.11**   Organizational identity

What is the organization here to deliver? This is to ask what is its primary process, i.e. what input is transformed into what output.

Who is involved? This is to ask who are its immediate suppliers and customers, who is performing this 'primary process', who controls it and who provides the context in which it takes place.

Answering this set of questions carefully and concisely helps individuals to work out not only the required organization's complexity but also the specific complexity relevant to them. It enables them to work out the structural requirements to achieve a declared purpose. Also, they can work out at a more personal level the immediate and distant interactions they need to manage in order to deliver their commitments.

By answering these questions they may avoid unnecessary interactions that distract them from a stated purpose. In short, the questions help them to compare their current strategies to manage complexity with those necessary to make the organization viable.

### Individual And Organizational Purposes

The differing purposes of the organization and the individual are not necessarily a source of conflict. They can be complementary, reinforcing principles of orientation.

Effective performance requires that organizational and individual purposes are aligned.

An individual with a weak sense of personal purpose may find that the experience of contributing actively to the formation of a group purpose triggers the will and capacity to develop a stronger sense of personal mission and values. Similarly, an individual in a leadership role with a highly developed individual purpose may inspire others to share something of his or her value system.

As individuals we naturally belong to several 'organizations', e.g. our extended family, circle of close friends, sports clubs, church group or local community action committee. We also belong to different organizational networks and management teams. Therefore an individual's organizing priorities, derived from his or her commitments in several different spheres of life, will not be identical to those of another individual, even though both are members of one particular organization. As human beings, we are by definition autonomous entities and must co-ordinate our actions with others in recognition of this.

It is, however, clear that we do not need to intrude into the full range of organizing priorities held by each member of a particular group to arrive at a common purpose for that group. What is required is adequate structural mechanisms for debate and interchange of ideas to enable all members to root a commonly held purpose for the group in their own personal value systems.

When these debates are inadequate, when individuals do not perceive a meaningful link between their own purposes and value systems and that of the task under discussion, then their motivation to contribute to that task will be weak. Individuals may 'go along' with the will of the more vociferous group members, perhaps to avoid upsetting others or to save having to ask embarrassing questions, but the interaction will not result in a high level of performance for the group as a whole. Dominant team member(s) may enjoy a temporary sense of power, but the longer term results will be a lower level of performance through a failure to tap into the latent energies of all the group members.

## More About Managing Complexity

As individuals, our understanding of the world is influenced by our own *immediate experiences* and *information about others' experiences*. Our ability to cope with complexity depends on how well we balance experience and information.

Consciously or not, people in organizations are continually striving to find and maintain a balance in coping with the complexity relevant to them. If I find myself in a situation in which I feel myself to be bombarded by different calls on my attention with insufficient means to respond to all these demands, I feel uncomfortable. I may try to recover my sense of balance by finding extra resources, delegating some tasks, hiring consultants, i.e., by *amplifying* my capacity to respond—or by choosing to ignore, temporarily at least, certain demands while I deal with others—thereby *attenuating* the complexity that I perceive in my situation. (See Figure 4.12.)

Managerial strategies to cope with complexity

amplify my complexity by getting the **commitment** of others while in conversation

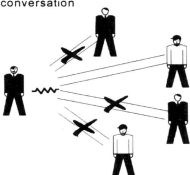

Attenuation of local complexity: Selection of **one conversation out of four**

**Figure 4.12**  Strategies to cope with complexity: local complexity operators

My performance will depend on how well I manage these balancing acts. For instance, suppose I select an operator to deliver certain supplies within an hour to another plant. By selecting the right operator I perform adequate attenuation; if the operator then does it, I perform adequate amplification. Thus by these two means I have managed effectively the complexity of my agreed task.

Operationally, in fact, in our local environments, we are each *attenuators and amplifiers of complexity* (i.e. complexity operators) vis-à-vis that environment. Our intentions and purposes, our visions and values, our expectations and preferences all help to determine how we maintain a balance with our local environment: which conversations we choose to have, how we conduct ourselves in those conversations, whether we gain support and commitment from colleagues or the opposite, and so on. We cope with distant information in a similar way: we pay attention to certain distant events while filtering out, consciously or otherwise, all the rest. Today we are increasingly dependent on distant information, i.e., on the experiences of others, to maintain balance in our interactions. Without this distant information it would be impossible for us to commit ourselves to tasks which depend on others for their performance.

As illustrated in Figure 4.13, I may get task amplification by getting the *support and commitment* of others. These others may be individuals or groups. They are shown in Figure 4.13 by drawing closed circles—the symbol we use for autonomous units. Equally, I may reduce the task complexity relevant to me by *trusting* that others will do whatever is necessary to perform the task successfully, leaving to my attention a more manageable residual complexity.

Task complexity is the outcome of task amplification and attenuation.

Amplification of task

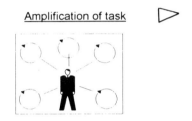

Creating the conditions for autonomy

Attenuation of task complexity:

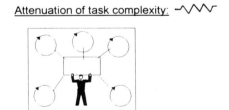

Residual complexity is manageable

**Figure 4.13**  Strategies to cope with complexity: distant complexity operators

My relevant complexity is then not the full complexity handled by myself and others but just the residual complexity left to me by them.

In all cases we need to ensure the integrity of the distant information. We need to ground its meaning for us in local experience of the distant situation—a point explored further in Chapter 5. Information cannot supersede the need for communications; if we do not support the information available to us with occasional communications we are likely to lose touch with the situation.

To overcome this problem we find the need to communicate with selected others who organizationally operate at a distance from ourselves in order to learn from their experiences. However, there are limitations to this way of extending our own experience. People cannot spend their whole time in it! Such communications can take place only occasionally.

It is in this balancing that we define the quality of our links with various organizational tasks. The bottom part of Figure 4.14 shows the local communications, and related complexity operators, between people in interaction: their interactive venue. In these interactions they ground, with different degrees of success, shared purposes for the organization they are constituting and thereby define the organizational task venue. At the same time they are construing their individual tasks; this takes place in their cognitive venue (Whitaker, 1992).

**Managers constituting their organizational
tasks through local and distant communications**

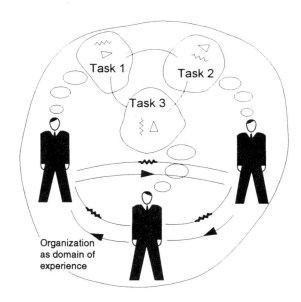

**Figure 4.14** Organizational complexity

The links among tasks in the upper part of the diagram show their distant communications with related tasks of their concern. Based on this, they can make effective use of information about these tasks.

### Balancing Local And Distant Information

As individuals we perform various roles in relation to different organizations. I may be referred to as 'colleague', 'spouse', 'parent', 'team member', 'football coach' and 'chairperson,' all within the same 24-hour period. These are all roles that I may assume in relation to the organizations of my concern.

How do we manage our performance in our different roles? We use 'local' and 'distant' information to help 'inform' our interactions so that we reach out and over time we learn to improve our performance beyond the boundaries of our immediate activities.

As with experience and observation, it is important to keep the two modes of operation in balance.

Mr Muller, for example, is very much a man in charge of his task; he believes first and foremost in maintaining good communications with the people in his immediate workplace. As regards what is happening elsewhere, he is totally dependent on distant reports; he neither goes to visit people elsewhere, nor is he interested in maintaining communication with them. His focus is purely local.

In his role as a manager, Mr Muller is likely to have problems in the long run, even if he appears successful in the short run. Because he does not interact enough with people in distant roles, his distant information is all second or third hand. He is unable to grasp the meaning of what is going on elsewhere. He lacks the context of the wider organization and the changes affecting it.

If Mr Muller has the role of managing director, his inability to assess accurately the meaning of distant information is likely to increase misunderstandings and breaks in communications. His 'inner cabinet' of supporters may form an effective screen against outside events, probably with devastating results for his company.

Problems with distant information are not, however, confined to managerial roles. If Mr Muller is a machine operator, his inadequate appreciation of the capabilities and skills available in the next department or his lack of appreciation of the customer's requirements may make all the difference between finding a timely solution to an unusual production problem and failing to do so.

Ms Schmidt, by contrast, prefers to spend her time checking directly the information she receives in reports from distant sources. She will postpone meetings with her immediate co-workers, or limit the time she spends in them, in order to have a deeper understanding of events elsewhere in the company and the market.

Ms Schmidt has a rich understanding of what is happening in the wider world but remains unaware of what the person at the next desk is thinking or feeling. She is 'out of touch' with the other members of her immediate work group. Ms Schmidt's good grasp of distant events will not be complemented by the commitment and action of the people close to her, making her as ineffective as Mr Muller at handling change in any of her life roles.

Achieving an optimum balance between these two extremes is not easy. We can see in principle that it makes sense to balance and validate our day-to-day information with access to more distant people, their experiences and concerns; yet in the face of the complexity posed by this multidimensional networking, or 'balancing act', we tend to retreat to the comfort zone of our preferred mode of operation. In this way we limit our potential for learning and adaptation, with negative effects on organizational learning.

> Individuals' processing of local and distant information need to be balanced for individual and organizational learning to take place.

# INDIVIDUAL AND ORGANIZATIONAL LEARNING

How do we make individual and organizational learning more effective?

As *individuals* we learn when we detect and correct 'errors'.

'Errors' are what we have earlier identified as 'issues of concern'. They are triggered by experiences that do not match our expectations. They appear against a background that is, for us, transparent.

It is, however, when we act upon these mismatches and reduce or eliminate the 'errors' that learning takes place. The distinctions we make in and about a situation affect our performance only if they are accompanied by actions. We learn when we produce effective actions from errors.

'Errors' may create defensive practices as well as new possibilities. At a deeper level, in order to learn, we may need to question the assumptions and views of the world that led us to experience particular errors in the first place. Changing these assumptions and views of the world is indeed at the core of individual learning.

In a learning situation, each of us is on the one hand developing, articulating and creating new distinctions, thus increasing the sophistication of our situational attenuation. On the other hand, we are developing new behaviours and practices to deal effectively with the distinctions made, thus creating the amplifiers for our action. As we learn we become more effective in making situational distinctions and in developing the necessary practices and skills to perform well in that kind of situation. Learning is manifested by our successful action in a situation rather than by our accumulated information about it.

We are, therefore, experiencing learning difficulties if we show great ability in developing constructs and models about a situation but limited ability in producing managerial practices based on those constructs and models. Equally, we are experiencing learning difficulties when we are unable to create new distinctions in a changing situation. Learning implies the balanced development of attenuators—a person's capacity to make distinctions—and amplifiers—the capacity to produce effective action.

*Organizational learning* is the creating, acquiring and transferring of distinctions and practices in the organization. It is effective if it increases the organization's fit to its environment. Organizational learning implies behaviour modification, including changes in relationships, in order to create the conditions for creating, acquiring and transferring distinctions and practices.

An organization is learning when people in it succeed in overcoming defensive practices, i.e., practices that reduce the chances of error detection or creation of new possibilities. An organization is learning when it evolves towards structures that on the one hand do not inhibit individual creativity and on the other do not overload or under-utilize people's skills.

In a learning organization the trend is towards distributed complexity. Bottlenecks—where people are overloaded—are eliminated. At the same time, problem-solving capacity is distributed; people's skills and capacities are developed throughout the organization. Self-organizing processes become aligned with global interests and people increasingly find that their own purposes and interests are synergistic with those declared for the organization.

As an organization learns, the issues of organizational concern change. People find that more and more they are in a position to create the organization's environmental complexity, rather than just to respond to external problems. More and more senior managers find that people within the organization have, independentl/ of them, the capacity to deal with most issues (Figure 4.13). In this context they hav∋ to deal with fewer issues, to the point where increasingly they find themselves creating possibilities rather than fire fighting internal problems.

Individual and organizational learning depend on working out ir dividual and organizational expectations, and if possible related criteria of performance.

Working out expectations and performance is not the result of unilateral views or decisions, but the result of being aware of our purposes and the wider environment of our actions. Knowing whether expectations are met over time does, however, require measurement of one kind or another. Mismatches in our expectations may trigger the need for inquiries. If these inquiries lead us to make more distinctions and these distinctions give way to new organizational practices, then we talk of organizational learning. On the other hand, if detecting errors merely triggers short term responses, avoiding the creation of new distinctions and practices, then there is little or no organizational learning and it is likely that problems will be compounded in the longer term.

Working out expectations and performance criteria, measuring organizational processes and producing responses to bring performance closer to expectations are the elements of the multiple learning loops constituting an organization. These loops provide the platform for personal and organizational learning.

Effective learning puts more complexity under the umbrella of self-regulating processes. Thus it at the same time reduces the complexity that individual managers have to cope with while increasing total organizational complexity. In this way it creates the space for both inventing the organization and inventing in the organization.

## Organizational Learning Through Co-ordinated Action

Vision and commitment are the key to realizing the potentials of an organization as a group of people.

Vision is what enables individual purposes to combine into a collective group purpose. It provides the accelerator, steering wheel and route map for the group, keeping it moving forward in a direction with which all group members can identify. Commitment provides the staying power—the maintenance of the engine, gears, brakes and other moving parts—that ensures the vehicle is capable of reaching the required destination.

Vision is created through conversations for possibilities among organizational members. These are future-focused discussions that prepare the groundwork and provide the momentum for change. Through them individuals discover a commonly desired future state. Commitment to the realization of conversations for possibilities is achieved when relevant participants can relate the ideas for change to their world of day-to-day experience. If they perceive the ideas for change to be so far-fetched as to be impractical, unrealizable, or in some way threatening, people will resist taking steps to implement the change, either because they cannot see how it can happen or because they do not feel inwardly that it is really desirable.

Therefore, conversations for possibilities need not only to take place in an atmosphere in which all participants contribute fully to the creation of a shared vision;

they also need to be complemented by conversations for action which ensure that the possibilities are fully tested for implementability in the light of the practical commitments and constraints raised by the participants.

What we are describing is in effect the learning loops experienced by people in an organization. Conversations for possibilities within a group may lead to commonly shared and articulated visions, desired futures and shared issues of concern. These conversations will rely on the participants' ways of thinking and explaining the world, i.e., their explanatory frameworks. The challenge lies, not in reducing all these frameworks to one shared by all, but in creating operational links among them in order to integrate their unique contributions around the articulated visions.

Achieving this will depend on the quality of the conversations. If a group is dominated by certain individuals, or if processes are inadequate in any sense, the chances for effective checks and balances are reduced. However in one form or another these interactions will support some conversations and hinder others; those surviving this testing phase trigger conversations for action, i.e. commitments, that in turn create new experiences, and so on. Indeed, this is a recurrent process in which conversations for action trigger new possibilities that in their turn trigger new conversations for action, and so on.

In other words, learning loops exist in an organizational context. Whether the participants are aware of it or not, learning loops are embodied in the organizational structure (this point is developed further in Chapter 7). If the participants are to improve the effectiveness of these learning loops they need to develop, maintain and improve their awareness of the organizational context in which their interactions take place.

They need to create mechanisms to grasp distant information concerning the purposes and actions of other relevant groups within the surrounding organization—otherwise their debates and activities will not take these into account. They also need to review periodically the mechanisms underpinning their own internal group processes to improve the quality of their debates and interactions over time. Are all the group members contributing fully or are there inhibiting factors that hinder open discussion? How can these be effectively addressed so that the group can achieve a still higher level of performance?

Without a language to gain insight into these working processes, groups of people in interaction run the risk of being trapped in vicious circles. Their discussions may lead to limited performance improvement in the short term. However, without the support of effective organizational processes they may lack the capacity to move on to new, higher levels of learning.

The chances are that a group operating in a poor organizational context will not have the necessary staying power to deal effectively with more complex organizational problems—those that require organizational amplification. These aspects of the learning process will be discussed in depth in the next three chapters.

## PROVIDING THE ORGANIZATIONAL CONTEXT FOR EFFECTIVE NETWORKING

We develop networks of interactions as we manage the complexity of our organizational tasks.

Our strategies for managing complexity fix the limits of effectiveness of our actions. Through our conscious and unconscious choices we create certain networks and exclude ourselves from others.

Yet because of the problem of maintaining balance in each individual's local environment, no network, however important to the organization as a whole, can grow effectively beyond a certain size: its members simply cannot cope with the intensity of maintaining continuous interaction with more than a limited number of people on the issues they confront in their day-to-day life. Spreading their resources too thinly over many fronts may make them ineffective in these interactions, perhaps creating chaos.

Instead, in practice operational networks tend to cluster around particular roles and functions, creating to different degrees local cliques and intra-functional cooperation, but not necessarily building up the required organizational interdependencies. Though in recent times we have seen a strong move towards multifunctional teams and workflow-based networks, in practice these teams and networks tend to slide toward hierarchies.

In the next section we will examine the characteristics of an organization that, while embracing current management trends, remains immersed in the traditional organizational hierarchy or pyramid. In the section after that, we examine an alternative to this restructured but in fact still hierarchical structure. This is the recursive structure.

### The Restructured Hierarchy

Consider then, an organization that has undergone restructuring to embrace multifunctional team work and horizontal flows of work, yet has retained its overall hierarchical structure. As we move down the pyramid, we observe different groups in action.

The top group, or clique, is busy deciding questions of business strategy. It is, however, not always aware that what its members know—albeit they are intelligent, experienced managers—is limited by their biology, that is, by their limited capacity as individuals. Moreover, their knowledge of the current and potential state of their organization and the environment that surrounds it is over-dependent on what others tell them, without further corroboration. Thus, self-important as they are, they are often unaware that their decisions are either groundless or are, in reality, the decisions of others within the organization—those that provide them with the options.

Groups around the middle layer of the organization are engaged in formulating operational policies for the lower levels in the light of the strategic aims laid down by the top group. These groups are networking frantically, but, again, are making decisions—or failing to make them!—about what should happen lower down the organization with a poor understanding of the operations that they think they have to manage and, even more significantly, with a lack of action capacity to cope with the ideas and possibilities coming from the shop floor. Moreover, they are fighting one another about who really is managing which operations and which work group should 'belong' to which manager. Nor can they seem to get enough attention from top management, which is always 'far too busy'; this is another source of competition between them.

Finally, as we approach the bottom of the pyramid, the 'worker' groups are bemused and skeptical about all this talk of 'empowerment'. What they are experiencing is cajoling from management to work in teams to solve work-related problems, accompanied by numerous directives and counter-directives, rearrangements of the teams and 'flavour-of-the-month' productivity campaigns.

What is happening is that all significant decisions regarding how their work should be organized are taken by the level above and nobody appears to listen very much to them. The truth is, their managers simply do not have the time to do all the networking that this would require. The result is, that except for one or two isolated examples of 'heroic brilliance' in the face of all odds, innovation is not really happening on the shop floor, the order processing department—or anywhere else.

Is it then inevitable that this organization must slide back to the notion of an organizational hierarchy or pyramid composed of the most important networks or cliques sitting on top of middle management networks that in turn sit on top of 'worker' networks? Not at all!

How, then, can we build workable and at the same time creative organizational networks? The 'undifferentiated network' is clearly impracticable. The organizational cascade of networks is hardly distinguishable from the traditional model that we are seeking to replace—hopefully, with a more adaptive organizational paradigm.

### The Recursive Structure

The answer lies in recognizing and respecting the autonomy of individuals and teams. The difficulty that every individual experiences in handling complexity leads naturally to a system of embedding autonomous tasks within autonomous tasks, rather than to a system of delegating responsibilities from one level to the next. We call this the recursive structure.

A recursive structure comprises 'autonomous units within autonomous units'. Each unit or network within the structure, inasmuch as it is producing the organization's task, rather than servicing or supporting this producing, should be a complete microcosm of the totality in which it is embedded: it should have all the functions of policy-making, intelligence gathering, control, co-ordination and implementation to enable it to manage, from start to finish, the processes for which it is held accountable. (In Chapter 5 we discuss these various management functions in more detail.)

Thus each unit or network does not merely implement policies laid down by the level above. It must create its own policies and exercise its own mechanisms for the adaptation and control of the tasks of its concern.

As we have said, the units or networks that are implementing the company's ascribed purpose are its 'primary activities'. The concept of recursion requires that these activities be structured as autonomous tasks within autonomous tasks. Embedded tasks are created and managed locally, rather than globally.

Not only does the level of detail at which tasks are managed increase as we move down the structure but the nature of these tasks is generated and managed locally. Thus the apparently much larger complexity of the whole organization is absorbed by the autonomous parts, leaving for higher management a manageable residual complexity—namely, the complexity of integrating the parts into a global task.

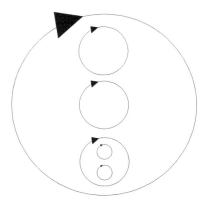

Autonomous organizations within
autonomous organizations

**Figure 4.15**  Recursive structure of organization: complexity unfolding

# Observers may construct the situation differently

**Figure 4.16**  Models of complexity

The autonomy of the parts has made their complexity, to a large extent, transparent to the whole. We have replaced the notion of an organizational hierarchy, in which a senior management tries to absorb more complexity than it can deal with, with a recursive organization structure in which the creation and management of complexity is distributed throughout the organization (see Figures 4.15–4.17).

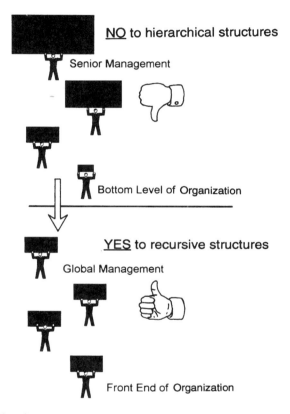

**Figure 4.17**   Hierarchical versus recursive structures

In complex environments, people's limited capacity to handle complexity makes recursive structures a necessity rather than a choice. If all 'primary activities' are permitted to develop these self-managing properties, then the organization's capacity for adaptation and learning is greatly enlarged. Flexibility and adaptation are built into the basic building blocks of the organization, so that these qualities in turn come to characterize the larger structure.

### Self-regulation And Self-organization

A recursively structured organization is one in which the relationships or networks between individuals are the outcome of self-regulation and self-organization.

But how is the coherence of the larger organization maintained? Is autonomy not dangerous to cohesion?

Thus the cohesion of the organization depends, ultimately, upon how individuals manage their work-loads. The more skilled we are in our interactions, the better we manage the balance:

- between being thrown into action and being observers of this action, and
- between our individual complexity (local information) and the situational complexity (distant information).

The better we manage these aspects the more likely we are to develop cohesion through shared purposes and meanings. The more we understand how to balance experience and information in line with our individual and organizational purposes, the more effective we will be in developing cohesive networks through increased awareness of personal and group interdependencies.

Of course, communication mechanisms and cultural context will influence organizational cohesion; but the stronger the characteristics of responsible self-management and co-ordination among and between individuals and groups, the more subtle and effective will be the use of these mechanisms. These aspects are further developed in the next chapter.

## VENUES OF ACTION IN AN ORGANIZATIONAL CONTEXT

In organizations every person interacts with others. It is in these interactions that they constitute organizations (see Figure 4.14).

Whether or not an organization will remain viable depends on whether these interactions trigger effective self-organizing processes. Organizations are constituted by interactive people exchanging their views about relevant situations and committing themselves to action of one kind or another. In these processes they declare tacitly or explicitly the purposes of these organizations, thus creating their organizational tasks.

Figure 4.18 is based on Figure 4.14 but focuses on one individual. It makes clear that for each individual there are three possible venues or platforms for their action; each individual has a *cognitive venue*, an *interactive venue* and an *organizational-task venue* (Espejo and Watt, 1988; Whitaker, 1992). These are depicted in Figure 4.18.

Note that Figure 4.18, in reducing the interactions constituting an organization into an individual-task loop, assumes that some form of meaningful agreement has been reached among the relevant participants as to the organization's purpose. If this were not the case then the task would be unlikely to have the commitment—or, acquiescence, in the case of an agreement that has been forced upon people—of the other participants, making it a construct relevant only to the individual.

The attenuators and amplifiers of Figure 4.18 suggest that the venues of action are embodied in the individuals themselves, in the networks of interactions between people and in the human and other resources constituting the organizational structure as a whole.

What of the cognitive venue? This is within the individual. An individual's knowledge space is shaped in the practices emerging from everyday interactions, i.e., in a

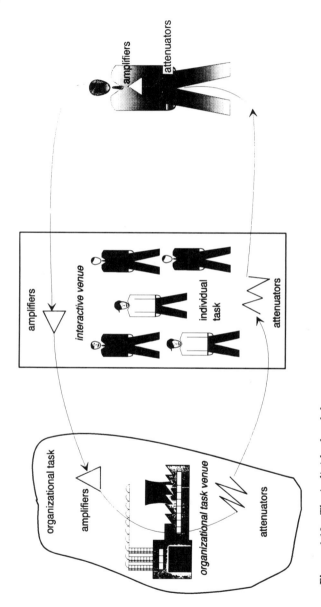

**Figure 4.18** The individual-task loop

history of recurrent interactions. Information is not enough to trigger effective action. It is the internal coherence, or structure, of the person, as emerging over time, that provides the space to be informed. Beyond that space the person may recognize a new distinction, may receive new information, but may not have response capacity. The information is simply not heard. To the extent that a person is developing new practices he or she is in a learning process. In other words, learning takes place when distinctions made are balanced by appropriate practices.

Any one person may, of course, construe a whole range of such individual-task loops. Moreover any observer, independent of the affected person him- or herself, may construe an individual-task loop. However, only those loops that are supported by agreed or authoritative declarations of purpose, transcending individual wishful thinking, have organizational meaning. As we have said, declarations of purpose may have implications not only for our own interactions but for the actions of others distant from us, if they are to produce the intended outcomes. Therefore a task, in general, is carried by an organizational network, not just a personal one. Often, of course, declarations of purpose are tacit, reflecting only tacit organizational images and agreements; this may make disagreements and conflicts more likely.

As far as the experience of people goes the three venues we have discussed are totally intertwined. Nevertheless they may be distinguished conceptually.

The *cognitive venue* is the personal domain of distinctions and practices. The important point here is that cognition is not the capacity to process information but the capacity to produce effective action. We know something if we are able to produce actions that are assessed as effective by others in a given domain of action. In this venue we develop, through learning, our capacity to interact and participate in co-operative work.

The *interactive venue* is that of negotiations and commitments, i.e., conversations, as well as that of expectations and intentions, i.e., relationships. It is the venue in which people constitute the organization. This is the venue of recurrent encounters, creating meanings for people's experiences, occasionally producing closed networks of self-organizing processes from which autonomous, viable organizations emerge. This is the venue in which people co-ordinate their actions and, through language, co-ordinate their co-ordination of actions. In this venue, willingly or not, we commit ourselves and get the commitment of others to future actions.

The *task venue* is embodied by the organizational resources. These do not exist, however, independently of others' purposes. The structure of the task venue emerges from people's purposeful action because organizational action implies the commitment of others and the alignment of individual purposes with those declared for the organization.

Historically, of course, because of our lack of understanding of self-organizing processes and autonomy, such alignment has proved difficult to achieve. Hence the task venue is often formed by managers declaring organizational purposes, tacitly or otherwise, without understanding their reciprocal link with the purposes of people in the organization. Legitimate declarations of purpose do not only depend on having the authority to make them, but also on not infringing the autonomy of the other people involved in the declarations.

Whether legitimate or not, such declarations lead, in general, to tacit or explicit agreements reached through interactions of one kind or another. For instance, corporate managers may declare purposes for the corporation without consulting the stakeholders. Their declaration defines the total organization as their task, while providing a framework for other autonomous units in the organization to declare their own purposes. These latter declarations also need to be grounded on relevant stakeholders, something that is less obvious, and less often practised, than declarations of corporate mission. Finally, from the interaction between the autonomous units emerges the 'purpose in use' of the organization, which provides the individual with his or her task venue.

We can look at this in another way. By ascribing purpose to an organization we are providing a reference to assess its complexity, i.e., a reference to enable us to work out the resources and relationships required to realize the corporate purpose. But, because the only practical way of assessing complexity is by involving those people experiencing the relevant relations, this assessment is a process rather than a quantification. In the task venue we assess the complexity of organizational work, based on the distinctions, promises and commitments made by all organizational members while in interaction.

## CONCLUSION: EFFECTIVE ACTION IN AN ORGANIZATIONAL CONTEXT

Effective action in the workplace that is beginning to emerge in today's corporations requires new skills and competencies that are fundamentally different from the command-and-control model of management. Understanding and applying these skills requires a paradigm shift in thinking, aided by a new vocabulary for articulating what performance means within this new organizational context.

Old behaviours in a flatter structure will not produce the step change in performance that is urgently needed; as this chapter of the book has emphasized, it is through a fundamental upgrading of our understanding of relationships and the management of complexity that the flexible, team-based structures that are emerging today will be given life and substance.

The primary skill which all members of the new organization will need to learn and practice in depth is the management of complexity. This primary skill encompasses skills in the management of conversations and the management of organizational processes. If we have a clear understanding of who it is we need to develop effective relations with, e.g., who are our customers and suppliers in different parts of the organization—and if we become skilled at generating creative learning opportunities in interaction with these other people, then we will have made significant progress in improving our performance.

If we also increase the awareness we have of our own action and the awareness we have of the wider context in which we are operating and learn to balance action with reflection and local interactions with relevant distant communications, our potential for self-development and organizational contribution is amplified by several orders of magnitude.

It is these qualities that need to characterize the new-style organization at all levels of its operations. Complexity occurs at every level, although the precise nature of the complexity will depend on the context of the organization or subsystem in question.

Creative problem-solving skills and competencies for handling interactions with other people are needed throughout the organization. By modelling these skills with our own behaviour, we can provide a powerful example for others to follow and the encouragement they need to transform themselves into effective communicators and problem solvers.

# Chapter 5

# Giving requisite variety to management: a discussion based on the viable system model

## INTRODUCTION

We are witnessing a fundamental change in our views about organization and management; new forms of organization and new practices of management are emerging.

The old hierarchical understanding of organizations, so powerfully entrenched in our minds, is not good enough for effective performance in a competitive environment. Flat structures, based on the work of autonomous teams that create the wealth of the organization while supported by services that make their operations effective, are widely espoused these days. Equally, managers are more and more aware that old functional structures need to be superseded by process-oriented structures, as they realize that the natural steps of a process have to be facilitated and supported by available resources rather than being constrained by functional fiefdoms.

Moreover, today's organizations are fighting against the rigid divisions of labour and artificial boundaries enshrined in institutions or departments; we realize that rigid distinctions about suppliers and customers or traditional departmental structures are unnecessary blinkers limiting our space of possibilities and action. These changes recognize the need for flexible, interdependent organizations if performance is to improve.

But improvements are not always forthcoming; the cost of creating interdependencies may be higher than the benefits they produce. It is not enough to redesign a process if its dependencies with other processes are not managed effectively; local optimization may give the illusion of total improvement. We need a holistic understanding of organizations and better strategies to manage complexity.

Thus it is becoming clear, albeit slowly, that effective organization implies autonomous units within autonomous units. This is the argument we want to develop in this chapter.

## The Emergence Of Recursive Structures

Over the last two decades the old functional structures of large organizations have been transformed. We now find divisions containing strategic business units, which in turn contain plants and self-managed market segments. Competitive pressures are pushing these changes; the benefits of creating local problem solving capacity are becoming apparent. We say—in the terminology of Chapter 4—that organizations are evolving towards recursive structures.

Recursive structures are emerging slowly but surely, though their full implications are not understood. They imply complementarity, rather than conflict, between the twin ideals of cohesive management and autonomy. They are necessary for current trends in management and organizational practices to bear fruit. For instance, recursive structures and management are necessary for an effective implementation of total quality, business process re-engineering and just-in-time supplies.

At the core of the recursive approach is the understanding that 'control' is not the unilateral imposition of a controller over a controllee but the outcome of self-regulation and effective communications; effective control is only possible when people are not only willing to co-operate but see an advantage in giving the best of themselves to the larger organization. It is in this sense that we use the word 'control'.

In this chapter we offer criteria for recursive management, articulated using the language of the viable system model (Beer, 1979; 1981; 1985).

### Plan For This Chapter

Though the idea of recursive structures has been with us for more than 30 years, its practical implications are still not understood. In this chapter, in order to make a contribution to this understanding, we will braid concepts with practice.

We will base our discussions on the management and organization of a particular strategic business unit (SBU) in a large corporation. By describing and explaining the observed behaviour of the SBU and discussing its strategies to manage complexity, we will compare the practice of management and organization in a concrete situation with systemic criteria for managing complexity. Our purpose is to derive general principles for management and organization.

Methodologically, the chapter is based on interviews and observations—the same as those used to support our discussions in Part One. The emphasis of these interviews was on detecting what managers recognize as interruptions in their normal flow of action. Such an emphasis on problems was, of course, intended as a platform to discuss structural improvements—not as a statement about the managerial skills of the people involved. In fact, the highlighted interruptions are in general the outcome of dysfunctional organizational relations, not of inadequate individual behaviour.

Our discussion recognizes that the SBU is embedded in a wider environment and in a larger corporation. The challenges for the SBU are achieving excellent performance in its environment, consistent with its long term viability, and synergistic interactions within the corporation, consistent with its own and the corporation's long term viability. Both challenges are discussed in this chapter.

The chapter has two main themes. The first is the conceptual framework provided by the viable system model (VSM); this will provide the theoretical tools we need.

The second theme is the application of this conceptual framework to the SBU. Here we attempt to braid concepts and practice. We give a description of the SBU based on interviews and general knowledge, together with system-analytic comments based on the VSM.

Each of these two themes is unfolded in five subthemes, as follows:

1. complexity and the management of complexity,
2. unfolding of complexity; linking strategy and structure,
3. the adaptation or policy making mechanism: inventing the organization,
4. the monitoring-control mechanism: inventing in the organization,
5. recursive structures and management.

## THE VIABLE SYSTEM MODEL: A MODEL OF RECURSIVE STRUCTURES

Organizations are composed of many interrelated people. Releasing the potentials of people and enabling them to handle autonomously the problems that they confront in their jobs is the way to provide organizations with the flexibility they need to survive in complex and rapidly changing environments.

Thus for an organization to be effective it needs to develop both the cohesion of the whole and the autonomy of individual participants.

But what do we mean by effectiveness? Effective organizations are those that are able to maintain viability, i.e., are viable systems. Such systems have their own problem-solving capacity. If they are to survive, they need not only the capacity to respond to familiar events such as customer orders, but the potential to respond to unexpected, previously unknown events such as the advent of new technologies or competitor initiatives.

The latter capacity is the hallmark of viable systems; it gives them the capacity to adapt to changing environments. While a catastrophic event may at a particular instant throw the viable system off balance, the fundamental characteristic of viability lessens its vulnerability to the unexpected, making it more adaptive to change.

Viability depends upon the organization's 'structure' though, as we saw in Chapter 4, this is a word that can be misunderstood. Often 'structure' is used to signify the formal hierarchical and functionally-based reporting relations shown on the typical organization chart. In our definition, structure incorporates the various roles that people adopt, the units, e.g., teams, departments, business units in which they participate, the resources that they employ, and the relationships between all these elements.

The organization's structure is thus viewed as a network of 'real-life' interactions, not as a static set of formal reporting relationships. Indeed the structure is like an X-ray of the actual—positive or negative—mechanisms supporting collaborative efforts in an organization.

Mechanisms, as we have said before, are stable forms of communication that permit the parts of an organization to operate as a whole. The structure of an organization can therefore also be defined as the set of specific mechanisms defining the interactions between the organization's parts.

Understanding its mechanisms is a way of understanding an organization's collaborative efforts and the scope for further collaboration. For this purpose we need to understand the management of complexity in viable organizations.

## Subtheme 1: Complexity And The Management Of Complexity

At the core of the VSM is the law of requisite variety. Broadly speaking, this states that a 'controller' has requisite variety—that is, has the capacity to maintain the outcomes of a situation within a target set of desirable states—if and only if it has the capacity to produce responses to all those disturbances that are likely to take the outcomes out of its target set. In other words, the variety of possible undesirable states of the situation must be equalled by the variety of responses that the controller can produce.

An example of this law is the case of a person driving a car. The person wants to keep the car on the road, and as the road twists and turns he or she responds to these disturbances by turning the steering wheel. She or he can be said to have requisite variety since they can apply the measures necessary to keep the state of the car within its target set, i.e., within a certain distance of the kerb.

If, however, the steering broke down and they could not respond to these changes, then the car would be out of control and a crash—a state outside the target set—would follow. This would be because the person did not have requisite variety.

Consider now an organization such as a business unit, represented in Figure 5.1. This organization does not operate in isolation; it has customers, competitors, suppliers of goods and services, neighbours, etc. Together these make up its environment.

The environment of the organization is largely beyond the knowledge and control of the people within it: they cannot know everything about every aspect of the world within which the organization operates—in fact, they can only know a fraction of what could be known. Similarly, management, i.e., those resources within the organization that oversee it and maintain its cohesion—cannot know everything about every aspect of the organization that they manage.

If, however, the organization is to continue to survive, i.e., remain viable within its environment—and management is to continue to control the organization, then the law of requisite variety suggests that the variety of the organization's management should at least equal that of the organization itself, which in turn should at least equal that of the environment. This is shown in Figure 5.2.

### Strategies To Manage Complexity

We have said that the environment is far more complex than the organization, which is in turn more complex than the organization's management. Their varieties, therefore, cannot equate. Yet the law of requisite variety seems to require them to.

This apparent paradox is resolved by recognizing the fact that of all the environmental variety, only part is relevant to the organization; namely, that which produces the disturbances that the organization has to respond to in order to maintain viability.

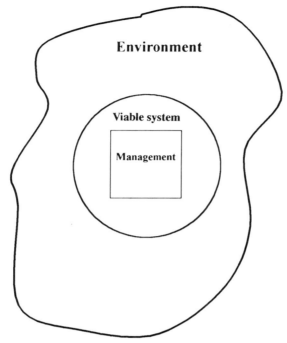

**Figure 5.1** Embedding

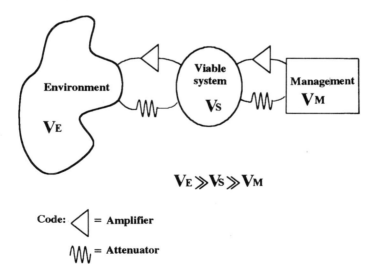

**Figure 5.2** Managing complexity

In addition, it may not be necessary for the organization to deal with all the complexity that is relevant to it since there may be agents within the environment that perform much of this activity. For example, suppliers—enabled by computer and communication systems—may perform a service for manufacturers by

supplying 'just-in-time'. In this way suppliers absorb an important part of the manufacturer's environmental complexity. However, the residual requirements that are
not dealt with by these environmental responses must be met by the manufacturer
itself. We call this the *residual variety*.

The same pattern occurs between a management and its organization. To say that
management 'controls' the organization is not to say that the varieties of the two are
the same, but that the residual variety left unabsorbed by the processes of self-
organization and self-regulation within the organization has to be absorbed by management. Complexity, or variety, is again dealt with by the use of management
amplifiers—such as delegation and obtaining the commitments of other people—
and attenuation, e.g., 'exception reporting', procedures and systems.

However, it is a common occurrence for amplification and attenuation processes
to creep out of balance. For example, the promises made by the promotional campaign cannot all be fulfilled due to lack of available stocks (here there is too much
amplification, leading to overload of the system), or the market segmentation in use
treats a vital, but varied group of customers as if they were all the same (a case either
of inadequate attenuation or of insufficient amplification).

Figure 5.3 shows the balancing of variety between the environment, the organization and its management. It is a hallmark of effective management to achieve this
balance at a minimum cost to the organization.

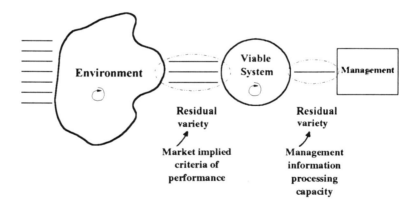

**Figure 5.3**   Residual complexity

### Subtheme 2: Unfolding Complexity: Linking Strategy And Structure

According to the dominant command-and-control model of management, organizations are structured as pyramids, with decisions about policy and direction taken at
the top and implemented through the lower levels of the organization. The total task
of the organization is broken down into smaller and smaller fragments, leading to an
increasingly narrow definition of tasks and an emphasis on functional specialization.
In this model implementation is implementation of tasks defined at the top; each
level merely adds resolution to the tasks handed down to it.

The viable system model suggest that organizations should work on a different principle; the principle of recursion.

How does it suggest this? The VSM is a general model of any viable system. According to it, viable systems (such as companies!) are themselves composed of viable systems, each having self-organizing and self-regulatory characteristics. Next, these viable subsystems contain further viable systems, and so on, right down to the level of the team or person delivering to the customer the organization's products or services.

Picture a Russian doll that contains within each doll not one, but twins, triplets, or even sextuplets of dolls, and this will give an idea of how powerfully variety is managed through this unfolding. This is what emerges from the need to create and manage whole tasks at all structural levels rather than just manage the fragments of a predefined task.

What emerges is a strategy to manage complexity that enhances the organization's capacity to invent and manage its environment. Of course, to make this unfolding a breaking-down of complexity management rather than a breakdown of the organization, a viable system requires resources to manage its cohesion. Therefore any organization, i.e., viable system, is constituted by both primary activities, i.e., viable systems within the viable system itself, and regulatory functions. These are the support, service and development functions.

Something resembling this unfolding of complexity, but in a form that is entangled and blurred, occurs naturally in organizations. It occurs as the outcome of uncontrolled processes of self organization, rather than of purposeful design. It is not described in the formal organization chart, which usually bears little resemblance to the organic processes of communication and control actually in use within the organization.

Figure 5.4 shows the unfolding of complexity for a hypothetical organization. The primary activities of the organization are those implied by its identity: why does the organization exist? What is it producing? What market areas is it serving? What are

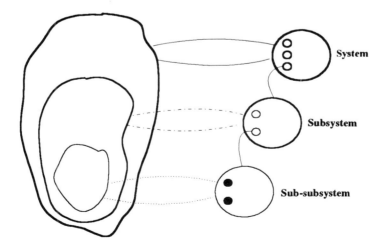

**Figure 5.4**   Unfolding of complexity

its core technologies? Answering these questions, which are often less obvious than they at first appear, helps to define the key transformation in which the organization is engaged; this is the primary activity of the organization. Establishing the activities producing this transformation in turn enables the modelling of the next level of recursion for the organization.

Subsequent levels are then unfolded, again according to the criterion of which are the primary activities, those that contribute directly to the organization's identity. The lowest level is the level at which the basic products and services of the organization are finally delivered to its customers.

The exact number of levels and the number of primary activities at each level will depend on the complexity of the organization's task and its control strategies. For example, how much decentralization does it wish to have? A highly centralized structure can be viable, but only at the cost of sophisticated co-ordination and support functions; the balance between effective centralization and decentralization is constantly changing with the development of information technology.

Each primary activity, and each primary activity within a primary activity is, by implication, a viable or autonomous unit. To continually ask, 'Do we want to make this activity viable?' helps to ensure that the focus remains on the organization's primary business.

Functions such as personnel, finance, marketing and IS generally fall into the category of regulatory functions within primary activities. They are important to the overall viability of the organization and are performed at different levels depending on the balance between centralization and decentralization accepted within the organization. Many of them will need to be devolved in some form to provide the support needed by lower-level primary activities. Modelling this interaction between regulatory functions and primary activities is an important contribution of the VSM.

The organization's primary activities are its *raison d'être*; they are the subjects of management control. Lower-level primary activities create and do what people at higher structural levels could not discover and do by themselves; it was beyond their capacity. This is the meaning of autonomy at all levels. Each primary activity creates and responds to chunks of complexity of its own and strives for its own viability in the same way as the parent activity strives at its more global level.

Thus in any viable system there is, in one form or another, a complementarity between control and autonomy. The challenge is to find criteria of effectiveness to make use of this complementarity in improving our organization's design.

The principle of recursion requires that all primary activities have their own local problem-solving capacity—or, in more strategic terms, their own policy-making and policy implementation capacity. Otherwise, they would not be able to maintain a separate existence in their environment. Thus the two principal mechanisms for viability are:

1. the mechanism for adaptation or policy-making,
2. the mechanism for monitoring control or policy implementation.

The next section will describe how these two mechanisms operate. For simplicity of presentation, we will refer, for the most part, to the operation of these mechanisms at the level of the corporation; however, it must be remembered throughout that the same principles apply to all viable systems, at whatever level of structural recursion they operate.

**Subtheme 3: The Adaptation And Policy-making Mechanism: Inventing The Organization**

An effective organization is one that not only 'does things right' but is also able to find the 'right things to do'. This capacity for adaptation of the mission and identity of the organization is normally associated with its strategic levels of management.

What is the appropriate contribution of policy makers? How can they increase the likelihood that their visions for the organization will support the organization's long term viability?

Senior managers are often confronted by seemingly impossible situations. For instance, as seen later in this chapter, it is not unusual for a board of directors to find that a new product, in which large sums of money have been invested, has no market, or is technically unfeasible; or that the new salary policy which they recently approved has led to damaging industrial relations problems.

In such cases, managers usually have an implicit awareness not only that they have been deciding on issues beyond their own immediate technical expertise but that important existing organizational resources—people with the necessary know-ledge to avoid the problem—were under-utilized in the debates that led to the critical decision.

It is not unusual for people in policy-making positions to feel that they are only rubber stamping what has already been debated and decided at lower levels in the organization; or that management briefings focus their attention on issues on which they do not have the required in-depth knowledge to pass judgement. In these conditions, policy makers may either abdicate their responsibility completely and blindly follow the advice of their subordinates or may take a 'strategic decision'—meaning, in this case, a leap in the dark—and hope for the best.

If most of the time policy makers are in the invidious position of deciding issues that are beyond either their comprehension or their resources, i.e., they have no time to tease them out, how can they keep control of these policy processes?

The concept of requisite variety suggests that the variety of policy makers is necessarily much lower than the variety of the organization of which they are members; they must, therefore, accept that much of the policy making they are accountable for is done within the organization. This does not mean that they should abdicate responsibility. It means that they should design the processes by which policy making is done; that is, should design effective attenuators to filter out from their attention most of this complexity, keeping within their concern only those normative aspects that nobody else can deal with because there is no one else to whom they can 'pass the buck'.

There are two main sources of complexity for policy makers: the organization itself and the organization's environment. The former is concerned with the 'inside and now' of conditions occurring within the organization, the latter with the 'outside and then' of actual or possible future environmental opportunities and threats. We refer to the two structural filters concerned with these two main sources of complexity as the organization's *control* and *intelligence functions*. Figure 5.5 illustrates this.

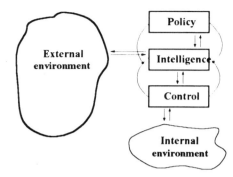

**Figure 5.5** The adaptation mechanism

The function of maintaining a balance between the control and intelligence functions and making final policy decisions is the *policy function* proper.

These three functions exist in one form or another in any viable organization. However, they are not necessarily related to well-defined entities on the organization chart. It is perfectly possible that one department, or even one individual, may have both an intelligence and a control function or that in a small organization, all three functions of policy, intelligence and control are combined within one individual.

The essential question is how to structure each of these functions and their interactions in order to make policy making more effective.

The basic design rules are as follows:

*Rule 1: Minimize The Information Requirements Of Policy Makers*

It is a common fallacy that the board must contain 'experts' in the industry, or the technology, or some other aspect of the business of the organization. This argument is related to the erroneous notion that the key role of policy makers is to make 'content' decisions.

If the role of policy makers is redefined as providing clarity about the overall direction, values and purpose of the organization, as well as designing, at the highest level, the conditions for organizational effectiveness, then it can be seen that providing technical expertise is not part of this role. Their understanding of technical issues needs to be broad rather than deep; sufficient to be able to understand and communicate with those responsible for assessing threats and opportunities in the environment and those controlling the current state of affairs in the organization, without becoming overwhelmed by detailed analysis.

In addition, the briefings reaching the attention of policy makers need to make minimal demands on their attention, consistent with their capacity to remain in control of the policy processes. Often, the thicker the management report, the less likely it is to be read with comprehension; not because the policy makers are stupid, but because they are being expected to get involved in operational details at a higher level of complexity than their own information processing capacity permits.

*Rule 2: Design Control And Intelligence Functions Of Similar Complexity*

The intelligence and control functions—respectively filtering conditions that are 'outside and then' and 'inside and now'—offer alternative, but complementary, perspectives on the same problems: those related to the definition, adjustment and implementation of the organization's identity.

Policy making is a process, the outcome of which is the choice of courses of action for the organization. The issues of concern to policy makers may have their origins in the policy makers themselves, or elsewhere in the organization. In the former case, there is a need to substantiate these issues with further detailed research from a variety of different perspectives; in the latter case, the ideas need to be subjected to detailed analysis and cross-checking from different points of view before they reach the top policy makers.

Effective policy making requires the orchestration and monitoring of organizational debates in such a way as to enable people to contribute to the best of their abilities to organizational adaptation and survival. It follows, from this and from the concept of structural recursion, that policy making takes place not just at the top of an organization but at all structural levels. Extensive debates within the organization among different and opposing viewpoints should produce informed conclusions and improve the quality of policy briefings. Policy makers should only be exposed to issues and alternatives that have been properly examined in this way.

A lack of balance between intelligence and control will damage the performance of the policy function. For example, if intelligence produces issues of policy relevance at a higher rate than the control function can cope with, then the policy makers may receive views of external possibilities unchecked by on-the-ground management; or if all the issues reaching policy are concerned with matters of internal efficiency, vital signals from the wider external environment may be overlooked. Decisions over-influenced by either of the two filters are likely to be both costly and ineffective.

*Rule 3: Make Intelligence And Control Highly Interconnected*

The effectiveness of the intelligence and control functions depends not only on the capabilities of each, but also on how well policy makers are able to monitor the interactions between these two filters.

If the filters were completely unconnected then policy makers would not only be receiving information independently from both sides, but would have the invidious task of performing all the cross-checks and balances themselves. The policy makers would be the only communication channel between two separate sets of people each of whom, in an organization of any size, deals with far more complexity than the policy function itself could possibly hope to cope with.

This situation may sound far-fetched, but how often do organizations establish large, centralized R&D departments detached from the rest of the organization? And how often is manufacturing brought into discussions on new product development as an afterthought, when the marketing and technical teams have already defined all the characteristics of the new product?

The two sets of filters, intelligence and control, need therefore to be highly inter-connected. When this is the case, most of the issues emerging from one side can be cross-checked with reference to the other before reaching the attention of the policy function. For example, while intelligence may suggest options to diversify the company, control may veto some of them on the grounds of operational and co-ordination costs.

In the light of the above considerations, the role of policy makers, or leaders at all levels of the organization, may be elaborated as follows:

- to identify the key issues of concern to the organization at a broad, macro level;
- to bring together into debate the right people with the right mix of skills; that is, to form teams and work units containing a balanced representation of the intelligence and control functions;
- to monitor the interactions of these elements;
- finally, to consider the alternatives and decide among them in the light of the organization's values and long term goals.

To discharge their responsibility competently, policy makers need not be experts or even knowledgeable about specific policy issues; they do need a good model of how the organizational structure works with reference to a clear vision of the organization's identity. In this way they may create the opportunities for everyone in the organization to get involved in inventing its future.

### Subtheme 4: The Monitoring And Control Mechanism: Inventing In The Organization

The contribution of the control function to the policy making debate is an accurate appreciation of the performance and capabilities of the existing organization.

The control function has, however, another contribution to make. It must see to the implementation of the organization's tasks. A requirement for it to do so—as well as for it to be an effective filter of the organization's internal complexity for policy-making purposes—is that it should be in control of the organization's primary activities.

Now the management operating in the control function is faced with what we term the *control dilemma*: having lower variety than the operations it must control, it cannot possibly maintain awareness of all that is going on within those operations; there is an 'information gap'. Yet management is still accountable for any loss of control that occurs in the operations!

The information gap often leads to a feeling of discomfort and uncertainty on the part of management. 'What is going on down there? How do I know what their preferences and thinking are? How do I know whether they are interpreting correctly my views? In extreme situations, how can I even tell if they're telling me the truth?'

This anxiety to know more leads to increased demands from management for special reports and investigations in order to keep 'in control'. In reality, however, these demands and instructions only serve to reduce the variety of the operations, making them less flexible, as people struggle to fulfil higher level requirements at the expense of adequately carrying out their own operations. At the very time that the operations need more flexibility in order to respond effectively to their own environmental pressures, managers' behaviour is reducing this flexibility.

Management cannot win with this type of control strategy—because of the law of requisite variety.

Control games with negative effects are a common phenomenon in these circumstances. These are interpersonal games in which, on the one hand, senior management uses the allocation of resources as a means of exercising control power and on the other, local management uses its better knowledge of the operations to manipulate senior management into unchecked decisions. Often, managers do not deliberately intend to start these games; they result from a structure of poor interpersonal interactions.

Summing up, the control dilemma comes about as follows. As organizations become more complex and sophisticated—due to market forces, technological developments or increased competition—so primary activities at all structural levels of the organization find themselves in complex, often turbulent environments. They need greater flexibility, i.e., greater ability to create their own complexity, in order to respond to this level of change. As a result, their managers are faced with larger information gaps. If, however, managers respond to the control dilemma with traditional control strategies, less flexibility and larger bureaucracies are created precisely when the need for greater flexibility has become most acute. A proliferation of control games is the result.

The problem can be redefined. How is one to avoid losing control of the all-important primary activities, despite having unavoidable, and in fact, ever increasing information gaps?

The answer again lies in following a few simple design rules.

*Rule 1: Minimize The Use Of Direct Commands*

To illustrate, Figure 5.6 shows the operation of the control function in relation to three operating divisions, which are to a greater or lesser extent interdependent by virtue of the fact that they belong to the same organization. They may interact operationally, by one providing inputs to another, or through the environment, for example through an overlap in the markets they serve. A key role of the control function is to achieve a degree of cohesion, and thereby added value, among these parts of the organization for which it is held accountable.

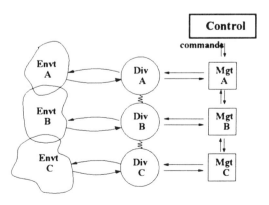

**Figure 5.6** Control dilemma: control as commanding

The central vertical command channel between the management of the control function and the management of each of the three divisions is the communication channel through which direct line management instructions are issued and resources are negotiated and allocated. In the other direction along this channel flows a regular stream of management reports which keep the senior level management in touch with events. As we have seen above, however, overloading this channel leads to control dilemmas.

One way of reducing the use of direct commands is by designing good 'exception reporting' systems, a process which computing technology is increasingly able to support. 'Management by objectives' also plays its part in helping the senior level management to distinguish 'the wood from the trees' and avoid too much interference.

Yet these devices are not in themselves sufficient to deal with the control dilemma and, moreover, they do little to address the problem of maintaining cohesion and developing synergy among the operating units. The next two design rules address these issues.

### Rule 2: Use Sporadic Monitoring—With Discretion

In our example, it is clear that the information provided by the divisional management will reflect personal biases and natural communication problems. There is a need to cross-check this information with an alternative source. This is achieved by developing a monitoring channel that runs directly between senior level management and the operations themselves, bypassing divisional management, see Figure 5.7.

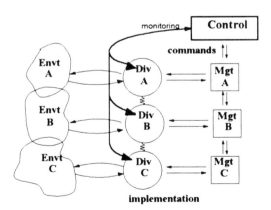

**Figure 5.7** Monitoring of primary activities

The control function needs an assurance that the accountability reports it receives from divisional management are not only an accurate reflection of the status of the primary activities from the viewpoint of their managements, but are also aligned with corporate interests. This is, at a simplistic level, the 'management by walking about' principle. Audits can take a variety of forms, from the obvious investigatory programmes to informal conversations and unscheduled visits. However, they must adhere to the following principles:

1. They must be sporadic rather than regular, anticipated events—otherwise they are not going to be effective in discovering what is really happening within the primary activities;
2. They must be infrequent, otherwise they risk undermining the authority and trust vested in the management of the divisions;
3. They must be an openly declared mechanism, of which everyone concerned is aware. The intention is not to play 'big brother', employing secretive tactics and games of subterfuge; it is simply to demonstrate an interest in knowing and understanding what is going on at first hand. If employed sensitively, cross-checks and audits should communicate a message of caring to those involved in the operations in question, without resulting in defensive behaviours from the intermediate level of management.

### Rule 3: Maximize Co-ordination Among Primary Activities

While, as we have discussed, the autonomy of the primary activities improves the flexibility of the organization, it also increases the likelihood of inconsistent responses. There are two ways of counteracting this. Co-ordination is necessary, either through direct supervision or through self-adjustment among the primary activities themselves.

The former method, though useful in many cases, may overload the control function, which has to serve as interpreter and bottleneck for all types of lateral communication. The latter method, on the other hand, may not allow optimization in the use of resources. It is, however, more likely to produce consistency among the primary activities over time.

The line of co-ordination, shown in Figure 5.8, is a powerful, high-variety function: the stronger it becomes, the less will be the residual variety needing the attention of the control function and the greater the discretion exercised by the lower structural levels.

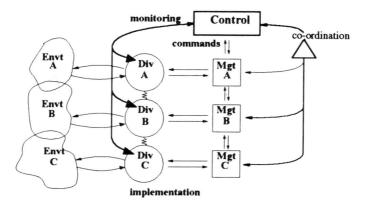

**Figure 5.8**  The monitoring control mechanism

The co-ordination function provides a common language that facilitates problem solving and lateral communication among primary activities. Co-ordination can be seen in the day-to-day actions of people, even more than through the organization's formal channels of communication.

Mechanisms can be developed by management that should and do support this lateral co-ordination. Such mechanisms are corporate guidelines, well developed cultural norms, operating and process standards and procedures of all kinds; also accounting methods, IT standards, shared databases, etc.

Though it should be the purpose of such mechanisms to enhance and support day-to-day co-ordination between people, they may be seen, especially in traditional, hierarchically structured organizations, as bureaucratic interference with people's personal freedom. In such organizational environments, 'standards' often appear as instructions coming down the line ('Here we go again—management throwing its weight around!') instead of lateral support, designed to make life easier in the longer term.

If, however, support functions can learn to behave in a supportive and receptive way, communicating their purposes with greater clarity, they may begin to change this attitude. In particular, guidelines clearly couched in different language from that of direct commands and instructions may find their acceptance increased. Finally, if an increase in the use of co-ordination mechanisms is accompanied by correspondingly effective autonomy of the primary activities of the organization at all structural levels, people may begin to appreciate the paradox: 'We are slaves of the system in order that we may be free!'

### Subtheme 5: Recursive Management And Structures

Figure 5.9 shows how the two main mechanisms for viability—namely, adaptation and control—are combined to define the organizational structure of a viable system.

Figure 5.10 shows how these mechanisms work in relation to the unfolding of complexity; it illustrates the principle of structural recursion. It is a complete model, showing all the recursions of a simple organization with two subsystems, i.e., primary activities, each of which contains three sub-subsystems. For the purpose of a more detailed analysis, a separate VSM can be drawn for each of the primary activities at each structural level, using a simple labeling system to keep track of the various levels of recursion.

What is the key proposition arising from our analysis of the characteristics of organizational viability? It is that in truly effective organizations, policy, intelligence, control, co-ordination and implementation are distributed at all structural levels.

In complex environments, people's limited capacity to handle variety makes recursive structures a necessity rather than an option. This becomes more necessary as environmental complexity increases. If all primary groups within an organization—meaning, those contributing directly to the organization's identity—are designed to have these self-managing properties, then the organization's capacity for adaptation and learning is enlarged.

The VSM offers a framework for effective organization. It allows us to work out the 'holistic' implications of particular practices. For instance, we might use it to adapt the organization to changing work practices. To do this, we would propose

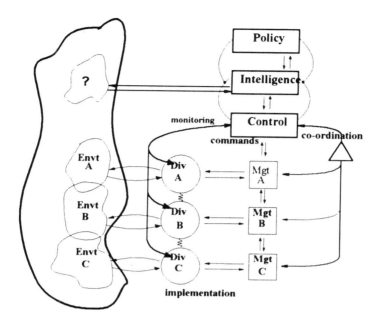

**Figure 5.9**  The viable system model

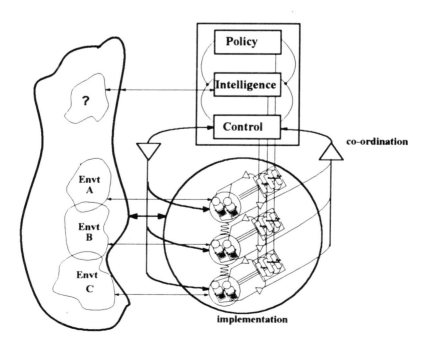

**Figure 5.10**  The recursive organization

and implement structural adjustments based on the VSM; for example, we would bring together those activities which naturally 'belong' to the same process, and which logically should be highly interconnected. Doing so would not only facilitate the adoption of more effective working practices, it would also suggest further lateral structural changes necessary to align each process with the organization's overall policy.

Our approach, based on the fundamental, logical principles we have outlined, contrasts with the cruder models and the experimental or expedient tinkering with organizational structures that characterize most current organizaional design efforts.

Since the VSM deals with the structure of communications within and between organizations, it can provide the framework for corporate information systems that are more closely related to the long-term aims of the organization and the information needs of its members at all levels of recursion.

In summary, the VSM is primarily a tool for diagnosis and design of organizational processes. By working, at a new level of depth and detail, on the control and communication processes required to invent and recursively implement the organization's mission, one can ensure that visions for the future are translated into effective interactions and co-operative work leading to practical business results.

## APPLYING THE VSM TO A STRATEGIC BUSINESS UNIT

We will now show how, by applying our discussion of the VSM to a strategic business unit (SBU) on which we have done research, we can derive some general principles for management and organization. Our discussion will again be organized around the five subthemes

1. complexity and the management of complexity,
2. unfolding of complexity; linking strategy and structure,
3. the adaptation or policy making mechanism: inventing the organization,
4. the monitoring control mechanism: inventing in the organization,
5. recursive structures and management.

At the end of each section, the principles arrived at will be stated in a general form and placed in a box.

We are concerned with an SBU in a large company, named X, the leader in its market. In Europe X has two plants, a strong central marketing unit and a large regional, country-based, sales network. The business unit, XTN, is one of seven business units in Division T of Corporation X. XTN's customers are mainly companies that convert its products, produced in large sizes and volumes, into products used directly or indirectly in retailing.

### Subtheme 1: Complexity And The Management Of Complexity

There are three kinds of relevant complexity for XTN as shown in Figure 5.1. These are *environmental complexity*, external to XTN, and two kinds of internal complexity—of the *organization* and of its *management*.

What, in XTN's case, does this complexity consist of?

*Environmental Complexity (External)*

XTN has to manage its interactions with several thousand customers, each with sophisticated and constantly changing requirements; also with a range of suppliers of raw materials and equipment. Competitors are of two kinds. A number of strong companies, using the same raw materials as XTN, compete directly with it. However, the applications for which its products are intended may use a range of alternative raw materials; users of these alternative raw materials also compete with XTN. All this commercial activity takes place in several countries, with different legal requirements. But perhaps the most significant pressures on XTN come from consumer associations, industrial customers, lobbyists and politicians concerned with the alleged immediate and long-term environmental impact of its products.

As we shall see, this complexity presents both threats and opportunities to XTN.

*Organizational Complexity (Internal)*

XTN has developed its organizational structure in the tradition of a large, well established, sophisticated and highly successful corporation. XTN has about a thousand people, with different degrees of training and skill. Its technology is complex and new products and processes are constantly being introduced. XTN has a strong R&D capacity.

Allocating orders to plants and machines and getting high quality production in time is a source of huge internal complexity. In responding to a large and changeable number of customer orders, the business unit tries to optimize the use of production resources while maintaining or enhancing customer satisfaction. Plants operate shifts in response to this challenge.

*Managerial Complexity (Internal)*

The direction of XTN is the ultimate responsibility of a leaders group, comprising production, R&D and marketing managers and a financial controller. The marketing function is led by a marketing manager responsible for six product managers; these in their turn are responsible for twenty market segment managers. A similar hierarchical structure is found in production, with plant and section managers and, below them, shift supervisors. The leader of the SBU is the former marketing manager.

Managers have the support of varied resources: secretarial support and services such as information systems, quality control, budgetary control and personnel add to their functional capacity. Though several of these functions and services are centralized at the corporate and divisional levels they are made available specifically to XTN.

*Systemic Comments*

The environmental complexity, then, is the complexity XTN must deal with. How, in principle, can it do so?

Figure 5.1 makes it clear that management is part of the organization and the organization is embedded in the wider environment. As argued in our discussion of

Figure 5.1, the complexity of the environment is much larger than that of the organization and the complexity of the organization larger than that of management.

It follows that there will always be relevant situations in the environment for
which XTN people will have no response capacity. For instance, some of the views of
environmental groups about its products, whether scientifically substantiated or not,
may influence public opinion and politicians beyond XTN's capacity to counteract
such influence. People in the environment may create unexpected complexity in
XTN's chosen domain of action—perhaps even without knowing that XTN exists!

Equally, individual workers and groups will see more operational detail, and
perhaps more possibilities, in their specific areas of action than their managers.
Machine minders, for instance, are likely to make far more day-to-day distinctions
about the specific machines under their control than their supervisors supervisors
simply cannot be with all the machines simultaneously, even given that they may
have a superior understanding of them.

Note that this fact says nothing about the relevance of the machine minders'
distinctions. One distinction made by the supervisor may make irrelevant a myriad
of theirs. It remains true that the machine minders will inevitably make orders-of-
magnitude more distinctions about their working environment than does their
supervisor.

In both kinds of interactions, therefore—between management and the environment and between management and the organization—there is an inherent imbalance of situational complexity.

However, for management to be at all effective it must respond to all relevant
situations within XTN. Likewise, for the organization to be competitive it must
respond to all relevant environmental situations, e.g., those that have an impact on
the 'benchmarks' it uses to compare itself with its competitors. These are performance problems that management and organizations need to deal with.

Strategies to achieve an adequate response capacity may vary substantially. Managers need to learn both how to enhance or amplify their problem solving capacity
and how to reduce or attenuate the organizational complexity relevant to them—as
in Figure 5.2.

Now organizational complexity may be reduced either by constraining local discretion or by empowering people to respond by themselves to problems. The latter
strategy has the advantage of increasing organizational complexity while, at the same
time, reducing the complexity relevant to managers. They get more for less. This
strategy relies upon the crucial idea of 'residual complexity' illustrated in Figure 5.3.

The idea of reducing the residual complexity managers must cope with applies
also to the interactions between XTN and its environment. XTN needs to achieve a
good performance by enhancing, i.e., amplifying its problem-solving capacity vis-
à-vis an increasingly demanding and sophisticated environment. Understanding
this environment and interacting effectively with it requires designing more and
more powerful attenuators of its complexity. Designing effective attenuators in
order to create opportunities and respond to threats is a challenge for the organization. By creating capacity in the environment to solve its own problems, XTN can
increase the complexity it matches in the environment at the same time as it reduces
the complexity it deals with directly. More of the relevant environmental issues for
XTN are dealt with by agents in the environment itself.

This is a way of increasing performance without increasing organizational resources. For instance 'just-in-time' agreements with suppliers, using electronic data interchange (EDI), may both take away from XTN a good deal of 'supply' complexity and improve its performance.

From this discussion we draw three general principles.

---

*PRINCIPLE 1: MANAGING COMPLEXITY*

Management of complexity requires matching distinctions in an action domain with appropriate actions.

*PRINCIPLE 2: REQUISITE COMPLEXITY*

Complexity is necessary to fight complexity; but the source of control complexity is in both the controller and the controllee.

*PRINCIPLE 3: BENCHMARKING*

A performer is competitive in an action domain if it is able to manage at least as much situational complexity as the best performers in that domain.

---

*Management Of Complexity In The SBU*

Having derived these principles, we intend to apply them to our SBU. First, let us ask how XTN's external and internal complexity is currently managed.

Consider the interactions between XTN and its environment. The image of XTN's products in the market is poor; they are thought of as environmentally unsound. This is affecting demand. The effect is compounded by an increase in competition from manufacturers of alternative products. To counter an 'anti-XTN products' campaign and avoid negative legislation the company has been active in forming industrial associations. The object of these has been to sponsor research to overcome some of the products' drawbacks and co-ordinate the industry's position in political debates.

It is, however, accepted in the industry that these responses only came about when the situation had already become grave. It took a long time for XTN to realize the power of pressure groups and their capacity to influence people's feelings. At first ecologists and 'greens' were dismissed as irrelevant or lacking in understanding. However, as their lobbying started to bite and industrial customers started to switch to other products, the industry had to take them seriously. The action of XTN and other industrial partners has averted the most damaging legislation. It has not, however, changed public views about their products. Major retailers are taking articles using XTN materials off their shelves, forcing suppliers to look for alternative materials.

The combined effect of these circumstances was for a time the stagnation of XTN's markets in Europe, and more recently their clear decline. Several former competitors of XTN have gone out of business. The industry's responses have also been unsuccessful in changing the animosity between politicians and industrialists. Overall, the political solutions adopted have confirmed the worst fears of both sides; they have proved to be ecologically unsound and economically inadequate.

In order to increase market share in a shrinking market without lowering prices, XTN is customizing its products, to the extent that each requested item in a customer order is in effect a 'different product'. This has led to a proliferation in the number of different products offered on the market. Product development is largely customer-driven; whenever a customer wants a new property in a product, a new product is developed. Any attempt to develop products within a market strategy has been abandoned. The general attitude has been reactive.

Now consider the internal interactions within XTN that have accompanied these developments. As customers have become aware of their new power they have not only expected customized orders but have changed these orders more often. Processing manufacturing orders in time and according to customers requirements has become more and more difficult. Customers are therefore experiencing increases in cycle time. Their response: to order earlier than before, with less precise knowledge of their own requirements. This has increased the chances of order changes before delivery time, which has made the allocations of orders to plants and machines increasingly difficult. The result has been to double the number of orders XTN has to handle from about 15 000 to 30 000 per year over the past three years.

Production planning and scheduling for the two SBU plants is done by central staff located in one of the unit's two plants. The staff's location in one plant has made them more responsive to that plant's problems and created resentment in the other plant.

The planned use of the individual machines is done with the support of a sophisticated linear programming software which is production-driven; its concern is to optimize machine utilization. Customer order management, however, is market-driven. Those controlling production lines have had to satisfy both requirements.

The problem is that machine optimization and market satisfaction are usually inconsistent interests. This is putting the production people under enormous stress. In practice, they have to make local adjustments to the instructions of production planning. Often they have to yield to the pressures of market segment managers who want 'their' customer orders in time. These pressures on production are further compounded by customers who, following the advice of market segment managers, anticipate their orders in an attempt to reserve machine time well in advance.

This behaviour is increasing even further the pressures on production planning, which has been diminished into a day-to-day fight to ensure on-time delivery of the 'most important' orders—where importance is defined, not by reference to an overview of the market as a whole, but by those market segment managers with most influence on the shop floor. The highly sophisticated software for production planning is 'refined' by the pressures on the shopfloor of the more influential market segment managers—which means, in practice, by the shouts of the managers with the loudest voices!

Discussions in XTN's leaders group, which meets every two weeks are focused on market segments and production lines. They spend a good deal of time discussing operational details of machine productivity and utilization as well as the relation-ships between market segments and machines, rather than overall strategy. An estimation shows that, compared with similar leaders groups in other business units, XTN's is handling only about 25% of relevant policy issues. This focus on segments and machines is reinforced by the information systems in place; these have the same focus.

The overall result: XTN was performing dismally. The survival of XTN was in question.

*Analysis Of Current Management Strategies*

The above is a *de facto* description of the strategies currently being used by XTN to manage the complexity of its external and internal interactions. Let us now examine these strategies in the light of the principles previously arrived at.

There is a need to think systemically about XTN's problems. Systemic thinking in this context means thinking about *loops*, that is, about two kinds of two-way interac-tions: the two-way interactions linking people in the environment with people in the organization and the two-way interactions linking the organization's management with its employees. These are shown in Figure 5.2.

Consider first the organization–environment loops.

An organization's performance is the outcome of its capacity to invent an environment—thereby attenuating environmental complexity—and to act in it, thereby amplifying the complexity of its own plans. In other words, it is the outcome of the complete loop: organization–environment–organization. If its performance is similar to or better than the performance of others in the same domain of action we recognize the organization as a good or excellent performer.

To perform well, the organization needs to learn about the environment in the relevant domain of action. For this purpose it needs good attenuators of environ-mental complexity; people in the organization cannot know, among many other things, all that the competition is doing nor all that lobbyists are planning. By necessity they must be ignorant of a good deal of what is going on in their environ-ment. In fact any attempt to 'know everything' will soon overload them. The chal-lenge is to be aware of what deserves to be ignored, and not to be ignorant of what is crucial to the organization's performance and viability.

XTN, like others in its industry, was slow in detecting important environmental messages. In fact, for a long time their behaviour ignored the 'greens', the environ-mentalists and the politicians sympathetic to them. During this period, XTN was attenuating their views in a drastic way; it was filtering them out.

This meant they were ignoring something that could not be ignored. Conse-quently, their response to the threat posed was slow and weak. The organization's responses did nothing to change the bad public image of the industry; amplification was insufficient.

At the same time, in order to improve its market share in a dwindling market, XTN has increased its capacity to know customers' requirements. It has made its attenuators of market complexity more sophisticated, thereby increasing its ability to make distinctions in the market. However, to make good use of these more sophistic-ated attenuators XTN needs to build up a response capacity that will enable it to

transform requirements into products delivered on time. As explained above, amplification capacity of this kind has been inadequate, producing longer cycle times and
higher costs. The effect of this weaker performance has been to make XTN's attenuators even more sensitive. Market segment managers are conveying more and more
orders to production as customers make their orders earlier and change their minds
more often.

There is plenty of channel capacity for customers to transmit their requirements.
The problem is delivering orders on time.

In this loop attenuators and amplifiers are out of balance; there are more and more
customers' requirements for which the company does not have response capacity.
There is no understanding of the systemic implications of the growing complexity in
customer requirements.

How can XTN respond to this growing complexity? Can it put back with the
customers more of the complexity without losing resolution or reducing performance? For instance, can it make orders more predictable and stable?

Now consider the organization–management loops.

Managerial performance is the outcome of its capacity to establish over time the
organization's capabilities and potentials (attenuation) and to get the best out of
available resources (amplification) in the chosen domain of action. In other words, it
is the outcome of the complete loop management–organization–management.

Debates in the XTN leaders group are supposed to define the SBU overall strategy.
However, the bulk of their discussions focus on the 20 or more market segments and
the similar number of fabrication machines. Their attenuation of the organization's
complexity is taking place at too high a level of resolution; that is, they are trying to
manage too much detail. This is making it impossible for them to deal with other
relevant organizational issues. Indeed, this situation suggests that the leaders group
needs attenuators with less resolution of markets and machines and more resolution
of global strategic business matters. As for the amplification side of this loop, such
behaviour implies that the actions of product and plant managers in amplifying the
leaders group decisions will be restricted by detailed instructions rather than empowered by general policies.

To a large degree this behaviour is the outcome of the management systems in use.
Communications between production planning, a centralized unit overviewing the
two plants, and the production lines on the shop floor illustrates this ineffective
amplification of management capacity. The purpose of production planning is to
match customer orders with production capacity within the policy frame of the
business unit. It is there to amplify management capacity. In XTN's case, however, it
is reducing the segment managers rich and detailed knowledge of markets and
customers to a few records feeding a linear programming model. This attenuated
knowledge is then amplified by the computer system, which plans machine utilization based on the expected contribution of each individual planned order.

The segment managers find that they have to adjust these plans at a later stage in
the process, as they become aware that the computer-generated amplification is not
dealing adequately with their customers' requirements.

Those on the shop floor are experiencing, in full, the complexity of customers'
requirements; they have to respond in one form or another to the various changes in
specifications. The planning system—which includes the linear programming

software and the human interface—produces unstable plans as small changes in specifications produce big changes in the orders' contributions. The system does not have the capacity to adjust schedules as orders change; this gives segment and plant managers the opportunity to use their more complete and up-to-date knowledge of customer requirements and plant capabilities to alter production schedules on the shop floor itself.

The costs of this informal amplification are a dysfunctional and expensive production planning system. Perhaps even more damaging, the system reinforces organizational conversations at the level of market segments and machines at the expense of more global conversations at the level of products, plants and business unit as a whole.

Our discussion so far has shown how the strategies in use to manage complexity in XTN are inadequate. In the remainder of the chapter we explain how to improve this management of complexity and so enable XTN to perform more effectively. In the meantime, we can state another general principle.

---

*PRINCIPLE 4: RESIDUAL VARIETY, OR 'GETTING MORE WITH LESS'*

Management may reduce the organizational complexity relevant to them either by constraining local discretion or by empowering people to respond by themselves to problems; equally, organizations may reduce the environmental complexity relevant to them by blinkering their vision or by getting the co-operation of people in the environment to respond by themselves to a wider range of possibilities. The latter strategies get more with less.

---

### Subtheme 2: Unfolding Complexity, Linking Strategy and Structure. XTN's Identity and its Structural Implications

XTN managers and workers are operating in a highly demanding environment which is testing to the extreme their response capacity. The leaders group is aware that it needs to focus XTN's efforts more sharply on the market.

Over time, as a result of ongoing conversations, the group has developed a shared view of the business identity. This shared identity is summarized in their own words as follows:

> XTN is a customer oriented strategic business unit producing synthetic materials for European markets that aims to minimize the strain on the environment of production and products through the controlled use, wherever possible, of the Corporation's own produced raw materials and manufacturing technology, incorporating all the necessary stages of refinement and finishing.

Further discussions based on this shared identity for XTN have emphasized the business unit's production capabilities.

What does the identity statement tell us? It suggests that XTN sees itself as being in the business of manufacturing and that in order to succeed it accepts the need to make its production processes viable. The concern expressed with all stages of refinement and finishing suggests that XTN wants to make its products viable in specific market segments. Finally, the focus on Europe defines the geographic coverage and environment of the business.

On a day-to-day basis, XTN's interactions with its market and the wider environment take place through its two production plants operating in two different countries and through its products, which are managed by six product managers operating from a third location. The two plant managers are responsible for production lines which use a sophisticated and expensive technology. The product managers are responsible for the commercial success of the various products.

Each product manager is responsible for three to four market segments. Under them, market segment managers, supported by the corporation's regional organization, interact with customers and are responsible for the efficient and successful processing of manufacturing orders.

XTN's identity statement is, of course, the outcome of and is supported by the resources made available to this SBU by corporation X. These are the resources that have created and continue to reproduce the organization's structure.

The espoused identity of XTN reflects the fact that corporation X has itself espoused a business-unit philosophy, according to which each SBU should be judged on its performance as an independent business. There is, however, a problem; X's espoused identity is not fully carried out in practice. It is not fully recognized by the regional subsidiaries, responsible for the operations of X in different countries.

Hence these regional subsidiaries tend to operate in a manner that does not properly recognize XTN's business autonomy. The corporation looks at results per plant and country; but according to the business-unit philosophy, it should not adopt the same criteria in looking at these two kinds of results. In the words of the leader of XTN:

> . . . results of the BU should be at the forefront of considerations, because X has deliberately adopted a BU-organization, not a matrix-organization. Consistency with this principle would make roles clearer. The role of BU management would be to optimize profit/contribution. The role of country management would be to optimize costs.

The problem is that X's practices are still supporting a matrix structure.

### Systemic Implications Of XTN's Identity

XTN's identity statement has specific systemic implications that are relevant to its structural arrangements. By clarifying them, we hope to clarify further the problems of managing XTN's complexity.

Such a discussion will also help us to a general understanding of the link between strategy and structure.

While by definition XTN is a strategic business unit that needs viability, the question is: does its structure support an effective autonomous business unit?

The statement of XTN's identity and related discussions suggest that it wants to make its production processes viable as well as its products in specific market segments. Questions emerging from this proposition are:

- Is it the intention to give plants the resources and structure to make them self-contained manufacturing units?

- Is it the intention to make the production lines within the plants self-contained, autonomous units?
- Are the products to be made viable?
- Are the market segments to be made viable?

If the answer to all these questions is 'yes', as appears to be consistent with XTN's espoused identity, then several implications follow.

The plants and production lines must be given local problem-solving capacity. Problems within the production lines must be sorted out by the people in the lines themselves. They must therefore have open communication channels with customers in order to develop an understanding of their needs. It is important for them to understand what kind of discretion is taken away from them by the plant management, and indeed by wider managerial levels; however, all the rest should be their concern.

The same logic applies to the plants; they must develop local problem-solving capacity within the framework of the wider business unit. Whatever happens within the plants should be the responsibility of this management level; hence it would be to their own advantage to have effective, autonomous production lines within the plants. This would amplify considerably the managerial capacity of plant managers. More problems should be dealt with locally, without requiring managerial attention. This would enable the 'residual complexity' of problems left unattended by people in the production lines to be minimized.

If products and segments are to be made viable, the political will must be developed to create autonomous product units and, within these, autonomous market segment units. These market segment units need to be given the resources and structures to transform themselves into autonomous problem-solving units. They too must have the capacity to solve all their problems from within, except in those areas in which discretion is taken away from them by wider organizational units. Indeed, the more effective the market segments are, the lower the residual complexity that product managers need to deal with and the larger the complexity they can create for products.

The market segments are responsible for satisfying customer orders. They therefore must be responsible for managing the various 'slices' of manufacturing that produce the various orders. If market segments units are to be autonomous problem-solving units, they must be responsible not only for managing the commercial aspects of order processing, but also for producing the orders for which they are accountable. Otherwise they will find themselves accountable for customer satisfaction related to orders but not responsible for the resources producing those orders. This de-coupling of the 'doing' capacity from the commercial capacity would undermine their local, autonomous, problem-solving capacity.

This conclusion, a consequence of answering yes to the above questions, suggests that production lines should be seen as embedded at the same time within the plant organization, i.e., within manufacturing and within the product organization, which is marketing. See Figure 5.11.

This analysis throws light on the problems with production planning described above. While the production organization is optimizing machine utilization, the product organization is optimizing order processing. At a later stage we will discuss

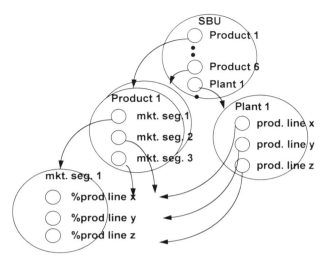

**Figure 5.11**  XTN unfolding of complexity

the managerial and regulatory implications of this need for dual regulation. Indeed, more implications of answering 'yes' to the above questions will emerge.

The embedding of autonomous units within autonomous units that we have described yields the model of XTN's unfolding of complexity shown in Figure 5.11. This unfolding results from recognizing the autonomous units embedded within XTN, itself recognized as an autonomous unit. The specific way in which complexity unfolding is a key consideration in the implementation of strategy; it defines the distribution of response capacity throughout the organization. In this case, production lines are the basic units producing XTN's products. Larger autonomous units also produce products, with each new level adding new value to the basic products and helping to develop synergy within the organization.

This way of unfolding complexity is a systemic implication of the identity statement and the distribution of resources in XTN. For as long as the purpose is to make viable both the strategic business unit as a whole and the manufacturing and product organizations within it, the managerial and structural implications of Figure 5.11 will constitute a good strategy for managing the complexity of XTN's task.

XTN's people do not have a clear grasp of the systemic implications of their identity and strategy. The corporation's functional history implies that managers see the business through functional spectacles as consisting of manufacturing, marketing and R&D, not as a total organizational unit. As a result, product-line capacity is shared between the manufacturing and product organizations in an improvised manner; market-segment managers accomplish it *de facto* by cajoling production-line managers and thereby circumventing organizational procedures.

*Relations Between XTN And Other Parts Of X*

Such are the implications of XTN's identity statement at the level of XTN itself. There are other implications.

Of great interest are the interactions between the regional and business units of corporation X. So far we have argued that XTN's two plants should be seen as embedded in the business unit. However, they are physically embedded in a geographic region. Does this mean that they should be seen as embedded also in the two regional subsidiaries of X?

What, moreover, is the relationship between the other regional units of corporation X, those without manufacturing capacity, and the business unit, XTN? Are the regional units corporate businesses? The fact that the corporation has espoused a business-unit focus rather than a regional focus or a matrix structure suggests that regional units should see themselves as being there to support the business units locally rather than to develop those businesses themselves. The regions are amplifiers of business-unit capacity.

It could be argued that regions are businesses in their own right in a 'business' different to the corporate business espoused by X, namely that of offering services to the latter, as do business parks or science parks. If this is agreed, then acceptance of the regional units as belonging to the corporation poses a challenge to the corporation's espoused identity. Does the corporation agree that it is in the 'business services' business? Has it decided that it should be?

In the next three sections we will develop further the implications of achieving 'autonomous units within autonomous units'.

---

*PRINCIPLE 5: DISTRIBUTED PROBLEM SOLVING*

An effective (viable) organization is one with distributed problem-solving capacity.

*PRINCIPLE 6: LINKING STRUCTURE AND STRATEGY*

An organization's strategy is created and implemented by its structure, that is, by the people and other resources constituting the organization's relationships. In particular, the specific way in which complexity is unfolded is key to business strategy; it defines the distribution of creative and response capacity throughout the organization.

---

### Subtheme 3: The Adaptation And Policy-making Mechanism: Inventing The Organization. XTN's Future

Let us ask: how does XTN currently carry out the function of strategic management?

The first point to note is that the majority of conversations in the leaders group are focused on specific market segments and machines, limiting their capacity to pay attention to more strategic concerns.

This is reinforced by the fact that XTN strategy is strongly influenced by corporate people, at the level of X, not XTN: the corporation's general board decides on special projects and to a degree approves investment budgets for each of the SBUs two structural levels below. In this process, the divisions, including division T to which

XTN belongs, are *de facto* bypassed, since they do not have the functional capacity to study strategy or steer the SBUs.

How does the board decide? It has the support of central staff, a powerful central office which undertakes investment studies focused on business units. Criteria for these studies and decisions are operational rather than strategic. For instance, poor operational performance is likely to reduce the chance of a particular business unit receiving further investment.

Regarding these decisions, managers make comments such as the following:

> Investment for an XTN product was approved without problems, although from both an ecological and a competitive stance this product was already doomed to failure.

XTN's concern for the future is expressed in its R&D work. It has a large R&D group located in one of the two plants, specifically developing XTN products and processes. However, there is evidence that about 50% of this group's projects are of conceptual more than practical interest. Innovation should, moreover, be seen in broader terms than R&D.

How does XTN project future demand? In effect, German and European Community environmental policies shape demand more than trade cycles do. Yet, as discussed above, XTN's ecological vulnerability and insufficient response—in common with the rest of the industry—to changes in people's values and attitudes have deeply affected its long term prospects.

XTN's business intelligence also seems to be inadequate. Intelligence is of no use if no action is taken. XTN produced an 'XTN-industry cost curve'; it failed, however, to develop the structural capacity for learning from it, i.e., for maintaining systems that would use the models it had developed.

The end result of XTN's lack of strategic awareness is that it has fallen into the 'trap of specialization', concentrating on high value products at the expense of overall adaptability.


*Systemic Comments*

We will begin now to disentangle the various interactions that have produced the above problems. First, let us make an important assumption: XTN wants to remain viable in its environment.

If we were talking about a business on its own, independent of a larger corporation, this assumption would be obvious. The business is likely to be fully, perhaps painfully, aware of its autonomy. It is wholly reliant on its own capacity for survival.

This sense of wholeness is likely to be less strong in XTN. Its management knows that important policy and strategic issues are taken by corporation X's board and that the necessary studies to support these decisions are made by central staff, beyond the boundaries of the business. Debates in the leaders group are focused on short term, internal operations rather than on long-term strategy, making the total business less tangible as an entity.

The discussions in the leaders group reflect the general tone of conversations within the business unit. The orientation and major concern of most people in XTN is with specific customer orders rather than the total business. Conversations that serve to integrate production and marketing within the business are weak. Most such conversations take place on the shop floor as market segment managers cajole production managers to give priority to 'their' orders.

Clearly, functional integration will not take place as long as the most significant forum for such integration is the leaders' fortnightly meeting. Integration requires orchestration of ongoing interactions between marketing, production and R&D. It is only if this integration continually takes place around global issues that the leaders' natural issues of concern will be holistic, and neither functional nor too detailed. Moreover, if effective integration is to take place, the leaders must use their grasp of XTN's identity, potentials and capabilities to orchestrate strategy debates throughout the unit. They have to match the people who have skills and knowledge relating to the 'outside and then' with those whose focus is on the 'inside and now'; then they must ensure that they communicate effectively.

Thinking in relational terms means asking such questions as:

- Are ongoing conversations consistent with our vision of the organization?
- Are they short-term oriented?
- Are they weakly grounded in the realities of the business?
- Are we creating the capacity to recognize threats and opportunities?
- Are we creating the capacity to develop strengths and overcome weaknesses?
- Is the allocation of resources to counter people's negative views about our products hindering the management of internal operations?

Answers to these questions should help leaders to allocate resources and develop communications so as to steer the organization more effectively.

Ways must be found to integrate the views of R&D, marketing and manufacturing at all levels of the business. If the ongoing learning of marketing, as they work with customers, is not affecting R&D, or if the designs of R&D are not being checked and balanced by manufacturing, then the likelihood of disparate developments will increase.

Cases of failed policies should be seen as platforms for learning. If an investment programme was approved on the basis of over-estimating demand, were people with relevant knowledge left out of the debates leading to that decision? As for those who were involved, did they offer a balanced representation of the 'here and now' and 'outside and then' perspectives?

Policy makers should devise specific mechanisms, such as working groups, *ad hoc* or permanent teams, and physical or technological layouts, to support a balanced contribution of those representing 'inside and now' and those representing 'outside and then' in policy debates. For instance, who represents the outside and then in debates underpinning the decisions of the corporate board? Assuming that this is the role of central staff and that XTN staff represent the inside and now, what mechanisms are used to integrate their perspectives? If it is accepted that the chances of such integration are small, what are the structural implications for XTN?

---

*PRINCIPLE 7: POLICY MAKING AS A PROCESS*

Policy making requires creating and maintaining a structural context for people in the organization to contribute to the best of their abilities to the policy process.

**Subtheme 4: The Monitoring And Control Mechanism, Inventing In The Organization. Managing XTN's Operations To Achieve Synergy**

Consider some of the observations made by XTN managers about the unit's internal operations. According to one manager:

> The main emphasis of control is on profits; the focus is on financial accounting. However, this system lacks in resolution capacity; at present it is not possible to work out the specific contributions of product lines and market segments. Efforts to improve this situation, by studying processes and cost drivers, lack the reference of a corporate framework.

> Systems across the company are inflexible. There is no corporation-wide system which adequately reflects XTN's product structure and resources. Management accounting information is lacking. Also, corporate systems furnish data about results with a big time lag. Operational planning is bureaucratic, estimations are too detailed and do not include enough calculations of risks, contingencies, and options.

The criteria used for performance measurement reflect this lack of resolution in the control systems.

> Sales staff operates on quantities rather than on profits. This is in spite of everyone being aware that contribution to profits and not prices should be used to steer sales performance. There is a lack of control measures. Aspects such as quality are not adequately measured. In general there is a lack of knowledge about the true costs of manufacturing and other operations.

This is compounded by the nature of the links between the SBU and central departments. One manager's comment illustrates this aspect:

> As production manager of XTN1 I receive from three different central departments different lists of cost centres within XTN1, which creates endless administrative difficulties. Costing standards and allocation rules are old fashioned.

However, there is an abundance of procedures and instructions.

> There are too many handbooks, specifications, and requirements for certification. People feel that they are over controlled. There are too many aspects of their daily operations that require higher level approval.

The different locations of manufacturing and marketing trigger the need for many meetings. Co-ordination is largely understood as cross-functional meetings. There is a proliferation of meetings and related traveling.

If we look at XTN's information systems, we find they have a functional orientation. Marketing and sales people use information systems different from those used by manufacturing people. This is compounded by shortcomings in the production planning system when it comes to relating commercial and manufacturing concerns. An additional problem is that one of the plants feels particularly disadvantaged since in their view the production planning team gives preference to the other plant—the one where it happens to be located.

The management of XTN, gauged by the activities of the leaders group, is not focused on the business as a whole. This implies not only a lack of focus on the SBU as such, but also that strategic thinking for production as a whole, or for products as a whole, does not take place anywhere.

Product managers make decisions about introducing new products with limited regard for their consequences in the production lines. There is a discrepancy between the goals espoused by managers, such as profit, quality and timely delivery, and the performance indices used by them, which are basically focused on quantity.

## Systemic Comments

As before, our concern is to make apparent the kind of organizational interactions that are implied by these comments of XTN's managers. Our purpose is to highlight shortcomings and suggest alternative ways of conducting interactions that might improve performance.

Managing the operations of the SBU implies more than co-ordinating manufacturing, marketing and logistics in order to satisfy customers with quality products and services in time. It implies managing the potentials of the resources involved. Consider what this means.

Current interactions within XTN are the outcomes of, among other factors, the leaders group's concern with specific market segments and machines, the increasing complexity of customer requirements, inadequate information systems and largely unco-ordinated and over-detailed corporate intervention.

By and large, the information systems within XTN reinforce the tendency for conversations to become lost in detail; this is particularly the case with the production planning system. Systems supporting global conversations, such as the financial accounting system, are not the same as those that would support conversations about products and market segments. There is a lack of information for conversations between the Leaders Group and those responsible for customer orders, and this lack is compounded by the functional nature of whatever information is available. Existing information systems offer information for manufacturing, marketing and finance, without supporting the holistic overview of the business or the businesses within it.

These facts make it natural for people to talk mostly about detailed orders, specific machine utilization of innumerable corporate procedural demands. It is much less natural for them to talk about the global operational needs of the business, the contribution of product lines or their strategic requirements, or the future of manufacturing plants, let alone about the strategic requirements of whole market segments or production lines. Conversations about investment requirements are by and large carried out between XTN people, divisional leaders and central staff, i.e., with people who are outside the business unit. Yet it is essential that these kind of conversations take place within XTN if there is to be effective implementation of its agreed identity.

Creating a context of conversations at different aggregation levels is a means of managing the organization's complexity. For instance, our hypothesized unfolding of XTN's complexity, shown in Figure 5.11, suggests the need to support conversations between the management of XTN and product and plant management. A prime purpose of these conversations would be to align the overall interests of the SBU with the specific interests of products and plants.

Their strategic interests need to be aligned. This assumes that both sides have strategies of their own and are clear about the resource implications of these strategies. Alignment of interests would take place through a process of resource bargaining leading to agreements about programmes for products and plants.

However, such bargaining requires that the two levels have a clear sense of their identity as autonomous units; in particular of their value-adding contributions to the business. Otherwise, business unit managers will see product and plant managers only as amplifiers of BU strategy, with no strategies of their own. XTN is, of course, implementing its strategy through products and plants, but it is not in the interest of the business to entangle the two levels of management. By blurring levels the amplification capacity of plants and products is inhibited. Autonomy, and the creation of 'separate worlds' at each structural level, is necessary for the organization as a whole to deal flexibly with complexity and change. Alternatively, an effective separation of identities between the different levels of management will have to be accompanied by effective negotiating mechanisms between them.

In order to define its own strategy the management of the global unit needs a realistic appreciation, from its own perspective, of the capabilities of the embedded units, and the way these capabilities change over time. XTN management needs to have independent information about products and plants. It cannot rely solely on what product and plant managers say about themselves. There will be much information relevant for XTN management that will be beyond the concern of product and plant management.

The management of the global units also needs to create the conditions for local units to interact among themselves in ways that they would not do naturally, were they left on their own. Precisely this is its value-adding activity.

If XTN is to be more than the addition of products and plants, it needs to add value to what they do; and this requires managing their interactions by creating synergy among them, that is, by creating the conditions for their mutual co-operation and the mechanisms for local problem solving. In all this we are saying that XTN management needs to develop communication channels for co-ordination.

The communication requirements outlined above are not met in XTN.

Discussions about the total potential of the business are limited; the conversations of XTN leaders are far too detailed in nature. Additionally, the distinction between XTN as such and its products and plants is blurred by poor information systems and entangled interactions—the responsibility to some degree of varied, over-detailed and often inconsistent corporate requirements.

The same picture emerges if we look at matters from the other side. While it is natural for people on the shop floor to deal with the complexities of time, length, weight, texture, colour and many more variables relevant to an order, it makes no sense to involve product or plant managers in these details. The more time they spend in them, the less capacity they have left for 'discovering' and 'realizing' the potentials of their own units. Even if these managers, in the course of their daily interactions, were to discover certain new potentials, they would have a limited chance of making them happen. Most of their energies, and the bulk of organizational resources, are consumed by the detailed requirements of the business. Indeed, there is room for improving the situational management of complexity.

The challenge is to create, within XTN, structures for conversations at different levels. Understanding how to create such structures requires an understanding of how to nurture autonomous units within autonomous units rather than hierarchical structures.

---

*PRINCIPLE 8: SYNERGY PRINCIPLE*

Managing an organization's primary activities means enabling their autonomous development and achieving their integration into the organization, i.e., the larger primary activity.

---

### Subtheme 5: Recursive Management And Structures

Consider these comments made by managers at different levels within the corporation—not merely within XTN. They serve to show us the nature of current processes between levels of management.

> The corporation's definition of its policies and strategies is business unit oriented. Therefore, potentials which are not captured by existing business units are undefinable and consequently excluded from consideration. Nobody is in charge of products going beyond our BU-structure. For instance, within industry T we have BUs for XTP, XTS and XTN. That is the reason why we do not think about other types of products for this industry.

The same kind of blindness exists regarding potentials not captured by a focus on products.

> Innovation is not happening as effectively as it should. When customer orders are not dealt with efficiently, the effects are felt throughout the organization. Poor response at the operational level affects customers' attitudes towards the company, which affects innovation since it is interactions with customers that account for about 80% of product innovation.

> Divisional management is seen as supporting corporate managers in relaying corporate policy to the business units. Divisions are not seen as businesses in their own right within the Corporation.

The last comment clarifies the corporate view of the role of divisions. Rather than being seen as units with their own proper autonomy, their management capacity is seen as essentially an amplifier of corporate policy.

This view of Division T's role in the management of its business units is reflected in the comment: 'R&D have been doing what they want; they maintain that their projects are going OK, but in fact, based on a consultant's report requested by the Division, they are doing little. Their projects are producing a good deal of "conceptual learning", but not much more'.

XTN does not sufficiently exploit complementarities or possibilities of co-operation with other related business units or support activities within the company. The leader of XTN makes the comment:

> The head of a BU should be in a position to integrate his actions into the larger picture of strategies and operations along the value chain within the company; in view of the way we are set up this is not possible.

Another comment:

> The leaders group does not have the support of management accounting systems with enough resolution to debate and carry out changes in the product range.

*Systemic Comments*

The interaction problems discussed above and in preceding sections recur at all levels of management within the organization. In this final section of Chapter 5, we want to illustrate the idea of 'recursive management' that is, the management of autonomous units within autonomous units.

Inventing the future of an organization and working out its strategy is the concern of all its people, at all structural levels. For XTN, its strategy and future should be as much the outcome of conversations within the plants (and within production lines within the plants) and product units (and within market segments within the product units) as of conversations in the business unit as such, represented by the leaders group and its support staff.

Indeed, conversations within a market segment unit, or a plant, are necessary for them to invent their own future. As they do this, however, they are contributing to the invention of the SBU, the division and the corporation.

For the corporation, its future should be as much the outcome of conversations at the corporate level as of the conversations within it; that is, within divisions, business units and so forth.

In corporation X, however, we find that corporate conversations are strongly focused on business units; business unit conversations are equally focused on production lines and market segments. This reduces the chance of distributed strategic management. Corporate management is inventing the corporation's future simply by adding together the futures of business units; it does not add value.

What then is the value that corporate management should be adding to the overall business? Should it be making detailed investment decisions as it does now? Is this an instance of unnecessary centralization? Decentralizing central staff resources to divisions and business units could have the double effect of creating autonomous divisions and disentangling interactions in order to make the business units more effective. Within XTN, which is the focus of our concern, management could be more focused on XTN itself rather than on the different market segments and production lines. Such a change might also enable products and market segments and plants and production lines to develop their own identities.

A systemic generalization can be made here: it is that a level of management unable to structure a task of its own is driven into a hierarchical relationship with the level above. It is driven to enhance, i.e. amplify the capacity of the level above instead of creating embedded units with its own management. This is the case of product and plant managers in relation to SBU managers; they are enhancing, i.e. amplifying their capacity rather than creating embedded units. The same phenomenon is also illustrated by the relationship between divisional and corporate management.

On the other hand, if a lower level of management structures a task of its own and creates the space for its continuous invention and adaptation, then it is *de facto* creating an autonomous unit within an autonomous unit. In this case the relationship with the level above is one between people who are each responsible for their own autonomous units; both levels of management are inventing the organization, albeit at different structural levels. Whether inventing at one level or the other is more difficult, or requires more skills, depends upon the particular situation.

When, however, we create autonomous units within autonomous units we must strike a balance between autonomy and cohesion. Sometimes people confuse autonomy with isolation. Far from this, autonomy is realized by full-fledged communication with the environment. However, the more complex this interaction with the environment becomes, the greater the challenge in maintaining cohesion.

At one extreme, the hierarchical view would imply that the 1000 people employed by XTN are all implementing the views of their leaders—including not only SBU leaders but also corporate and divisional leaders. These leaders are doing the thinking for the rest. The recursive view of autonomous units within autonomous units differs from this. It sees XTN as the outcome of people at several levels inventing the business; thinking and creation is distributed throughout the organization. Entrepreneurship is brought forth from within XTN.

The challenge for XTN is to align local interests with global interests; for instance, the interests of market segment managers and the people they represent with the more general interests of product managers and the people they represent—which happens to include responsibility for market segments. The global unit must be more than the addition of its embedded units. A global unit is unnecessary unless it adds value to the business.

We should remember that the basic products of the organization are being produced by its most elementary autonomous units. The argument for keeping these units is that the larger (embedding) unit can make products that are more than the addition of the basic products. The benefit for the organization of managing the interactions between the basic products must be larger than its cost. For as long as the higher-level products satisfy additional aspects of customers' needs it will make sense to maintain the cohesion of the elementary autonomous units. Of course, this management—the production of higher-level products—may entail discontinuing basic products, relating them differently, adding new properties to them, making them more accessible or just making them cheaper.

XTN provides a good illustration of a generally 'non-recursive' organization. Its information and communication processes are such as to blur the value-adding processes of higher management. Managers, from the leaders group downwards, focus on the basic products and processes. The increasing complexity of customer needs is pushed down to the shopfloor, without recognition of the advantages to be found in adding value recursively. Despite claims to the contrary, this behaviour is producing entangled management and reinforcing a hierarchical mode of operation. The result is increasing costs and poor performance.

What, then, does recursive management entail? How is it possible to create the conditions for autonomous units within autonomous units? What is required to disentangle interactions in order to create separate but aligned management levels?

First, it is necessary for autonomous units at all structural levels to be able to 'invent' their own, legitimate *raison d'être*, as discussed earlier in this chapter in relation to mechanisms for adaptation. How can higher levels add value to the organizations' basic products? They must not only invent their own purposes; they must implement them by creating the conditions for value-adding interactions between the autonomous units embedded within them.

Second, it will inevitably happen, in one form or another, that a global unit will negotiate over time with its embedded autonomous units their respective visions and

possibilities—as described in our discussion of the monitoring-control mechanism. It is in these negotiations that interests are aligned. In recursive organizations it is through communications, rather than information, that control processes are set in place. High-quality interactions depend not only on people 'having information' about each other but on mutual understanding, respect and trust. Interactions should help people to appreciate their potential contributions to the common interest.

In general, there are a number of existing or potential autonomous units within any autonomous unit. For instance, XTN has six products and two plants. Within each product we find three or four market segments; within each plant we find several product lines. This one-to-many, asymmetric relationship often creates pressures on the management of global units, leading them to hierarchical, information-based, rather than recursive, communication-based relations.

In a less structured situation than XTN's if each unit pursued its own interest without paying attention to the totality, the outcome would be loss of cohesion; each would go its own way. But where cohesion is by and large secured by the fact that all of the units belong to a strong corporation, as in the case of XTN, the result may be an increasingly autocratic organization, dominated by its leadership. In the long term this is a recipe to under-perform. Systemically, the problem is how to design a recursive structure; how to create the structural conditions for effective organizational conversations.

Such a design entails the design of communications rather than merely of information systems. It is important for people to distinguish interactions aimed at the alignment of tasks with more global tasks from interactions intended to co-ordinate actions within an overall task that has been agreed. The quality of the former interactions is crucial to the implementation of organizational tasks. If there is not enough channel capacity to support them, hierarchical relations will dominate and tasks will be defined from above, creating not only lack of commitment but also tasks that people find less interesting and involving.

For global management the challenge entails:

- negotiating and agreeing tasks with embedded autonomous units, defining the resource implications of these agreements and seeing that tasks are implemented, modified and implemented as agreed;
- increasing the capacity of local autonomous units to work out by themselves and among themselves the implications of the negotiated tasks, thus reducing as much as possible their independent demands on global management, i.e., reducing the residual variety left for this management to cope with.

Managing tasks, that is negotiating resources and monitoring their execution, requires global management to develop an independent appreciation of local units' capabilities and performance. It is not possible for global management to rely only on what local management says; their monitoring is necessary. As we have explained, monitoring is not motivated by suspicion. Such independent appreciation is necessary even if local management is a model of candour. Accepting the need for independent appreciation tends to reduce communication breakdowns and misunderstandings.

The fact is that both global and local autonomous units operate in complex environments, which create new situations for each of them all the time. They are creating their independent 'separate worlds'. Local managers, precisely because of this independence, lack the context to appreciate the global meaning and relevance of their experiences; this can only be assessed by global managers. This, however, makes it necessary for global managers to have occasional, unattenuated access to local situations. Without these local communications, they will not be in a position to assess the meaning of local tasks, and the chances of an alignment of global and local interests will be reduced. The chances of breakdowns, as the two sides realize that they are talking about different things, will increase.

The negotiation of tasks and resources should be intertwined with the monitoring of local tasks. When this point is not understood, managers tend to base negotiations on meetings, reports and management information systems, missing the point that such media are, by design, unable to capture the complexity of people's 'separate worlds'.

In XTN there are no monitoring mechanisms of this kind; this makes the formation of autonomous units within autonomous units hard to achieve. Middle-level managers see no scope for autonomy and tend to operate within the hierarchical framework of corporate-divisional-SBU management.

There is in XTN no effective 'invention' of tasks at intermediate levels, as is clear from the experience of product and manufacturing managers. They experience multiple, predictable breakdowns in their interactions as product managers make decisions about new products with limited regard for their consequences on the production lines. XTN managers are aware of inadequate resource bargaining processes, with no checks on the plausibility of bottom-up plans and poor co-ordination between them.

To enhance local problem solving, and thereby exploit organizational synergy, it is necessary to create the context for horizontal communications. In general terms, it is the quality of people's moment-to-moment co-ordination of actions that, more than any other factor, determines the performance of different organizations. Better moment-to-moment co-ordination of actions implies easier communications, less demands on channel capacity and, above all, more effective alignment of local and global interests.

In pursuit of effective co-ordination of tasks, it makes sense for global management to take away from local autonomous units discretion in all those functions, i.e. support services, that are not central to the units' negotiated tasks. Standardizing these functions for all units provides them with a common language to facilitate cross-functional and across-units communications, making it easier for the parts to understand each other's needs and requirements. Designing these functions in such a way as to effect co-ordination by mutual adjustment, rather than by direct supervision, enhances the problem-solving capacity of the organization as a whole.

---

*PRINCIPLE 9: RECURSIVE ORGANIZATION*

An organization's effective performance in its environment requires a structure of autonomous viable units within autonomous viable units.

---

*PRINCIPLE 10: CHAINING SEPARATE REALITIES*

In a recursive organization, control is achieved through effective interpersonal communications rather than just by information transmission. This principle makes necessary the monitoring of local activities by global management.

*PRINCIPLE 11: COHESION AND SELF-REGULATION*

In a recursive organization, cohesion requires increasing the capacity for local communications to take place; that requires creating the structural and cultural context for co-ordination of communications.

---

# GIVING REQUISITE VARIETY TO MANAGEMENT AND ORGANIZATION

The aim of this chapter has been to show how complexity is a guiding principle for organizational design. The central idea has been that of recursive structures and management.

This idea is creeping into our current practices; cell structures, autonomous teams and the like are becoming increasingly fashionable. Yet its practice is not fully understood.

We have argued, also, for control as a matter of communication processes and not as a matter of extrinsic intervention. This emphasis on communications rather than information has important implications for the design of control and information systems. We should be more alert to people's conversations and pay more attention to the connection between them and the development of autonomous units within autonomous units.

Perhaps the most striking example of XTN's lack of understanding of this point is provided by its planning of shop floor activities. Conversations between market segment managers and production line supervisors are not in alignment with the production planning information systems. This system was, in fact, designed with total disregard for organizational conversations. The problem is made more acute by the entangled nature of these conversations.

If, however, our assumptions about XTN's complexity unfolding are accepted, the production planning system will have to be aligned with this unfolding. The system has to support conversations at different structural levels and avoid diving into the shop floor in one stage. In this way it may be possible to increase substantially the channel capacity between manufacturing and marketing, thus increasing XTN's capacity to respond to the increasing complexity of customers' requirements. The response capacity is, no doubt, on the shop floor, but the problem is to co-ordinate the management of production lines with the management of various 'slices' of production lines by market segment managers. Conversations are needed to define global priorities between product and market segments and the negotiation of these priorities with production lines so that they can decide specific production plans—

rather than leaving this to the computer system! A system designed for such conversations is likely to have far more capacity to respond to customers' requirements than today's heavy-handed, top-down production planning combined with uncoordinated pressures from different market segments.

This example shows how to disentangle interactions and, also, the practical implications of recursive management. Hopefully, the arguments of this chapter will show that this understanding is not only a way to increase organizational performance but also a way to develop people's commitment to the organization.

## Postscript

During the last two years company X has carried out substantial organizational changes. Corporate management has not only acknowledged internal criticisms but used them as the building blocks for developing the new corporation X. They realized that people were prepared for and expected change. The majority of people in X have accepted the need for these changes. A number of them have realized that the magic of skilled incompetence has lost its power and that the comfortable ties of bureaucracy had to be removed in favour of autonomy and personal responsibility.

There is evidence that developing an entrepreneurial culture is working; transformation is taking place. These are instances:

1. The huge central staff has been reduced to a very small group of people, mainly supporting the board's activities.
2. The corporation's regional (country) organizations are no longer profit centres. The SBUs are in charge of global strategies and global results.
3. Powerful centralized functional departments like accounting and engineering have been largely integrated into the divisions.
4. The divisions are now autonomous primary activities with adequate resources and information systems support. Divisions are responsible for SBUs and plants; they have been constituted as true primary activities.
5. The chief executive has led establishing a strategic management process as an 'open learning loop' (his words) in which senior management and experts control the centrifugal forces of increasingly autonomous divisions.
6. XTN was well prepared for this new structure and, most importantly, is back making profits.

Something else is important to mention about XTN. The public and political perception of XTN's products has improved. This change is, to a large degree, the outcome of the SBU leader's efforts. He has played the role of the 'innovative butterfly' in the chaotic communication process of many interest groups.

## List Of Principles

We conclude by putting together in one place the principles of management and organization derived in this chapter.

*PRINCIPLE 1: MANAGING COMPLEXITY*

Management of complexity requires matching distinctions in an action domain with appropriate actions.

*PRINCIPLE 2: REQUISITE COMPLEXITY*

Complexity is necessary to fight complexity . . . but the source of control complexity is in both the controller and the controllee.

*PRINCIPLE 3: BENCHMARKING*

A performer is competitive with others in the same action domain if it is able to manage at least as much situational complexity as the best performers.

*PRINCIPLE 4: RESIDUAL VARIETY OR 'GETTING MORE WITH LESS'*

Management may reduce the organizational complexity relevant to them either by constraining local discretion or by empowering people to respond by themselves to problems; equally organizations may reduce the environmental complexity relevant to them by blinkering their vision or by getting the co-operation of people in the environment to respond by themselves to a wider range of possibilities. The latter strategies get more with less.

*PRINCIPLE 5: DISTRIBUTED PROBLEM SOLVING*

An effective (viable) organization is one with distributed problem solving capacity.

*PRINCIPLE 6: LINKING STRUCTURE AND STRATEGY*

An organization's strategy is created and implemented by its structure, that is, by the people and other resources constituting the organization's relationships. In particular, complexity unfolding is key to business strategy; it defines the distribution of response capacity throughout the organization.

*PRINCIPLE 7: POLICY MAKING AS A PROCESS*

Effective policy making requires creating and maintaining the structural context for people in the organization to contribute to the best of their abilities to the policy process.

*PRINCIPLE 8: SYNERGY PRINCIPLE*

Managing an organization's primary activities means enabling their autonomous development and achieving their integration into the organization, i.e. the larger primary activity.

*PRINCIPLE 9: RECURSIVE ORGANIZATION*

An organization's effective performance in its environment requires a structure of autonomous viable units within autonomous viable units.

*PRINCIPLE 10: CHAINING SEPARATE REALITIES*

In a recursive organization, control is achieved through effective interpersonal communications rather than just by information transmission. This principle makes necessary the monitoring of local activities by global management.

*PRINCIPLE 11: COHESION AND SELF-REGULATION*

In a recursive organization, cohesion requires increasing the capacity for local communications; that requires creating the structural and cultural context for co-ordination of communications.

# Chapter 6

# Organizational Learning

## INTRODUCTION

A fundamental prerequisite for the survival of an organization in a changing environment is the ability to adapt to change. This is the essence of 'learning'. The organization requires an organizational learning capability.

However, such a learning capability is not enough. Competing companies are learning too. Thus the speed of learning is also important—one must be able to learn faster than the competition. *Similar to Nonaka.*

To design an effective learning capability for the organization has thus become one of the central management tasks of the present day. It will continue in the future.

In the last chapter we discussed the necessary structural conditions for organizational learning. They may be summarized as: *team-learning through co-ordinated action embedded in recursive structures.*

In this chapter we focus on the process of learning itself. Our analysis will point out the differences between individual and organizational learning, the ways in which individual learning is important for organizational learning, the role of mental models, the main obstacles to individual and organizational learning and what remedies may help to overcome them.

### An Integrated Approach

Various authors have discussed organizational learning using different conceptual frameworks and models. We will attempt to integrate a number of these into a single approach, drawing especially upon the following:

- the OADI-SMM model of Kim (1993);
- the concept of organizational learning of March and Olson (1975);
- the concept of double-loop learning of Argyris and Schön (1978);
- the concept of organizational learning through mental models (Argyris and Schön, 1978);
- the concept of organizational disciplines of Senge (1992);
- the viable system model (VSM) (Beer, 1979; 1981; 1985).

Though we shall borrow from these conceptual frameworks, we shall not provide detailed descriptions of them. These are available from the references.

# THE LEARNING CAPABILITY OF AN ORGANIZATION

What does learning by an organization mean?

It describes a process, linked to individual learning, whereby organizations acquire skills and experience. Parts of this process may be independent of human minds; nevertheless, individual learning processes are obviously central. Ultimately, an organization learns through the learning of its individual members.

On the other hand, individuals may learn without their organizations doing so; that is, the organizational routines that individuals follow may be unaffected by the knowledge they have in their heads.

We have to elucidate this and show how individual learning is fostered and made part of organizational learning. Drawing upon Kim (1993), we begin by describing how individuals learn.

### Individual Learning

What does 'learning' mean, as applied to an individual?

It can be defined, in line with our views in Chapter 4 and in Kim (1993), as enhancing the potential for effective action. As such, it comprises the acquisition of knowledge and skills. It has two aspects:

- operational learning or *know-how*; that is, the capability of bringing about a desired situation;
- conceptual learning, or *know-why*; that is, the understanding of experience, or insight.

'Learning' therefore has two closely associated meanings: what is learnt, and how what is learnt is understood and interpreted.

According to Kofman (1992), the learning process can be described as an *OADI cycle*; that is, as Figure 6.1 shows, it cycles through the following stages.

- O   observe      take in specific experiences
- A   assess       reflect on the observations
- D   design       form of abstract concepts (models)
- I   implement    test the concepts against reality

In brief, this cycle functions as follows: the observation of events or experiences is reflected upon and conclusions or hypotheses derived; these give rise to concepts and models of individual realities. If the concepts and models are tested against reality, the learning cycle begins again with the observation of these experiments and their results.

We are thus able to agree with Kim (1993, p. 38). We define individual learning as an increase in an individual's capability for effective action. It takes place by the individual repeatedly going through a learning loop described by the OADI cycle.

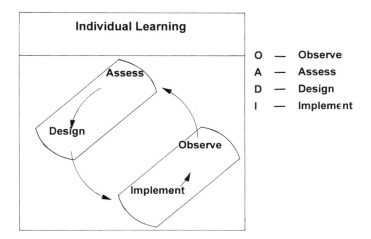

**Figure 6.1**   OADI cycle of individual learning (Kofman, 1992)

### Single- Versus Double-loop Learning

The OADI cycle does not, however, make a distinction that we shall need to make—that between single- and double-loop learning (based on Bateson, 1972). Single-loop learning consists of solving problems as they present themselves. A reaction based on single-loop learning can be compared to the reaction of a thermostat as it detects deviations from the prescribed temperature and turns the heat on or off. Note that the thermostat does not analyse the reasons for any variance, whether it be the varying outside temperature, bad insulation, a newly-opened window or a fire destroying the installation. The control model built into the thermostat is static and makes very few distinctions.

To tackle the more basic problem of why a problem, i.e. a variance exists in the first place, one must break the limitations imposed by asking the 'wrong' question. Instead of merely asking how to react to temperature variances, one must ask why these variances exist to the extent that they do.

In an organizational context, this means to shift attention from the question

- how to solve the problem

to the question

- why does this problem exist in the first place?

or even to the question

- why did we stick for so long to a solution we had found to be inadequate?

Answering the last question will need a discussion of the assumptions made by individual managers and their perceptions and roles. The group dynamics will also have to be analysed. To prevent repetition of the problem-generating syndrome certain assumptions, behaviours or values of individual managers or the group will have to change. In such cases we speak of double-loop learning.

**Individual Mental Models**

Learning of any kind is often connected with memory: what we have learnt is stored in our memory. In this view learning describes a form of acquisition, memory a form of storage of data or knowledge.

The cognitivist view is that what is stored in an individual's memory encompasses a mass of data and information. To sort this out, it is important to distinguish between, on the one hand, data or facts, constituting *passive* memory, and on the other hand, our mental models, through which our memory can be *active*.

Data are structured knowledge that can be called up; for instance, the price of a share on a certain day or the maximum daytime temperature. By contrast, mental models are constructs embodying ideas about the functioning of our environment. They therefore have a great influence on our actions.

Mental models represent individuals' implicit and explicit understanding of the world, i.e., their world-view. They control the individual's search for data and information and define how these are used.

The above suggests that models cannot usefully be classified as 'right' or 'wrong'; rather, they should be thought of as 'helpful' and 'unhelpful'. Examples of helpful scientific models that were valuable as they were created include the Copernican model of planetary motion, Einstein's theory of relativity and Forrester's system dynamics models. For us the viable systems model (VSM) is a helpful model of organization.

By contrast, prejudices—which may be described as generalizations derived from a too restricted basis of assumptions—represent examples of simple but relatively unhelpful mental models. 'Unhelpful', at least, in generating insight or understanding of a situation; 'helpful', perhaps, in winning beer-hall battles or even elections.

We can distinguish mental models involved in conceptual learning from those involved in operational learning. The former can be called 'framework's, the latter 'routines'.

*Frameworks* are used for conceptual learning. A framework describes the methods used by individuals in solving an organizational problem. Examples include frameworks for value process information management; examples of frameworks will be found in Part Three of this book.

*Routines*, on the other hand, are used for operational learning. An important part of the memory of an organization comprises its standard operating procedures (SOPs). These specify what the organization has learned to do in the operational sphere. Examples are the individual stages of order processing or annual planning.

Note that while routines may exist in organizational handbooks, they must be learned by individuals before they can be implemented.

Having distinguished between the categories of operational and conceptual learning, we can associate the four stages of the OADI cycle with these two categories:

*Operational learning* is associated with 'observing' and 'implementing'. This is because the steps for implementing a particular job are a matter of operational learning for the individual. Once in the individual's memory they become, over the course of time, a routine—as, for instance, with the steps in replacing the toner cassette of a copier.

Knowledge of routine activities improves over the course of time, and the routine undergoes adaptation as individuals become more expert, i.e., reach higher levels on their 'learning curve'.

*Conceptual learning*, on the other hand, is associated with the 'assessing' and 'designing' stages of the OADI cycle. This is the kind of learning required for the building and adaptation of the individual's mental models. It comprises the understanding of the reasons why these procedures and routines are necessary, and the construction of mental models that reflect this.

At different times, individual elements of the routine or the routine as a whole may be called into question; this happens, for example, during business process re-engineering projects. Such questioning may lead to new concepts and mental models, or even to whole new paradigms. As a result, discontinuous advance becomes possible.

Learning that does not proceed simultaneously in both categories, conceptual and operational, may be seriously defective. Thus operational learning without conceptual learning, i.e., 'practice without theory' has the disadvantages of a 'trial-and-error' process. Conceptual learning without operational, learning, i.e., 'theory without practice' may result in scholastic theory that lacks a factual basis.

We shall later discuss these two phenomena in an organizational context, where we will call them *superstitious* and *superficial learning*.

Figure 6.2 shows a simple model that describes the interaction between the individual's mental models and the categories of conceptual and operational learning in the OADI learning cycle. These categories may also be related to the concepts of 'single-loop' and 'double-loop' learning. Thus single-loop learning is represented by the OADI cycle described above. Double-loop learning consists of changes in an individual's mental models.

Individual learning in effect consists of enhancements of individual mental models. From these individuals derive, in the conceptual sphere, updated frameworks within which to design improvements. In the operational sphere, they derive updated routines and procedures with which to implement such improvements.

## Organizational Learning: The Sharing Of Mental Models

Thus far we have a picture of what is involved in individual learning. What then is organizational learning?

We can define organizational learning quite simply, following the definition of individual learning, as *an increase in the organization's capability for effective action*. Since, however, we have said that all learning is ultimately by the individual, the question arises: when does individual learning become learning by the organization, i.e., how does it increase an organization's capability for effective action?

We need a picture of organizational action in relation to individual action. March and Olson (1975, pp. 147–71) have given such a picture set out in Figure 6.3.

The March and Olson cycle functions as follows: individual beliefs or convictions regarding an organizational problem situation lead to individual actions. An individual tries to solve a problem situation by triggering the appropriate organizational response. This organizational action leads to responses and reactions in the

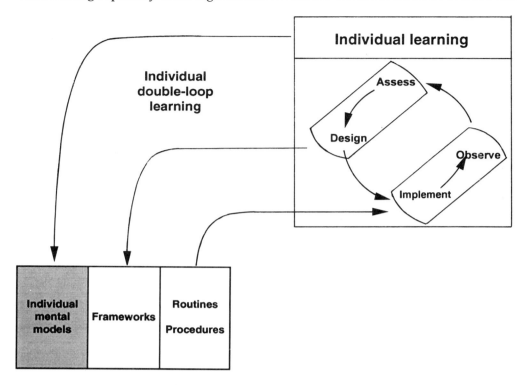

**Figure 6.2** OADI model of individual learning (Kim, 1993)

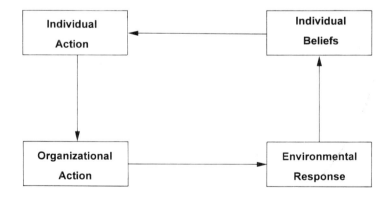

**Figure 6.3** Model of organizational learning (March and Olson, 1975)

environment; the learning cycle is completed when the environmental responses result in a change of the individual beliefs and convictions.

Clearly, learning by organizations is more complex and dynamic than learning by an individual; the learning process, in particular, is fundamentally different. Argyris and Schön (1978, p. 9) point to an essential dilemma in trying to understand it.

There is something paradoxical here. Organizations are not merely collections of individuals, yet there are no organizations without such collections. Similarly, organizational learning is not merely individual learning, yet organizations learn only through the experience and actions of individuals. What, then, are we to make of organizational learning? What is an organization that it may learn?

They go on to postulate a theory whereby organizational learning largely takes place as a result of actions by individuals whose actions are based on a common understanding. Such individuals have a *shared mental model (SMM)*.

Based upon this, Kim (1993) has built an integrated model of organizational learning, the OADI-SMM model shown in Figure 6.4. This essentially combines the above models as follows. We begin with the OADI cycle of individual learning. Next, we take March and Olson's model of organizational learning and replace its box for 'individual beliefs' by our OADI model. We then add Argyris and Schon's theory that organizational learning takes place on the basis of shared mental models and incorporate also their concept of 'double-loop' learning. This concept—double-loop learning—is considered in both its individual and organizational aspects. In both aspects, it is interpreted as including the questioning of preconceived notions.

It now becomes clear how individuals can learn independently of the organization. The individual learning cycle, which takes place via individual double-loop learning, is essentially a process of changing individual mental models. This has an effect on the organization's learning if—but only if—it influences the organization's shared mental models.

Insofar as individual mental models are integrated into shared mental models they are capable of influencing organizational action. This is how *organizational double-loop learning* can take place.

Note the following points:

- As in individual learning, organizational learning often requires people and organizations to 're-learn'. They must 'forget' and acquire knowledge anew if they are to drop their attachment to familiar models and concepts. At the level of individuals there are sometimes emotional and intellectual barriers against this, which of course can hinder organizational learning.
- In organizations, too, a distinction can be drawn between data and (shared) mental models. The data comprise the items filed or stored, such as correspondence, vouchers, etc.
- The functioning of an organization requires a wide-ranging variety of mental models, the most widely used being documented and retrievable in information systems. They include, for instance, models describing:
  - the functioning of a piece of machinery,
  - the control of production parameters,
  - order processing,
  - the competitive environment,
  - reactions of customers when confronted with increased prices,
  - frameworks for strategic management,
  - frameworks for effective organization,
  - etc.

The part of an organization's memory that is relevant for organizational learning is the active 'memory'; that is, the shared mental models, whether explicit or implicit,

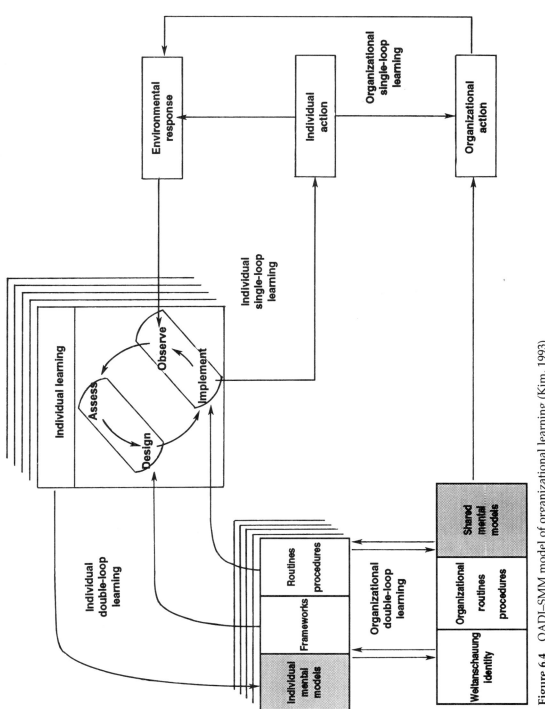

Figure 6.4  OADI–SMM model of organizational learning (Kim, 1993)

tacit or expressly assumed. These determine what an organization takes into account, how it reacts and what it remembers.

Clearly, the learning capability of an organization depends on the learning capability of its individual members. It also depends, as we shall see, on the organization's communications system.

Thus individual learning is necessary for organizational learning, but not sufficient. Mental models must be shared. A critical factor in designing processes whereby such sharing takes place is that individual models must to a certain degree be *made explicit*. When they are made explicit, learning within the organization becomes less dependent on the individual.

Later, however, we shall find that there are limits to the explication of shared mental models.

### Why Are The Shared Mental Models Of An Organization So Important?

Consider two cases. In the first, all data and documents belonging to an organization disappear overnight. In the second, all employees in an organization are replaced by outsiders. Clearly it will be easier to get the organization 'up and running' again in the first case than in the second.

In the first scenario, the organization's passive memory has been erased but its shared mental models have not; in the second, all individual mental models and the links between them, which after all give shared mental models their particular meaning, are no longer available to the organization.

Even in the most extensively bureaucratized organizations, having masses of procedures and regulations, there are many things that are not defined.

The intangible and generally invisible assets of an organization lie in the individual mental models that, as a whole, contribute to the shared mental models. Without these mental models and the multitude of sophisticated interfaces that have evolved over the course of time between individual employees, an organization is capable neither of action nor of learning. It is the shared mental models that make the rest of the organizational memory—in other words, the data—usable in the first place.

## OBSTACLES TO ORGANIZATIONAL LEARNING

The OADI-SMM model clarifies the process of organizational learning. It also explains a number of familiar organizational frustrations, enabling us, following Kim's work, to see them as *obstacles to organizational learning*.

The 'obstacles' to be reviewed in the light of the OADI-SMM model are shown in Figure 6.5. Here they are classified according to whether they impede single- or double-loop learning, as follows:

*Obstacles to single-loop learning:*

- role-constrained learning
- audience-restricted learning
- superstitious learning

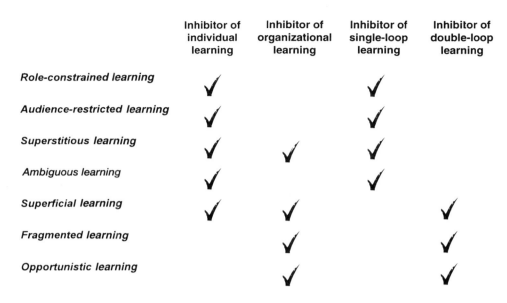

**Figure 6.5** Learning obstacles

- ambiguous learning.

*Obstacles to double-loop learning:*

- superficial learning,
- fragmented learning,
- opportunistic learning.

The obstacles are also shown in Figure 6.6. This figure will serve as a guide to our discussion. It shows in what part of the OADI-SMM learning cycle each obstacle has its effects.

We shall find that it is often possible to diagnose faults in the organization's learning loops by observing the type and nature of the frustrations we call 'obstacles to organizational learning'.

## Linkages Between Different Obstacles

How shall we proceed? We intend to discuss each learning obstacle in turn, then illustrate it by a number of examples.

Before doing so, we should issue a warning. Life is less clear-cut than theory. Distinguishing between different kinds of learning obstacle is analytically useful. In real life, however, they do not occur in isolation from each other. One kind may generate another. Deficits in single-loop learning may generate deficits in double-loop learning and vice versa. Hence, our examples often illustrate several kinds of learning obstacle at once.

Nevertheless they will be given labels, e.g., RC1, AR2, indicating the type of obstacle they primarily illustrate.

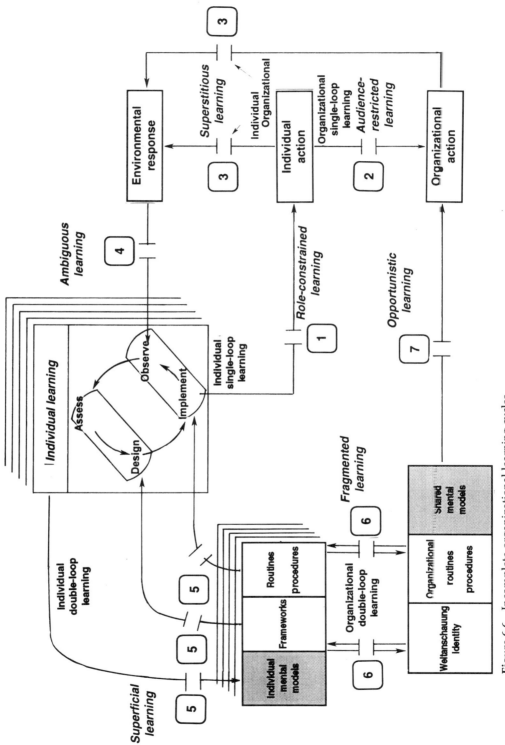

Figure 6.6  Incomplete organizational learning cycles

## Two Obstacles To Single-loop Learning

First we discuss *role-constrained* and *audience-restricted* learning. These share the property that:

> individual conceptual learning takes place but operational learning is inhibited.

With role-constrained learning, this happens primarily because individuals do not translate their knowledge into action; with audience-restricted learning, it is because though they do so, the organization fails to respond. This appears clearly in Figure 6.6. Let us see how it works in each case.

### Role-constrained learning

This is a kind of 'non-behaviour' on the part of individuals in an organization. Individuals do not take appropriate action within the organization although they have the knowledge, in an abstract form, that they should do so. Hence, individual conceptual learning is not converted into individual action.

Assume organizational actions have been taken, an environmental response has been received and individual managers have learned something from this, either by observing and analysing the response or by acquiring new knowledge, e.g., on a management seminar. What they have learned has changed their beliefs or basic assumptions. If they do not change their actions accordingly, their insights are lost to the organization. This is role-constrained learning.

It may easily lead to 'fragmented learning' by the organization as a whole. As discussed below, this is learning in which mental models are not adequately shared. Indeed, models that are not used by individuals in the organization can hardly be shared.

Role-constrained learning may be found even in cases when individuals make some attempt to implement their knowledge. This is because successful organizational learning may require more than one iteration of the learning loop (see example RC3).

From a systemic viewpoint, this kind of learning defect occurs when an individual does not generate enough variety to control or change a given situation. This may be because the individual cannot do so—perhaps through being overloaded, as in example RC2—or, due to low motivation or opposite interests, prefers not to do so. This is the case in example RC1.

*Example RC1: internal emigration.* Mr B is a staff employee whose apparently sound suggestions have constantly been ignored by the line management. As a consequence of his frustration, he has abandoned the idea of making any suggestions at all. In the company he is still regarded as an efficient employee.

Mr B has shifted his attention outside the company, where he is active in several community groups and organizes local cultural events. When in the company, he has managed to organize his daily routines in a way which minimizes their interference with his other interests. His new learning and experience outside the company will not profit the organization because they will lead to no action by him. This individual has given up efforts to produce change. In effect, Mr B has detached his individual learning loops from those of the organization.

If there is a culture in a company or in a department that frustrates people for whatever reason—if, for instance, new ideas are discouraged rather than supported—then there will be many who, like Mr B, are 'working to rule'. People can be very creative in undermining the system. Thus individual learning changes individual action, but not on behalf of the organization, rather against it.

*Example RC2: overloading.* Mr P of the patent department is informed about a forthcoming patent of a competitor in a field that may or may not be of considerable interest to a business unit. Mr P himself is not able to judge the significance of this patent. Informing the business unit requires preparation and the possible answer will add to a workload that Mr P already has difficulty in coping with. In this stress situation he simply forgets to inform the business unit.

Consequence: the competitor gets its patent through without difficulty, although this could have been prevented. A stimulus from the environment was not properly dealt with.

*Example RC3: risk aversion and 'once is not enough'.* The marketing manager Mr M tries to improve the size of the average order by imposing a minimum order size. He communicates this idea to his salesforce at the next sales meeting, and the idea seems to get acceptance. The salesforce informs the customers. After a while, analysis shows that the order size has not improved.

What happened: the introduction of a minimum order size requires taking the risk of some orders being withdrawn. No one in the organization, not even the marketing manager himself, was willing to take this risk. When salespersons confronted him with the decision either to accept a small order or to lose the customer, the order was accepted.

Here, the first iteration seemed to be successful, but the second failed because the manager himself did not take appropriate action in his capacity as an individual. The implementation lacked requisite variety. By accepting small orders he annulled his former action.

Later—see example SF1—we shall explain this behaviour on the part of the marketing manager. It is a case of 'superficial learning'.

### Audience-restricted learning

This describes a 'non-behaviour' on the part of the organization as a reaction to the efforts of an individual. No actions are taken, although appropriate knowledge has been spread or orders given.

Assume organizational actions have been taken, an environmental response has been received and some individual managers have learned. They now start to act as individuals and try to change special aspects of the organization's behaviour. Audience-restricted learning takes place when the organization proves immune to their efforts and does not change its behaviour. Either the people whose actions are necessary to produce the required changes do not have requisite variety, as in example AR2, or the variety is attenuated in a way that prevents the changes from taking place—see example AR1.

People often try to test how earnest the will to change really is. The spoken word alone, which may be sufficient for individual learning—as, for instance, in the case of a university lecture—is usually not sufficient in an organizational context. It has to be accompanied by culturally approved signals and actions. Sometimes it is not the people but the cybernetics of the situation that test whether the will to change is serious, see example AR4.

Audience-restricted learning implies that conversations between the individual and the other members of the organization either lack necessary amplification variety or take place in an organizational context not adequate for the purpose.

We have seen, in example RC1, how audience-restricted learning can lead to role-constrained learning on the part of people whose ideas and efforts are ignored.

Audience-restricted learning is encouraged in an organizational context where auditing and monitoring procedures are not in place (see Chapter 5). Such procedures may be the only way to detect audience-restricted learning in the long run; communication gaps need to be detected, that is, communication loops need to be closed.

*Example AR1: 'bloody intellectuals'.* A manager tries to emphasize the role of quality (leadership, vision, strategy, process design, etc.) and to influence his colleagues. He lays stress on quality in his speeches, delivers lectures, organizes seminars and even calls in consultants. If the people in the organization do no accept his ideas ('he's a bloody intellectual, just let him talk'), his efforts will not lead to the desired organizational actions.

There can even be a worse case. Sometimes people successfully camouflage their resentment of new ideas by using culturally accepted methods. Thus they may start a discussion about theory in order to prevent action, or adorn reports with 'new' phrases to hide their inactivity.

This is an example of methods of variety engineering being used to delay or obstruct learning. Specifically, amplification variety is being absorbed by the generation of 'obstructive' variety.

*Example AR2: abstract concepts.* Something similar can happen if people accept exhortations without further questioning, e.g. to 'produce quality' or become a 'quality organization', but these abstract concepts are not amplified in such a way that people at different levels of recursion know what their roles in the 'quality organization' are to be and how the transition will be managed. As a result, they are helpless and left alone.

*Example AR3: 'not invented here'.* Ideas from persons outside a specific department are ignored by those inside the department just because they come from people outside. This is the 'not-invented-here' syndrome. Ignorance is, for them, a simple and attractive variety attenuator. It is, indeed, an efficient one—though not effective.

*Example AR4: pressures from outside.* A marketing manager of a large firm tries to shift the customer focus. He wants his salesforce to spend more time visiting large customers, and uses organizationally accepted procedures to bring about this change in their behaviour. After some time it becomes evident that salespeople are ignoring his efforts, although when he talks to them they seem to understand his reasons.

What happened: large customers confront the salespeople with professional purchasing departments who have their own expertise, set high technical standards and bargain for fractions of a cent. Small customers give salespeople a feeling of being important. They are accepted as specialists able to solve problems with 'their' products; negotiations often take place with the owners themselves, who may be locally important people. Talks usually have a more personal or familiar atmosphere.

Compare this with example RC3. There the manager himself attenuated the variety of his action by initiating a change which he did not, by his own individual actions, accept. Here, the variety used by the manager is appropriate to start the action; he is consistent. However, the environmental response requires an additional iteration of the learning loop, i.e., it is such that additional amplification is required.

*Example AR5: 'what is he up to?'* Mr E has hitherto managed his department in an authoritarian way, as suits his personality type, but now begins reading books and attending seminars in an attempt to understand cybernetics and co-operative ways of management. He does change his former authoritarian behaviour. He feels, however, that people are not open to him; he is met with suspicion everywhere. In the end he reverts to his former style.

What happened: because of their former experiences with him, people could not believe that there had been a true change in Mr E's behaviour. Being unprepared to accept his new style, they concluded that it was a technique being used by him to get access to critical or personal information. They wondered what he was up to.

**Further Obstacles To Single-loop Learning**

Next on our list of defective kinds of learning are *superstitious* and *ambiguous* learning. These have in common the property that:

> operational learning takes place in an individual or organizational context, but conceptual learning is hindered.

With superstitious learning, this happens because of defects in people's mental models, i.e., unrealistic models for the intended actions. With ambiguous learning, it is due to inadequate measurement, i.e., feedback, of the effects of actions taken.

Again, we take a closer look at these types of defect and give a number of examples.

*Superstitious Learning*

Here learning is inhibited by the absence of necessary concepts, models or theories concerning individual or organizational actions and environmental responses to them. The conclusions drawn may or may not be correct. They may well not be, because the underlying models are unhelpful to the organization. One of the bases for learning—the conceptual basis—is missing.

When managers have all the information they need to get a picture of the situation yet are unable to interpret it correctly, e.g., are unable to see causal relationships between organizational actions and environmental responses, this normally implies that their mental models of the situation are inadequate. When, for lack of a better alternative, they repeat their accustomed actions without knowing why, this is more akin to magic ritual than to conscious, rational action. Hence the term 'superstitious' learning.

This kind of defect can occur in individual or organizational single-loop learning processes. In the case of individual learning, it means, as we have said, that the models used by an individual are insufficient to interpret the connection between organizational actions and environmental responses. In the case of organizational learning, the shared mental models, i.e., the visions, procedures, and routines used by the organization, are insufficient.

There are strong connections between superstitious learning and the still-to-be-discussed superficial and ambiguous learning; often they are found together. The basis of superstitious learning is inadequate models; but to improve our models requires overcoming what we shall call 'superficial' learning. Next, the impetus to change models is usually derived from the observation of an environmental signal, the interpretation of which does not fit into existing frameworks. But to measure and assess such signals correctly requires overcoming 'ambiguous' learning.

These connections exist because, given the huge variety of the organization's environment, a good model is required to discriminate between environmental signals that are worth observing and interpreting and those which may be neglected. In the case of superstitious learning, environmental reactions may be ignored—as in examples ST1 and ST3 below—because the individual's mental model has a blind spot. Worse: it may happen that people know of but choose to ignore information that is felt to be unpleasant or painful. Again, this is a case of ignorance being used as a variety filter. Example ST4 illustrates this.

*Example ST1: outdated models.* After a continuous fall in profits and prices, the manager of the largest competitor in a business segment decides that the prices for his products are too low, so he tries several times to increase them. He is an experienced manager who has been in this business a long time. The steps to be followed with a price increase are organized as a standard operating procedure (SOP) and can be done with mechanical precision:

1. inform salesforce
2. send a letter to customers
3. visit customers and explain the situation.

Although the organization follows these rules, the situation worsens. Sales plummet and prices fall. The policy has to be changed. What happened: the manager changed his policy in reaction to the market, but had no adequate model to explain why this reaction should be considered appropriate. Further research revealed two important inadequacies in the models he was using. First, he was unaware of a late but important change in market conditions; the products were now threatened by substitution. Naturally, a rise in prices merely accelerated this. Second, benchmarking of the competition showed not that the firm's prices were too low, but that its production and marketing costs had become too high. Obvious signals generated in the market were ignored—a case of ambiguous learning—because the model in use did not recognize their importance, i.e., the root cause of the problem was superstitious learning.

*Example ST2: planning rituals.* Consider the complex bureaucratic planning procedures found in large enterprises. The planning procedure starts as early as April. Step-by-step, each step comprising two or three iterations, the projected sales by product and customer, the projected costs and the investments are consolidated in the centralized planning system. Many people have to participate, more or less willingly, in the planning procedure. Several hundred thousand planning items have to be considered. The aim of the planning procedure is to produce, for the next 3–4 years:

- the company-wide coordination of the different business units;
- integrated forecasts setting the financial expectations of the board.

Consequence: when the planning cycle, which began in the second quarter of the year, has come to an end in December, the plan for the following year is presented to board members and finally approved. By the end of January, usually, the plan has lost its credibility. Neither of its two goals is achieved.

Why is this? Such an organizational effort to plan the future has two major faults. The first is in the implementation of the procedure itself. The amount of detail required means that a long time is needed, by the end of which the data are outdated. The basis for this is the underlying planning philosophy, which assumes that more detail will improve the quality of the prognosis.

The second major fault is the non-recursiveness of the approach. Plans of the most diverse levels of recursion, from divisions and business units to single products and customers, from whole plants to single machines, are collected and consolidated via a complicated mathematical model. The output of the model, i.e., the consolidated material and financial flows, simply lacks meaning. Why? Because what is lacking is an appropriate recursive interpretation of the consequences of actions taken at various levels.

A socialist planned economy is basically similar—with an important difference. In the case of the private company the plan is ignored quite openly by those whom it affects—although, of course, this has to be camouflaged for others' benefit. Hence, besides the waste of resources put into it, the plan itself seldom has disastrous consequences. In the case of totalitarian planning, long-term consequences are likely to be more disastrous. The party bureaucracy has an image to lose. It tries to enforce adherence to the plan by all means, which may encompass all the elements a totalitarian regime has at its discretion.

*Example ST3: blind spots.* A manufacturing company receives mounting complaints: deliveries are notoriously late. As a reaction, a management team identifies obvious capacity bottlenecks. Efforts to improve the situation are agreed within the management responsible. Over the years, by investing in efficient machinery, output is increased substantially. Late deliveries stubbornly persist.

What happened: the company's global production process consists of two processes: production, with an overall utilization of 105%) and customizing (overall utilization 70%). The heavily automated production process limited the output, but the customizing process was the time-consuming factor of the operation. Its low overall utilization did not reflect a severe shortage in manpower and equipment when handling the many speciality products of the company. For the problem of delivery service, the models used by the managers were not adequate. The shared models of management did not include the temporal aspects of the production processes.

In the production, yield is a critical cost-driver. Management was aware of this, so daily measurements were made of the yield of each production machine, measuring yield as 'output per unit of raw material input'. Production worked hard to increase the yield so defined, and it went up from 80% to about 95%. Certain managers— among them some quite clever people—thought that, in addition to a 15% saving of raw materials, there would now be 15% more capacity available. The opposite occurred: output capacity was 5% lower than before. An enquiry was started.

What had happened: in order to increase yield, production had installed recycling facilities to reuse material directly at the machines; as a result, about 75% of scrap produced could be reused. What had not changed was that the machines still needed about 120% of raw materials to produce 100% of output—though the former now consisted of 100% raw materials and 20% recycled scrap.

A lot of money had been saved by reusing the scrap; however, no additional capacity was available, i.e., throughput per hour was not increased. Worse: because recycling became so easy, machine operators unconsciously relaxed their hitherto tight control of the machines and produced about 5% more scrap than before. Because it was recycled, this increase in the amount of scrap did not impair the yield. It did, however, have the effect of increasing the average production time by 5%. This was not measured in measuring the yield.

It is worth considering this example a little further. The people on the shop floor, working as an autonomous team, increased the yield without adopting the shared mental model of the management. This is an example of what we may call 'opportunistic' learning. The basic flaw in management's understanding lay in limiting themselves to measurements of yield defined as 'output per unit of raw material input'; this should have been changed to 'output per unit of all material input'— including labour time. The superstitious learning of management, based upon this definition, could not be questioned as long as the environmental response, i.e., the increase in production time, was not measured. Thus this was also a case of ambiguous learning.

*Example ST4: hidden assumptions.* A manager wants to maximize earnings by focusing on speciality products with a high contribution. In the first quarter he is successful as he sells more of his favourite products; however, overall earnings decline. So in the second quarter he tries even harder; still overall profits decline. This goes on for years.

What happened: when calculating the contribution of each product, the manager used the standard calculation system of the company. As with many calculation systems, the fixed costs of each cost centre were spread over the different products according to the amount of each product processed. This meant that speciality products and small orders appeared to make a high contribution—since they were assigned small proportions of fixed costs—while the contribution of standard products appeared relatively low. The calculation did not reflect 'costs of complexity', such as setup times. For many of the smaller products and orders these costs of complexity more than offset their apparently greater contribution.

The model used by the manager, i.e., higher contribution leads to higher profits, was basically correct. It was the model used by the organization to calculate contributions that was inadequate for its purpose. Again, therefore, we have a case of ambiguous learning. As long as the manager tacitly assumes that calculation model is adequate, he will remain in the situation of individual superstitious learning: he will achieve results that seem to contradict his actions. What is needed is for the manager to overcome superficial learning by changing his model of the situation, via double-loop learning; that is, he has to abandon his tacit assumption.

Incidentally, though this manager has recently changed his policy he remains unconvinced of the inadequacy of his model.

*Example ST5: more hidden assumptions.* As a reaction to declining profits, the management of a firm that has been market leader for several years tries to implement a high-price policy in a regional market: Western Europe. This halts the fall in prices and profits for a short time, but the company loses market share—a result that accords with the models and expectations of management. However all are surprised when during the next economic crisis the company is nearly forced out of business.

What happened: the policy adopted was based on the assumption that the market was truly a regional one. Although the writing on the wall was clearly visible, management chose to ignore early-warning symptoms of the development of the business towards a more global market, in which high prices in Western Europe were virtually an invitation to potential importers and competitors.

Obvious information to this effect had been deliberately ignored by management. Why? This particular management team had been successful in the stable regional environment that had existed earlier. To acknowledge a new situation would have necessitated painful discussions and actions that would have shaken to its foundations the complacency of members of the team.

*Example ST6: 'success is ours'.* Mr F, in his role as marketing manager of a business unit, evaluates the success of his business teams by two measurements: sales volume and contribution to profits. But he is not happy with these measures. Whenever sales volume increases or the prices go up, the business teams claim the credit: it is thanks to their efforts. When sales volume or prices go down, they assert that 'the market', competitors or other factors are responsible. As long as Mr F has no model to separate the effects of the actions of the business teams from what happens in the market, no evaluation of the efforts of individual business teams is possible—even if their sales and contributions are measured.

Mr F is in a situation of individual superstitious learning. The business unit team is in a similar situation of organizational superstitious learning, if it tries to evaluate the marketing department as a whole without an adequate model.

*Example ST7: 'the organizational chart is the organization'.* The board of an international company has introduced global business units responsible for its product lines, and on the other hand defines the regional companies as profit centres As a consequence, there is a never-ending discussion about who is responsible for the marketing strategy for product A in region B: is it the business unit responsible for product

A or the subsidiary responsible for region B? These conflicts become important topics on the board's agenda.

What happened? The decision to introduce global business units into the existing matrix structure was taken in a crisis situation, having been recommended independently by several consultants. At the time, however, the board had rather vague ideas about the consequences. The shared thinking of most board members was in terms of organizational charts and matrix structures, their organizational models being strongly based on the 'mechanistic' metaphor discussed in Part One.

Epilogue: two years after this decision, the regional companies lost their status as profit-centres. A deepening crisis, together with the accession of new members to the board, resulted in a revision of its organizational models.

*Example ST8: ignoring information.* There are countless cases in which obvious, accessible information is ignored. Either it does not fit into the picture, i.e., the models, of the world that we use or, more simply, we do not want to be bothered with that problem just now. The following examples are chosen at random:

- driving a car whose tires have worn out;
- violations of human rights in countries one wants to trade with;
- environmental consequences of individual behaviour;
- the threat to American and European industry by Far-Eastern competition.

*Ambiguous Learning*

We have referred to ambiguous learning several times in our discussions. It is a type of 'non-learning' caused by failure to measure the responses to actions, i.e., the feedback. Even though the model used to solve a problem may be adequate, if the outcome of an experiment is not adequately measured then any conclusions drawn are unsupported by data. Examples of ambiguous learning occur, therefore, in the case of organizational actions whose success or failure is not quantified or cannot be quantified.

This is of central importance. The content of the models used in an organization defines what will be measured. Now what is measured, whether the underlying model is adequate or not, is an important part of the organizational model. It will have consequences in the actions of people and the awareness of management—just because it is measured. It is 'hard data'.

Sometimes, however, 'hard' data may provide 'soft' facts—as we shall see in example AB4 below.

Note that when information is lacking concerning the output of an organizational action, this is a case of ambiguous learning. When, however, there is no documentation of the input of an experiment, this is a case of what is below called 'superficial' learning. This means learning that does not lead to appropriate changes in mental models or organizational procedures.

*Example AB1: missing information (1).* In a particular firm, a number of organizational changes have been made with a view to reducing delivery time from seven days to three days. If the effects are not quantified and constantly monitored, the success of the measure cannot be assessed. After a while the organization may fall back into its former behaviour, so that no learning will have taken place.

*Example AB2: missing information (2).* The manager of a company's salesforce receives no information as to whether particular deals were profitable, for fear of information leakage; he receives only overall profit information. So he manages order acquisition activities according to a number of self-defined rules, based on order quantity or price. The overall amount of each product sold is left to be determined by the marketing plan.

The marketing manager is naturally very unhappy with the manager of the salesforce, who is seemingly unable to acquire profitable orders.

*Example AB3: late information.* Consider the weekly production runs in a polymerization process. The machine operator, who has to constantly fine-tune the machine parameters to guarantee stable operations, receives the result of quality inspections one week late in the form of average values. He is unable to adapt his behaviour to the results of these inspections.

*Example AB4: distorted information.* Distorted information can have effects similar to no information, except that they are less easy to detect.

Example ST4 can be cited here. Here, a manager's superstitious learning was the result of a faulty system for calculating the contributions of different products. We add this remark: the manager trusted the distorted information he received from this standard system. If it had not been available, he would probably have developed a system tailored to his needs.

*Example AB5: lack of reliable measurements.* For a long time environmental concerns could be ignored by industry because goods such as air or water were accessible free and neither the pollution, nor its effects nor its costs to society were measurable. The impending destruction of the ozone shield could be disputed as long as no reliable measurements were at hand.

*Example AB6: high costs of information: throughput time.* Most companies have not installed measurement systems for throughput time, but rely on occasional reports to assess the quality of their overall delivery service. Until recently the necessary re-engineering of existing programs, accompanied by additional hard and software requirements, made such measurements costly. They were introduced mostly by companies who regarded delivery service as a core competency.

*Example AB7: high costs of information: real-time MISs.* Real-time management information systems (MISs) have also been installed rather late and reluctantly partly for the same reasons. Although the degree of flexibility required by such systems still poses problems, the underlying concepts have been available for some time. The cybernetic advantages they bring are many, not only in cases such as example AB3 above, but in the process of adaptation at all levels. Part Three of this book looks into these systems.

This and the previous example cite costs as a factor discouraging investment in needed information. However, in an organizational context, lack of investment in measurement is usually accompanied by defects in the organization's shared mental models. In our experience, costs are rarely a decisive factor. What is crucial is that responsible managers should be clear about their intentions and goals.

### Obstacles To Double-loop Learning

As seen in Figure 6.6, obstacles to double-loop learning occur in the cycle through which mental models, individual and shared, are updated and revised. They are of three kinds: superficial, fragmented and opportunistic learning.

Of these, only the first kind—*superficial* learning—operates on the level of the individual. Individual double-loop learning is inhibited by superficial learning. We will now discuss this type of defective learning, and illustrate it with examples.

### *Superficial Learning*

Superficial learning occurs either when individual double-loop learning does not occur at all, i.e., when models or procedures are not revised although they should be, or when such learning is not simultaneously operational and conceptual. This means that either the procedures are not revised in accordance with changes in individual's mental models or vice versa, i.e., procedures are changed in a way not supported by mental-model changes.

Thus it means that a potential increase in knowledge is lost both to the individual and to the organization, either because the necessity to change a mental model has not been recognized or, if it has, the mental model has changed but the individual has no idea of when and how to use it. The appropriate use of the model has not been recognized.

In both cases the capacity for action has not improved.

The most simple case is that in which superficial learning derives from defects in storing and retrieving knowledge, i.e., data and models. More difficult cases arise, however.

The necessary new model may be unavailable or exceed the individual's learning capacity. Existing models may be regarded as proven, e.g., because 'that's the way we've always done it'. Changes in familiar patterns may be required and these are often felt as painful.

At a deeper conceptual level, a change in paradigm may be needed that an individual is simply unable to comprehend, e.g., a change from a strictly division-of-labour standpoint to a holistic process-oriented one. Alternatively, changing one's model may cast doubt on one's past actions, i.e., in practice it may mean confessing to an error, with associated fear of losing face.

Any one of the learning obstacles we have encountered in single-loop learning may lead to superficial learning as a consequence. This works as follows. There will be no impetus for individuals to change mental models they may regard as quite successful if disturbances to their picture of the world are avoided. And how may they be avoided? By setting up obstacles to single-loop learning!

Specifically, disturbances to individuals' worldviews are avoided if:

- individuals do not try out new, different modes of action—as in role-constrained learning;

- the influence of individual actions on organizational actions is not clear—as in audience-restricted learning;
- there is limited understanding of connections between individual or organizational actions and environmental responses—as in superstitious learning;
- environmental responses are not observed—as in ambiguous learning.

It may be a difficult and time-consuming process to shake out deep-seated assumptions from a manager's model, absurd though they may seem from the outside. If the company does not have the time for this, it may be necessary to change the people involved.

If individuals' models have changed but they cannot use them because of their organizational roles or functions, we again encounter role-constrained learning.

Additionally, superficial learning easily leads to fragmented learning, in which the organization fails to learn, though some individuals in it do. This happens because if certain individuals do not change their models or practice, the organization as a whole may be unable to do so.

*Example SF1: no will or ability to change (1).* Consider again the manager, Mr E, of example AR5 above. Mr E has hitherto run his department in an authoritarian manner, in accordance with his personality, but is now trying to understand cybernetic and co-operative ways of management by reading books or attending seminars. If the intellectual change in his ideas is not reflected in his behaviour, and he still manages his department in the same way as before, he will not experience any results from his conceptual insights because he will not be implementing them.

*Example SF2: no will or ability to change (2).* Mr M, the marketing manager of example RC3 above, exemplifies the same problem. He too had changed his intellectual model of the market, but deep in his heart did not really believe it. When encountering a situation that, according to the revised model, needed a new decision, he did not feel secure. Instead, he reverted to his former procedures.

*Example SF3: no will or ability to change (3).* In another example, Mr P of the patent department has not long ago attended a seminar at the request of his boss. The topic of the seminar: to explain the benefits a company could reap if the identity of the patent department could be changed from 'legal procedure service' to 'competitor intelligence'. Not liking to change his habit of working, Mr P does everything to convince his boss that this would be a mistake. The consequence: no change in the way the patent department works.

*Example SF4: missing documentation (1).* During a normal production run, a change in several production parameters—of which there are about 150—is detected. Afterwards it is found that the product produced during these variations has exceptionally good properties. Unluckily, this random 'experiment' cannot be repeated because the variations of the production parameter during a normal production run are not documented.

*Example SF5: missing documentation (2).* When planning monthly sales for the next year, the market department of a business unit belonging to a large firm recognized the seasonal variation in sales for each product. When, however, this plan was put into the central planning system of the company, the seasonal data was lost: the planning system allowed the input of yearly figures only. Because reporting procedures relied heavily on the figures given by the central plan, this had the following grotesque results:

1. In the short run, the market manager had to explain the deviations of the sales figures from the central plan projections at every meeting of the business unit. This represented superficial learning by the other members of the business team inasmuch as their model, by which they interpreted the sales figures, remained unchanged.
2. In the longer run this very procedure became institutionalized. Whenever there was a deviation to explain, the marketing manager could evade further questioning by using the 'killer' phrase 'seasonal effects'. This represented an institutionalization of superficial learning, as the procedure had been changed in a way that did not allow any member of the business team to learn about the market.

Note that if, in such a case, the marketing manager were to improve his model of the market while the business team as a whole did not, we would have an example of fragmented learning.

*Example SF6: missing documentation (3).* A plant producing 50 000 t of plastics manages its logistics in the standard fashion. There is an economic downturn of five years duration; production is reduced to 30 000 t. The management is changed. When the next upturn comes and the plant's production is back to its former levels there emerges a host of troubles with logistics, resulting in very high costs.

What had happened: during a long period of steady growth, the former management had become thoroughly experienced in handling the logistics of producing 50 000 t. This experience was so well shared amongst them that they did not bother to analyse their actions and, of course, did not write them down. When during the downturn the former management was replaced, this 'implicit' knowledge of large-volume logistics had disappeared; it had to be 'explicitly' reintroduced by an external consultant.

*Example SF7: limited understanding (1).* Consider a scientifically trained manager who can only grasp the impact of organizational problems if they are presented to him in clear-cut formulas or in the usual two-dimensional graphs (which often in reality represent causal-loop diagrams). For him, only 'hard figures' have meaning. He cannot grasp organizational problems for which this model is not appropriate. He may be a good chemist, physicist or engineer; he is hardly a good manager.

*Example SF8: Limited understanding (2).* The board of a large company is discussing the investment plans of a subsidiary company. It has spent five hours evaluating a number of minor projects, each requiring less than $5 million. For several hours the discussion has dragged along, dealing with profit lines, cash flows and return on investment.

The last project is a $100 million development project. Suddenly the majority of members of the board become alert. There is a feeling of excitement in the air: voices talk about molecular design, chemical formulas and reactions, product properties and the design of reactors and laboratories. The project is agreed in less than 15 minutes. All board members think they have made a wonderful decision. They do not foresee what might have been foreseen—that the project will be scrapped after six expensive years.

What happened: most of the members of the board had gone through a scientific education. Some were still struggling with their understanding of the unfamiliar and 'unscientific' fields of marketing and economics. The board had acquired a reputation for critical analysis of investment projects. The moment this project came up most were glad they could talk about something familiar. They therefore relaxed their watchfulness just a bit.

## Problems With Organizational Double-loop Learning

We come, finally, to two kinds of defects that occur in the process of double-loop learning at the level of the organization, rather than that of the individual. These are *fragmented* and *opportunistic* learning. It is when learning is defective in these ways that:

> organizational double-loop learning is inhibited.

*Fragmented Learning*

Consider first what is meant by 'fragmented' learning.

This is the case of conceptual 'non-learning' by an organization. Here, individuals learn and change their mental models, but the models of the organization do not change. The models of individuals do not become part of a shared model.

In this case, if individuals are lost to the organization, learning also can be lost: the two kinds of loss are the same. This may easily happen in organizations where knowledge is not distributed freely but is used to secure organizational power and influence. Universities provide institutionalized examples; typically, the individual specialist skills of professors, for instance in management, are not used by the university to solve its management problems.

Individuals may have learned and may be bringing about improvement in a situation, but if they cannot change the organization's shared mental model, their efforts will last only as long as they are there. Managers generally do not act alone but have a team around them. The members of such a team each have their own mental models, which are shaped by different skills and experiences. The intersection of these individual models forms the basis for the team's discourse, through which its members act with each other. Thus it determines the regulatory variety of that unit. The intersection of these models can, intrinsically, be very small or even null. This leads to a correspondingly low regulatory variety and a limited basis for organizational learning.

For a concrete example, suppose that the individual mental models of a group of people have an overlap of 80% with one another; that is, there is a probability of 0.8 that one of them will understand a random communication from another related to their mental models. This is actually a high figure. Yet in a group of five people the intersection—the probability of all understanding a random communication in the same way—will be no more than $0.85 = 0.33$; that is, 33%. It is, of course, entirely possible that in a group of two people the intersection of their mental models may be a null set.

Even, if this intersection is not null, it is extremely probable that a model shared by a group of people will not be suited for solving the problems they confront. In such a situation, it is unhelpful if an individual—generally the group leader—endeavours to impose his or her own mental model as the model of the group. This is unhelpful because, in all probability this model:

- has arisen from the functionally oriented background of that individual and is not relevant to important aspects of the problem;
- is a regulatory model of relatively high complexity derived from individual experience, and therefore cannot be transmitted in full to others;
- must fail, by virtue of the way it is transmitted, to reflect the various experiences of the group; that is, it will undergo a kind of 'immune rejection'.

Something comparable happens if a group of persons responsible for dealing with a problem within the organization, e.g., a business unit team, is unable to adopt a shared mental model for reasons such as the following.

- The necessary new model is not available or exceeds the learning capacity of the group.
- Important individuals are unwilling or unable to adapt their own mental models. A problem with any type of group work is how 'loners', who may be outstanding technically, can be integrated into a team without obstructing the working capability of the group. 'Loners' often have mental models of adequate variety that they are unable to share with the group.
- A shared mental model has never existed, because the horizons of experience or the personalities within the group are too divergent; hence they are unaccustomed to having a shared model.

An organization usually puts a lot of effort into building shared models. A corporate vision is helpful—though not, of course, if the members of the board are the only ones that know about it. Handbooks setting out organization and procedures also contribute. Formal information systems do also.

Finally, the greatest part of what makes shared models possible is constituted by the cognition of individuals and their day-to-day interactions and communication.

*Example FR1: lost knowledge (1).* Organizational learning can be lost if important 'carriers' of this knowledge leave without proper replacement.

In one example, a specialist within order processing had developed exceptional competence in solving logistical problems. He embodied the organization's experience and knowledge in this field. However, due to unexpected retirement he could pass on only a fraction of this knowledge to his successor. The latter had to start virtually from scratch and the experience was lost to the organization.

*Example FR2: lost knowledge (2).* Something similar may happen if a key person is lost to a competitor. The fierceness of the struggle between General Motors and

Volkswagen around the person of Mr Lopez may signify that the former believes itself to have lost, in this individual, a crucial part of its organizational capability. It seems that Mr Lopez was a manager with the rare ability to provide cohesion—and so prevent fragmented learning—while simultaneously bringing change to the organization.

*Example FR3: restricted access (1).* Many learning efforts in an organization are wasted because they are neither documented nor stored in such a way that other people or departments can profit from them.

For example, when analysing the logistics problems of a business unit in a large company one may find that the necessary data, such as daily production and shipment information by packaging, are hard to access even though they are, in principle, available to anyone who is interested. This is because a comprehensive view of the data is restricted to the logistics department, located outside the business unit, and, on a technical level, access to it requires special programming knowledge available only in the information systems department—again outside the business unit. Hence to access the data the business unit has to undertake costly and time-consuming bargaining with these two departments. For its day-to-day work, the business unit has to rely on information to which it has easy access.

*Example FR4: restricted access (2).* Another common case is this. The results of a study are used to improve the functioning of department A, after which the study vanishes in someone's desk. Department B with similar problems does not know—especially if the company is large—that a study of this subject has been undertaken, still less what were its results. It therefore commissions a study of its own.

*Example FR5: restricted access (3).* Manager D hires a consultancy firm to analyse a production planning problem. The analysis shows that, though marginal improvements can be made, substantial benefits are possible only by restructuring the customer service organization. Now the manager does not want to get into trouble with customer services. As the leader of the steering committee, he convinces the consultants to concentrate on marginal improvements and camouflage the report. The consultant's report is loudly praised and the marginal improvements implemented with much publicity. The important parts of the report vanish in the desk of Mr D.

Note that this behaviour on the part of manager D affects two loops. At the level of individual single-loop learning, Mr D reduces his own ability to learn more. At the same time, by camouflaging the report he fails to share its results with the rest of the organization; this is a case of fragmented learning in relation to the organization's double-loop learning.

*Example FR6: different models in use (1).* Fragmented learning also occurs when the management group of a company cannot decide which organizational model, e.g., tayloristic or cybernetic, to build their actions upon. Different schools, experiences or temperament may account for such divergencies of view. The result is that managers, caught in different perceptions, may misunderstand each other's role and misinterpret each other's actions.

*Example FR7: different models in use (2).* Does the use of different theories seem a far-fetched example? Unresolved differences in the interpretation of company strategy may have similar results—as, for example, when the marketing manager wants to serve the low-price, large-volume segment of a market while the production manager attempts to specialize on high-price products.

*Example FR8: different models in use (3).* The identity of a business unit was changed from a 'production' orientation to a 'quality-and-customer' orientation by the management of the unit. The unit's day-to-day work did not change, although the new identity was communicated widely and the employees knew about it. It remained 'lip-service'.

What happened: the information and performance evaluation systems of the business unit remained unchanged; they still reported quantity instead of quality. Thus an important part of the organizational shared model had not changed.

*Example FR9: personal bottlenecks (1).* A manufacturer has several production sites located throughout Europe. The production manager tries to control all processes as far as possible by himself; he prefers not to delegate, or grant the local management freedom in implementing improvements. Every new idea generated in his own group—the size of which is about 500 persons—has to be evaluated and approved by himself before it can be implemented.

Consequence: the manager, in fact, defines himself as the bottleneck for the learning of his group. Much of what could belong to the shared model of the organization is filtered out by this procedure. Most of the learning done in the organization remains fragmented.

*Example FR10: personal bottlenecks (2).* A project in business process re-engineering is carried out. When the implementation phase begins, it slowly emerges that while most of the lower-level people are pleased about the pending changes, their boss is not. He uses all the tricks he can to delay and inhibit progress. By redirecting the tasks and communications of people in his department he successfully undermines organizational learning by destroying the necessary communication links. Most of the learning results of the project remain fragmented in the minds of individuals, without deeply affecting the organization.

Note, in general, that acceptance of changes in mental models is highly dependent on individual experience. It may happen that an individual or a group is no longer able or willing to undergo this adaptation. It is then possible to change mental models, and so sustain the learning capacity of the organization, only by replacing team members.

Such a change of personnel should be seen as a change in the composition of a team, not an evaluation of the individual's abilities. Changing the membership of a team is a widespread practice in sports such as soccer, football, handball or basketball; here, beneficial effects of change are exploited by the replacement of players during a match or the surprise change of a trainer in mid-season. It often happens that players who have been effective in one team can achieve only average results in another, and vice versa.

*Opportunistic Learning*

Consider next what is meant by 'opportunistic' learning.

This may also be called 'organization-constrained' learning; the appropriateness of this name will become clear in the next chapter, where we analyse the various learning obstacles from the viewpoint of complexity management. What happens is this: though the design or implementation of organizational actions is directed at realizing a substantiated or imagined opportunity, it is inconsistent with the organization's shared mental models.

How does this happen? Typically, when a team is formed to implement an autonomous project. Though the project may be based on a shared model within the team, the team itself is often detached from the customary procedures and thus also from the shared mental models of the organization.

We have to distinguish, in such cases, between organization-constrained learning itself and 'autonomous-team learning', i.e., learning by setting up a team to conduct a project. The latter is not, in itself, a learning obstacle. Rather it is an acknowledgement that the rest of the organization has difficulty with the proposed action. It means that a team is formed to build up a new business, factory or product that will finally become a primary activity for the business. Why? Entrusting the task to a team may be necessary for reasons of time. Often the opportunity cannot wait for the organization as a whole to change—perhaps because the project is critical for competitive reasons. Alternatively, it may be that the organization as a whole resists the change—as in examples OP1 and OP3. Here, the rationale for an autonomous team is: 'if others won't or can't . . .'

If the project works out well the learning of the team may, in the long run, provide guidelines along which the rest of the organization can be redesigned. What must be recognized is that they are bound to lag behind in speed of learning. It must also be recognized that such a team, liberated though it is from many organizational constraints, must adhere to basic security guidelines. If it does not, the results can be devastating—as in example OP2. Good cybernetic judgement is needed to distinguish between those constraints that can safely be relaxed and those that cannot.

In organization-constrained learning, by contrast, the actions of a team are bureaucratically restricted by other parts of the organization. Example OP4 illustrates this.

Though what we have called autonomous-team learning is not a defect, provided it is seen as the first stage in a process of organizational learning, yet it is important to realize its limitations. These become clear when we consider that from the viewpoint of the sharing of mental models, autonomous-team learning can be regarded as a case of fragmented learning. Inconsistent models are being used in different parts of the organization. The cybernetic analysis of learning obstacles in the next chapter will clarify this point further. The implications of autonomous-team learning are also similar to those of role-constrained learning. This is because the team has detached its own learning loops from the 'standard' learning loops of the organization.

*Example OP1: project teams.* Examples of autonomous project teams, with the advantages and accompanying dangers that we have discussed, are given by Kim; he looks at GM's Saturn project and IBM's project to develop the PC. In both cases, teams were deliberately set up to bypass the standard organizational procedures, which were seen as a hindrance to the accomplishment of specific tasks. According to Kim (1993, p. 46):

> They wanted to sever the link between shared mental models and organizational action in order to seize an opportunity that cannot wait for the whole organization to change (or for which it may not be desirable for the whole organization to change).

*Example OP2: speculation.* Well-known cases of losses incurred by the finance management units of certain large companies—among them Metallgesellschaft and Proctor & Gamble—illustrate the severing of a link between the usual reporting and risk assessment procedures in these companies. Combined with the wish to seize opportunities that cannot wait, this can lead to disastrous results.

*Example OP3: autonomous production teams.* Example ST3 of superstitious learning involved a production team that, by making improvements, gave the production process characteristics that were not recognized in the models held by management. This was opportunistic learning.

*Example OP4: the political weight of the centre.* A business unit has developed and implemented an elegant, integrated software tool to help management allocate costs, assess contribution margins and calculate profits. It does this about five years earlier than the central planning department is able to present its own software tool for the same purpose. Though the latter is much inferior from the viewpoint of the business unit, the central planning department dictates that the unit's own system be eliminated. Thus central intervention has killed an innovation.

Why has this happened? The business unit's software development was an example of autonomous team learning. The intervention of the central planning department made it a case of organization-constrained learning.

## CREATING ORGANIZATIONAL LEARNING

We have analysed the major obstacles to organizational learning. Let us now ask: How can these obstacles be overcome?

In this section we propose a detailed answer to this question. In outline, it consists in taking the following three steps:

- *Step 1:* See what is needed to unfreeze the organization; that is, to reduce its 'organizational defensive pattern'. As we shall see, this means unblocking the learning loops of individuals.
- *Step 2:* Develop the disciplines of a learning organization. This means, develop the capacity in individuals to unblock organizational learning loops.
- *Step 3:* Use the insight and capacity gained through the preceding steps to overcome specific obstacles to learning.

Do these steps suggest that learning proceeds in a linear way? If so, the impression is mistaken. We are concerned with learning how to learn. As learning itself is a self-referential process, learning how to learn cannot be described in simple cause-and-effect recipes. Within the limitations of the language we use, which is based on a *linear* model of the world, we must try our best to describe *nonlinear* phenomena.

This non-linearity means that if, at some point, you receive the impression that we are discussing logical steps already passed—then you are right!

There is, moreover, another kind of contradiction between what we are trying to say and the manner in which we say it. This chapter contains advice on how to overcome specific obstacles to organizational learning. Yet the form in which we have to present such advice often compounds the problem—for reasons mentioned above.

To be implementable, advice should:

- contain a causal theory that points to specific forms of action;
- illustrate this through action strategies, actual statements and examples;
- include the values that must guide the action strategies.

We hope to fulfil these criteria.

## Reducing An Organizational Defensive Pattern

In the three-step procedure outlined above, step 1 is to see how an organizational defensive pattern can be reduced. What is an 'organizational defensive pattern'?

It is a phenomenon identified by Argyris (1990, p. 64) as arising from a specific way of interpreting social virtues such as 'help and support', 'respect for others', etc. He proposes that these virtues are often interpreted according to a model—he calls it Model 1—that inculcates behavioural patterns that hinder change. To implement change, the organization must be 'unfrozen'; that is, these behavioural patterns must be changed by the adoption of a different model—Model 2. The nature of this model and its comparison with Model 1 are described in Figure 6.7. Model 2's interpretation of social virtues is consistently one that creates relationships of mutual respect and openness, in which both parts are willing to question and challenge, without inhibitions, or any other form of defensive pattern, what the other says.

Figure 6.8 sets out some of the organizational practices that result from Model 1. These are as follows.

First, there is 'skilled incompetence'. According to Model 1, individuals seek 'to be in unilateral control, to win, and not to upset people'. From this it follows that they should limit the degree to which they intervene in another person's sphere of action. Social action strategies therefore consist mainly of 'selling', 'persuading', and 'face-saving'. The carrying out of these strategies leads to a dilemma ('You can't save a person's face while telling them that') and a paradox: to implement the strategies effectively requires a theory-in-use according to which the recipients of the strategies are expected to be 'submissive, passive, and dependent'; that is 'to act in ways that are ineffective by the very terms of Model 1' (Argyris, 1990, p. 13).

The organizational consequences: people act in such a way as not to upset others, censoring their speech and reactions to one another. This, in the guise of respect and support, strengthens the obstacles to individual single-loop learning. Thus organizational members are largely unaware of the effects of their accustomed actions. Their competence in doing what they are used to—in actions that are 'automatic,

| Social Virtue | Model 1 Interpretation | Model 2 Interpretation |
|---|---|---|
| Help and support | Give approval and praise to others. Tell others what you believe will make them feel good about themselves. Reduce their feelings of hurt by telling them how much you care, and, if possible, agree with them that the others acted improperly. | Increase the other's capacity to confront their own ideas, to create a window into their own mind, and to face their unsurfaced assumptions, biases, and fears by acting in these ways toward other people. |
| Respect for others | Defer to other people and do not confront their reasoning or actions. | Attribute to other people a high capacity for self-reflection and self-examination without becoming so upset that they lose their effectiveness and their sense of self-responsibility and choice. Keep testing this attribution openly. |
| Strength | Advocate your position in order to win. Hold your own position in the face of advocacy. Feeling vulnerable is a sign of weakness. | Advocate your position and combine it with inquiry and self-reflection. Feeling vulnerable while encouraging inquiry is a sign of strength. |
| Honesty | Tell other people no lies or tell others all you think and feel. | Encourage yourself and other people to say what they know yet fear to say. Minimize what would otherwise be subject to distortion and cover-up of the distortion. |
| Integrity | Stick to your principles, values, and beliefs. | Advocate your principles, values, and beliefs in a way that invites inquiry into them and encourages other people to do the same. |

Figure 6.7   Interpretation of social virtues (Argyris, 1990)

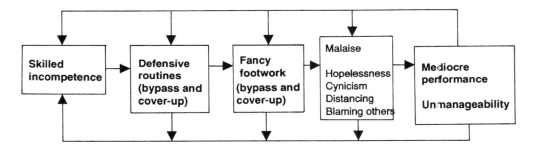

**Figure 6.8**  Organizational defensive pattern (Argyris, 1990)

spontaneous, and taken for granted'—is accompanied by an unawareness of their function and consequences. Thus we find 'skilled incompetence'—a combination of skilled behaviour and unawareness of its effects.

Next, the behaviour associated with skilled incompetence leads to 'organizational defensive routines'. These are organizational actions or policies 'that protect individuals or segments of the organization from experiencing embarrassment or threat'. In doing this, 'they prevent people from identifying and getting rid of the causes of potential embarrassment or threat'. They are 'anti-learning, overprotective and self-sealing'. Such routines are difficult to change because concerned individuals feel helpless about them. This is because the attempt to engage defensive routines will usually activate and strengthen them, and a concerned individual does not want to be seen as making the situation worse.

The result is that organizational routines are usually not engaged, but bypassed. For the bypass to become effective, it has to be covered up. In such a situation, drawing a logical inference is difficult; feedback is attenuated. This fosters the learning obstacles that hinder conceptual learning in the case of both individual and organizational single-loop learning.

Finally, 'fancy footwork' consists of a number of maneouvres that permit individuals to be blind to inconsistencies in their actions, to deny that these inconsistencies exist or to place the blame on others without holding themselves responsible. Analysis of actions thereby remains superficial and mental models are unchanged by the fact that outcomes are ineffective.

Consequently, the learning obstacles that hinder double-loop learning by individuals and organizations are strengthened. There is superficial, fragmented and opportunistic learning.

These coexisting and self-reinforcing types of behaviour—skilled incompetence, defensive routines and fancy footwork—constitute an 'organizational defensive pattern endemic in human organizations. It is caused by the theory-in-use and social virtues that most individuals learn during their early years. These combine to create skilled incompetence, which, in turn, creates organizational defensive routines, fancy footwork, and "malaise" (Argyris, 1990, p. 63).

Malaise is defined by Argyris as a situation of prevailing mediocrity, where performance, commitment, and concern for the organization is reduced and 'excellence will be, at best, an ongoing fad destined to progressive deterioration'. At the same time, the defensive patterns creating this situation are not confronted 'because the players do not know how to do it effectively' (Argyris, 1990, p. 45).

What are the cybernetic effects of such organizational malaise? We have seen that the learning loops in an organization have to be redesigned constantly, either due to changes in the environment, e.g., in technology, markets or competitors, changes in organizational tasks and people or the fact that the installed learning loops in the organization are producing new knowledge with decreasing frequency—'sclerosis'.

Such sclerosis of the learning loops must be prevented. Basically this can be achieved in two ways: by changing the mode of interaction with the environment or by changing the mode of internal operation.

Making changes within the learning loop is equivalent to a continuous redesign of this loop. The following changes form part of this process of redesign.

- Alterations in the organizational environment, e.g., new products, new markets.
- Trying-out of new individual and organizational activities, e.g., TQM (total quality management).
- The influx and processing of new information into existing loops.
- Changes in the individual and shared mental models via, for instance, a new vision.
- Replacement of personnel, e.g., by fluctuation or job rotation.
- Breaking up of existing learning loops and introduction of new ones, e.g., by defining new organizational units, business areas or projects.

It is obvious that a strong organizational defensive pattern will hinder this continuous input of 'novelties', though these are the motor of organizational learning. Thus it will foster sclerosis.

To unfreeze the organization we must find ways of overcoming the organizational defensive pattern. As this is based on a specific interpretation (Model 1) of social values, that interpretation must be changed. It must be supplemented by a new interpretation—Argyris' Model 2—that makes it possible to deal with Model 1's defensive routines.

Figure 6.7 shows Argyris' view of the differences between these models.

**Six Disciplines Of A Learning Organization**

The interpretation of accepted social values given in Model 2 encourages a change of behaviour that makes single- and double-loop learning for individuals easier in their organizational environment. Such a change strengthens feedback and self-reflection, and thus, albeit indirectly, lowers the hurdles that impede successful organizational learning.

Lowering hurdles is not enough, however, if there is no one to jump. Senge (1992) has identified five disciplines of a learning organization through which successful individual learning is transformed into organizational learning. To these we will add a sixth. Instilling these six disciplines in an organization can give it the capability to move from Model 1 behaviour toward Model 2.

The first discipline is *personal mastery*—described by Senge as 'the discipline of continually clarifying and deepening our personal vision, of focusing our energies . . .' We have to be aware, that what we see is as 'reality' is an interpretation based on our positions both as an observer and participant, and out limited information processing capacity.

To manage in accordance with a Model 2 interpretation involves a certain degree of personal mastery, at least to the extent of:

- an ongoing awareness of other people's behaviour;
- an ongoing awareness of one's own behaviour;
- valid mental models of interaction to encourage enquiry and self-reflection.

The second discipline is that of *mental models*. Mental models, as conceptualized by Senge, are 'deeply ingrained assumptions, generalizations, or even pictures or images that influence how we understand the world and how we take action.' Models 1 and 2 are conflicting mental models of how to act individually in an organizational environment. For the process of organizational learning models are needed that are valid or helpful and can be easily adapted to new insights gained during the learning processes.

The third discipline is that of a *shared vision*. This is 'the capacity to hold a shared picture of the future we seek to create . . . When there is a genuine vision, people excel and learn, not because they are told to, but because they want to'

A shared vision is a special case of a mental model. It is a model shared between people that describes a desirable future for the organization. The vision can be used as the basis for the definition and implementation of strategies—a complex recursive process that is described in more detail in Part Three below. To 'become a learning organization' may be part of a shared vision.

*Systems thinking* is the fourth of Senge's disciplines. This is 'a conceptual framework, a body of knowledge and tools that has been developed over the past 50 years, to make patterns clearer, and to help us see how to change them effectively. Though the tools are new, the underlying worldview is extremely intuitive . . .'

Systems thinking, in Senge's terms, is a tool for the creation and validation of dynamic models. It obviously allows deeper insights into complex systems than linear cause-and-effect reasoning, but is also more difficult to learn—at least for persons trained in the Western style of thinking.

The fifth discipline, *team learning*, is necessary for the attainment of a shared vision—which is the third discipline we have already discussed. Thus the various disciplines depend upon each other.

Team learning starts with 'dialogue', the capacity of members of a team to suspend assumptions and enter into a genuine 'thinking together'. It is vital because 'teams, not individuals, are the learning unit in modern organizations'.

For this, team members must have the ability to share mental models—and this requires dialogue. Here, Senge draws attention to the fact that dialogue (dia-logos) means a free flow of interpretations within a group, enabling the group to obtain insights that would remain hidden to the individual. By contrast, the customary discussion that takes place at the majority of management meetings is merely a pushing around of ideas in a competition that has only one winner. Irrespective of who wins or loses in such a discussion—even though the winners may think to themselves, 'We put it across them again'—both have, in fact, lost. This is behaviour in accordance with Model 1.

The sharing of mental models also requires that these models be made explicit. Now there are fundamental problems involved in making mental models explicit; these are problems of transduction, transducers and channel capacity, as seen in various examples given by Beer (1979, pp. 123f.). Problems arise, according to Beer, because what is understood is not what is heard, what is heard is not what is said and what is said is not what is meant.

Also necessary for the sharing of mental models is an environment relatively free from the influence of organizational defensive patterns.

The sixth discipline required, according to Espejo (1993b), by a learning organization is that of *effective structures*. For effective problem solving or change in organizations, it is not enough to have good 'dynamic models' or to 'improve debates' or to 'make change culturally feasible'. It is necessary to take into account the 'detail complexity' of the organization, that is, whether there is requisite variety for the problem solving and related learning.

Effective problem solving necessitates an *effective operational domain* for the problem solvers *to create issues of concern* and *implement* the change.

From our perspective, these effective structures are those of the VSM—the viable systems model that we have already encountered in Chapter 5. Organizational learning, defined as increasing the capability of an organization for effective action, can take place in the VSM in all loops. Correspondingly, organizational learning capability in the VSM is disrupted if one or more of the necessary components have shortcomings. If, for instance, the communication channels, the transducers or the regulation models used in the mechanisms for adaptation and monitoring control fail to exhibit the necessary variety, such shortcomings in the regulatory loops of the VSM correspond to incomplete learning loops in the OADI-SMM model.

## Specific Obstacles To Learning And How They Are Overcome

We are now equipped to show specifically how the obstacles to learning that we have identified can be overcome. What is required, as we know, is to adopt a Model 2 interpretation; for this it is necessary for the organization to abide by the six disciplines. Let us see how this is done in the case of each obstacle to learning.

*Role-constrained learning*, as we know, means that individuals required to act in a certain way are unable to do so. In this case those concerned must acquire *personal mastery*. They must learn how to act effectively in their organizational context, i.e., how to communicate and 'pull the ropes' so as to get their ideas and propositions through. This 'elementary practice' can be compared with the learning you have to do if you are a stranger in a new country; that is, you must learn the 'landscape', consisting of plants, products, processes and bureaucracies; the 'language', consisting of the organizational models and procedures in use; and the 'culture', i.e., the organizational defensive patterns used.

Following the shared vision of the organization—if one exists—will make it easier for the individual's ideas to be accepted. Actions should be guided by the interpretation of Model 2, which, in the long run, can reduce the impact of the organizational defense patterns encountered. To overcome role-constrained learning, individuals should be given tasks with clear criteria of performance and provided, when necessary, with the help of a mentor.

Clear criteria of performance can be of double use in this context. They both give the individual transparent guidelines as to what is expected and enable the detection of role-constrained learning situations.

The conscious use of mental models together with an ongoing improvement of these models based on observation of the responses received—thereby preventing ambiguous learning—will enhance the quality and speed with which this learning obstacle is overcome. This is especially so if actions are supported by effective structures.

In *audience-restricted learning*, people who are the recipients of actions do not act according to expectations; either they cannot or they will not. This can be attributed mainly to organizational defenses, inhibitors and camouflage. To overcome these, Model 2 recommends improving the quality of conversations by presenting ideas in more convincing and culturally accepted ways, while at the same time encouraging self-reflection on the part of those addressed. Argyris (1990, pp. 109f. and 138f.) provides many examples of discussions in this mode.

This, however, may be unsuccessful without improvements in the monitoring-control mechanisms throughout the organization; it is necessary to close the loop, i.e., to present results to those who may want to test the sincerity of the advocates of change and, of course, to open up discussions in order to overcome sabotage or camouflage. For this a model is needed which will point to what needs to be measured, thereby underlining the sincerity of the intention to change and detecting sabotage or camouflage.

Simply using better presentation techniques and stronger informational amplifiers would be a Model 1 solution—not Model 2.

The use of models in overcoming audience-restricted learning may ensure that *superstitious learning* does not occur. This kind of obstacle occurs, as we have said, when models used do not adequately reflect the dynamics or the cybernetics of the situation. In this case, organizational conversations have to be redesigned so that the emergence of adequate models is made more likely. Hidden assumptions have to be overcome by self-reflection and self-examination, in accordance with Model 2. Otherwise defensive routines will hinder learning.

People must learn how to get access to existing models or how to generate new ones. They must also, if superficial learning is to be prevented, know when and how to use them. The first step could be to talk to people in the market or in the company who have differing opinions about the effectiveness of specific actions. Ask for their opinions, question their assumptions and compare them to your assumptions.

Experts in most areas that are relevant will probably be available inside the company. If not, make a survey or hire a consultant. Often, for example, a great deal of uncollected and unsystematized data on competing products, the behaviour of customers and competitors in the market is available within one's own organization. There are also simple but good standard models with which to explain this behaviour, e.g., models dealing with 'substitution effects', the 'experience curve' and the 'industry cost curve'.

The need to avoid superficial learning when creating models is discussed below.

In the case of *ambiguous learning*, the measurements used do not have adequate variety. Here the solution may lie in improving measurement procedures, which encompass monitoring, auditing, and management information systems. Systems thinking and effective structures are the disciplines that enable the right kind of measurements to be made, i.e., those that have adequate and appropriate variety. Here again, the organizational defensive pattern protecting hidden assumptions—

such as the assumption that performance is not measureable—and distorting the free flow of information will have to be overcome, as seen in Model 2.

Measurements are dependent on mental models and structures-in-use. If the models and structures on which measurements are based are inadequate, these have to be improved. Otherwise, we fail to prevent superstitious learning. Usually more data is available than is used by the organization.

*Superficial learning* occurs if procedures are not revised when mental models are changed or, vice versa, if procedures are changed without a corresponding change in mental models. In the simplest case, it can be overcome by enhancing the memory of individuals and organizations; that is, by storing routine procedures in information systems; designing easy ways to store and retrieve models and data; and improving access to knowledge and databases. All this will help to support the generation of adequate models and their dissemination at a fast rate.

According to Model 2, the capacity for self-reflection—involved in personal mastery—is needed. Models and their basic assumptions have to be clear in the individual's mind.

To devise and validate models, some of the techniques related to systems thinking (e.g. microworlds) might be helpful. Individuals should start to learn with simple models on paper or on a PC, describing situations in logical or qualitative ways. If unavailable in the unit to which the individual belongs, the organization may contain many persons who can help with model-building; otherwise, consultants can be hired. General models should be adapted to the desired purpose. If necessary or helpful, models should be quantified to the extent possible. The influence of the organizational defensive pattern on model-building has to be minimized.

But model-building, however excellent, is not enough. Models must be tested. Either an individual or an organizational action has to be explicitly based on the model. Both role-constrained and audience-restricted learning must be avoided. Finally, to avoid ambiguous learning the outcome of the experiment has to be measured.

Examples of model-building and testing in relation to strategic management and information management are discussed in Chapter 9.

If a special regulatory model used by the organization lacks requisite variety, individual learning loops can be modified. This may mean changing structures or the model coded in a person's brain, perhaps by changing the person, or changing the model coded in computer software, perhaps by changing the software. It depends upon what is causing the problem.

The available standard programs for spreadsheet calculation include many features that make data-handling and modelling easy. Simulation and system dynamics are other powerful tools to produce high-variety models and insights into the dynamics of complex situations; see especially Forrester (1968), Morecroft and Sterman (1994), Richardson and Pugh (1981) and Roberts (1978).

*Fragmented learning* is learning by individuals only, not by the organization to which they belong. To overcome it, individual mental models and skills have to be transferred to the organization as a whole. If, however, strong organizational defensive patterns are left untouched, such a process will not succeed; it will hardly be worth trying.

The process itself is a process of communication and requires mastery of all the disciplines of a learning organization, in particular of effective structures. Personal mastery is needed to encourage inquiry and self-examination, bringing to the surface the hidden assumptions and biases of individual mental models. A shared vision has to be developed in the process of team learning. Systems thinking has to be used to create and validate shared mental models. Finally, implementation requires effective structures.

Shared mental models are an emergent property of organizational communication. It is not the case that the same model has to be present in all minds; what is necessary is that people communicate in ways that produce models. As time goes by, more and more complex personal models will develop. Sharing a model does not mean the transfer of a model from one person to another, but the development of a dialogue that permits a better co-ordination of individuals. The problem, therefore, is to design communications in the organization that are likely to generate adequate shared models of co-ordinated actions.

Possible outcomes of this process are the following. Ideas about the future of the organization should lead to the development of its *vision* and *identity*; discussion about the role of a business unit in its competitive environment should become its *strategy*; progress in organizational modelling should lead to *business process re-engineering* and *new information systems*; progress in technology or science should lead to *new products*; and new knowledge created and disseminated throughout the organization should be embodied in *new products, services, structures and systems*. These are the outcomes described empirically by Nonoka and Takeuchi (1995).

One way of enlarging the intersection between the mental models of different groups is to provide training and experience to enable the participants to improve themselves in the organizational disciplines concerned. Systems thinking and team learning, for example, may be learned by designing 'dialogues' in which participants assume, in turn, the roles of team member and moderator or trainer. Familiarization with models that are both relevant and simple, as well as the planning of shared knowledge and shared experience, are also helpful.

Training may be provided not only through formal training assignments, but also through inclusion in projects, project groups and teams and through the experience of job rotation.

A number of methods for organizational improvement explicitly endeavour to enlarge the intersection of individual mental models in a specific problem context through shared experience of problem understanding and problem solving. We mention in particular TQM (Total Quality Management) as described by Flood (1993); IBM's CFM (Continuous Flow Manufacturing) an equivalent of business process re-engineering; and the KVP$^2$ (Continuous Improvement Process) at Volkswagen, described by Deutsch (1993, pp. 65–9). And, of course, we have to mention 'Team Syntegrity' (Beer, 1994).

*Opportunistic, or organization-constrained learning* occurs when actions are directed at a substantial opportunity that is not part of the organization's shared mental model. To transform mental models shared by a subset of the organization into action by the organization as a whole requires a driving force to support change. Otherwise any change will not be taken seriously.

What is required for such a driving force? A *shared vision* must be the guideline along which to act—a vision that has emerged from an organizational discussion of how the organization sees its role in the future. *Shared models* constitute a map of culturally acceptable communications and actions in the organization which show the possible ways to achieve or prevent change; these must be built up in favour of change. Finally, a force-field of change is needed to generate the energy to overcome the self-stabilizing feedback mechanism of organizational lethargy and resistance. To be successful, it must be realized in *effective structures* to implement required changes, including the necessary changes in the organizational chart.

According to Model 2, the organizational defensive pattern resisting change can be reduced and frictions and discussions made easier when the self-reflective capacities of those involved in the change are tapped.

While a shared vision and shared mental models can be assumed to be the result of overcoming fragmented learning, the new element here is the force-field. This is a necessary element, and can only be generated by the sincere and open commitment of the company's top management to the change project. Both features—shared vision as well as top-management commitment—are necessary when trying to overcome situations of organization-constrained learning in which powerful departments unite behind defensive routines and fancy footwork.

## Dilemmas Of Organizational Modelling

At this point we must introduce a counter-theme that will be developed in the next chapter.

We have described various obstacles to learning and shown how to overcome them. Now in all the steps to be taken, a central role is played by the generation and dissemination of models. Model-building itself is not easy. It is a skill that may have to be learned.

In addition, three *dilemmas of modelling* confront the organization. It is important to understand the nature of these dilemmas.

They arise from the fact that there are very different requirements for models used for *regulatory purposes* and those an organization must use for *learning purposes*. The latter are the SMM (shared mental models). As a rule these two kinds of models cannot be the same. Our three dilemmas arise from the different complexity needs of these different models.

The first dilemma lies in keeping the balance between:

- the complexity the organization must have in order to generate the requisite variety to cope with its tasks;
- the complexity of the cognitive models needed to describe adequately the dynamics and cybernetics of the organizational situation and so provide the basis for effective action in the task domain.

What is the dilemma here? It seems obvious that one's cognitive models of organizational reality should be as good as possible. Yet the consequences of generating and working with models that are too perfect or too complex, encompassing too many entities, can easily be a 'cancerogenous' growth of logical entities. Why? Because the reality is constantly changing. No model will be able to describe the changes adequately for long periods. If you try to stick to an outdated model, you will have to build ever more daring logical bridges to cross the gaps between the reality and the model.

In the end this leads to the exclusion of reality in the models that had been generated to describe it. This may be called the scholastic dilemma. The only way to get out of it is to start anew with a simpler, more adequate model.

William of Occam is credited with having stated the rule *'Entia non sunt multipl-canda praeter necessitatem'*. ('No more things should be presumed than are absolutely necessary'.) In the same vein, it is said that 'You don't need to be a weatherman to know which way the wind blows.'

The same truths hold for an organization. If it tries to stick to outdated models of the environment and its own functioning—such as, for instance, an organization matrix—it will be forced to construct ever more organizational artefacts in order to understand and cope with reality. This will lead to a cancerogenous growth in organizational departments and units. Each supposedly 'synergy-creating' unit will consume a part of the regulatory variety of the primary activities management. Thereby the autonomy of these units will be reduced a little further, until at some point the management attention and resources that are supposed to support these units will stifle their autonomy and creativity.

Conclusions may then be drawn as drastic as the following about the universe and the Earth.

> . . . if there's any real truth it's that the entire multi-dimensional infinity of the Universe is almost certainly being run by a bunch of maniacs . . . because without that fairly simple and obvious piece of knowledge nothing that ever happened on Earth could possibly make the slightest bit of sense.

This is adapted from Adams (1985, pp. 83–90). In fact this is not a citation but a combination of two independent statements from Adams' book. For the interested reader they are:

> I mean, yes idealism, yes the dignity of pure research, yes the pursuit of truth in all its forms, but there comes a point I'm afraid where you begin to suspect that if there's any real truth it's that the entire multi-dimensional infinity of the Universe is almost certainly being run by a bunch of maniacs; . . . [pp. 83–84] And this computer, which was called The Earth, was so large that it was frequently mistaken for a planet—particularly by the strange ape like beings who roamed its surface totally unaware that they were simply a part of a gigantic computer programme. And this is very odd because without that fairly simple and obvious bit of knowledge nothing that ever happened on Earth could possibly make the slightest bit of sense. (p. 90)

Have you never been tempted to draw similar conclusions about your department, company, political party, city, country or church?

Let us now state:

---

### The Organizational Complexity Dilemma

The greater the complexity with which an organization is structured to cope with complex problems, the more the variety that is squandered on building models to explain its internal nature and functioning. Correspondingly less variety is left to deal with its environment.

---

One answer to this dilemma is to keep the organization simple, especially when dealing with complex problems. This may be done by the means Peters (1988) prescribes, viz., by simplifying and reducing structures, reconceiving middle managers' roles and eliminating bureaucratic rules. In fact this is the hallmark of recursive structures.

Note that the strategy of splitting up large organizations into smaller, more flexible and adaptive parts has its analogue in nature. To adapt to changing environmental conditions, lower organisms divide themselves physically. Beer (1979) points out that human institutions, by contrast, 'expand variety by contemplating rather than creating alternatives. They reduce variety by mental elimination . . .'

In this way organizations 'simulate the amplification and attenuation of variety engineering by contemplating the future that "lower organisms" achieve by manipulating recursions', i.e., by going down one level of recursion and absorbing complexity by physically dividing themselves. The 'manipulation of recursion levels is cybernetically far more powerful.'

Consider now our second dilemma. It arises from keeping a balance between the complexity of the models needed for process regulation and the necessity to communicate at least some aspects of the models in order to share them.

The Conant-Ashby theorem states, Conant and Ashby (1970), that every controller must contain an adequately rich model of what it regulates. We can now reason as follows.

If the regulator consists of more than one person, the regulatory model must be a shared model and shared models must be simple in transduction and acceptable by the cultural background, otherwise they cannot be effectively communicated.

On the other hand, if a regulator has to control a complex situation, its control models must not be simple; even complex machines use fuzzy controllers or neural network controllers!

The dilemma is compounded by the fact that if the organization is to learn from it, the model must be explicitly stated.

We can state the dilemma as follows:

---

**The Regulatory Models Dilemma**

The more complex the regulatory models in use, the lower is the possibility of sharing them and the less likely is organizational learning. Control cannot, however, be maintained with simple models.

---

The solution must be that, regardless of the complexity of your own regulatory models, you should keep the models you have to share simple, otherwise no one will understand them. Stick to the essential variables.

Moreover, regardless of the complexity of the environment: organizational learning requires that simple models be made explicit. Otherwise, only individual learning can take place.

In this connection, note that a clear statement of vision can be communicated, and if it inspires people, will take away much more 'unwanted' variety than hundreds of pages of explicit rules. In addition, it may generate 'wanted' variety in problem solving.

The general conclusion must be that organizational learning cannot take place by making explicit complex regulatory models. On the other hand, individual learning is not hindered by the use of complex models, where appropriate.

The balance is kept by recognizing that under many circumstances it is unnecessary for regulatory models to be shared. Specialists can be made responsible for the design and operation of complex regulatory models. You don't, for example, know the individual lines of code of the computer program you are working with; your regulatory model concerns the use of the mouse and keyboard. Our third dilemma is a consequence of the first two.

Organizational learning happens by sharing simple models, but regulatory models are complex. This leads to the following:

---

**Shared Models Dilemma**

Organizational learning requires shared models. But it does not take place through the sharing or understanding of the individual, complex, regulatory models coded in the brains of organizational members or in the code of organizational computer software. It follows that organizational learning is impossible.

---

If, indeed, we insist on organizational learning on the one hand and on generating requisite variety on the other, how can organizational learning happen at all?

The answer is stated by Beer in his 'regulatory aphorisms':

> it is not necessary to enter the black box
> to understand the nature of the function it performs;
> to calculate the variety that it may potentially generate.

The models that are simple enough to be shared and can thus enable organizational learning are not the regulatory models themselves but statements about the interfaces between them. They describe the task domains of the managers.

Managers need not understand each other's regulatory models. It is unlikely, in fact, that they are able to do so, because the models in their cognitive domains have developed under different influences of knowledge, experience and interactions. Their different roles prevent them from sharing their interactive domains.

It is not needed. Managers only need to understand the nature of the tasks each performs and the variety each can generate with respect to the other

A vision is usually a statement about interfaces; that is, it is about the relationships to be striven for between the firm and its customers—as well as other stakeholders—and between individuals or groups in the firm.

# Chapter 7

# The cybernetics of individual and organizational learning

## INTRODUCTION

The purpose of this chapter is to integrate the frameworks and models of the previous three chapters into a single methodology for problem solving. The framework for effective action in an organizational context presented in Chapter 4, the viable system model of Chapter 5 and the OADI-SMM framework discussed in Chapter 6 will be related in one approach to the diagnosis of individual and organizational learning and the design of more effective learning cycles. We call this approach the cybernetic methodology (Espejo, 1993b).

The key idea behind it is to relate each learning loop to the organizational context in which it takes place. This makes it possible to dissolve many problems by creating a context for effective learning. The emphasis shifts from particular learning episodes or problem situations to learning how to deal with a class of situations, i.e., on 'learning how to learn' rather than on the characteristics of particular cases. Using the terminology of Chapter 5, the emphasis is on giving 'requisite variety' to effective individual and organizational learning, rather than on fire-fighting particular situations.

Learning is an ongoing concern. The challenge is to make it a positive experience that becomes more efficient as time goes by and situations emerge and recur. This is a must for modern organizations in an increasingly competitive environment.

Methodologically, the problem is to know how to work out the relevant organizational context for each individual and each class of issues of concern. This is what the idea of 'recursive organization', discussed in Chapter 5, allows us to do; we use it to bring out the idea of 'recursive learning'. This simply means that it is not enough to concentrate problem-solving capacity at the corporate level of an organization. It must be distributed—although actually, it is always distributed in one form or another. The problem is rather to ensure that its distribution is adequate and makes the best use of available organizational resources. This the cybernetic methodology allows us to do.

The plan for this chapter is as follows. First, we will discuss further how to transform individual into organizational learning. We will emphasize how to answer the question: What is the learning about? Organizational learning depends on the articulation of domains of concern and supporting learning through effective structures.

Second, we will discuss the management of complexity and introduce in more formal terms a framework that links individual action, organizational action, environmental responses and performance. Third, we use this framework to typify individual and organizational problem situations. Perceived problem situations emerge from action loops of individuals, through the organization to the environment and back to individuals.

Next, we will revisit the OADI-SMM model, equipped now with more advanced ideas of complexity and a more focused concern on particular domains of action. The outcome will be an enhanced and slightly modified version of the OADI-SMM model that will, we believe, prove to be more useful.

Finally, we will introduce the cybernetic methodology. This makes it possible to relate each learning loop to its organizational context. The straightforward argument is that a learning loop starved of complexity, i.e., of channel capacity, is more likely to be an incomplete learning cycle than one with adequate complexity.

## INDIVIDUAL AND ORGANIZATIONAL LEARNING

In Chapter 4 we made a clear distinction between individual and organizational learning. In Chapter 6 we took this further, agreeing with Kim's definition of individual learning as 'an increase in the individual capacity for effective acticn' and organizational learning as 'an increase in the organization's capacity for effective action'. We then used the OADI-SMM model to make the further distinction between operational and conceptual learning; that is, between know-how and know-why.

Crucial to organizational learning is the transformation of individual learning into organizational learning, and for this purpose it is necessary to work out the 'whats' or domains of shared action. These whats are more than common objectives; they entail the shared worldviews through which people attach commor meanings to their actions, thus supporting their co-ordination of action.

Our concern in this chapter is therefore methodological; the question 'What is the learning about?' comes to the fore.

The point here is that individuals or organizations operate in particular domains; they have limited capabilities and can develop competencies only in certain areas. If, therefore, learning is to increase their capacity for effective action, it must be for effective action in those domains; and when we make an assessment about an individual's or an organization's capacity for effective action we need to make it for a specific domain—not as a blanket statement about everything.

The definition of the 'what'—what domain of action?—is particularly important for organizational learning. Individuals may learn and become highly effective in their domains of action without becoming highly conscious of them. This may also be the case for organizations; however, it is less likely here, since organizations learn through people's co-ordinated actions. In order to learn, organizations must do two things. They must focus individuals' capabilities on shared concerns and find mechanisms to enable them to co-operate.

These are two crucial and interrelated issues. To work out shared concerns is to work out a domain for learning. To find mechanisms for co-operation is to give capacity for learning interactions to take place. In other words, the problem of organizational learning is not merely one of sharing mental models. Those mental models, if they are to affect organizational action, must also be supported by structural mechanisms that enable the co-ordinated action of individuals. We refer to this as the structural embodiment of shared mental models. We will discuss it further when we revisit the OADI-SMM model.

Our first concern is with the task of working out a common domain of action so that learning can take place. This is not unproblematic. As individuals working in an organizational context we constantly find that a key obstacle to our action is high uncertainty as to what are the agreed action domains. We spend much time and effort trying to work them out. Unfortunately, we often approach this resolution process with poor frameworks. For instance, we may dismiss those who do not agree with our views and attempt to bulldoze away their contrary views from a position of power. This creates resentment and conflicts. Later we may find, either because of breakdowns or a weak sense of commitment leading to poor performance, that a revision of the situation with those affected becomes necessary. Eventually, after a painful process, some kind of agreement is reached concerning the conversations in progress and the conditions of satisfaction for them, i.e., about the action domain.

Effective individual and organizational single loop learning depend on a tacit or explicit knowledge of action domains. They provide the platform to detect errors and develop practices to overcome them.

Of course, there are in any organization many situations with clear, well-accepted common objectives, and shared meanings for them, where we find that individuals and organizations are good at single-loop learning. They are comfortable in knowing what to do, even more comfortable in knowing how to do it. It is not threatening for them to constantly improve well-defined tasks, given that underlying policies, assumptions and theories are not questioned.

As long as this behaviour produces satisfactory environmental responses people feel comfortable and unprepared to change. However, intractable problems arise when environmental responses are not good and, at the same time, people feel frightened or inhibited from questioning the worldviews that underpin their existing tasks. In such conditions individual double-loop learning is impaired, let alone organizational learning.

To transform individual learning into organizational learning it is necessary both that individuals play one or more organizational roles and that they share some kind of organizational task. Individuals may be effective single- and double-loop learners but may be poor contributors to organizational learning. This may be the case either when their domains of effective learning are not those implied by their organizational roles or when the organization's structure does not support their direct or indirect required interactions. Indeed, either because the organizational context does not offer them the opportunity to interact effectively, or because the outcomes of their interactions are not supported by enough resources, they will find it hard to remove uncertainty, to question assumptions and to perform organizational tasks; both organizational and individual learning are impaired. Clearly, organizational learning will only take place when individuals find a framework for communication.

It is through this framework that an identity for the organization may emerge, agreed tasks for co-operation may be declared and organizational routines may be introduced.

The outcome of interactions may be a total breakdown in communications! In other words, a framework for (direct and indirect) communications is not sufficient for organizational learning. Yet it is necessary. Without it, there is no possibility of learning. It is also necessary to consider that each individual brings to the organization a complex personal history. Each is constituting a personal reality that needs to be related to the realities being constituted by others in order to constitute the organization itself. But there is no way in which these realities can be fully shared. Their complexity is too large for this to be a possibility—and even if it were possible it would not be desirable. The wealth of an organization is in the diversity of its people and not in their uniformity. This point is well accepted today, yet what is far from being understood is how far to go with this sharing in order to achieve an effective integration of viewpoints thus avoiding either cosmetic interactions or too detailed interactions.

It is with this in mind that we need to understand the idea of shared mental models; recall the shared mental models dilemma in the last chapter. Organizational learning does not mean that everyone evolves the same mental models, only that everyone knows how to relate to each other in such a way that they amplify their mutual capacities. To achieve this, it is first of all important to routinize everything that can be made a routine. Indeed, it is important to do this for every single aspect that is not seen by individuals, and organizational units, as central to their concerns—a point we made in discussing the co-ordination function in Chapter 5.

Why should some functions and not others be routinized? Routines and procedures can be enablers or inhibitors of organizational learning, depending on whether or not they are sensitive to the purposes ascribed to the organization and the purposes of individuals. For all aspects that are not central to the purposes of the organization (and recursively of its primary activities), routinization should enable, not constrain, the interactions that are necessary to enhance the individual's action. But how can we say which are the necessary interactions? Only by sharing a common understanding of the domains of action of the organization (and recursively of its primary activities).

Above all, what is needed is to share an understanding of the organization's identity—which means more than sharing a common view of its mission. The organization's mission needs to be grounded in a worldview, or *Weltanschauung*, in which people share important stories, metaphors and visions.

Such a shared worldview is the critical anchor for organizational learning. It provides not only a common direction for individual's actions but also an orientation for their necessary interactions. Of course, there is a circularity in this argument; the interactions that are possible help to articulate a shared worldview which is then used as an umbrella to define the interactions that are necessary. This circularity of causation is inherent to the process of constituting an organization.

The above argument concerning shared mental models is particularly useful when we consider recursive structures, with their distributed and constantly adaptable nature. It is within the framework of the multiple, tacit or explicitly agreed, identities of the organization's primary activities that people give meanings to issues of concern. These issues themselves need to evolve their own identities; for as long as they need to be shared, their identities are the platform that supports effective interactions and organizational learning.

## MANAGEMENT OF COMPLEXITY

Let us now show in more depth how individual and organizational learning are related to the management of complexity. Discussing learning loops from the point of view of complexity management will enable us to deduce some necessary conditions for effective learning.

First, we need to review some fundamental concepts concerning organizational and individual action which, as we have seen, are closely related to learning.

Our actions affect our surroundings, which in turn affect us. In other words, there is a structural coupling between us and our environment.

Our interactions with our individual environment may be construed in terms of environmental responses to our actions—responses that may reinforce or change our beliefs, embodied in our models of the world. These models provide the platform for our action. This is our learning loop. But in organizations we act upon the organization's environment as well. We do this through other people. A market segment manager in a large company acts upon this environment through the activities of manufacturing; he is not the producer of the products he is marketing. In such cases, closing the loop between the individual and the environment takes longer; our direct actions may trigger a myriad of related actions that are construed as the organizational action. These actions then produce environmental responses. In our example, the market segment manager may fail to get repeat orders because of poor product quality.

The many individual–organization–environment–individual loops natural to any organization define the organization's learning loops. Let us look at these in more detail.

In all cases, whether we are talking of individual or organizational learning, our actions affect other people who, to a greater or lesser degree, are beyond our immediate interactions. Therefore it is often the case that the effects of our actions are the outcomes of cascading actions, involving distant people. We cannot see, let alone experience, what is happening within them. We may see a logic in their responses and hypothesize a model linking our actions to the responses we observe; we cannot peep into those others. In other words, we are interacting with the environment through a 'black box'.

From our perspective, particularly if we are acting through others, the problem is to control the outcomes. As said before in previous chapters, these others are on the one hand amplifiers of our action, on the other hand attenuators of environmental responses. Most of the time, disturbances—another term for environmental responses—are absorbed by others. Therefore they are irrelevant to us. What we do need to consider are those disturbances that are relevant to our performance but not absorbed by others within the organization—without forgetting to consider those disturbances that are being absorbed by others but ought to be handled by us.

To understand how we handle these disturbances we need to apply the concept of 'requisite variety' developed in Chapters 3, 4 and 5. Our purpose is to clarify the link

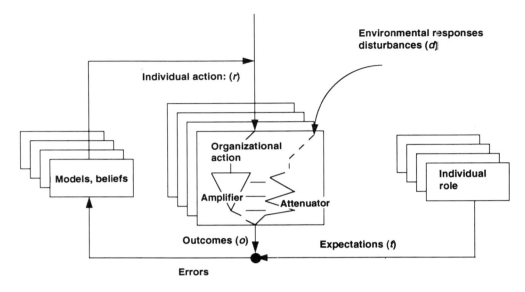

**Figure 7.1** Management of complexity

between individual strategies for managing complexity and the trarsformation of individual learning into organizational learning.

### Applying Requisite Variety

We have requisite variety to manage a situation—represented by a black box—if the variety of our responses $r$ is enough to cope with all disturbances $d$ that potentially can take the black box out of course; that is, that can produce outcomes $o$ outside the target set $T$ of expected outcomes. Figure 7.1 illustrates this.

The market segment manager has requisite variety to manage the segment (which encompasses the slice of manufacturing related to the segment) if he has enough responses $r$ to cope with all the contingencies $d$ likely to take the outcomes of the market segment out of its target set $T$.

When there is insufficient variety in our responses, vis-à-vis the expected or required performance, we must work out ways of solving the problems that ensue either by increasing our capabilities to perform complex activities or by finding ways to simplify them. This is a learning process that takes place most of the time intuitively—though we are not always aware that our efforts to increase our capabilities should be related to our efforts to simplify the complexity of our task.

In order to manage the situation, the market segment manager needs, first, an adaptive understanding of how contingencies are absorbed by the (relevant) organization, i.e., needs an evolving model of the interactions between the black box' and the environment; second, the manager needs a capacity to act upon the (relevant) organization in order to achieve required performance over time.

In general, assuming that we have a well-defined task, successful problem solving and learning requires that we should have responses $r$ to all those environmental disturbances $d$ for which others in the situation do not have response capacity and for which a response is necessary if we are to achieve an adequate performance $T$. If we have fewer responses than those required by the complexity of the situation, then we will not manage the situation satisfactorily.

If, on the other hand, we have more responses than those required by the situation, it may be that we are misusing our resources by giving too many to this particular task.

Requisite variety is concerned with the minimum necessary conditions to achieve an acceptable performance. It is about the amount of regulation that is necessary to achieve acceptable, competitive performance in a selected action domain. Since this acceptable performance is a moving target that is constantly being modified by new competitive requirements, we derive from this a picture of 'learning' as an ongoing process that strives to maintain requisite variety, i.e., outcomes within the set defined as competitive performance.

## Insufficient Variety: The Engine For Learning

A common experience for all of us, particularly in today's highly interconnected world, is that we, as individuals, lack variety to deal with the complexity we experience in relevant situations. We are in a permanent state of insufficient variety. Indeed, we commonly accept that we depend on others to do what we require to be done—but in accepting this we must also accept that we cannot experience or see the complexity that is experienced and seen by them. Moreover, even with all this amplification we still experience insufficient variety.

As a strategy to attain requisite variety we either try to reduce the variety of contingencies that we deal with, i.e., we try to reduce (attenuate) the task complexity—or we try to amplify our action capacity. Or we may do both! Attenuation we do either by ignoring contingencies—thus reducing our performance—or by classifying contingencies into a smaller number of groups and ignoring the differences between contingencies within a single group. We then make a single response to all the contingencies within a single group, which means that in some way we must delegate the task of actually making a separate response to each separate contingency. We overcome insufficient variety by attenuation of problem complexity and amplification of our response capacity. In this latter case it may be possible to achieve more with less involvement; but this is a learning problem.

## Requisite Variety And The Management Of Complexity

Based upon these concepts, let us now discuss, in more general terms, how we 'control' a black box such as that in Figure 7.1. As we have seen, doing so may be equated with solving problems and with learning.

To control a black box, we observe over time the flow of its outputs and make distinctions within this flow. We call the states thus distinguished 'outcomes' ($o$); they define the set of actual outcomes O. These outcomes define the situational complexity $we$ see in the situation.

Of the whole set of outcomes, only a subset is likely to be perceived as adequate. We define this subset, tacitly or explicitly, by our perceptions of stability in the relations between the black box and the environment. This is the target set $T$.

If defined explicitly, this set will generally have a smaller number of states than those necessary to maintain the black box's stability; provided stability is maintained, the individual is free to define a subset of desirable outcomes within the target set. However, it may be necessary to enlarge the set of outcomes defined as desirable when we recognize that the smaller set is unachievable.

The more stringent are the criteria of performance the fewer states belong to the target set. 'Perfect' regulation would be the case where there is an effective action for every contingency. This means we are able to produce a corrective response for all disturbances threatening to produce an outcome different from the desired one; we have an optimal response strategy for all eventualities. Whether this is an ideal is not the point. The point is that as we learn, whether as individuals or organizations, our capacity to hit the target set increases. Or in different terms, the more stringent becomes the target set the more pressing is the need to learn; that is, the more we depend on effective actions. This is the case in an increasingly competitive world. In general, the set of response actions is called the 'response set' R.

The minimum number of necessary responses will depend upon several factors. First, it will depend upon the level of performance desired—greater performance demanding greater response capacity. Second, it will depend upon the number of factors likely to occur to upset the stability of the situation. These factors that affect significantly the outcomes of the situation go to make up the 'disturbances' set D. The greater their number, the greater again must be the set R.

The third factor affecting how large R must be for a regulator is the 'absorptive' capacity of situational actions. We have seen, in our discussion of insufficient variety, that the regulator needs to be able to give one and the same effective response to more than one disturbance—otherwise the responses $r$ will be swamped by the variety of disturbances. The 'absorptive capacity' $a$ is the average number of different disturbances that a response can effectively deal with. The greater the coefficient $a$, the less need for variety of responses. This absorptive capacity relates to self-regulation and self-organization, which are closely linked to organizational learning; as the organization learns to learn its capacity to deal with classes of situations becomes larger; that is, $a$ becomes larger.

For example one standard letter, once implemented, may be sent in response to many different letters of complaint or enquiry. Before, each complaint or enquiry required a different response. The regulators, i.e. we as problem solvers, 'absorb' many disturbances through one and the same response.

It is a fact, of course, that for any system there will be many possible disturbances for which the system has no adequate response. A company cannot and does not generally prepare for the possibility of being attacked from the air by a hostile power. A country's armed forces cannot cope effectively with an all-out nuclear attack. None of us could cope with the sun exploding. But short of such drastic eventualities, a company may constantly try to foresee new opportunities and threats and proceed to prepare responses for them. Indeed as an organization learns it develops more and more effective actions to cope with an ever more demanding environment. Thus the set $D$ of disturbances is not fixed in time. In other words, new disturbances emerge all the time; the disturbances we see depend on the models we have of our action domains and the selected criteria of performance, defined by the set $T$. These models define the distinctions we make in the situation.

While often we get involved in wishful thinking and are prepared to define arbitrary goals, the set $T$ is not defined arbitrarily. It is the outcome of the demands coming from the multiple relations relevant to us, and of course it is in constant evolution. As long as we experience stability in our relations we are, for the selected action domain, within our target set. If the responses $r$ produced to offset the disturbances $d$ maintain outcomes within the set $T$, then we have *de facto* control capacity, i.e., requisite variety. On the other hand, if the actual outcomes $o$ go out of $T$, then we have lost control. However, as we learn it becomes more and more likely that $O$ (the set of outcomes) will be within $T$.

### Revisiting Residual Variety

There is yet another, perhaps more interesting way of looking at the absorptive coefficient $a$. This brings in the important concept of 'residual' variety, through which we gain further insight into what 'control' means and how the organization can learn to exercise it.

We have said that the coefficient $a$ reflects the capacity of the average response to 'absorb' the variety of a number of different disturbances. However, likewise, and at the same time, it reflects the capacity of the average response to generate, i.e., amplify, response variety in the situation itself; that is, one response generates a number of other responses in the situation itself, which absorb disturbances before they become relevant to the person or organization. For example, suppose corporate management creates a primary activity—an $r$—to deal with a particular market segment; once it is implemented, corporate management may, to a large degree, forget about the segment and still each customer may receive a particular response! One response 'creates' and 'absorbs' *uniquely* many disturbances.

This is also the strategy of getting customers or suppliers to do part of the organization's task. For instance, telephone banking is one organizational response that involves customers managing the complexity of banking, thus off-loading it from the bank. This is an example where a strategy amplifies the organization's complexity. Another case: consider the accounting data reaching the head office of a company—a company whose head office consists of a small unit controlling a large number of very large subsidiaries. The head office may be routinely concerned only with accounting data; it may not even take cognizance of what business each (very large) subsidiary is in—only of the average financial performance of businesses in the same financial category. It is natural to call the variety of the accounting data the head office deals with the residual variety of the company; after all the rest has been taken away by a myriad of self-regulating processes within the subsidiaries. From the viewpoint of head office this is a strategy to attenuate the subsidiaries' complexity.

We learn over time which are the subset of disturbances that require special, highly selective responses. These are our *critical success factors*.

Therefore, if a company survives in its environment, i.e. has requisite variety, this does not mean that its variety is as great or greater than that of its environment. On the contrary, of the huge number of possible environmental states, the large majority will be either irrelevant to the company, or if relevant will be absorbed by interactions within the environment itself. In either case, the large environmental complexity is dealt with by a few, general responses on the part of the company.

Only the residual variety that remains—the complexity that is not absorbed in the environment itself—must be absorbed by selective responses of the company if it is to remain viable.

While the company remains viable it is this residual variety that will be consciously and selectively matched by the company's variety. This is the set of disturbances $D$ for which the company needs to produce selective responses $r$ in order to keep the outcomes of the company within the set $T$, consistent with its viability.

The same argument of residual variety is valid for individual learning; the complexities that are equated are those defined by our action capacity and the residual variety that is relevant yet not absorbed in the situation itself. This is the complexity that we have to cope with. If we cannot cope with this variety then stability, with reference to a set $T$, may be lost.

This argument makes it clear that the more effective is the absorption of variety in the situation itself, the less problematic that situation is. We can see that in organizations this absorption of variety within the situation relates to learning processes in which self-regulation and self-organization are seen as the dynamo of the learning.

### Problem Solving And Organizational Learning

We have related organizational learning to the management of complexity and to the control of a 'black box'. Let us now ask: how is it related to problem solving?

Learning depends on effective problem solving, though problem solving may happen without learning. The logic of our argument is that as we search for ways to maintain stability in our interactions, i.e., as we search for ways to maintain the outcomes $o$ within a target set $T$, we are searching for responses $r$ to disturbances $d$. In this process we may develop new models of the world and new practices to respond to disturbances. If this is the case we are learning; we are becoming more effective operators. Moreover, if we are able to co-ordinate our actions using a common platform, i.e., if we are able to create and share a vision and develop co-ordinating frameworks and practices for our action then we may recognize ourselves as constituting a learning organization.

Thus we rely on the ideas of complexity and management of complexity for our discussion of problem solving. That discussion will provide a platform for the cybernetic methodology.

In this section we want to show that as problem solvers we need to find effective ways of reducing situational complexity at the same time as we improve performance; that is, we need to learn how to do more with less. From our perspective this is systemic management. Relating amplification and attenuation to problem solving helps us to keep in view the total individual–organization–environmental loop.

How do we absorb the complexity created by our actions?

### About Problem Situations: Issues of Concern

In Chapter 4 we made it clear that breakdowns—or breaks in expectations—in the course of conversations were responsible for 'issues of concern'.

Issues of concern are the source of complexity in our daily life. If the world posed no problems or challenges, we would be operating in a transparent world with no complexity, where creativity or learning would not be necessary.

Problem solving consists of managing the breaks we experience; it is learning how to create effective responses to them. Following the logic of residual variety, our situational complexity is defined by those breaks that make a difference to us; that is, by those issues for which we have to create responses.

For a group of corporate managers, complexity is defined by the breaks beyond the organization's self-regulating capabilities. For the total organization, complexity is defined by those breaks that the organization chooses to deal with in order to develop its competitive advantage, or is forced to respond to in order to remain in business. In each case—for us as individuals, for the management group or for the organization as a whole—these breaks are critical success factors.

## Issues Of Personal (Individual) Concern

Just as we recognize individual and organizational learning we distinguish issues of individual and organizational concern. The former relate to our own performance in the organization, the latter to organizational performance.

Issues of personal concern are breaks that we have to deal with if we are to cope with expectations concerning our contribution to the organization. They relate to our organizational performance; they concern us individually. Such issues, as they emerge, trigger the need for us to develop new distinctions, practices and capabilities. They concern the complexity directly relevant to us. We cannot leave this complexity unattended unless we are prepared to disappoint others. They are the trigger of our learning processes.

This complexity emerges from our interactions with others; that is, from breakdowns in our interactions. Stability in interactions between ourselves and others depends on mutual expectations about each other. We all have both informational and normative expectations (Luhmann, 1985). If as a result of an interaction we simply adjust our expectations about others, then the change in expectations is informational and not necessarily problematic; this is a case of single-loop learning. After the interaction we know more about the other side. If, on the other hand, we experience a break in our expectations, then the change in our expectations is normative and problematic in nature. In other words, the change in expectations is not based only on insufficient information but is grounded on views of the world, norms, beliefs and values which we do not find easy to adjust. The solution to this requires effective double-loop learning; it requires that we question our views of the world and as a consequence, modify our norms, values and beliefs.

Effective action requires developing personal skills and conversational capabilities to overcome normative breaks. If, for instance, we inhibit others or are unable to get their commitment and genuine support for action we are in a non-learning situation. Figure 7.2 offers insights about the interdependence between distinctions (attenuation) and practices (amplification) necessary for learning. Each of us needs to develop the necessary competencies to become effective organizational actors. These competencies relate to our cognitive, interactive and task venues, discussed in Chapter 4.

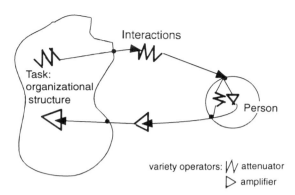

**Figure 7.2**   Task, interactive and cognitive venues

Figure 7.2 is an abstract representation of a person who is part of a task, together with his or her relevant interactions relating him/her to the task of concern. It shows *de facto* attenuators and amplifiers relating the person to the task; these are the cognitive, interactive and task venues. These variety operators relate to competencies, or lack of them, of various kinds. Thus, for instance, the following competencies represent attenuators in the cognitive venue: perceptual objectivity; listening skills; logical thought; conceptualization; and self-control. Examples of amplifiers in the cognitive venue are: creativity; systemic thinking; diagnostic use of concepts; clarity in expression; speed of response.

Individual competencies that represent attenuators in the interactive venue are: ability to select relevant conversations; ability to get valid informatior in conversations; ability to assess the meaning of interactions. Amplifiers in this venue relate to the person's ability to get the commitment of others while in conversations.

In the task venue we find attenuators such as the person's ability to operate high quality monitoring communication channels, thus increasing his or her chances of knowing about the organization's capabilities and performance and tneir ability to induce confidence in the market and thereby create the conditions for effective communications with the environment. In all these cases the person is making the structural attenuation of complexity more effective. A fundamental amplifier is leadership; that is, the ability to create the conditions for individual and team empowerment, the ability to create a culture of trust and mutual respect—thus reducing the need for direct supervision—or the ability to induce structures that define organizational potentials. Thereby a person makes the structural amplificaticn of complexity more effective.

Developing practices that make the most of issues of personal concern requires the balancing of attenuators and amplifiers. For instance, it does not make sense for us to develop great conceptualization skills—thereby becoming excellent in attenuating situational complexity—without developing our abilities to make diagnostic use of concepts—thereby amplifying our action complexity. Again, it does not help to know which conversations to open if we fail to get the commitment of the people we talk with. Equally, it is no use increasing our abilities to know about the organization's capabilities and the organization's environment if we fail to create the conditions to act upon this information by motivating people and unleashing self-regulating and self-organizing processes.

Thus, a balanced development of attenuators and amplifiers is necessary for effective individual learning. As we develop these skills we increase our learning capabilities and our action becomes more effective.

## Issues Of Organizational Concern

Consider next issues of concern to the organization. These relate to organizational performance and are fundamentally structural and cultural. Organizational issues relate to grounded practices and frameworks, beyond specific individuals; they relate to past organizational learning and may require unlearning this learning.

Dealing with these issues does not depend so much on improving individual competencies as on improving the organization's competence to learn and to provide a context for learning. Such issues are, nevertheless, rooted in the interactions of people in the organization.

If, independently of their individual capacity to hold effective conversations, organizational norms inhibit people from expressing their true views and feelings about a situation—if there are topics that cannot be discussed or there are particular 'correct' ways of thinking—then agreements will tend to be weak, in spite of apparently stable interactions. This is likely to increase the chances of painful organizational breakdowns.

Such breakdowns emerge from constraints on individuals that prevent them from questioning beliefs and expectations. The prevention of organizational breakdowns often requires, among other things, questioning and overcoming organizational norms that support defensive behaviours. People in the organization need to overcome, as a community, behaviours that inhibit open communications, distort information flows and punish those who dare question 'organizational truths'. This is necessary in order to have a learning organization. Unfortunately, individuals and organizations are often poor at this kind of learning, i.e., at the double-loop learning described by Argyris and Schön (1978).

While the overcoming of restrictive norms requires, in the first place, individual double-loop learning, this learning will not become learning by the organization as such unless its structure supports the effective transformation of individual into organizational learning. Without effective structural mechanisms for sharing mental models, the chances of grounding new norms, beliefs and values in the organization are reduced. This, in turn, reduces the chances of effective organizational action.

Not only double-loop, but also single-loop learning by the organization—i.e., doing better what the organization has already agreed upon—depends upon effective structures and communications. Many breakdowns emerge because the structure does not support the commitments we make while in conversations. For instance, a market segment manager accepts an order but manufacturing has different priorities; the outcome is a dissatisfied customer. While at the individual level we need to learn that often the satisfactory completion of conversations depends on the successful completion of many distant conversations taking place throughout the organization, at the organizational level we need to learn how to create effective communication mechanisms. When the market segment manager commits the organization to deliver an order by a certain date, he is making assumptions about a wide range of subsidiary conversations; at the very least those of manufacturing and logistics. This point is illustrated in Figure 7.3, where we can appreciate that the successful completion of the salesman's conversation with a customer depends on a myriad of organizational conversations, implied by the diagram's outer loop. However good might be the manager's individual learning, if the structures are inadequate, the overall organizational performance will be inadequate; organizational learning is necessary as well.

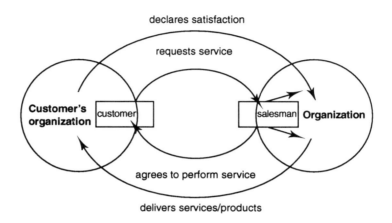

**Figure 7.3**    Customer–supplier loops

Whether our concern is with single- or double-loop learning, organizational tasks are the outcome of conversations in which people commit themselves to particular courses of action. The quality of these conversations is crucial to individual and organizational performance. Many of the breakdowns experienced in organizational work are rooted in a poor grasp of the structures underlying these conversations (a problem of individual learning); but they are also rooted in weak structures that hinder necessary communications (a problem of organizational learning).

These are common organizational issues of concern. They are themselves rooted in the processes by which the organization's structure is constituted. Indeed, as was made apparent in Chapter 5, a source of these breakdowns is the inability of existing communication channels to accommodate the complexity of the process implied by the organization's tacit or declared purposes, i.e., the organization's task venue. This may manifest itself in breakdowns that are rooted in poor or inadequate declarations of purpose or in weak structures to support tacit or explicit declarations of purpose.

In summary, issues of organizational concern emerge when we examine the structural and cultural context of issues of personal concern. They are breakdowns rooted in the organization's norms, values, views of the world—or *Weltanschauungen*—and structure. This is in contrast to issues of personal concern that are rooted in individual competencies.

Since the organization is the context of people's interactions, issues of organizational concern do affect people's performance at the local level. However, it is this very performance that defines, once aggregated for all people, the organizational context of their action. Understanding this reciprocal relation, or circular causality, between structure and action, in particular the types of issues of organizational concern emerging from this relation, should lead to individual and organizational learning.

## Types Of Individual And Organizational Issues

Based on the ideas of management of complexity, we distinguish four types of issues of individual and organizational concern.

First, we may distinguish *identity problems*. These are breakdowns triggered by lack of clarity about the situation itself; the action domain is unclear. Such problems require 'inventing the world' and bringing forth new situations. They depend on 'conversations for possibilities'.

Often we are unclear about organizational purposes; what is the organization for, what business is it in? Being aware of the institutions we work for does not necessarily mean that we are aware of the organizations we belong to. We may conflate recursive structures. We may recognize the corporation as a whole as a business but not the specific division we are working for. The better defined is the relevant organization's identity, the more clear it will become what resources and communications channels are required to succeed with its vision and purpose; this was made clear in our discussion of the viable system model. A clear identity is the platform for organizational learning. Articulating our situations is, in addition, an identity problem, facilitated by sharing a vision.

Next, we can distinguish *response problems*. These occur when the resources supporting amplification of commitments are inadequate. Performance is then perceived as inadequate. The individual or organization's resources to perform agreed tasks are seen as insufficient. Such problems arise from an imbalance between attenuators and amplifiers. The individual, or the organization, are making distinctions for which they have no response capacity. Their operational capacity, i.e., their amplification capacity, is not enough.

The health system is an example of an organization that, almost universally, has response problems. This is because distinctions about 'illnesses' and possible cures are growing much faster than operational capabilities. However hard the system works, the ever-increasing gap between our expectations, i.e., our increasingly sophisticated attenuation of health needs, and operational response capacity, viz., the amplification of the health service, will continue to create dissatisfaction. In spite of improved levels of service, the overall performance will be perceived as declining, making unresolved issues of personal concern that much more likely. In the language of requisite variety, the target set $T$ is becoming more stringent, with the result that organizational responses $r$ are not matching the increasing rate at which environmental disturbances $d$ are buffeting the organization.

While this is a typical response problem, organizational learning does not only mean increasing response capacity. In general, it means managing expectations and balancing responses and disturbances more effectively.

*Environmental problems* occur when situational attenuation is relatively inadequate. The people in the organization are not recognizing enough distinctions in the task's environment, i.e., not distinguishing enough disturbances. Great though their re-sources may be, they are unable to match expectations because poor attenuation of task complexity is impairing their performance. The individual or the organization is then not learning well enough how to allocate available resources.

A typical case is that of a 'successful' company that has increasingly unsuccessful products or services through its failure to recognize changes in people's needs and concerns. While such companies may have more than enough resources to deal with production requirements, their inability to adapt or develop new markets may hinder their chances of targeting these resources effectively. However hard people within the organization work to make the resources productive, the chances are that they will not succeed; that is, they will finally be unable to overcome issues of organizational concern.

In the end, *performance problems* occur when individuals or the organization have weak links with their environment. It is not clear what they consider to be adequate performance in their selected action domain. Their learning is impaired because they do not know how to decode signals coming from the environment. Our last com-ment about health systems above suggests that they may also have, intertwined with their response problems, performance problems.

## THE OADI-SMM MODEL REVISITED

Let us now revisit the OADI-SMM model introduced in Chapter 6 from the perspec-tive of the management of complexity and with a methodological concern.

We have argued that organizational learning requires more than the sharing of mental models. Shared models can only be the bridges between multiple, complex, individual models; since organizational learning implies making the organization's action more effective, the problem is to share models as a means of co-ordinating people's actions. Learning, therefore, requires the creation of mechanisms for co-ordinating individuals' actions.

Learning depends on how adequate is the embodiment of these mechanisms. This embodiment is the structure of the organization; that is, its stable relations—consisting of both resources and relationships. Without this structure there are no communication channels to support co-ordinated action. We may expect that the more effective this structure is, the more effective will be the organization's action; that is, the more effective will be its learning.

However, individuals are the ones who learn and it is only through their co-ordination of actions that the organization learns. We see this point as being at the core of the OADI-SMM model discussed in Chapter 6. Our concern is to increase the diagnostic power of this model by clarifying its relation to the organization's structure.

### Revision Of The OADI-SMM Model

In Chapter 6 we explained and gave many examples of obstacles to individual and organizational learning. We now want to relate these obstacles to complexity management.

Our discussion will be supported by Figures 7.4 and 7.5, which illustrate 'incomplete organizational learning cycles' and the individual, interactive and organizational task venues of action.

The complexity of our cognitive venue is defined by our practices (amplifier 1 in Figure 7.5) in particular action domains. These practices emerge from the distinctions we make (attenuator 1) in each domain. We may make distinctions for which we develop no practices. This is the case of *role-constrained learning*, our transformation of distinctions into practices is inhibited for one reason or another, and hence our action is inhibited. While this mismatch may be natural, it becomes a learning problem once a relevant observer—ourselves or our peers—assess our performance in the selected action domain as inadequate. This is a performance problem; our actions $r$ are not producing outcomes $o$ within the target set $T$.

We naturally interact with others in the organization; this is our interactive venue—see Figure 7.5. In general, organizational tasks can only take place through other people. Even our individual tasks often depend on co-operation with others. Our ability to get the best out of these interactions will affect organizational action. For instance, if we do not succeed in getting the explicit or tacit commitment of people to carry out expected organizational actions, i.e., if amplifier 2 is weak, then we have a case of *audience-restricted learning*. This problem is made more acute if people do not express their views clearly as, for example, when they adjust their views in accordance with what they expect we want to hear. (In this case, attenuator 2 is not working.) We then lose touch with organizational action; our learning is restricted by the audience. The problem emerges when we assess that poor performance is due to inadequate organizational actions (an organizational response problem). For instance setting unrealistic targets, where people know the targets are beyond their capabilities, coupled with organizational defences, may trigger this kind of restricted learning; people know that the expected organizational action is beyond the available resources, yet are not prepared to say so. These are characteristic response problems, in which amplification of the organization's response to its environment is inadequate.

From Figure 7.5 it is clear that a good deal of individual learning in organizations requires closing the loop individual–environment through the organization (the organizational task). This, indeed, is also an assumption of the OADI-SMM model. Through our interactions (amplifiers 2) we may get some kind of organizational actions (amplifiers 3) which produce environmental responses which affect our beliefs and models. We recognize these responses through the attenuators 3.

This may be the source of learning problems; to understand the link between organizational action (amplifiers 3) and environmental responses (attenuators 3) represents a challenge for any of us. We are forced to reduce to a simple causal loop the very large complexity of many people and organizations interacting with our organization—to the point where we say 'this individual's actions produce this organizational action which in its turn produces this environmental response'. This is a huge attenuation of complexity, filled with danger.

The problem is not only the difficulty of producing good models of complex and often unpredictable behaviours but the uncertainty of the action domain itself. What is our action domain? Are we clear about the purpose of our action? How do we align this purpose with organizational purposes? In these circumstances *superstitious and ambiguous learning* are highly likely, as an inadequate attenuator 3 makes it

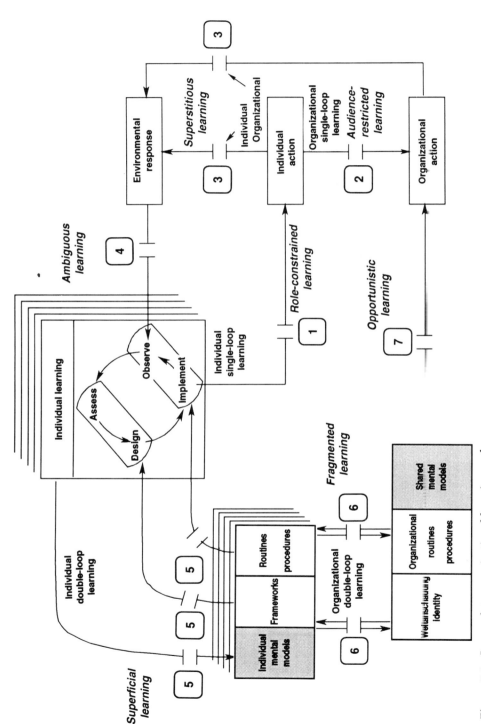

**Figure 7.4** Incomplete organizational learning cycles

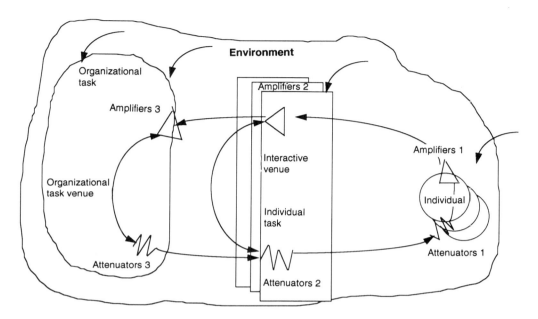

**Figure 7.5**   Individual-organizational task loop

difficult to establish which are relevant disturbances for our purposes. We are failing to make distinctions in the environment. Learning is then incomplete because of environmental problems.

In fact, good causal models, with a good grasp of circular causality, relating multiple variables with an in-depth understanding of relationships, might yield a good understanding of the dynamics of the situation. These models may help us to link several apparently unrelated disturbances, thus reducing their complexity and making the situation more manageable. Archetypal situations of this kind are discussed by Senge (1992). If, on the other hand, we use models that are static or overemphasize the short term, the chances of *superstitious learning* will increase.

Our situational assessment depends on the disturbances we pay attention to. This assessment is in effect a definition of the outcomes set $O$ and the target set $T$. If there is no consistent measurement of outcomes—perhaps because we do not know how to measure these outcomes, perhaps because of delays in the transmission of information, perhaps for some other reason—then we are faced with *ambiguous learning*.

But, to be useful for organizational learning models must be grounded in shared views about the action domain. While such grounding may exist for a wide range of well-established action domains, by definition it will not exist for as yet undefined domains. We must depend upon organizational double-loop learning for that kind of grounding to take place. In other words we have to ground in the organization our new views, frameworks and practices concerning the situation. We confront an identity problem.

We often find ourselves pushed into double-loop learning. This is the case when we recognize threats and opportunities; that is, when we perceive or anticipate outcomes outside the target set $T$. Either we are not performing in our chosen action domains or we are visualizing new possibilities. Whatever the trigger may be, it often compels us to challenge the basic assumptions of our action. It is at this point that we get into double-loop learning; that is, into a questioning of our worldviews as well as of the frameworks and practices supporting our action.

This kind of learning depends to a large degree on individual styles and concerns (see Chapter 4) but it also depends on the organization's structure and culture.

Organizations that create constant operational pressures, starve people of necessary resources to consolidate new learning or do not reward innovative, long-term behaviours do inhibit double-loop learning. Even if we discover new models about the world, in such an organization we may have neither the personal stamina nor the structural support to translate them into new frameworks and practices. This is then a case of *superficial learning*. In Figure 7.5, our attenuators 1 have changed but not our amplifiers 1; we continue to operate within the old frameworks and practices.

It remains true that once we begin to work in an organizational context some kind of organizational double-loop learning has to take place. This is the process by which we share our views of the world, invent new ways of sharing the organizational context of our action and create the structures that make possible this sharing. Our assessment as to whether these structures are adequate or not depends on agreements as to the organization's purpose. Often structures are inadequate because we do not know how to declare legitimate purposes or do not know how to translate them into functional structures. In the first case, we experience the difficulty of aligning our own interests and purposes with varied, unstable and perhaps inconsistent organizational purposes; in the second, we do not know how to use self-organizing and self-regulating forces in their support.

Creating an identity for the organization, and its entailed structure, is part of a learning process facilitated by creating a context for effective conversations. Often we do not know how to create this context for organizational double-loop learning; the result is *fragmented learning*. The viable system model and, as we will see in the next section, the cybernetic methodology provide a framework to overcome this obstacle to learning.

The viable system model reminds us that organizational learning is happening, in one way or another, in all primary activities that possess autonomy—often in spite of the people involved. The recursive nature of the model makes it clear that learning loops exist within particular primary activities and therefore that the most significant organizational context for individual learning may not be the total organization, whatever that may be, but a much smaller primary activity (if we are referring to a large corporation). We will see that the cybernetic methodology makes clear the link between this individual learning loop and the organizational context of learning.

Finally, the viable system model points to one or two changes that need to be made in the OADI-SMM model. The recursive, Russian-doll nature of any viable system indicates that what may be considered to be fragmented learning depends on the level of recursion being considered.

If, for instance, a company forms a new team responsible for a new business and this team develops new frameworks and practices of its own, inconsistent with those of the rest of the organization but is successful in producing the intended result, we may consider this a case of successful—let us call it 'positive'—*opportunistic learning*.

On the other hand, if the team is not an autonomous primary activity but a support (regulatory) team for a larger primary activity, its opportunistic learning may be dysfunctional with the rest and therefore appear as an example of fragmented learning, hindering organizational double-loop learning.

What then, from the perspective of complexity, is the difference between 'negative', i.e., ineffective, opportunistic learning and fragmented learning? They are the same. On the other hand, it becomes clear that *organization-constrained learning* is a learning obstacle in the same way as role-constrained learning is an obstacle to individual learning.

The general point that needs to be understood is that the learning of primary activities at all levels of recursion may be constrained by their structural embedding. For instance, the actions of people constituting a primary activity operating within an over-centralizing larger primary activity may be inhibited as a result of perceiving the centralizing culture of the larger organization.

These considerations lead us to modify the OADI-SMM model as in Figure 7.6. Here:

- we recognize a new learning obstacle—organization-constrained learning;
- we identify 'negative' opportunistic learning with fragmented learning;
- we no longer see 'positive' opportunistic learning as a learning obstacle. Indeed, it is a curious feature of the OADI-SMM model that it should be seen as such. It is as well to get rid of this feature.

# THE CYBERNETIC METHODOLOGY

## Introduction

We now have a model to relate individual and organizational learning. The next stage is to develop a methodology to use it; we will call it the cybernetic methodology (CM). This methodology was developed by one of the authors—Espejo (1993b)—during the 1980s and has been tested for a number of years. For our purposes here it will be adjusted to the language of the OADI-SMM model.

The cybernetic methodology is summarized in Figure 7.7. Here learning is related to the process of problem solving. This process is shown as going through two loops simultaneously dealing with two aspects of problem solving. These are the content of the particular problem situation, that is, the issue of concern, and the structural context in which it arises and through which it is dealt with.

Since our concern is methodological the outer loop of Figure 7.7, called the 'learning loop' shows how one deals with issues of concern, while the inner loop, the 'cybernetic loop', shows how one can and should at the same time deal with its context, i.e., with the concomitant issues of organizational restructuring. We are relating each learning loop to its organizational context.

The different stages in Figure 7.7 provide only a sketch of the cybernetic methodology, to be filled in by our discussion. Our aim is to show how it provides a framework for problem solving in an organizational context. It will also make possible a better appreciation of the interrelationship between individual and organizational learning.

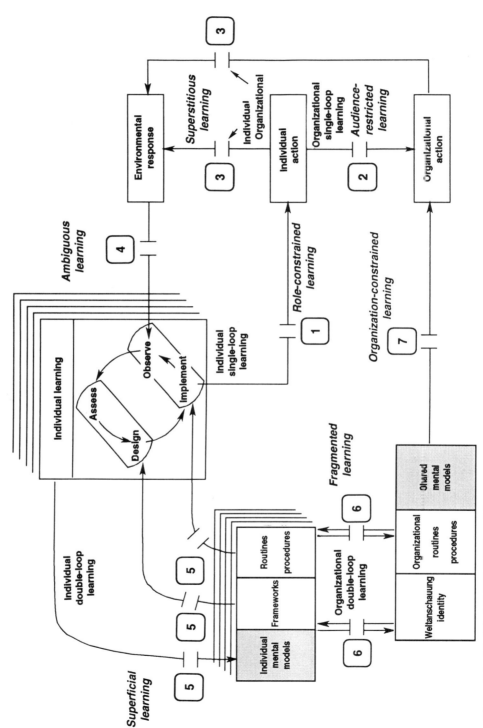

Figure 7.6  Modified OADI-SMM model

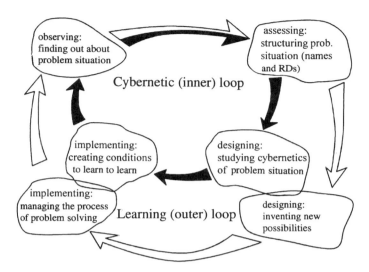

**Figure 7.7** The cybernetic methodology

What, however, does effective problem solving require? Specific conceptual solutions, though necessary in the end, are never sufficient. Organizational problem solving requires also managing transformation processes, based on people's competence for action. Of course both aspects are intertwined. Specific conceptual solutions emerge as participants create, discover and share meanings for their experiences. Producing these solutions is the outcome of appreciative processes (i.e. assessments) and transforming them into actions is 'managing the process of problem solving' (i.e. implementation). They take place in the outer loop of Figure 7.7. As expected, being a learning loop, the outer loop reveals the OADI model.

Meanwhile, the inner loop concentrates on studying and improving the structural context of these learning processes; that is, on diagnosing and overcoming structural weaknesses. Quite naturally problems and related learning difficulties are triggered by inadequate resourcing of organizational interactions and weak relationships. Of course, both aspects, content and structure are totally intertwined. We separate them only to clarify the use of the methodology.

In the following discussion we make the distinction between individual and group learning. Individual learning specifically refers to the experiences we all have in organizations; as we interact with others we experience issues of personal (individual) and organizational concern. The challenge is increasing our capabilities for effective action in these circumstances. The cybernetic methodology offers guidelines for this purpose.

Group learning refers to a formal or informal group of people sharing over time common concerns, or situations, even if they do not know what these concerns are or cannot agree about their meaning. If members of this group belong to the same primary activity then their interactions are producing organizational learning (even if often this learning may turn out to be fragmented learning).

**Individual Single-loop Learning**

All of us are members of many organizations. Inevitably we will need to learn our way in each of them. Some aspects of this learning may relate to personal concerns others to our organizational roles. In what follows we explain how to facilitate individual learning, particularly with reference to significant issues of concern, that is, those issues that are seen as critical success factors. Methodologically conceptual learning (know-why) and operational learning (know-how) depend on knowing what the learning is about, that is knowing the domain of action.

The learning loop of Figure 7.7 helps to clarify the 'what'. This 'what'. as we might expect, is closely intertwined with the 'why' and 'how'. The loop is made up of four activities: finding out about the problem situation (observing), structuring problem situations (assessing), modelling these situations (designing) and managing the problem-solving process (implementing).

*Finding Out About The Problem Situation*

We all have different strategies for experiencing the world. Some of us are more action-oriented and therefore less inclined than others to reflect upon our experiences. However, unless we become effective observers of our environments we will be overwhelmed by its complexity and therefore will be less effective in our action. Also, with reference to our organizational roles, some of us pay more attention to local aspects, others to distant, global aspects. We argued in Chapter 4 that some kind of balance between these two extremes is likely to support a better management of complexity. Of course this assumes we know what is local and what is distant; that is, it assumes a grasp of the organizational context of our action.

To be effective observers, we need practices to create rich pictures of problem situations. Tools like the cognitive mapping of Eden (1989) and the rich pictures of Checkland (1981) help to organize individual complexity and also to create maps of our experiences. Indeed, models of the organizational complexity relevant to our action, such as those presented in earlier chapters, should help us in finding out about the context of the problem situation. Complexity entails all aspects of significance, whether aesthetic, ethical, political, cultural, structural or any other.

*Structuring The Problem Situation*

It is natural for us to structure experiences according to our personal histories and background. History provides the space, or clearing, to make sense of experiences. We all develop a worldview or *Weltanschauung* (W) that gives meaning to these experiences. This structuring is done, most of the time, implicitly; we are unaware of the assumptions and natural blinkers produced by our histories. Of course these blinkers are shared by groups and communities with similar histories and backgrounds. Indeed, over time we develop consensual domains that influence our appreciation of situations. When assessing a situation these are the views of the world that emerge most naturally. Most of the time they serve us well, since they give us a handle to understand our experiences. They represent our accumulated learning.

Methodologically, when we want to capture the meaning of a situation as it is grounded in a community of observers, we may use the idea of 'naming systems' discussed by Espejo (1994). In essence, the idea is to define the process or transformation that we see as reflecting what the situation is. The significant aspect of a system is that it is intended to reflect the situation as it is seen by a relevant community of observers. Sometimes these systems express people's espoused views, not necessarily corroborated by external observers of the situation. At other times they express theories-in-use, as observed by an independent observer. *System names* express in one form or another the complexity seen and recognized by participants in the situation. In Appendix 1 we give more technical details of naming systems.

*Modelling Systems*

To work out this complexity we break down the process into a number of activities, those producing the named transformation. These are descriptive models of the situation as seen by the people concerned. Quite naturally we see the complexity most directly relevant to our roles and personal traits. Therefore there are many possible descriptive models of the same system, let alone of the same situation. Moreover, depending on our organizational roles and our observing strategies we will emphasize some things at the expense of others.

This is a common communication problem. It is often found, for instance, between a marketing manager and a production manager. While the former is more likely to emphasize activities related to customers, the latter is more likely to emphasize those related to optimizing the use of production resources. Equally, if our concern is with people we are more likely to see individual problems than organizational performance problems. This may well be the contrast between the viewpoints of a human resources manager and a finance manager. In any case, comparing descriptive models about the same situation from different viewpoints, or for one viewpoint with best practice, may help us in designing necessary actions.

*Managing The Problem-solving Process*

The outcome of designing necessary actions has to be the production of desirable change. Assuming that there is a fundamental agreement about the nature of the situation, i.e., assuming that the participants share a common culture and therefore name commensurable systems, still we are faced with the problem of getting their commitment to produce the necessary changes.

It is at this stage that we get involved in conversations for action in order to manage the process of problem solving. At this stage we are thrown into action. The more effective we are in overcoming individual single-loop learning obstacles, i.e., role-constrained, audience-restricted, superstitious and ambiguous learning, the more likely it is that we will experience stability in our interactions and a satisfactory performance. As conversations for action produce changes, we experience new situations and therefore our 'observing' is modified. We are in a (single-loop) learning loop.

## Individual Double-loop Learning

However, often the problem is that we cannot assume that other situational participants will share our views or models of the situation, nor that they will make commensurable assessments. In methodological terms, either there are no grounded systems to support learning or if there are, they are not adequate. The former is the case when the people we are interacting with either have very different views about the situation or are not prepared to accept our views. The latter is the case when, even if there is this grounding, the current organizational performance suggests that these views and models are not good enough. In these circumstances the problem is creating a new focus, or new foci, for our views about the situation. At this stage we get involved in conversations for possibilities; we try to remove current constraints with the purpose of discovering new possibilities. We are now in a process of idealized design (Ackoff, 1978). A methodological tool for this purpose is the production of root definitions as advocated by Checkland (1981). We need to create new, insightful views about the situation; these are hypotheses about it. We are now talking about holons—to use a term of Checkland and Sholes (1990)—and not systems. Holons are ideas or distinctions that, as Espejo (1994) points out, are still not grounded in the day-to-day network of commitments. It is this ideal nature or root definitions of holons, that allows them to support conversations for possibilities. In Appendix 2 we offer more technical details of holons and root definitions.

If our strategy is to explore the situation with the support of root definitions the design stage will take the form of producing conceptual models. These are models defined by the logical activities necessary to produce the transformation named by the root definition, with no reference to the activities taking place in the concrete situation. In this sense they are unconstrained by current resources and practices. If as a result of these models we discover new possible actions and their performance improves the situation then we are creating new frameworks and learning new practices. This is a case of individual double-loop learning. In the longer run this individual strategy may work for the individual but not for the organization. Organizational learning requires, as we know, sharing mental models and therefore organizational double-loop learning. We will come back to this type of learning later.

## The Cybernetic Loop And Individual Learning

We now refer to the inner loop of the cybernetic methodology set out in Figure 7.7. Problem situations or breaks are not isolated events; they emerge from networks of communications. The chances are that we will experience more breaks if these networks are inadequate for their intended (implicit and explicit) purpose. Therefore the cybernetic loop is intended both for diagnosing inadequate communications and designing effective ones.

Of course, this is a learning loop as well. However, in this case the learning is about creating effective communication structures. This is a means of learning how to learn. By learning to create effective structures we learn to deal more effectively with everyday organizational instances and situations. This is not different to the experience of learning how to use a dictionary in order to learn the meaning of most words, except that in this case the 'dictionary' is changing all the time; the task of creating effective structures is never-ending. Hence the loop.

Methodologically, we use similar tools to those defined above; that is, naming systems and root definitions. In addition we use the ideas of recursive structures and the viable system model. Each of us is part of several, or many primary activities, i.e., organizations with autonomy. For each of our roles we can define a 'system in focus' or primary activity. This is the systemic context of our learning. We observe our day-to-day experiences in it and develop 'rich pictures'; we assess this context by ascribing a purpose to the primary activity—methodologically we do this by naming a system—and diagnosing the system using the VSM. We design the context by inventing new purposes for the organization with the support, perhaps, of root definitions and recognizing the need for new structures, again using the VSM. Finally, we create the conditions for effective problem solving by implementing desirable and feasible structural changes.

It is easy to appreciate the shortcomings of this change process if it remains an exercise in individual learning. For instance, this may be the case of a general manager who gets new learning skills from a consultant, makes use of them, but fails to share his or her new mental models with others affected by these structural changes. These are likely to experience superstitious learning. However, more often the problem for the general manager will be audience-restricted learning.

The cybernetic loop can also be single- or double-loop. If the design is focused on continuous improvement, i.e. on improving the structures relevant to existing processes, then we are talking about single-loop learning. On the other hand if the design is focused on inventing new processes, i.e. on inventing the organization and creating new structures, then we are talking about double-loop learning.

### Group and Organizational Learning

Our focus is now on group and organizational learning. We are concerned with situations in which groups of people, representing different interests, histories and backgrounds, do the ongoing observing, assessing and designing of situations. Methodologically this is the most interesting case of learning. This is indeed the case of organizational learning.

### The Learning Loop

The simplest case of group learning is when there is commonality of perspectives. If the group members share a common understanding of the situation or are not prepared to question dominant views, then their case is similar to individual single-loop learning. We call this 'single-viewpoint organizational learning'. The group may produce agreed assessments and designs for the situation; their conversations will be conversations for action rather than for possibilities. Methodologically, we proceed as in the case of individual single-loop learning. As long as the group and the related organizational performances are perceived as adequate, the chances are that this loop will not be disrupted. However, as we will discuss below, the cybernetics of the situation may reveal problems ahead.

The most difficult case of group learning is the most common one; this is multiviewpoint organizational learning. This is the case where participants do not share a common history and background and therefore bring to the interaction their own peculiar experiences and interpretations; their own realities. In such cases, each participant is likely to experience a different system in the same situation. Their understanding of what is the case will be different. The weaker is the organizational culture, the more likely it is that people will express different *Weltanschauungen* in their contributions to debates; this may be a symptom of insufficient organizational learning.

According to our discussions in Chapter 4, channels with 'larger capacity' will be necessary for effective communication. However, this is a point relevant to the cybernetic loop. What is relevant to us now is that different group participants will produce different assessments of the situation; therefore they will have to find means to bridge their differences. Root definitions may help in this effort. Rather than trying to clarify the complexity that is seen by each participant—something that is impossible in any event, as noted in Chapter 6 when we discussed the regulatory models dilemma and the shared models dilemma, the problem is to create shared holons among the group. These holons, and their related conceptual models, are the shared mental models necessary to produce organizational double-loop learning. Instances of this kind of holon are a vision—as will be described in Chapter 10—and issues of concern agreed by the group.

Holons provide a platform for the group to design activities. If the group is an *ad hoc* group, meeting only occasionally, the chances are that this design will be of a superficial and general kind. This superficial learning may make it more difficult to manage the process of problem solving, since it may not be clear how to transform these designs into new organizational routines and procedures. Indeed, managing the process of problem solving means managing the interactions among all those affected by the implementation of these designs. This illustrates the difficulties of organizational learning based on *group learning processes*.

### The Cybernetic Loop

The design of the cybernetic loop is of particular interest in the case of group organizational learning. In this case we encounter:

1. the problem of relating the group to an organizational context or primary activity—note that here we are assuming an organizationally based group, and,
2. the problem of effective group interactions.

For a group with an agreed purpose and stable organizational role the former problem is equivalent to the cybernetic loop for individual learning. Studying the cybernetics of the situation requires naming the primary activity in which the group is embedded, studying the communications relating the group to other participants in this primary activity and, also studying the overall quality of the primary activity's structure. For the group to improve this structure implies that it must learn how to learn. It might do this, for instance, by establishing more clearly its required membership, in order to align its functionality with that of the total organization.

Additionally, the group needs to create the conditions for effective problem solving. If implementing the outcomes of their designs implies the contribution of other organizational members, structural mechanisms to get their commitment will be required. Failure to create these conditions is a common cause of failure in implementation, i.e., of organization-constrained learning. The complexity of implementation requires more than *ad hoc*, short term, action programmes; it requires mechanisms to learn how to learn.

If the group is not stable or does not share a common purpose then individuals or subgroups must either accept—tacitly or explicitly—that they will be more concerned with their own learning or they must make an effort to create an identity and appropriate structure for the group. In the latter case the problem will again be to align the group's interests with those of the primary activity, i.e., the organization. If this is not done, people in the organization will experience fragmented and organization-constrained learning.

In either case, whether the group is stable or not, methodologically we have to think in forms of creating effective group dynamics. If, for instance, the group has a large number of participants and a hierarchical structure the chances are that any assessment and design will be dominated by those in positions of power at the expense of the rest. This is bound to produce implementation problems. Structural designs like team syntegrity (Beer, 1994) can help to improve the cybernetics of the group itself and thereby create the conditions for effective problem solving. Equally, the problem of membership is fundamental and must be addressed in order to align group and organizational interests.

Organizational learning takes place when we succeed in sharing mental models and creating organizational routines and procedures. This sharing and creating depends on effective communications; organizations with good cybernetics make these more likely. Groups of one kind or another emerge in all organizations. Whether they are formal or informal is often a matter of culture and individual behaviours. In either case, the above discussions apply and provide the methodological orientation to support problem solving and learning.

## SUMMARY

In this chapter we have developed a framework for the diagnosis of organizational learning problems and for the design of improved learning conditions. The management of complexity, the OADI-SMM model and the cybernetic methodology have helped us in this task. The resulting framework is one that focuses attention on particular action domains. Conceptual learning—why do we do things as we do—and operational learning—how do we do what we do—are related to a particular action domain—what it is that we are learning about. The cybernetic methodology provides the integrating framework.

We contribute to organizational learning by learning as individuals and by constituting effective organizational contexts for our action. These two aspects are interrelated. For instance, people's unwillingness to co-operate or their negative attitudes toward each other may be influenced by the inadequate capacity of the communication channels between them, rather than by incompatible beliefs or their view that there is no ground for working together. Organizational learning is an emergent property of the organization's structure and culture but relies on individual learning.

This chapter has also made a link between organizational learning and the cybernetic methodology.

The cybernetics of an organization affects our shared models. We develop mental models as we constitute our individual realities; each of us is continually constituting something different. Our linking together of our experiences is supported by these mental models. They enable us to relate to each other and co-ordinate our actions.

They are not descriptions of reality. They cannot be, because there is no one reality to map. Instead, mental models help us to relate our experiences; they trigger synergistic behaviour. Mental models are not even common denominators of reality. They are bridges linking our inherently untransferable personal complexity. This point makes clear the relevance both of communications and of models of communications, i.e. models of the organizational structure such as those in Chapter 5. These are models of the networks of communications linking inherently untransferable personal mental models. Individuals have their own models and through communications they trade and share meanings; as they create or discover common *Weltanschauungen* they create the mechanisms to align these personal models. Only simple models are shared with others, in the sense of being the same.

This is a problem of alignment. For instance, sharing a vision does not imply that everyone will do the same; it may imply that everyone recognizes a particular way of linking their strengths to those of others in the organization.

One of the achievements of this chapter is the concept of recursive learning. This sees our problem as the creation of space for the effective constitution of our unique, separate realities; that is the way to get the best out of us. At the same time, the problem of organizational cohesion makes clear the need for a mechanism—specifically, it is the mechanism of monitoring-control—that will produce bridges between these separate realities. This is why we need to share *Weltanschauungen*, or mental models. Doing so helps us to align our local and global efforts.

Individual learning takes place in particular domains of action; the domains in which the individual develops competence. This is a crucial methodological point. Effective action can only be assessed by others once an action domain is explicitly or tacitly declared.

The idea of single-loop learning relates to performance, response and environmental problems; that is to problems for which the 'what' is clear. The problem here is to develop more distinctions and practices within a given framework. Within any framework there is always space for improvement—a fact that provides the underpinning for the total quality movement, or TQM.

The idea of double-loop learning relates more to identity and innovation problems; that is, to problems for which we need to develop new frameworks and change fundamentally existing practices. If we do not know what the problem is then we are dealing with 'soft' problems; that is, problems for which we need to work out the what and how. That happens through appreciative processes. This concept may be seen as underpinning the many forms of business process re-engineering.

Improving individual learning, i.e., making our actions more effective, requires taking into account our conversations, i.e., our interactive venue also and the context of our actions, our task venue. For instance, a good deal of superficial learning takes place because we do not have the time and resources to consolidate new mental models into new practices. Significant new experiences, if they are not supported by structures enabling new practices, are not transformed into individual double-loop learning.

If we accept that the key to the learning loop in the cybernetic methodology is the discovery and articulation of new *Weltanschauungen*, i.e., of new shared mental models—then we could say that the emphasis of the methodology is on overcoming fragmented learning. This is an important insight: *Weltanschauungen* are basic mental models that we need to share in order to co-ordinate our actions. We could say, then, that the cybernetic methodology is focused on the alignment of individual learning with organizational learning.

In this sense the outer, learning loop of the methodology, when focused on the creation of new possibilities, is intended to create and anchor individual mental models in a shared space of action. When the focus is on implementation, the need for a common *Weltanschauung* becomes even more significant. It is within the framework this provides that people have the chance to create autonomous responses.

The loop that runs from individual beliefs to individual action to organizational action to environmental response relates to particular organizational and individual domains. It is in this sense that the distinction between interactive and task venues in Figure 7.5 has proved to be useful. It is important for each of us to work out the meaning of the individual–organizational task loop. It is within that framework that we may discover the shortcomings of our learning processes.

However, this must be seen also as a structural problem. One of the most common obstacles for organizational learning is what we have identified as organization-constrained learning.

## APPENDIX 1: SYSTEMS AND NAMING SYSTEMS

Systems are grounded ideas. They are shared by the people in conversation and reflect the natural meanings they attach to particular situations. For instance the word hospital may bring forth the idea of a place to 'cure people's illnesses'. This is the system 'hospital'. A system name is an explicit statement of this grounded understanding. System names are used to explore the complexity of the situation. The name highlights the transformation seen as taking place in the world by a community of participants. Such a name should answer the following questions:

- Transformation: What inputs are transformed into what outputs?
- Actors: Who carries out the activities entailed by the transformation?
- Suppliers: Who are, or would be, the suppliers of inputs to make possible the transformation? 'Inputs' are products that are not only necessary to perform the transformation, but are also directly negotiated by the actors in the system.
- Customers: Who are, or would be, the immediate customers for the outputs of this transformation?
- Owners: Who have or would have an overview of the transformation?
- Interveners: Who define or would define the context for the transformation? Interveners are people who affect the scope of the transformations because they allocate resources for them, are competitors or are concerned by some of the secondary effects of inputs or outputs, e.g., its ecological effects. Since the number of interveners can be large, only the most significant ones need be recognized.

In naming the system one describes not only the transformation that is involved, but also the participants as construed by a particular viewpoint. The mnemonic TASCOI is used here to check that all participants have been identified.

System names can be names of organizational units, companies, activities, tasks or any perceived closed network of people in interaction—provided it has an identity. The actors and owners implied by such system names do not necessarily correspond to the formal members of an existing institution. For this reason, it is important to give clear descriptions of each participant and their role in the system.

The main function of TASCOI is to help in managing the complexity of the task; it is a manager's tool. The full mnemonic should be used to define a system for managing conversations about a particular problem.

# APPENDIX 2: HOLONS AND ROOT DEFINITIONS

A holon is an ungrounded idea; that is, an idea that is not shared by the relevant group in conversation. We use a root definition, as advocated by Checkland (1981), to express a holon. Root definitions are intended to offer insightful views about a situation with no reference to its actuality. They offer hypotheses in order to open up discussions about possibilities relevant to the current situation.

The most significant function of a root definition is to define an insightful purpose for the situation. In an example discussed before, in Chapter 4, it is one thing to construe the work of a group of people in a quarry as 'cutting stones'; it is another thing to see them as 'building a cathedral'.

A well-formed root definition should shed light on:

C: the system's customers, i.e., the beneficiaries or victims of the system's output;
A: the actors responsible for the transformation carried out;
T: the transformation of specified inputs into specified outputs that characterizes the system's behaviour;
W: the *Weltanschauung* or worldview that underlies this definition of the system;
O: the system's owners, i.e., those who enable the transformation to continue;
E: the environmental constraints under which the system operates.

The mnemonic CATWOE may be used to recall the components of this definition. Holons are not intended to represent the grounded views of any participant, merely to offer an insightful view about the situation. It is because of this characteristic that the problem solver, in producing the root definition, has to make the 'W' explicit; in this case we are not given a participant whose grounded views provides the meaning to the name. The 'W' should make clear the tacit assumptions about the situation that are made by the problem solver in order to create a new possibility.

It is evident that root definitions have to avoid foreclosing options. They have to create new appreciations of the problem situation. If, for example, the problem situation is charging for parking space in a city centre, it might be construed as a 'system for keeping cars out of the city centre' or a 'system for resolving conflicts on land use in the city centre' rather than the more obvious but less percipient: 'system to charge for car parking in the city centre'. Often it is the unexpected, less obvious transformations that are of interest to the problem solver.

An obvious problem may hide others that are more subtle and relevant. On the other hand, a transformation perceived as non-problematic may conceal unexpressed aspects related to the participants' undeclared purposes and values. Thus the need to discuss the 'W'.

# Part Three

# Recursive Management

# Summary of Part Three

## FROM SYSTEMIC CONCEPTS TO EFFECTIVE ACTION

The mission of Part Three is to apply the concepts of complexity, structural recursion and organizational learning, introduced in Part Two, to the design of management processes.

It is here that we will make clear the meaning of systemic management as it is understood in management cybernetics. This is what does—or should—underlie the revolution currently taking place in the theory and practice of management. To show this, we will draw upon recent work in strategic management, comparing and contrasting it with what we have to say.

How does Part Three relate to the material in Part Two?

In Part Two, the structural conditions that must be met for people to be able to contribute to the best of their abilities to the organization's performance were laid out. Now we must ask: *What are the structural and behavioural conditions most likely to support organizational fitness?*

For this purpose a corporation must be able to control and transform itself; that is why in the preceding chapters we have assigned priority to self-control, self-organization, and self-transformation. The question is not 'How do we control organizations?', but 'How can we design organizations that achieve viability and development?' or: 'How can an organization attain integral fitness?'

Managers of one company defined its corporate fitness in terms of being 'fast, lean, and strong' (in the original German, as 'Schnell-Schlank-Stark'). But what, if it continues 'bad' and 'dumb', at the same time? A systemic concept of organizational fitness must embrace standards of 'intelligence' and 'ethos'.

A theme already introduced in Part One will become important. There, we mentioned that the 'managerial steering cycle' is not oriented toward only one type of objectives, such as profits. In order to be comprehensively 'fit', an organization must pursue objectives at different logical levels.

In Part Three as a whole, the frameworks and tools provided in Part Two will be developed and applied to the issues of managerial concern discussed and illustrated in Part One; in this way we hope to offer insights into how to achieve 'integral fitness'.

We will emphasize three issues that are crucial for organizational effectiveness:

- the mastering of complexity

- recursive structures and processes
- organizational learning

In doing so we will cite the postulates for effective management developed in Part One as they become appropriate.

### Organization of Part Three

Part Three has three chapters.

In Chapter 8, we shall lay out a comprehensive set of steering criteria for 'organizational fitness'. This is grounded in a systemic model of management developed by Schwaninger (1993; 1989). These 'strategy' criteria will then be linked to the structural criteria developed in Part Two and elsewhere—particularly in Bleicher (1992) and Espejo (1993c). Together, strategy and structure provide a powerful framework for information management; this topic is introduced by the end of the chapter. The overall emphasis is on providing the prerequisites to enable managers to cope with complexity effectively; this is what we call 'recursive management'.

Based on this outline, Chapters 9 and 10 will discuss the design of management processes at the normative, strategic and operative levels and at different structural levels. This discussion will be oriented toward application.

Chapter 9 covers the management of primary processes; that is, of the processes that produce the products and services defined by the organization's policies and strategies. The emphasis is on implementation; this is the operational domain of 'process management', the fulcrum where visions are realized—efficiently or inefficiently. A crucial aspect will be the recursive nature of normative and strategic management. Why do we need recursion levels and how do we establish them? We should not decide how many levels we need on the basis that there happens to be a general craze for 'lean management'; levels should be there if complexity management requires them and they generate added value. The touchstone for achieving high performance in the operational domain is excellence in the modelling, layout and management of primary processes, helped by powerful enabling technologies. It is in this sense that Chapter 9 offers a framework for information management.

Chapter 10 will focus on a higher structural level within the organization—the level of the meta-management of primary activities. Thus it is focused on the company as a whole; that is, on the first level of recursion. This chapter should help to clarify the distinction between the management of an organization's primary processes and the management of the businesses that are embedded in the organization, i.e., of the organization's primary *activities*.

The chapter is written from the viewpoint of a manager concerned with the improvement of a medium or large sized corporation's management processes, making significant use of the knowledge and experience available from management consultancies while keeping in mind structural and organizational learning considerations.

# Chapter 8

# Enabling Systemic Management

Managers are facing new problems in their quest for organizational fitness. As environments become more complex, foresight, adaptability and learning become critical features for a social system to survive and develop. Established models of organizational control are insufficient to cope with this proliferating complexity.

## ON STRATEGIC MANAGEMENT

### The Limitations Of Traditional Approaches To Organizational Effectiveness

'What is it that makes an organization efficient?' 'What is the grounding of organizational effectiveness?' These are recurrent questions that preoccupy managers and management research. Various answers have been given, depending on the underlying models adopted. Some have been controversial or of dubious value.

Chiefly, the role of efficiency has been overestimated, leading to a neglect of higher-order levels of fitness. To put it more precisely: short-term thinking has frequently driven out a long-term orientation. Despite the growing body of literature on corporate strategy, a team of leading researchers from the Massachusetts Institute of Technology observed that American industry was 'handicapped by shrinking time horizons and a growing preoccupation with short-term profits' (Berger *et al.*, 1989, p. 25).

These authors ask why US firms are 'less willing than their rivals to live through a period of heavy investment and meagre returns in order to build expertise'; we are reminded of John Ruskin's lament, put forward more than a hundred years ago: 'We pour our whole masculine energy into the false business of money-making' (Ruskin, 1865, p. 88).

This is not to deny the importance of profits as such. In the long run, no business can survive without being profitable. Profits are a prerequisite to the maintenance of investment and the substance of a company. In Peter Drucker's cutting words, profits are 'the costs of staying in business' (Drucker, 1980, pp. 28f.)

If profit is a necessary precondition for survival, profit-mindedness is not sufficient to guarantee the viability of a company. On the contrary, as discussed in

Schwaninger (1990a), the frequently-quoted goal of 'profit maximization' may turn out, in the long run, to be an obstacle to rather than an orientator for superior performance. In a context of rapid change, the levels of profits or even of stock prices are inadequate orientators of organizational effectiveness.

We may resort to an analogy: assessing the effectiveness of a business by the level of its profits is like measuring the temperature to decide what season one is in; for this purpose the calendar, not the thermometer, is the appropriate source of information. As with temperature in relation to climate, profit is an inherently short-term orientator in the world of business. Long-term patterns are driven by different causal factors and relationships—as is evident in the newer approaches to the evaluation of companies, based on assessing, as in Rappaport (1986), how different strategies impinge on cash flow as a basis for calculating net present value. To deal adequately with these factors, a different logic and language are necessary.

Let us be clear on this matter. Profitability is far from worthless as an indicator for management. Since Fra Luca Pacioli introduced double-entry bookkeeping in 1494, most firms have made use of this valuable instrument; they continue to use it, in a more or less unchanged way, to keep track of revenues, costs and resulting profits.

Despite its usefulness, it is likely to mislead managers if they draw from it lessons which it cannot deliver. The profit-and-loss statement is an appropriate model of the economic state of a business at the operational level. However, signals drawn from it to orientate strategy may point in precisely the wrong direction. In the light of such recent insights from planning theory as Gälweiler (1990) and Drucker (1980), it is wrong to consider profits as a strategic goal—despite what is implied by much of the literature on strategy. Schwaninger (1984) explains this in more detail.

Yet many companies are still 'steered' mainly on the basis of traditional accounting figures—in part because of legal requirements that forbid the incorporation of uncertain future incomes into the balance sheet.

In times of economic stability and periods of continuous growth, the shortcomings of these approaches to control do not 'come to the surface'. But in a context of instability and dynamic transformation, corporations mainly managed from the perspective of 'profit-mindedness' easily become victims of their own myopia. This is demonstrated by a growing failure rate of companies in industrialized countries as a consequence of increasing turbulence in the world's economy during the past decades.

As the difficulty of ensuring organizational viability has grown, traditional concepts of control have increasingly become obsolete.

There is no doubt that management scientists have made substantial efforts to treat organizational effectiveness in a broader perspective. The abundant literature on this subject has produced interesting propositions. Judgments on the 'state-of-the-art' by Cameron and Whetten (1983, p. 1), Goodman and Pennings (1977, pp. 2f), Miles (1980, pp. 353f.) and Zammuto (1982, pp. 21f) have found it to be incoherent and unsatisfactory. Conceptual and theoretical research has, therefore, on the one hand largely directed its interest to specific aspects of organizational performance; for example, the various contributions to the 1995 Academy of Management Review discuss raising productivity, ecological performance, social and ethical performance, etc. On the other hand, empirical studies have generated interesting insights about the interdependencies between strategy, structure and performance—in Hagedorn and Schakenrad (1994) and Markides (1995)—and between culture and organizational effectiveness, particularly in Kotter and Heskett (1992).

Summing up, a new understanding rooted in a more comprehensive view of organizational fitness is needed, one that will integrate the many perspectives of organizational theory; this is pointed out in Cameron and Whetten (1983, pp. 274f).

Two areas of scientific progress appear to be of particular relevance in meeting this requirement: management cybernetics and planning theory. Our aim in this chapter is to offer some insights about an evolving approach to organizational fitness which has emerged from a synthesis of concepts drawn from these two areas.

## Steering Criteria For Organizational Fitness

Effective self-control implies a dynamic equilibrium, at a satisfactory level of performance, between a corporation or organizational unit and the milieu in which it operates. But which variables define adequate performance?

This is not only a problem of control, it is a fundamental epistemological question: a matter of what we can know and how we can use our knowledge.

Traditional control models took their bearings largely or exclusively from the goal of 'profit'. It has been demonstrated that such models no longer meet today's requirements. Under the 'evolutionary pressure' of increasing complexity and turbulence, important progress has been made with regard to the criteria of competent management.

The essence of this progress is based on the insight that a system must govern itself with the help of control variables that may contradict each other because they belong to different logical levels: the levels of operational, strategic, and normative management defined in Schwaninger (1989). As shown in Figure 8.1, there are interrelationships between these levels; specifically, the control variables of the higher logical levels exert a pre-control influence on those of the lower levels.

We will discuss the three levels of management one by one.

## Operational Level

The control variables essential to the operational level are *solvency* and *profit*.

We have been aware since Pacioli's introduction of double-entry bookkeeping that these are two distinct objects of thought and action. (It is interesting to note that until then, this was not known.)

For centuries, bookkeeping has been a mature tool, capable of furnishing proper models of the operative reality of a firm. The interrelationships of the variables which form part of a profit-and-loss statement—revenue, costs and profits—are straightforward and part of the common body of knowledge of administrators; the Dupont scheme of indices dates back more than 70 years and is basically still in use. The same applies to the basics of cash management: if income and expenditures are not in balance during a given period, the shortcomings must be compensated by surpluses from earlier periods or by credits.

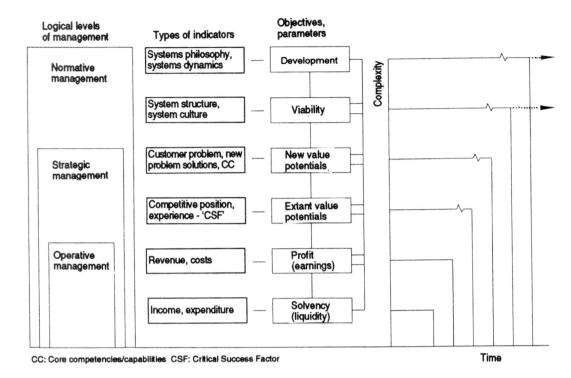

**Figure 8.1** Objectives and control variables at different logical levels of management (Schwaninger 1990a)

Profit has a pre-control function in relation to solvency. By this we mean that if over a longer period profits do not appear, it becomes increasingly difficult to close the liquidity gap and the probability of bankruptcy grows.

These mechanisms have not changed, even though technology has made available more sophisticated tools to get to grips with the dangers inherent in the profit-liquidity link, as well as to optimize management of cash and for profit. Among such tools we include all the systems usually subsumed under the term 'operations management'; these are systems, whether human, material or financial, that have evolved to optimize the planning and use of resources. An example is the MRP (manufacturing resource planning) system described by Wight (1984).

The traditional models for allocation of resources were almost exclusively orientated toward profit and liquidity. But profit behaves in an inherently short-term mode, and its level is largely predetermined by parameters of another nature.

Good managers have always known that the attainment of operative goals requires preconditions that have to be created in advance. Practitioners and writers in many domains of management have become increasingly aware of this. Attempts have been made to link operative and strategic logic, e.g., in production (Underwood, 1994), logistics (Bowersox *et al.*, 1992), and marketing (Kotler, 1994). Based partly on these attempts, we will present a comprehensive theory that incorporates the relevant higher-order criteria.

## Strategic Level

Just as profit largely determines solvency, 'value potentials' pre-control profit.

What are value potentials? According to Gälweiler (1990), they are defined as the set of all applicable business-specific, prerequisites, that must be realized when profits are to be achieved.

Value potentials are more than just a new word; they represent operational and calculable categories. Their patterns of behaviour can be foreseen and influenced, i.e., 'controlled'.

They must, however, be controlled separately from profit and solvency, on the basis of independent criteria.

Recent work in strategic management has clarified the nature of these criteria and shown, for instance, how to apprehend the critical success factors—such as market share, relative market share, quality or customer benefit, cost, price, speed or flexibility—in a given business system. The approach that consists of identifying 'laws of the marketplace', pursued by SPI-Strategic Planning Institute and PIMS Associates, has led to substantial insights as to the factors which influence profitability and cash flow in the medium to long term, and to what extent.

The PIMS methodology rests on a large database, which incorporates data from more than 3000 strategic business units (SBUs), representing businesses of all kinds. This number includes only SBUs that are represented with full data sets ranging over at least four years. Counting also limited and shorter-range data sets, the PIMS database is much larger. The box gives an overview of the most important general insights into business strategy to which the PIMS research has led.

---

### General Insights Into The Behaviour Of SBUs

1. The behaviour of a 'business' (represented by one of the SBUs sampled) is characterized by regularities and is therefore largely foreseeable.
2. Certain laws of the marketplace hold for all kinds of business. They express themselves in key success factors, which are of essential strategical importance.
3. These key success factors account for about 70% of the variance in the return on investment (ROI) in the medium term.
4. The interrelationships of these factors are complex. They can reinforce or weaken one another. Their interplay is hard to assess on an intuitive basis.
5. In this connection, the differences between products are of subordinate relevance. Their characteristics account for only part of one of the factors.
6. The effects to be expected due to these regularities ensue over the longer term.
7. Sustained business success can only be expected, if the 'fundamentals' are in balance. These can be assessed quantitatively.
8. Most of the strategic factors are robust. Variations in the data are only problematic under certain conditions.

After Malik (1987, p. 60)

The box below lists and reviews eight key factors which were identified with the help of multivariate analysis—for details of which, see Buzzell and Gale (1987).

---

**Eight Key Strategic Factors, In Order Of Their Impact On Sustained Profitability**

1. *Investment intensity*
Definition: Investment per dollar of value added
Impact: High investment intensity is always negative for ROI

2. *Productivity*
Definition: Value added per employee
Impact: High productivity is always positive; it is indispensable in case of high investment intensity

3. *Relative market share*
Definition: Own market share as a proportion of sum of market shares of three largest competitors
Impact: High relative market share is always favourable. It is particularly important in case of:
- high marketing intensity
- high R&D intensity
- weak trade cycle

4. *Growth rate of market served*
Impact: High growth rate is
- positive for absolute profit
- neutral for relative profit
- negative for all cash flows

5. *Relative quality*
Definition: Share of sales from products with superior quality minus share of sales from products with inferior quality
Impact:   Positive for all financial variables
          Indispensable if market share is low

6. *Rate of innovation*
Definition: Share of sales from products that are not older than three years
Impact:   Favourable up to a certain level of share of sales, though as a rule only when market share is high. Innovation above a certain level of share of sales is negative for ROI

7. *Vertical integration*
Definition: Value added per dollar of sales
Impact:   Positive only in mature, stable markets; negative in fast growing or in shrinking markets

8. *Customer profile*
Definition: Number of direct customers that account for 50% of sales volume
Impact: A relatively small number of customers (depending on characteristics of the industry) is favourable

Source: Buzzell and Gale (1987); Malik (1987).

---

This research gives us valuable clues as to the management of new value potentials. It has to include making changes in established patterns, taking into account the dynamics of customer problems, solutions to those problems, technological substitution and the value chain.

This involves innovation. Often it requires a redesign of the business system; that is, of its processes and related structures. Hamel and Prahalad (1994) have emphasized that too often strategic efforts rest on established modes, whereas the essence of genuine innovation is rethinking the system completely—as noted in Part One. Often this leads to the emergence of new modes of doing business, creates new opportunities and even reshapes entire industries.

A general heuristic for reframing and redesigning a business system is given in Figure 8.2. This depicts the invariant structure of any business system, (to our knowledge the term 'business system' was coined by McKinsey Associates, see Buaron (1981)) based on the following dimensions which in principle define any such system: products or services, technologies, distribution channels, customer groups and customer problems, i.e. user problems and user needs.

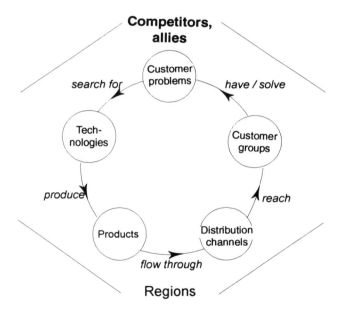

**Figure 8.2**   Invariant structure of business systems (Schwaninger 1994b)

All five of these elements have to be configured or reconfigured in such a way that suppliers and other partners are included in the process. Competitors have to be considered carefully; they may even become new partners. In many cases, regional differentiation is important.

Often, substantial customer benefit and sustained competitive advantage—or even better, uniqueness—can only be created if the whole business system is renewed. At this point, not only the elements but more so the relationships between these elements are questioned and reinvented. In principle, such interrelationships can be distinguished between any of the elements listed, not only along the arrows of the simplified graph.

Substantial innovations are usually based on changes in more than one component, sometimes also on an elimination or addition of certain components. What we have said so far relates to strategy at the level of the business unit. What of the corporate level?

At this level, strategic methodologies have made progress in recent years. In particular, the need to distinguish between success factors relevant at the level of subsystems, e.g. the SBU, and overarching core competencies or capabilities has been emphasized by Pümpin (1989), Prahalad and Hamel (1990) and Stalk, Evans and Shulman (1992); core competencies have to be managed at the next higher, e.g., the corporate, level. This is an aspect that we will explore in this chapter and return to from a more managerial perspective in Chapter 10.

For strategic business units a mature methodology has become available. This methodology has made more transparent and controllable the essential variables of the strategic level—as, a long time ago, bookkeeping did for the operational domain. Gälweiler (1990) for the most part, but also Porter (1980; 1985), Schwaninger (1989) and several other authors have elaborated on this new methodological concept. The support for strategy at the corporate level has grown into a relatively mature methodology as well—as discussed by Pümpin (1991), Hamel and Prahalad (1994) and Kleindorfer and Schoemaker (1993), although the heuristic devices available inevitably remain more general and abstract.

The main ideas of core competency- or capabilities-based strategy (we use 'core capabilities' and 'core competencies' as synonyms, refraining from the distinctions between the two terms, occasionally made in the literature, e.g., by Stalk, Evans and Shulman (1992)) can be summarized as follows:

1. The building blocks of corporate strategy are not primarily products and markets, but core processes.
2. Competitive effectiveness is, in the long run, based on transforming core processes into core capabilities. Over time, these capabilities can materialize at the 'fronts' of different and often unexpected business units—giving rise to 'strategic surprise'.
3. Strong capabilities are often based on a sophisticated combination of 'soft' factors, i.e., intangible, human ones, and 'hard' factors such as powerful information systems.
4. Creating and fostering these competencies or capabilities requires substantial and sustained investments which, in a sense, 'break up' the established boundaries of traditional functions or SBUs, establishing unorthodox links.
5. As managing overarching core capabilities transcends the customary discretion of organizational units (in the language of Part Two: of the primary activities of an organization), building them up requires powerful promoters, i.e. the CEO or, better, the whole board of an organization.

But, after all, how do we define a 'core capability' or 'core competency'? There are at least six distinctive features by which it can be recognized as in Schoemaker (1992):

1. It has evolved slowly through collective learning and information sharing.
2. Its development cannot be greatly speeded up, even by doubling investments.

3. It cannot be easily imitated by or transferred (sold) to other firms.
4. In the eyes of the customers it confers a competitive advantage.
5. It complements other capabilities in a synergetic fashion ('2 + 2 = 5').
6. Investment in it is largely irreversible, i.e. the firm cannot cash it out.

The assertion that the management of core competencies is the essence of strategy at the corporate level is backed by innovation-oriented studies: Utterback (1994) has emphasized the challenge of 'mastering the dynamics of innovation'. On the grounds of long-term empirical evidence and solid conceptual reflection he confirms that organizations must consistently embrace innovation, even when this appears to undermine traditional strengths. He pleads for continually renewing core capabilities, while abandoning the logic of past successes: innovating incrementally is not enough because, in the long run, the regeneration of a corporation's business relies on radical innovation.

According to Hamel and Prahalad (1994, p. 23), a 'strategic architecture' is needed 'that is less concerned with ensuring a tight fit between goals and resources and . . . more . . . with creating *stretch goals* that challenge employees to accomplish the seemingly impossible'. In our language, the requirements of building up new core competencies to ensure new value potentials may contradict those of extant value potentials, but in the long run, they must have priority if viability is to be sustained.

In summary: profit is not a strategic control variable, and consequently not a strategic aim. Rather, its appearance or absence is a consequence of good or bad strategies.

This divergence from the traditional view, which regards profit, or other monetary values related to profit, as the fundamental corporate objective has also been expressed to a certain extent in more recent attempts to integrate finance theory with strategic considerations. The methodologies developed for assessing shareholder value of companies calculate the net present value; this is derived by Rappaport (1986) and Copeland, Koller and Murrin (1994) from discounted future free cash flows—the cash sums that a corporation can potentially generate at various points in time—as a function of various possible strategies. The crux in these assessments is not, as it may seem, the calculus, which relies on sophisticated accounting techniques; it is a proper knowledge of the variables that pre-control profits and their interrelationships.

### Normative Level

Insights into the reference variables of normative management have also improved. The research which has led to this is primarily based on systems theory and cybernetics and once more presents independent criteria for the assessment of the viability and development of organizations.

Viability, understood by Beer (1979, p. 113) as the ability to maintain a separate existence, i.e., a distinct configuration by which a system can be identified, can be assessed on the grounds of structural considerations that are not bound by the orientators of the strategic and operational levels. In our view, the most advanced theory for assessing the viability of an organization in structural terms is Beer's viable system model (VSM), outlined in Chapter 5.

The principle underlying the VSM is that organizations need to learn how to manage complexity. The VSM itself provides criteria for this management as follows:

- Functions of and relationships between the organizational parts are defined precisely.
- Deficiencies in this structure are diagnosed; that is, it is shown how poor interplay of the parts, missing elements or insufficient capacity of certain parts diminishes or jeopardizes the viability of the organization.
- The structure outlined is recursive, i.e., it applies to organizational units at any level.
- The autonomy of subsystems and the cohesion of the whole are simultaneously maintained.

This model is an excellent device for diagnosing and maintaining the degree of viability of an organization, independent of the steering criteria of the lower levels—strategic and operative. What else is available for the normative level?

As far as the 'soft factors' of organization are concerned—factors referred to under the common denominator of 'culture'—Deal and Kennedy (1982) and Schein (1985) have elaborated models that appear, for the time being, more appropriate for description and diagnosis than for design purposes. Beyond that, the emerging paradigm of the 'learning organization', initiated by Argyris and Schön (1978) and further developed by Senge (1992), has the aim of outlining a developmental and transformative orientation to structure as well as to culture. This book—in particular Chapters 6 and 7—itself makes a contribution in this field. Undoubtedly, however, it is the overall capacity to disentangle complexity conferred by the VSM that most helps the user to recognize stakeholders and differing structural levels and thereby to manage more effectively the issues of values, preferences and interests.

From a systemic point of view, however, we need to adopt a still more advanced position. An organization must and should aim at *viability beyond survival*.

What does this entail? Systems thinkers have increasingly become interested in designing evolving structures in which an organization's identity may completely change, rather than in sticking to viability in the narrow sense; this, after all, has often led to the self-maintenance or self-production of systems which show a dysfunctional behaviour vis-à-vis the total organization. This effect is sometimes referred to, e.g., by Beer (1979), as 'pathological autopoiesis'; that is, the self-maintenance or self-production of a system despite a negative balance of its effects on the larger whole.

Progressive managers are increasingly adopting a systemic viewpoint in which they enlarge their reference system, eliminating narrow boundaries: this is corroborated by the growing rate of economic, juridical and structural transformations of companies with the aim of creating new, viable organizational entities. 'Development' in the sense used by Russell Ackoff is a good term for such viability beyond survival.

At the level of development—defined by Ackoff (1994, p. 65) as a system's growing ability and desire to fulfil its own and others' needs—the quest of an organization is in fact viability beyond survival. At this level, indicators become even more hazy. Yet social system theories can provide important insights into how to diagnose a system's propensity for development as a function of such properties or philosophical principles as openness and instability, or by taking into account the pattern of a system's trajectories or dynamics. Criteria such as catalytic reinforcement, consensus, self-governance and learning can help one to judge whether a change process qualifies as 'development' or not; see the discussions by Etzioni (1968) and Jantsch and Waddington (1976).

In sum, the field of indicators at the normative level is multifaceted; social, political, cultural and ecological aspects have to be taken into consideration, giving adequate space to ethical and aesthetic concerns for the pursuit of ideals such as beauty, truth, good and plenty; see Ackoff (1981). Multiple constituents and viewpoints ascribe different purposes to a social system, which leads to an emphasis on different criteria of fitness. For a corporation to be viable in the long run, the legitimate claims of these different stakeholders must be met adequately. Clarkson (1995, p. 112) describes it as follows:

> The economic and social purpose of the corporation is to create and distribute increased wealth and value to all its primary stakeholder groups, without favouring one group at the expense of others. Wealth and value are not defined adequately only in terms of increased share price, dividends, or profits. Managers can no longer be held responsible for maximizing returns to shareholders at the expense of other primary stakeholder groups.

The normative base of this theory is ethical. Yet, as Donaldson and Preston (1995) have shown, it is even supported by the theory of property rights.

The concept of 'control' which applies at the level of normative management is in a certain sense incompatible with the understanding derived from traditional sciences. Instability is no longer a feature to be eliminated completely; in a sense and to a certain extent it is a necessary and valuable precondition for development—as pointed out by Prigogine (1989). Control—meaning self-control—must nevertheless maintain it within acceptable levels and frequencies.

The coming turbulent decades will increasingly demand 'control by development', 'control by learning' or 'control by transformation'; and each of these kinds of control will have to be essentially self-control. Effectiveness will, more than in past decades, consist in the ability of organizations to learn to develop—and to learn this not just at the lowest level but at the higher levels, such as 'learning to learn' and 'double-loop-learning', discussed in Chapter 6. Thereby they will reorientate and transform themselves.

Some publications, e.g., by Ramanujan et al. (1986) indicate that serious research efforts are under way to operationalize the 'soft' organizational variables and their interrelationships with 'hard' performance figures, although there is still a long way to go. The following two examples will be of interest in this context. First, the comprehensive empirical studies of more than 3000 business units comprising the PIMS database, described in Buzzell and Gale (1987), indicate, as mentioned earlier, that strategic variables account for 70% of the variance in ROI (return on investment); only 30% is explained by variables representing operational decisions and tactical skills. Secondly, a study by Hansen and Wernerfelt (1989) of a smaller sample of Fortune 1000 firms leads to the conclusion that the impact of organizational factors on profit rates is twice as high as that of economic factors.

# THE CHALLENGE OF SYSTEMIC MANAGEMENT

We have learned much from a survey of the control variables and their pertinent criteria. It must be noted that they cannot be compared in every respect, since they belong to three different logical levels; ultimate consistency can be achieved within, but not between these levels. In logical systemic terms, this is to say that the strategic level uses a metalanguage relative to the operative, as does the normative level relative to the strategic and the operative levels. The variables regulated at one level are the pre-control parameters for the next level down.

Figure 8.1 illustrates that operational, strategic and normative management are by no means three subsystems detached from each other; rather, each higher level envelops those below it.

A rigid view of this embedment would, however, be too static. While a normative framework expresses a certain identity, this identity encapsulates a huge set of possible strategies. Moreover, at a certain stage strategy-making may find new ways of relating to the environment that reach out beyond the borders of the identity defined by the current normative framework.

In many companies, such attempts at redefinition are out of the question, *a priori*. This is a trait that sooner or later turns out to be pathological. The distinctive features of an identity and its normative implications must be reviewed over time. Most industries are subject to fundamental change; boundaries between industries collapse, so that organizational intelligence demands that the company be reinvented, in the process forgetting, i.e., 'unlearning' outdated recipes for success and building new competencies. Constant creative tension between normative management and strategy-making are thus necessary for a company to evolve. The pertinent connection is not an algorithmic one, but one that must express itself in a strenuous process of organizational discourse. In a study which we shall revert to later, Collins and Porras (1995) have given an empirical account of this 'dynamic interplay between core ideology and the drive for progress' (p. 85).

Figure 8.1 further demonstrates that the relevant time horizon increases as we move from operational to normative management. At the same time, the factual horizon is also extended, as is the complexity which is managed. The dotted arrows indicate that certain principles relevant to normative management, e.g. ethical and aesthetic ones, are largely timeless.

The diagram also shows that the concerns of the higher levels are not detached from those of the lower ones. A company can only survive if it is in possession of value potentials that are actualized; that is, converted into profits. An equilibrium between the sacrifices incurred in building up value potentials and reaping their fruits is a further necessary precondition of viability that normative management must ensure.

At the three levels of management, different criteria of organizational fitness—or, to speak more generally, of systemic effectiveness—apply, as shown by Figure 8.3:

1. at the operational level, the criterion is that of economic efficiency, mainly in terms of profitability;
2. at the strategic level, it is effectiveness in both the competitive and the co-operative sense;

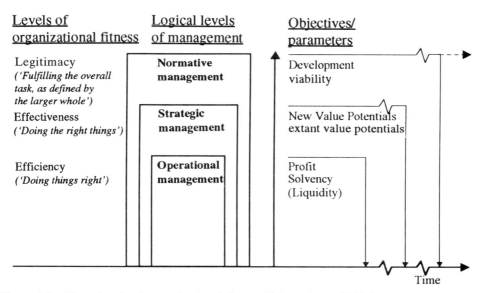

**Figure 8.3**   Three levels of organizational fitness (Schwaninger 1994a)

3. at the normative level it is legitimacy, defined as the potential to fulfil the claims
   of all relevant stakeholders.

The key duty of an integral or systemic management is to meet all three requirements
in the long run. In other words, the challenge consists in assuring that the corporation is
*successful* in operational terms, *intelligent*—that is to say, on course—in strategic terms
and a *valuable* contributor to the larger whole in terms of normative management.

In order to achieve such a delicate task a corporation will require—as has been
illustrated in detail in Schwaninger (1993)—considerably more highly developed
mental models and more complex control systems than the simple feedback systems
traditionally used.

The hierarchy of control variables delineated here results in a *multilevel* control
structure, as shown in Figure 8.1; Schwaninger (1993) represents the same thing in
terms of feedback, feedforward and pre-control loops. Our figure makes it clear that
one and the same state of affairs cannot be pre-controlled by means of the variable
by which it is controlled. If, at the operative level, control is exercised in the interests
of profit—by means of the relevant control variables, revenue and costs—then profit
cannot be pre-controlled by means of these traditional accounting variables. For pre-
control other variables are required. These are the extant and newly developed value
potentials, which in turn are pre-controlled by viability and development. It has
been argued by Jackson (1989, p. 428) that the use of 'control models' such as the
VSM prevents organizational learning, leading to 'increasing dominance of history'
as in de Zeeuw (1986, p. 139). A concept of control that embraces development as a
goal defies this argument in principle, although it cannot guarantee that there will be
learning in every organization that uses the concept.

That is why we assert so strongly that profit is not a strategic goal. A closure of the
hierarchy of control variables is provided insofar as final liquidity outcomes at the

operational level not only result from higher level pre-controls, but can also pre-control higher level 'parameters' to a certain extent. For instance, not only an organization's innovative capabilities, but also the liquid financial resources actually available to it might play an important role in its strategic and normative decisions. Substantial own funds can add a degree of freedom in the building-up of value potentials.

## ORGANIZATIONAL FITNESS IN ACTION—SOME EMPIRICAL EVIDENCE

Surprising systemic manifestations can occur in social organizations whose potentials are realized. However, from a cybernetic perspective processes of corporate development are not the outcome of chance. They are company-wide processes obeying an evolutionary logic. As such they can, within limits, be influenced in the sense of a 'planned evolution'. In this process, as has been shown in empirical pilot studies by Schwaninger (1989; 1993), the catalytic reinforcement of dynamic forces in the organization plays a crucial part. On a higher level, however, the development process itself should the object of design and control measures, if evolution is to be virtuous; see the discussion by Krieg (1985).

Rigorous exploratory research by Schwaninger (1988; 1989) has shown that the application of the systemic framework of organizational fitness presented here is likely to enhance the learning of an organization significantly. In the cases analysed this was due to the fact that the corporations were managed on the basis of a multilevel system of orientators as illustrated in Figure 8.1. This strikingly enhanced the 'intelligence' of the organizations, i.e., their openness, learning and adaptability, and it facilitated change. Even under difficult circumstances, fundamental corporate transformation towards better performance, viability and development was possible. The crucial point was that managers consciously detached themselves from conventional, one-dimensional control approaches and instead oriented their actions by a comprehensive, systemic concept of organizational fitness.

The authors' joint research, discussed in the preface, that was the point of departure for this book corroborates these results in a less rigorous manner.

As far as the priority and the pre-control function of the control variables of the higher logical levels in relation to the lower ones is concerned, strong empirical evidence corroborating earlier theoretical works by Drucker (1980), Gälweiler (1979; 1990) and Schwaninger (1984; 1993) has been brought forward by several large studies. Some of these have already been cited, e.g., the PIMS and Utterback studies of Buzzell and Gale (1987) and Utterback (1994). Studies that corroborate the pre-control function of the steering variables of the normative level have resulted from two extensive investigations in the USA:

1.  Under the title *Built to Last*, Collins and Porras (1994) have published the results of their enquiry into the 'successful habits of visionary companies'. They observed, over several decades, the evolution of a set of 'visionary companies'; these are the premier institutions or 'crown jewels' in their industries, widely admired by their

peers and having a long track record of making a significant impact on the world around them. They compared these with a control set of companies that are also good but 'don't quite match up to the overall stature of the visionary companies' (p. 2).

They concluded as a result of this study: 'They are *more* than successful. They are more than enduring . . . Visionary companies attain extraordinary *long-term* performance' (pp. 3f.). To illustrate this, they point out that equal investments of $1 in two general-market stock funds, one for the comparison companies, and one for the visionary companies of their sample, made on January 1, 1926, with later reinvestment of all dividends and appropriate adjustments when the companies became available on the Stock Exchange (in the study, all companies were held at general market rates until they appeared on the market) would have obtained the following results. The $1 in the general market fund would have grown to $415 on December 31, 1990; the $1 invested in the group of comparison companies would have grown to $955, more than twice the general market. However, the $1 in the visionary companies stock fund would have grown to $6,356—over six times the comparison fund and over 15 times the general market; for details, see Collins and Porras (1994, pp. 4f.).

Contrary, however, to a widely taught doctrine, profit maximization is not their dominant driving force. 'Through the history of most of the visionary companies we saw a core ideology that transcended purely economic considerations. . . . they have had core ideology to a greater degree than the comparison companies in our study' (p. 55). The authors consider the dynamic interplay between core ideology and the drive for progress, set out in Table 8.1, to be one of the most important findings of their study.

**Table 8.1** Core ideology versus drive for progress (Collins and Porras, 1994)

| Core ideology | Drive for progress |
| --- | --- |
| Provides continuity and *stability* <br><br> Plants a relatively *fixed* stake in the ground | Urges continual *change*—new directions, new methods, new strategies, and so on |
| *Limits* possibilities and directions for the company to those consistent with the content of the ideology | Impels constant *movement* toward goals, improvement, an envisioned form, and so on |
| Has clear content: '*This* is our core ideology and we will not breach it' | *Expands* the number and variety of possibilities that the company can consider |
| Installing a core ideology is, by its very nature, a *conservative* act | Can be content-free: '*Any* progress is good, as long as it is consistent with our core' |
|  | Expressing the drive for progress can lead to dramatic, radical, and *revolutionary* change |

2. In a large empirical investigation, Harvard professors John P. Kotter and James L. Heskett (Kotter and Heskett, 1992) tried to ascertain the link between corporate culture and performance. Starting from a sample of 207 firms from 22 US industries, the authors examined in detail subsets of 22 and 20 firms respectively to test specific theories concerning culture and performance. Their studies showed the

incompleteness of the theory that strong cultures lead to high performance. A strong culture can have detrimental effects on performance if the values adhered to inhibit proper alignment with the milieu.

How do they propose that the theory should be amended? Their results strongly suggest that an orientation toward the main stakeholders of an organization discriminates strong from weak performers.

Firms with cultures that emphasized all the key managerial constituencies (customers, stockholders, and employees) and leadership from managers at all levels outperformed firms that did not have those cultural traits by a huge margin. Over an eleven-year period, the former increased revenues by an average of 682% versus 166% of the latter, expanded their work forces by 282% versus 36%, grew their stock prices by 901% versus 74%, and improved their net incomes by 756% versus 1% (p. 11).

This study led the authors to specify the characteristics of two ideal types of culture—'adaptive' and 'non-adaptive'—set out in Table 8.2.

**Table 8.2** Adaptive versus non-adaptive cultures (Kotter and Heskett, 1992)

|  | Adaptive corporate cultures | Non-adaptive corporate cultures |
|---|---|---|
| Core values | Most managers care deeply about customers, stockholders, and employees. They also strongly value people and processes that can create useful change, e.g., leadership up and down the management hierarchy | Most managers care mainly about themselves, their immediate work group or some product or technology associated with that work group. They value an orderly and risk-reducing management process more highly than leadership initiatives |
| Common behaviour | Managers pay close attention to all their constituencies, especially customers, and initiate change when needed to serve their legitimate interests, even if it entails taking some risks. | Managers tend to behave somewhat insularly, politically, and bureaucratically. As a result, they do not change their strategies quickly to adjust to or take advantage of changes in their business environment. |

Both studies underline the importance of normative frameworks that emphasize a complex stakeholder value orientation, as opposed to a narrow profit or shareholder value orientation, and a constant quest to bring about the necessary changes. This is emphasized in our postulate P1. Organizations have to develop vision and strategy, and adhere steadfastly to their core values, when realizing them; this is in accordance with postulates P2 and P3. In addition, there is at least one more significant insight that the Kotter and Heskett study provides. In pleading for 'leadership from managers at all levels' it underlines the argument of this book in favour of recursive management.

Our own explorative, empirical studies, upon which this book is based, lead us to make an even stronger point.

1. Firms that espouse strong cultures but do not amplify leadership at all levels block their development toward better performance.
2. A corporate culture must be embedded in a structure that supports leadership at all levels if it is to bring about organizational learning and development.

These aspects will be explored further in the last section of this chapter. There we shall concretize our argument for recursive management processes—briefly stated in postulate P2.

# ON STRATEGY AND STRUCTURE

### Processes Of Systemic Management

Up to this point, the argument for simultaneously maintaining control over the steering variables at all three structural levels has remained largely within the factual logic of 'what the company does' or intends to do. These are the organizational tasks defined by the policy and strategy processes; and there is a need for these processes to make the right decisions. Chapter 4's discussion of the role of 'purpose' is relevant here.

But making the right decisions, though necessary, is not sufficient. Of 27 firms threatened by technological change and studied by Utterback (1994), only seven adapted successfully. Utterback comments (p. 225)

> But the irony is that these firms all made the right decisions to enter with the threatening innovation. They were simply blocked by organizational impediments and the constraints of established patterns of thought and action.

The next step, therefore, must be to combine the factual logic of defining policies and strategies with the formal logic of *structure*. How have management processes to be designed so as to generate and realize sound strategies? Only when such processes have been designed can we consider adequately the socio-psycho-logic of *behaviour*.

Structures must be designed so as to support 'virtuous' behaviour—by which we mean behaviour that is favourable both to viability and to the ethical and responsible development of an organization.

Linking task-setting, i.e. purposes, and structure: management as conversational processes.

As we postulated in Part One, a fundamental requirement for the management of complexity is that there should exist effective structures, allowing organizations to create opportunities for themselves as well as to respond to disturbances and change; this is stated in postulate S1. We have outlined the structural constituents and principles of the viable system model (VSM). It offers a basis upon which to design organizations capable of coping with complexity and change.

Here we must point out that the activity of 'coping' needs to involve management processes that enable an organization to adapt, learn and develop, even under difficult circumstances. Nobody can possibly anticipate all the different kinds of

situations that will be faced in the history of a concrete company. Yet if an organization is to become viable, somebody must at least outline structural mechanisms
capable of fostering the emergence of meaningful tasks and virtuous behaviours. It is
necessary that any—and everybody who is part of such an organization should be
supported by a structure that leverages his or her individual creativity, thereby
supporting individual and organizational development, and, if necessary, transformation. This requirement is stated in postulate S6.

The text in Chapter 5 has, in the context of the VSM, described the necessary
mechanisms—named 'adaptation' and 'monitoring-control'—in a fairly abstract
manner. How can they be brought to life?

For this purpose, we have to 'marry' them with the OADI cycle of learning
described in Chapter 6. This is defined by the components *Observe, Assess, Design*
and *Implement*. Chapter 6 dealt with the obstacles to this process of learning. We
wish now to emphasize the conversational features inherent in the learning process.
Figure 8.4 illustrates this aspect.

The model outlined in Figure 8.4 represents, in a nutshell, a structural blueprint
for the management of a primary process. Primary processes, as we have said in
discussing the VSM and as will be elaborated further in Chapter 9, are those that
produce the organization's products and services. Our concern is the management of
this process.

Structurally, this management is represented by the control, intelligence and policy functions described in Chapter 5; processually, it is represented by the levels of
normative, strategic and operational management. A company's fundamental asset
for effective adaptation and control lies in the possession of multiple viewpoints; but
these cannot be allowed to disrupt its activity. Channelling different viewpoints into
coherent action is a prerequisite for coping with the complexity, both external and
internal, that the organization faces; postulate P4 states this.

This channelling cannot be accomplished by any mechanical algorithm. It has to
be achieved through negotiating common goals and agreements between people in
the various management functions.

The logic of these processes, as explained in Chapter 5, is straightforward. The
control function brings its issues and priorities into the process; they are by and large
driven by concerns of productivity and synergy within the parameters given by,
first, the actual strategy and, second, the structures as they are and will be in the near
future. Here, the restrictions are abundant. On the other hand, the intelligence function brings in considerations derived from detecting opportunities in the evolving
environment. Its concern is with maintaining a fit between the organization and its
environment in the long run. Intelligence strives to explore and create possible
futures.

Discrepancies between the actual and the possible are inherent in the discourse
between control and intelligence. What intelligence considers to be 'fit' will often be
perceived by control as a 'misfit' or, at least, as some suspicious form of 'stretch'. We
have here a dialectic between 'stretch' and 'fit'; it can be mastered in a 'virtuous'
manner only if certain conditions are fulfilled:

1. The conversations between the two functions must be balanced; that is, neither of
   them must dominate the conversation in a manner unchecked by the other.

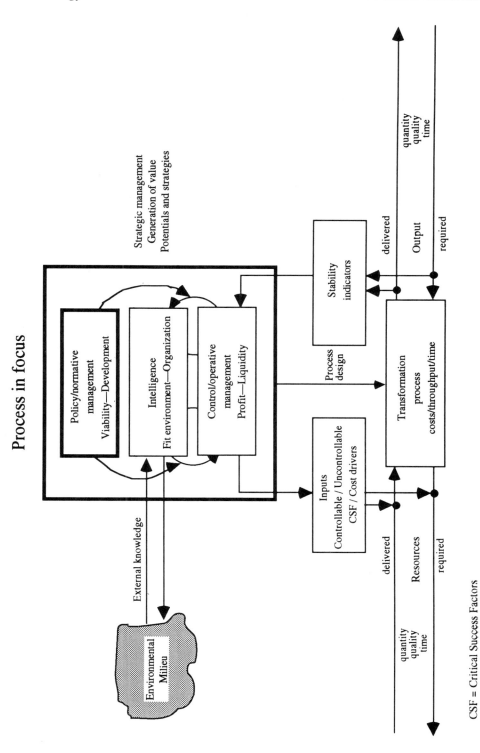

CSF = Critical Success Factors

**Figure 8.4** Management as conversational processes

2. The individuals and groups involved in these conversations must have learned the principles of effective action in an organizational context; that is, they must have learned to be effective learners—as described in Chapter 4.

The latter requirement involves, in particular, an awareness of the implications of one's own actions, as required by postulate I5. It involves also an ability to deal appropriately with distant as well as with local information; that is, to balance action and observation. It requires mature personalities, capable of respecting different viewpoints, arguing constructively and learning.

Single-loop learning is often, in this case, insufficient. In many cases such a dialogue requires an ability to make new distinctions, making it possible to learn entirely new modes of operation with which to reconfigure the organization. This is the requirement for double-loop learning stated in postulate P6. It is an ability that can be fostered through training.

The function of policy is to moderate the interaction between control and intelligence, thereby facilitating the generation of new value potentials and strategies.

A good example to illustrate this mechanism may be found in the issue of environmental responsibility, noted in Chapter 2. A well-developed intelligence function will be concerned with the need for the organization to develop a sustainable ecological balance with its milieu—as postulate P9 specifies. Therefore those responsible for this function will argue for investment in new, environment-friendly products and techniques, preferring 'clean' to 'dirty technologies'. It will resist 'end-of-pipe' technologies. On the other hand, those responsible for control will in principle defend the least expensive solutions, arguing that the organization should abide by minimal legal standards. In recent years, some advanced companies have learned a lot through such conversations; their outcome has been a completely new vision of the organization. A well-known example is Ciba, a large chemical company, which has given itself an innovative normative framework. In its vision statement formulated in the early nineties (Ciba-Geigy, 1991), the company declared the objective of ensuring prosperity beyond the year 2000 by striking a balance among:

- responsibility for long-term economic success,
- social responsibility,
- responsibility for the environment.

Ciba's management is currently working intensively to implement that philosophy through leadership. It is determined not to maximize any one of the three dimensions of responsibility at the expense of the others, but to optimize them jointly, thereby generating high levels of benefits to all major stakeholders. In cases such as this, according to Utterback (1994), only 'full commitment by top management to renewing the business of the firm—together with patience and persistence in that commitment—will have a chance to succeed' (p. 227). Committee systems and organizational requirements that diffuse responsibility inordinately need to be recalibrated. 'Investors must be educated to the new direction of the firm, and reminded that greater rewards are only associated with greater risks. Otherwise new initiatives will almost inevitably be starved for resources, allowing competitors to establish formidable positions at the expense of the once-preeminent industry leaders' (p. 230).

In our theoretical language, the mechanism of adaptation functions as follows:

1. It relies on powerful filters—the intelligence and control filters described in Chapter 5. The intelligence function filters issues and potential solutions out of an astronomical complexity of signals picked out from the evolving milieu, using a sensorium that must be rich in perception and powerful in making relevant distinctions. The control function filters priorities out of both continuous and intermittent flows of events, mainly from inside the organization. In many of the cases we have studied these filters were insufficient, i.e., the wrong signals were picked up and irrelevant information was generated. We attribute this to inadequate conceptual knowledge of the 'language' appropriate to each case; that is, to inadequate knowledge of the uses of strategic and operative orientators and their logical differences. The second section of this chapter discussed the appropriate criteria for operational and strategic effectiveness.

2. Adaptation requires intensive interactions between control and intelligence. These should generate meaningful conclusions and feasible solutions, leading to progress in action. In practice, control and intelligence are often out of balance. In these instances,

    a. if intelligence is relatively weak, the strategy process will not be vigorous enough to generate adequate innovation and change;

    b. if it is control that is too weak, strategies will be unrealistic or irrelevant.

3. It is the job of the policy function to moderate the interaction between intelligence and control. It must be concerned to ensure that the varieties generated by each function are approximately in balance and to create a context for appropriate conversations to take place between them. If there is balance, policy can cope adequately with the residual variety that results from these conversations. In order to provide a context for effective conversations, policy must in the first place have knowledge of the players involved; secondly, it must know what systemic management is all about.

Policy must choose between the options generated in the interaction between intelligence and control. The criteria for making these choices are set by the policy function itself.

The policy function is normative. It defines policies and directions based on its own vision—or sometimes, lack of vision—values, preferences and intentions. It is an expression of the interests and values of the stakeholders in the organization. Policy shapes, in one form or another, the identity of the organization. It ascribes purpose; thereby it defines its own strategic intent. It provides, explicitly or implicitly, answers to questions such as: What is the organization all about? What is its mission? Its core competencies? Its business areas? What values does it stand for? What destiny does it pursue? Which responses, among those that are available to the organization to cope with opportunities and threats, are consistent with its identity and intent?

Obviously, identity is a constant amidst change, but it must evolve as well. Therefore, the strategy process outlined here is a dialectical one, a continual quest for a balance between preservation and transformation.

While the mechanism of adaptation is very much about learning new modes—and, also, forgetting outdated ones, as in our postulate P6—the mechanism of monitoring control is about an organization learning to do better what it already does. This requirement is stated in postulates I3 and P5.

Among the outcomes of management conversations are definitions or redefinitions of the organization's primary processes; this is the essence of organizational development. Such redefinitions may lead to changes in primary activities, i.e., in the way the company is divided into strategic business units. We will deal with these topics in greater depth in the next two chapters.

The conversational processes between the control function and the managements in charge of primary activities are based on the principle of mutual adjustment. The chief object is to negotiate operational goals for and allocation of resources to the primary activities. At the same time, these processes involve defining and redefining the identities, norms and strategic intents of subunits in the context of the larger whole. Due to the limited capacity of the vertical communication channel, interactions should be largely limited to these core issues. The channel should only exceptionally be used for issuing commands, i.e., only when the cohesion of the whole is threatened by developments in the realm of the subunits.

To help avert such threats, the co-ordination function, as we have said before, fulfils the task of fostering cohesion among the sub-units by such means as information systems, standards and personal interaction. Finally, the monitoring function helps to assess whether that cohesion is really achieved, and to what extent, as well as detecting exceptional situations.

In the cases studied our most frequent diagnosis has been that of an overload on the vertical command channel, caused partly by the fact that co-ordination and monitoring systems were unsatisfactory. This was mainly a matter of mechanistically designed information systems and poor understanding of the different systemic roles of the various channels. A major challenge in most organizations is to design co-ordination and monitoring processes that have sufficient capacity.

## LINKING STRUCTURE TO CULTURE AND BEHAVIOUR: MANAGEMENT AS A RECURSIVE PROCESS

A policy or strategy is only as good as its carrying out. Appropriate structures are needed to facilitate the realization of strategy by supporting functional behaviour at all levels of the organization.

As we showed in Chapter 5, the viability of an organization is determined, first of all, by whether it has command over specific management functions that must work together in a manner precisely defined by Beer's theory. This system of management functions having been identified, can be shown to be recursive in nature. Viability can, in principle, be structurally located in each workteam or workplace.

A most important consideration is related to this. It is that normative and strategic management are not limited to the domain of the corporate board. On the contrary, they must be found in each unit. We will show that the essential tasks of management are not and should not be reserved to the board of a corporation. They consist of a fundamental steering process that is inherent to each level of an organization, from corporation to business to work team or project. There is need not only for operational but also for strategic and normative management in any viable subsystem, i.e., each primary activity, of an organization; for each subsystem has to meet the criterion of viability.

The cybernetic theory of organization advocated here contradicts oft-repeated comments that 'vision is the concern of the entrepreneur' or 'strategy is the duty of the board of directors'. Vision is a function of the normative management of every viable unit. Recognition of this fact is a hallmark of structures that foster autonomy and local problem-solving capacity—as required by postulate S2—and thereby provide conditions for people to develop themselves and to find and create new possibilities. The latter is required by postulate S4.

Strategic thinking is necessary even in the smallest units, if such units are to be conceived of as viable wholes. That is why there has to be a 'meta-management' at all levels of recursion that makes use of orientators other than those of the corresponding 'management'. This is a level of management that is concerned with the viability of the larger organization, i.e., with its management, as well as with the 'meta-management' of the primary activities, i.e., with enabling them to remain viable.

In small units, it is often the case that the operational, strategic and normative functions of management, as well as the basic activities themselves, are all discharged by the same persons. In spite of this, it is vital for any unit that it should not restrict itself to the operating functions—assuming that the unit in focus is supposed to be viable. It must be so led that the steering variables of all three logical levels are taken into consideration and simultaneously kept under control. This must hold true even when inconsistencies arise between these steering variables.

It is incumbent upon the management at each level of recursion to define for its own purposes the specific orientators appropriate to its level and to realize a corresponding 'integral' leadership. Figure 8.5 illustrates this in a highly simplified manner. Starting from a more abstract scheme than the one in Figure 8.1, examples of steering variables and orientators are presented that might be appropriate for three levels of recursion—an enterprise, a subsidiary and a business unit within the subsidiary. The orientators shown at the different levels would help those involved in any of these recursion levels in several ways. They would be helped:

- to understand the links with the other recursion levels and the need to strive for autonomy and cohesion at the same time—as in our postulate S5;
- to appreciate the meaning of core competency, viability and development, as required by postulate R3;
- to look outward, developing an appreciation of the meaning of customer and market orientation as in postulate R1;
- to grasp the need to develop synergistic alliances with suppliers, customers, competitors and other external stakeholders. This is the requirement of postulate R4.

The broken line tries to illustrate the point that for an organization, communications and information about its primary activities at recursion levels other than those in its immediate neighbourhood can be of relevance. The dotted lines indicate that in principle the logic of this model can be transferred to further recursion levels. Thus it holds good for networks representing more complex systems i.e. ones that have more recursions.

The same logic applies also to the concept of the 'virtual organization'. The word 'virtual' comes from *virtus*, meaning virtue. It refers to an organization that can, in

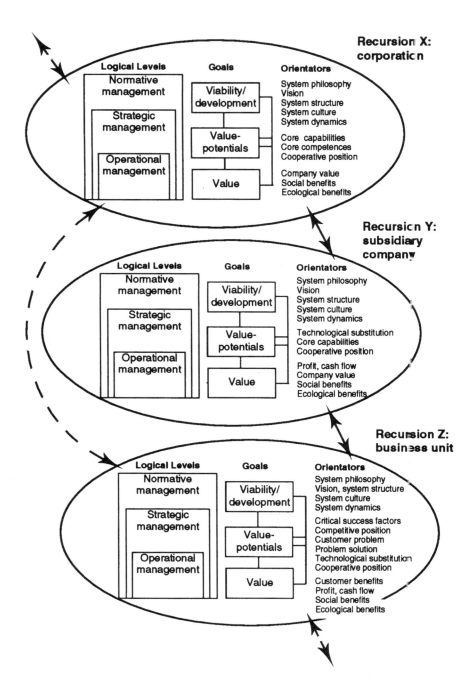

**Figure 8.5** Operational, strategic and normative management as distributed functions (Schwaninger 1994b)

principle, materialize its 'virtuous' potential in many different forms. Using available resources, project teams can be formed in many different constellations, tailor-made according to the function that needs to be carried out. What is significant is that in this connection, the meaning of the word 'available' can be expanded almost indefinitely. What is not available 'in-house' can often be acquired through partnerships and co-operation.

The logic of Figure 8.5 applies here inasmuch as the goals of 'viability' and 'development' are meaningful also in connection with projects, as has been pointed out by Davies *et al.* (1979) and by Schwaninger (1994b). Even projects having a limited life-span need a specific identity during the period of their existence. One important difference should be mentioned: looking at the situation from the inside, the question 'what is to become of us when the project is completed?' may be of burning importance for the members of the project team.

Figure 8.6 shows how the system of regulatory variables for an integral management illustrated in Figure 8.5 can be transferred to the project level.

Applying the recursive approach to management outlined here will open the space necessary to create a capacity for cultural transformation, as required in postulate R7. In this way the path towards more open and participative structures can be pursued.

## STRATEGY, STRUCTURE AND INFORMATION MANAGEMENT

### Linking Culture, Behaviour And Task-setting: Management As An Evolutionary Or Revolutionary Process

By linking behaviour and task-setting we close a loop established throughout the two preceding sections.

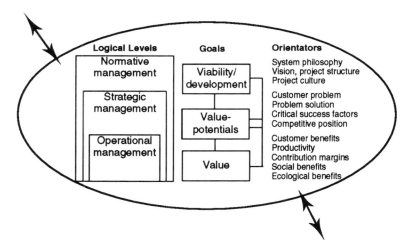

**Figure 8.6**  Reference variables for an integral management of projects (Schwaninger 1994b)

If task-setting must be supported by structures to result in functional behaviour, the functionality of that behaviour must be continually validated by linking it back to the tasks that the organization must accomplish. That is the way, ultimately, to the excellent performance described by postulate P1, achieved by implementing quality and continual improvement in all activities as in postulate P5.

For this purpose, appropriate methods and tools for organizational design and information management are necessary. Current executive information systems (EISs), equipped with graphic and reporting capabilities, are often not adequate. Many of their features, e.g., for exception reporting, drilling down into the data or accessing external databases and communications, are not consistent with effective managerial processes. To take one example: an emphasis on drilling down into detailed data ignores the need for autonomy at all levels, bypassing as it does the necessary conversational processes between structural levels.

For management information systems to be effective they must be aligned with an effective organization structure and must help to focus the attention of managers on conversations that are relevant to the tasks for which they are responsible. These are the criteria underlying the management support system called CyberSyn, described in the appendix to this chapter. Implementing this system requires, first, a study of the organizational structure in a diagnostic mode. Then it requires the initiation of a process toward improving the structure in all areas where change is desirable and feasible. Only then can the definition of indices of performance for individual managers and their connection with data processing systems be meaningful.

For the purpose of studying the organizational structure in a diagnostic mode, the VSM has proved to be highly useful, as in Espejo and Harnden (1989) and Espejo and Schwaninger (1993). A stringent procedure has been developed for carrying out such an investigation; this is described by Espejo (1989a, 1989b), Chapters 5 and 13. The outcomes of such a study are diagnostic points—areas where communication mechanisms and information flows in the organization are inadequate and require improvement.

This is a highly technical study, based on interviews and the analysis of organizational data. It is, however, in the management of the process of improving these mechanisms and flows that the difficulties of aligning information systems with an effective organization structure become apparent. Schuhmann (1990) discusses these difficulties with reference to a concrete application of CyberSyn in a large German company; we will be discussing them further in the following two chapters.

The result of implementing more effective structures is that people in the organization obtain more flexibility and capacity to participate in organizational processes; this is because they are now operating in a context that provides better communication channels and more appropriate checks and balances. Such a context supports the distribution of information needs throughout the organization. The more effective the organization, the more evenly distributed are these information needs—as noted by Espejo (1990). In other words, the traditional structural aberration, in which senior managers are overloaded with information while people at lower levels are underloaded, is replaced by a structure that irons out these imbalances. This transformation can be greatly facilitated by the design and implementation of effective information systems—meaning information systems that support management processes that allow all members of the organization to participate creatively in it.

In particular, all should have the opportunity to participate, within the scope of their autonomy, in conversations about future possibilities and current actions. It makes no sense to leave all the responsibility for creating the organization's future in the hands of senior management. The structure should allow everyone to have visions in the domains of their competence, to transform these visions into plans and these plans into everyday actions; inventing and creating the future, including the identity of their tasks, is the right and responsibility of everyone in an organization. For each of them, planning should not be a matter of forecasting or guessing what is going to happen so that the organization can plan a response; it should consist of responsible conversations that construct the organization's future. Today's conversations are a means of feeding forward a desirable future.

The above views will be seen as impractical while organizations continue to measure results in the way they do today. As we have said, it is extraordinary that for the last 500 years, since Luca Pacioli introduced double-entry bookkeeping, the same system of performance measurement should have remained in place. Yet in many companies, the key assumptions about an organization made by double-entry bookkeeping and accounting remain unchanged. The major concern still is to measure results with a historic perspective, rather than with a view to the future. The assumption underlying such an emphasis on past information is that the organization operates in a relatively stable environment, where it can be realistically assumed that the future will be an extension of the past. Everyone knows, however, that this assumption is not realistic today. Even if accounting methods are used with a view to the future, as when enterprises rely on discounting future cash flows to assess whether possible investments are likely to be profitable or not, the procedures used generally lack requisite variety to distinguish between futures that are normatively desirable or undesirable.

At a deeper structural level, sticking to traditional accountancy systems as the main tool for measurement may have the effect of reproducing inadequate management processes. The structural balance between intelligence and control is likely to be biased toward the latter. This may be the case even if there is an understanding that the situation should be otherwise. For example, discounted cash-flow analyses tend to favour investments in incremental change, where costs and payoffs can be more reliably forecast, than investments in radical innovation. According to Utterback (1994, p. 226): 'Discounted cash-flow analysis provides no room for the unexpected surprises that destroy existing businesses.'

From this discussion, the interrelated nature of management processes and information systems is becoming apparent. There is no doubt that in a changing world, in which the constitution of the 'outside and then' requires increased attention in order to survive, it is necessary to have information systems that measure not only the short-term results of people's activities but also take into account their abilities to transform their long-term aspirations and possibilities into reality.

An emphasis upon viability should precede profit orientation. Beyond that, viability should be thought of as more than a matter of mere economic survival. Environmental factors such as social values and attitudes are concerns that may influence the acceptability or otherwise the obsolescence of particular enterprises in the long run.

Criteria of viability are meant to be a pre-control for profits, as pointed out above. And as a matter of fact, the criteria of viability offered by the VSM support each of the above propositions. Current measurement systems, on the other hand, and their related information systems, often obscure not only the need for a balance between the 'outside and then' and the 'inside and now', but also the need for a distribution of autonomy throughout the organization. Concepts like profit centres may ameliorate, but do not overcome the problem: first, because in principle, their focus is still on short-term orientators; secondly, because they are seldom attached to 'small' enough tasks, i.e., to those undertaken at low structural levels in the organization. These arguments suggest the need for an 'accounting system' that highlights autonomy and brings forth conversations about possibilities and actions at all structural levels.

One such measurement system, set out by Beer (1981), is based on the concepts of *actuality, capability and potentiality*, understood as organizational concepts closely intertwined with the VSM. What follows is an explanation of this measurement system.

The three values—actuality ('IS'), capability ('COULD BE') and potentiality ('OUGHT TO BE')—of a chosen variable permit us to define three indices: the indices of achievement, latency and performance. They are related as shown in Figure 8.7. If the definition of potentialities and the measurement of capabilities and actualities are made for all autonomous activities at all structural levels in an organization, then they constitute a comprehensive system linking behaviour to task-setting.

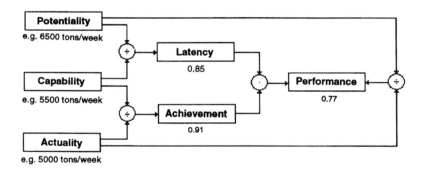

**Figure 8.7**  A system for measurement

At this point we must ask: which are the activities that must be autonomous in an organization?

The answer depends on the identity, vision and strategy of the organization. Autonomous activities are defined by answering the question: which are the activities in which the organization must excel—be world champion—if it is going to be viable as a whole?

As technology pushes down the competitive edge into smaller and smaller activities, large organizations need to adjust their answers to the above question. If, with reference to any specific activity, however small it might be, the answer is that the organization expects or needs to make it viable, either today or in the future, then, it is not enough to work out a competitive edge for it today, it is also necessary to enhance its core competencies and to endow it with a viable organization structure.

Of course, the creation of an effective enterprise depends on the quality of the organizational conversations producing the above answers. If the structure underlying these conversations is good, i.e., if it is a structure dictated by the need for autonomy and the need to have a mechanism for adaptation, then the likelihood is that these answers will be more appropriate and have more chances of succeeding. In that case, most people in the organization will at the appropriate level and with appropriate checks and balances be involved in the conversations, thus increasing their commitment to the outcomes. In a nutshell, these conversations will be the embodiments of a mechanism that simultaneously fosters autonomy and cohesion, as required by postulate S5.

The underlying value of a system of measurement based on actualities, capabilities, potentialities and the unfolding of complexity is that it offers a means of balancing short- and long-term criteria of performance throughout the organization. For all autonomous activities, at all structural levels, achievement refers to current results and latency to 'realistic' commitments to developments necessary to actualize the mission of the organization. Performance effects a balance between the two. Moreover, these concepts provide a platform to relate task-setting, structure and behaviour.

*Potentiality*, or what the organization ought to be doing is only meaningful as a result of discussions concerning core values and possibilities. It is the policy function that provides a normative framework for organizational activities; it ascribes purposes to the organization. The clearer the normative framework, the more likely it is that effective organizational debates, cross-checking the intended 'outside and then' with the current 'inside and now', will take place. The normative framework helps to establish the boundaries of each of these environments. The clearer it is, the more likely it also is that meaningful and useful definitions of potentialities will emerge.

These potentialities provide directions in which to develop the organization's resources. This means two things. It means leveraging extant resources. It also means increasing, if necessary, the resource base of the company, thereby opening access to new ones. It is the concern of the intelligence and control functions to work out investment plans and development programmes to realize the latent resources of the organization; that is, it is conversations between these two functions that will transform vision and intent into plans for action by building shared levels of aspiration and consensus concerning actions to be taken.

*Capability*, or what the organization can do with the resources currently at its disposal requires adequate control mechanisms for its successful measurement. These should allow managers to know what resources are available as well as to monitor the allocation and use of operational resources. Otherwise, the definition of capabilities becomes an arbitrary definition of targets. Knowledge of capabilities is necessary to define the scope for improvement in the organization. It is the responsibility of the organization's control function to achieve the best use of the available resources, i.e. to move actualities closer and closer to capabilities.

*Actuality*—what the organization is doing today—is measured for all those variables perceived by management to be essential for the control of organizational activities. The perception as to which variables are essential will depend on the structure; the more the 'outside and then' is represented in the organization at all structural levels, the more the essential variables will evolve from operational to strategic. They will evolve from traditional accountancy-based variables such as income, expenditure, revenues and costs toward including, in addition, variables that measure the organization's capabilities, e.g., measures of its ability to solve customers' problems and critical success factors such as competitive position and market share. As more attention is given to strategic variables, the potentialities associated with the more operational variables become clearer.

It is the logic of complexity unfolding offered by the VSM that gives power to the above measurement system. The definition of actualities, capabilities and potentialities should concern not only the organization as a whole, but also all the autonomous activities that produce its identity; that is, all the activities in which the organization must excel if it is to remain competitive.

This suggests that appropriate indices of achievement, latency and performance must be defined and measured at all levels in the organization. It follows, therefore, that potentialities, however difficult their definition might appear at lower structural levels, are meaningful and valid at every level. Their relevance is not confined to higher levels as is traditionally believed.

The 'outside and then' is thus the responsibility of all structural levels. Once it is devolved in this way, the measurement system becomes a means to leverage the activities of people throughout the organization. Everyone is concerned with the short, medium and long term. From the point of view of organizational development we have a system to generate the complexity needed by the organization and thereby to support its long term viability.

These measurements will, in the short term, depend upon existing information systems in the organization. In the long run, however, they should be a driving force to support the development of all information flows required for viability.

In practice, the variables to measure are those that managers perceive as essential to the performance of organizational tasks. It is these essential variables that constitute a driving force for the development of new information systems. This view seems to be consistent with well-established methodologies for information systems development such as the critical success factors of Rockart (1979). However, the need to emphasize structural viability and conversations for possibilities and action is not yet fully appreciated. Information systems have to be much more than reporting systems; they must support functional behaviour.

Let us now discuss in some depth the handling of indices of performance. Technical aspects of the definition of these indices have been discussed by Espejo and Watt (1979), Espejo and Garcia (1984) and in Syncho (1990). Our discussion, inspired by the remarks of Beer (1979) on the subject of measurement, will highlight the significance of the indices as a system for enabling recursive, task-oriented behaviour.

Figure 8.8 shows an interpretation of the indices from a structural viewpoint. The following points need to be made about how the system does or should work.

1. The policy function defines criteria of performance (C1) in line with the identity of the organization and its vision of the direction it should follow. These measure (M1) the results of interactions between management—consisting of policy, intelligence and control—and the organization's operations; that is, the operational capabilities of the whole organization. The criteria of performance are defined in the form of potentialities that are consistent with the normative framework, i.e. the vision, mission and identity ascribed to the organization, established by the policy function. Changes and expectations of changes in organizational capabilities, as a result of resource allocation and policy implementation, are measured and reported to corporate management. Corporate managers, if they are to follow the execution of their policies, need to concern themselves with actual and planned changes in the indices of latency, i.e. in the ratios between capabilities and potentialities. They need not be involved in the interactions between management and those responsible for operations at lower structural levels. It is enough to establish that the organization is realizing its potentialities.

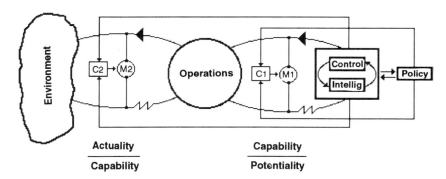

**Figure 8.8** Linking behaviour to task-setting—interpreting indices structurally (Espejo 1993c)

It is natural to expect that all kind of problems will emerge in this process, not least adjustments in the potentialities themselves as a result of new conditions. The system of measurement depends for its effectiveness on two factors: the quality of the organizational conversations supporting the definition of potentialities and the capacity of the control function to establish changes in organizational capabilities. However, provided the policy function monitors the conversations between intelligence and control in the manner we have explained and the control function is effective in monitoring operations—keeping an eye on both structural and processual requirements—the measurement system will be meaningful and useful.

2. Corporate management establishes criteria of performance (C2) to assess the results (M2) of interactions between the organization and its environment. These criteria of performance are the capabilities of the variables implied by the managers' critical success factors. The measurements to be made are achievements, i.e. ratios between actualities and capabilities, for all these variables.

Corporate management—the control function in particular—do not need to be involved in the details of interactions between operations and the environments in which they take place; that is the concern of the operations themselves. However, they need to know the extent to which the capabilities of the organization are being realized by the operations. Capabilities define the direction and space for improvements. They are not, however, targets. Achievements measure the degree to which the environment, e.g. the market, is supporting the realization of the organization's capabilities. Provided the control function has a realistic assessment of the organization's capabilities and is able to measure actualities in real time the measurement system will be capable of supporting the effective management of operations.

It should be noted that a 'corporate management' exists in all autonomous operations, at all structural levels in the organization. Such management is not exclusive to the highest structural level. The same measurement system, therefore, applies at all levels in the organization.

When it comes to solving the technical problems of data processing and reporting, a number of alternative approaches are possible. Most EISs, however, are implemented without an understanding of the need to manage complexity or the requirements for doing so. This shortcoming most likely underlies the facts that their usage is limited and that 'In a number of organizations there is a move to expand the range of performance indicators used (in the EIS), usually away from the standard financial measures' (Fitzgerald, 1992). Perhaps CyberFilter (Syncho, 1990) is one of the few packages that offers an explicit link between management processes and the design of management information systems (see Appendix 3).

As a management system CyberFilter depends on the management processes responsible for the definitions of potentialities and the assessments of capabilities. As an information system it is based on the following criteria:

1. Reports are aggregated at the level appropriate to each manager. Only by exception will a manager receive reports about unresolved problems at lower structural levels. The indices relevant to managers depend on the structural level at which they operate and their functional responsibilities. In the case of general managers, responsible for autonomous operations, the indices relevant to them will relate to the discretion exercised by them at their particular structural level in the organization. In the case of functional managers, the degree of aggregation of their indices is defined by the requirements of the autonomous operations that their functions serve.

2. Information is filtered in such a way that not all changes or discrepancies are reported to managers—only the significant ones. 'Significance' is assessed as follows. CyberFilter makes reports when it detects either incipient instability in the behaviour of an index or significant discrepancies between actualities and the improvements planned to bring them closer to capabilities.

3. Reports are as close to real time as practically possible. It makes no sense to wait until the next periodic report to alert a manager that a significant change has occurred or is likely to occur. Indices are updated as soon as the necessary data is available. Anticipatory reports are made available whenever possible, whether in the form of short-term forecasting or in the form of information that problems in the development of the capabilities of the organization are anticipated. Thus managers are alerted to events that may hinder anticipated changes in the future.

What has been described here, in rather abstract terms, is a mechanism that links behaviour to the tasks that have been set. The core task for an organization facing a turbulent environment is to continually implement change, as required by postulate R8, without losing order and orientation.

Effective leadership is increasingly based on conceptual and interpersonal rather than technical competencies, as in postulate I6. Managing the conversations, often in a multicultural context, that define core values and criteria of performance or through which resource allocation is negotiated may involve conflict and stress. A culture able to use conflict constructively will favour the attainment of higher levels of order; that is, 'metastability'. That is a major aspect of the challenge to the interpersonal competence of future leaders. The challenge to their conceptual competence will lie in improving the mental models supporting the management process, understanding the structures underlying the manifest behaviour of the system managed and becoming ever more skilled in shaping them for the benefit of the organization.

## SYNTHESIZING THE LINKS: MANAGEMENT AS A SYSTEMIC PROCESS

To conclude this chapter, we will synthesize the links between task-setting, structure and behaviour, thereby emphasizing some of the systemic properties of the management process.

First, the management process is multidimensional. In Figure 8.9, we have depicted only three of its dimensions: 'task-setting', 'structure' and 'behaviour'. These represent key aspects. They are, in fact, the dimensions that define the columns of the 'St. Gallen management concept', a framework for structuring management issues developed at the University of St. Gallen and described by Bleicher (1992).

Second, it is a multilevel process in logical terms. We have analysed in detail the three levels of operative, strategic and normative management. In Figure 8.9, these are implied and suggested in, for example, the task-setting circle, where corporate policy (as part of the normative management) and strategy (as a component of strategic management) are separately represented. Furthermore, identity and vision (components of integrative normative management) are given a central position in the scheme.

Third, the components of the scheme are interrelated. This has been sufficiently laid out in the preceding sections.

Fourth, management is a recursive process. In principle, the whole scheme applies to any level of recursion of a firm, even though some of the terms may contain bias towards the higher levels of recursion.

These terms give an overview of the domains in which the management process can catalyse corporate transformation. At the task-setting level, the emphasis is on reshaping profile and thrust and on revising principles and norms that govern the behaviour of the corporation (or organizational unit) both internally and in relation to its environment; here we find the development of core competencies and the reconfiguration of businesses. At the structural level, the levers of transformation are structural change, the redesign of processes and management systems, the use of

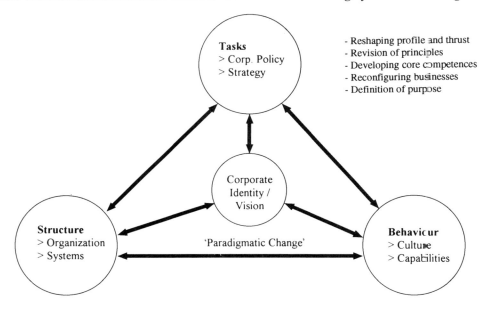

**Figure 8.9**   A framework for corporate transformation

resources—particularly time—and, in many cases, a reconsideration of the composition of the team. Finally, the possible impulses for transformation at the behavioural–cultural level can be subsumed under core categories such as reframing, revitalizing, empowerment and energizing.

Note that the quality of management and of organizational transformation is a dependent variable of the mental models that management and the people in the organization can build upon, as required by the theorem of Conant and Ashby discussed in Chapters 3 and 6. This is so in all three domains.

The considerations in this book have emphasized structural aspects, but the discussion has shown how they are intertwined with purpose, i.e., with task-setting, and with behaviour, i.e., with action. After all, changing an organization cannot be achieved by pulling levers in one domain only. A virtuous transformation leading to ever more vigorous viability and adaptability involves synchronous development in all three domains—conversations (task-setting), structure and behaviour. As the time constants inherent in each one of these domains are different  managing a transformation is a highly delicate task. Strategies can be reinvented fairly quickly, whereas structural transformation takes more time. The variables that react most slowly, however, are the behavioural ones. Consequently, the management of organizational transformation and learning poses high demands on the conceptual skills of leaders, as is evident from postulate I6.

# APPENDIX 3: THE CYBERFILTER/CYBERSYN PACKAGE

## THE KEY CONCEPTS BEHIND CYBERFILTER/CYBERSYN

This appendix outlines the key ideas and thinking that lie behind CyberFilter and CyberSyn; our aim is to give a greater understanding of the link between strategy, structure and information management.

### Background, Assumptions And Terminology

CyberFilter is a software tool designed to simplify the management of organizational tasks. The system filters out irrelevant organizational data in order to:

- alert managers to current changes in critical aspects of their tasks;
- help the planning of today's activities so as to achieve desirable results in the short, medium and long term;
- alert managers to current and anticipated discrepancies between plans and actuality.

CyberSyn is a tool designed to relate the activities of one manager to the activities of others in the organization. It facilitates:

- the modelling of the organization's structure;
- the transmission of alerting and action messages between managers.

Individual managers use CyberFilter, which is a distributed, PC-based software system. The interactions between these individual CyberFilter applications are supervised by CyberSyn—a software system maintained and run by the organization rather than the individual. CyberSyn does not take decisions for the manager; rather, it reports problems and provides a means to report responses and later retrieve them. In addition it permits the user to define desirable futures and to check how current behaviour may affect intended performance in the future. In this sense the program is both an exceptions-reporting and a planning system.

The aim is to improve managers' effectiveness by reducing their information needs without hindering their performance. Without such a tool, too much of a manager's time may be absorbed by irrelevant data, increasing the chance that they will leave unattended the most important data. More effective information processing enables a manager to be more distant from the tasks of his or her concern without losing any control.

The assumption is that managers perform the following three activities:

- They define, in agreement with others in the organization, expected task performances, i.e., goals, objectives, targets to be achieved.
- They detect and, if possible, anticipate inadequate performance before it becomes problematic.
- They take actions to achieve agreed performance, i.e. to produce responses that keep measured variables within acceptable limits.

The program supports these three activities. First, it helps to focus managers' attention on tasks for which they are required to define short-, medium- and long-term objectives. Second, it produces alerts of different kinds and relevance when these objectives appear to go out of control. Finally, it permits detailed investigation of out-of-control situations.

## Organizational Tasks

For the purpose of defining adequate measures of performance, users need to have clear what are the tasks of their concern in the context of the organization.

The tasks of an organization lie in producing the services or products that it offers to its external clients. The units producing these services or products are the organization's primary activities. CyberFilter is intended to support their control. Note that it is not intended to support the control of the organization's internal procedures.

It is intended to control results at several structural levels of the organization.

At the most global level, the total organization is responsible for an aggregated set of products or services to customers. Next, divisions may be responsible for producing different types of service or product. Strategic business units (SBUs) may be responsible for specific products and market segments. Plants may be responsible for processes at a fourth level and within the plants, sections will be responsible for specific product lines and processes. All these levels have the capacity to manage organizational tasks at different levels of aggregation. They define the organization's unfolding of complexity.

This unfolding of organizational tasks is common to all kinds of enterprises. In local government, for example, each local authority offers a global set of services in its own right. Within it, 'housing' and 'technical services' could be tasks at a second level, and within technical services, 'building control', 'development control', and 'refuse collection' could be tasks at a third level. Finally, within each of the services, any autonomous unit responsible for the delivery of a particular service could be defined as the fourth level.

## Defining Indices

To define indices is a relatively cheap and simple way of overcoming inundation with data, increasing the probability of getting relevant information and improving the potential for effective control.

Indices have essentially two roles—*indication* and *control*. First, they are used to *indicate* relevant information—where by 'information' we mean data that is capable of changing the behaviour or perceptions of its recipient. Data that is not information in this sense can be considered irrelevant.

To make the most effective use of the limited cognitive capacities of individual managers, indices have to be designed in such a way as to minimize the amount of irrelevant data impinging on managers, maximize the amount of relevant data recognized by them and minimize the time-span between the reception of data and the real-world processes that gave rise to them.

Second, in order to enable *control*, indices need to contain information about the stability of the process or system in focus. They have to inform whether a situation can be considered as 'stable' or if there is a deviation that will require managerial action. Only in the latter case should a message be sent to the manager. Data that remain within the control limits are registered and stored but do not create a signal to management; this is consistent with the principle of 'management by exception'.

Relevant information has to be adequately communicated via an appropriate information system—one that recognizes (a) managers' commitments to certain stability levels and (b) the information needs appropriate to tasks at different levels of recursion. On this basis it should:

- provide, during normal operation, information about achieved levels of stability for purposes of planning and control,
- point out, at times of exceptional operation, important statistical deviations and distribute alarm signals to all the relevant people.

What should differ between the different levels of recursion are the key variables that managers need to know about to control organizational tasks.

How are these key variables selected? This is a matter of *defining critical success factors*.

Individual managers control tasks from the perspective of their responsibilities. 'General managers' control tasks as wholes, 'functional managers' control them from the perspective of their functional responsibilities. A managing director is concerned with the performance of the organization as a whole (that is the task he is controlling) and should, therefore, be interested in variables such as overall productivity, financial performance and global sales. On the other hand, a finance director, while concerned with the same task, i.e., the company as a whole, will have a more in-depth interest in variables related to the company's financial performance.

Implementing the program depends upon managers agreeing as to the key variables to be measured. They can be established through a 'critical success factors' exercise.

For a manager to keep a task under control means to keep the chosen key variables within acceptable levels of performance. Provided practical ways can be found of measuring these variables, the CyberSyn/CyberFilter system will be of benefit.

## Measurement

CyberSyn and CyberFilter are designed to use a particular system of measurement; it is, however, one that draws upon and supplements the wide range of measures already used in organizations. All organizations have a system of measurement of one kind or another. The more sophisticated and well-developed this is, the easier will be the implementation of the CyberSyn/CyberFilter system.

The three building blocks of CyberSyn/CyberFilter measurement system are the concepts of actuality, capability and potentiality set out in Figure 8A.1. Actuality is the current value of the measured variable; capability is the best possible value that the variable could take, given present level of resources and organizational constraints; finally, potentiality is the value the variable could take if constraints were removed and resources developed.

### What To Measure

Primarily, the concern of the system is with controlling results; these, therefore, must be measured. In practice, however, measurements can be made in terms of inputs or intermediate processes if these can be accepted as satisfactory proxies for results.

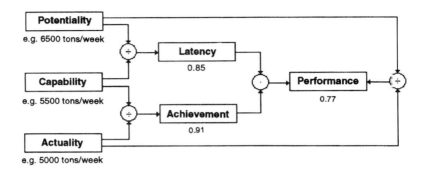

**Figure 8A.1**   CyberSyn/CyberFilter measurement system

For example, in a number of cases the quality of the input may be a good predictor of the quality of the output, so that by measuring inputs we may anticipate problems with outputs. This is particularly the case when the measured input is human resources. In other cases, internal processes may give a better proxy measurement of the output than the output itself. This could be the case for output variables difficult to measure in the short term, when instead it is possible to measure the output of a representative intermediate process. For instance, while in the short term the measurement of a plant's production output may be affected by unavoidable delays in recording the values of finished products, the measurement of machine usage for certain critical machines may be a good indicator of this production.

In other situations, the number of times that a particular transaction takes place in a given period may be a good indicator of future results. For instance, in certain circumstances variation in the number of payments received per unit of time may be an indicator of variations in a company's cash flow.

Whatever is measured, the purpose in all cases is to have measurements that allow the user to detect and, if possible, anticipate changes in the behaviour of the key variable—results.

### How To Measure

We have said that CyberSyn/CyberFilter uses a particular system of indices. The power of this system is its generality. Its purpose is to make the best possible use of the limited information processing capacity of a manager.

It makes sense to simplify as far as possible the presentation of information. The system transforms all data inputs, i.e., actualities, into two-digit pure numbers that vary between 0 and 1. In all cases, whatever is measured, 1 is best and 0 is worst.

Actualities are compared with capabilities and potentialities. In this way we form the following three ratios:

*Achievement* is defined as:

- *the ratio between actuality and capability* in cases where 'better' means 'more', e.g., when measuring production per day;

- *the ratio between capability and actuality* in cases where 'better' means 'less', e.g., when measuring hours required to do a job.

*Latency* is defined as:

- *the ratio between capability and potentiality* when 'better' means 'more';
- *the ratio between potentiality and capability* when 'better' means 'less'.

This index is a measure of possible developments into the future, inasmuch as the index of latency measures how far the system can go by removing constraints and allocating resources.

*Performance* may be defined quite simply as the product of the indices of achievement and latency. Alternatively, it is:

- *the ratio between actuality and potentiality* when 'better' means 'more';
- *the ratio between potentiality and actuality* when 'better' means 'less'.

Again, this index can only vary from 0 to 1, and the closer it is to 1, the better the performance.

## Example

Suppose the index of production is tonnes per day—so that 'more' is 'better'. We might have the following figures.

| | | | | |
|---|---|---|---|---|
| Potentiality: | 1000 | | | |
| | | Achievement: | .60 | |
| Capacity: | 600 | | | Performance: | .40 |
| | | Latency: | .67 | |
| Actuality: | 400 | | | |

*Measuring Actuality*

The system aims at measuring all key variables at time intervals determined by the user's time cycles. Raw, or 'atomic' data, produced by the organization's information systems, are processed in different forms and for different periods to produce 'actualities'. These actualities are filtered out of 'real-time' data concerning transactions of the primary processes, e.g., order processing. They are generally taken from the information systems, e.g., the order-processing system that service primary processes at various levels of recursion.

*Measuring Capability*

Capability can be measured in different forms and with different degrees of sophistication. An in-depth study of an organization, division, plant, or section's resources and operational constraints may permit a scientific definition of capability values. On the other hand, if there are no resources for such studies, capability can be defined as the best value ever achieved by the actuality of the particular key variable, either within the firm or by the best comparable firm—an example of 'benchmarking'.

In general, capability is not the same as the design capacity of a machine. Rather, it is the best that the machine can do in practice given existing 'shop floor' constraints. Capability can and will have different values at different times. For example, the capability of a plant may change with the product mix or as a result of a planned maintenance programme.

*Measuring Potentiality*

Potentiality is the value that a variable ought to take once appropriate policy decisions about resources allocation have been implemented. These decisions may be based on considerations external to the process as such or may be directed by the need to make better use of current resources. An example of the former case would be when potentiality is defined based on new value potentials. In the latter case, potentiality might be defined with reference to bottlenecks in the manufacturing process. Note that whereas the current values of capability are constrained by these bottlenecks, potentiality is defined by the value that capability ought to take if these bottlenecks were removed.

Potentiality relates to the resources the organization is prepared to commit to support its long-term development. Therefore potentiality relates to organizational decisions; it relates to changes in capability as a result of allocating development resources to key variables.

If there is no clear way of defining potentiality, then it may be assumed to be either the same as capability or, in cases where it is clear that improvements in capability are possible, a tentative value, e.g., 30% above capability, may be fixed while decisions are made.

**Alerts**

The periodical measurement and recording of key variables generates a time series that is analysed by the system to detect significant changes and make forecasts. This analysis requires that the variables measured show stable behaviour, i.e., their underlying probability distribution must remain the same over longer periods of time. CyberFilter assumes that the manager keeps these variables under control so that, by and large, their behaviour is stable.

Indeed, if the 'manager-variable' loop is effective the behaviour of indices should be stable, producing significant changes only exceptionally. Changes in the behaviour of key variables are recognized by a combination of statistical and managerial criteria; that is, managers set the criteria as to what should count as 'change' and the program performs statistical analyses of the data to detect such changes.

*The CyberFilter Alarms*

CyberFilter has an alarm function that transmits critical deviation information to the managers of relevant units. Managers require measurements of the stability or instability of the systems that they, in their roles as managers, are accountable for.

Using the statistical algorithm of Harrison and Stevens (1971), CyberFilter analyses the time series for each index and evaluates it according to its behaviour. Figure 8A.2 shows how behaviours are classified. The following states are identified as giving rise to different kinds of expected behaviour.

- *Stable*. This means the current value is fluctuating around the expected value, i.e., the current statistical mean value of the time series. Expected behaviour: no change expected.
- *Transient*. The current value is outside the expected range. However, there is a high probability that the next value will be inside the normal range. Expected behaviour: after a short period of turbulence, stable behaviour at the former level is expected to resume.
- *Unstable*. The current value is in a succession of transient values. Expected behaviour: turbulence will occur for a longer period. Predictions are not possible or meaningful at the moment.
- *Slope down*. The current value is on a downward slope. Expected behaviour: the index is following an unbroken downward trend.
- *Slope up*. The current value is on an upward slope. Expected behaviour: the index is following an unbroken upward trend.
- *Step down*. The current value is stable at a lower level, i.e., a lower mean value. Expected behaviour: the index has reached a new lower level and will remain on it.
- *Step up*. The current value is stable at a higher level, i.e., a higher mean value. Expected behaviour: the index has reached a new higher level and will remain on it.

The use of an appropriate statistical model to analyse the time series gives managers the chance to detect incipient instabilities earlier than if they were trying to do so by themselves, e.g., by skimming over long rows of numbers of a standard report or trying to evaluate graphical representations of figures in order to detect changes with their eyes. Figure 8A.3 illustrates this.

Each new value updating a time series is tested statistically to detect whether it implies a 'change' or 'no change' with respect to the previous value. If the judgement is 'no change' then that particular value is ignored; if the judgement is 'change' then an alert is triggered. The program is able to identify which type of change is occurring.

If alerts are reported, CyberFilter helps the manager to examine the situation. The manager may, for example, enquire about the history of the index, view filtered historical information in the form of stability graphs or compare plans with actuality. CyberSyn also helps in relating this alert to variables relevant to other managers in the organization; in this way it is possible to work out the details of a global problem. This is done as follows: CyberSyn consults the control loops described in the VSM and, based upon these, communicates information about the states of indices to the manager in charge of the operation and to all managers in neighbouring primary activities that depend on this information. Thus CyberSyn's distribution of information follows the communication lines in the VSM.

## Planning

Managers need to establish whether current levels of achievement and latency are acceptable in relation to other organizational activities and the environment. Thus

Stable: The actual value confirms the expectations: No change expected.

Transient: The actual value is outside expectations, but there is a high probability for the next value to be stable at the previous level.

Unstable: The actual value is in a sequence of transient values. Behaviour not predictable.

Slope down: The actual value confirms a downward trend.

Slope up: The actual value confirms an upward trend.

Step down: The actual value confirms the attaining of a lower level then before.

Step up: The actual value confirms the attaining of a higher level than before.

**Figure 8A.2** Behaviour of indices

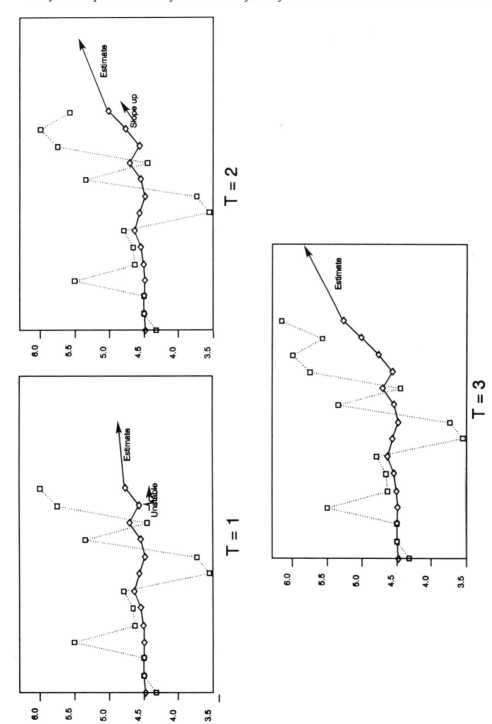

**Figure 8A.3**  CyberFilter: breaking the time barrier

they have to negotiate with managers of other primary activities and with their meta-management acceptable levels of achievement and latency, consistent with their views of the present and the future. The outcomes of these negotiations are plans defining levels of achievement and latency for the key variables selected.

A great strength of CyberFilter/CyberSyn lies in the support it can give to local, distributed planning. This springs out of the measurement system in use. Related to the concepts of actuality, capability and potentiality, two forms of planning emerge.

The first is *planning for capability*, or middle-term planning. In general the value of the achievement index is short of its best possible value i.e., unity. In other words, there is a gap between actuality and capability. Since capability is the best realistic value an essential variable can take, it makes sense to plan toward this value or to understand the reasons for the gap. CyberFilter asks the manager for the assumptions made in defining the current value of capability and for views about the current gap; these are in the form of annotations to the definitions of actuality and capability. The manager's options for improving achievement are to reduce the value of capability or to decide on new response strategies that will improve actuality. The latter is usually better.

*Planning for potentiality*, or long-term planning, is the second form of planning to be considered. The program permits managers to make explicit the assumptions that are made in defining the current value of potentiality. Thus it is a tool in a long-term planning system under which managers both negotiate resources to develop the organizational potentials with which they are concerned and plan changes of capability toward the defined potentiality. Such planning might involve the allocation of extra resources in the form, for example, of investment, or it might involve structural changes or technological innovations.

### Final Comments

CyberFilter offers a coherent approach to the measurement of organizational results in a number of different time frames. Contrary to the normal accounting methods, which only measure results with reference to the past, CyberFilter permits the measurement of results both with reference to the current situation and to the future that the organization wants to create. Thus the definition of potentiality encourages the measurement of results with reference to what is recognized as a desirable future; and CyberFilter produces anticipatory reports to alert managers about present conditions that may affect long-term plans. At the same time, the measurement of capability encourages the defining of budgets and plans with reference to existing resources; and CyberFilter produces variance reports for these budgets and plans. Finally, the measurement of actuality aids the detection of trends; and CyberFilter produces short-term alerts to do the fine tuning of organizations' activities.

Technically CyberFilter/CyberSyn is not new; its basic filtering concepts are at least 30 years old. Yet its capability as a management tool has increased with recent information technology. CyberFilter exists as a prototype to support specific developments in concrete organizations. CyberSyn is a methodology, based on the viable system model, to support the development of an organization wide information system.

# Chapter 9

# Primary Processes and Information Management

## INTRODUCTION

Part Two offered a view of action in an organizational context. Its conclusion was that effective action depended on individual and organizational learning and that overcoming learning obstacles required, among other disciplines, an effective organizational structure. The outcomes of Part Two were a learning and a structural model and a problem-solving methodology. Part Three began with Chapter 8, where we made a link between normative, strategic and operational management and structural and informational requirements. The CyberSyn/CyberFilter approach and tools were introduced.

Our aim in this chapter is a more specific focus on the management of primary processes, and in particular on their information and communication requirements.

Organizations are networks of recurrent interactions, driven by people's alignment of concerns and interests. These alignments are the outcome of recursive processes in which individuals, teams and organizations negotiate their interests.

Primary processes are the basic instances of such recursive processes. These are the processes that produce the products and services of the organization.

In this chapter we unfold a template of general validity for the management of primary processes. This elementary template offers:

- a way of conceptualizing the management of primary processes as learning processes;
- an understanding of internal and external recursive communications between primary processes.

The outcome will be a framework for the management of information in organizations.

Our focus is on the management of the processes that recursively produce the organization. We will show how business processes relate to the recursive structure of the viable system model (VSM), and how the goals of the organization, e.g., those emerging from strategic or value management, guide processes all the way

from the shop floor to the board. Each primary activity is responsible for a primary business process; that is, for the production and maintenance of a product or service for its customers. These are the processes that define the identity of each primary activity.

# PRIMARY BUSINESS PROCESSES

## About Processes

First, what do we mean by a process, and in particular a primary business process?

A process—better, perhaps, called a process chain—is a chain of coupled activities directed toward producing a particular output. In the case of a primary process, this output is either one of the enterprise's products or an intermediate component of one. In a process chain, the output of any process is an input for another.

Processes are thus generally characterized by

- An agreed performance output, which encompasses:
  - a volume, i.e., quantitative, target, not always easy to define,
  - with quality features relating to the output that is to be achieved,
  - and a time frame within which this output is to be achieved.
- A certain utilization of resources, which encompasses:
- human resources,
- the consumption of materials, energy, etc.,
  - a defined level of quality for resources of all kinds, such as is necessary for achieving the performance output,
  - a defined period within which resources must be made available in order to achieve the performance output;
  - resources to cover the financial costs of obtaining resources;
- A certain expenditure of time, inasmuch as the whole process requires a certain process or throughput time from the ordering of the output through the conversion of the resource inputs to the delivery of the outputs to the client.
- A crossing of borders between different primary activities and primary activities and organizations in the environment.

## Primary Processes

Among the processes taking place in a business, the primary business processes are those responsible for the products or services that define the company's identity. They are constituted by a myriad of elementary, basic activities. However, being more general, higher-level processes, they are or should be more than the addition of basic processes; each new level of aggregation, in order to constitute a recursive level, should add something 'of its own' to its basic processes. For instance:

- At the most basic level, a primary process may be the outcome of integrating the 'self-contained' manufacturing activities of an operator or a team with, at one end, the supplies needed to support this manufacturing activity and at the other end, the movement of its products to the next stage of the process.

- At the next level up, the process in focus may, from the manufacturing perspective, include the 'self-contained' manufacturing activities of a plant together with the procurement of external supplies for it and the transportation of its products to a warehouse. We will then find the lower-level operator—or team-based primary processes embedded in this process.
- At the same level, viewed from a marketing perspective, the process may include the processing of orders from a particular market segment, including the allocation of these orders to machines and the distribution of finished orders to clients. Notice that this process includes—though the organization chart may not say so— a 'slice' of 'self-managed' manufacturing; that is, it includes the manufacturing necessary to fulfil the orders emanating from this market segment.
- At the next level up the process in focus may include the definition of customer problems, the design of products and services to solve those problems, the procurement of key inputs for the whole business unit (BU) and distribution activities across the BU. All the lower-level primary processes are here regarded, as in all the earlier examples, as black boxes embedded in this primary business process.
- We can continue this characterization of primary processes into still higher levels of recursion. At the next level up we may find divisions managing technological interrelations between business units; at the level above that, a headquarters responsible for managing the company's core competencies and its business portfolio. Primary processes for divisions will be responsible for producing a network of interrelated products; thus they will encompass the primary processes of the related business units together with the reconfiguration of existing products, the creation of new ones and the exploitation of economies of scale. The primary process of the company as a whole entails all the above processes; in addition, it may entail the building-up of core competencies across divisions and their reconfiguration into new portfolios.

The point is that each level should add value to the activities of the levels below; if this were not the case it would be an unnecessary structural level. Chapter 10 will illustrate the value added by corporate management to a large global company. Of course it is not unusual to find structural levels that, rather than adding value, take value away from their constituent processes. This would be the case of a business group or corporation whose value is lower than the sum of the values of its embedded business units. In this case, the relevance of the group as a whole is questionable—though not necessarily that of its divisions or business units.

### Control Of Primary Processes

We can visualize the management of a process as the management of a black box. It consists of a control loop. In its simplest form, such a loop contains the following elements, shown in Figure 9.1. As we will show, they correspond to the elements of the OADI cycle of individual learning.

*Stability Indicators: Corresponding To The 'Observing' Phase Of The OADI Cycle*

Stability indicators support the 'observing' of a process. This process is by and large self-controlled, but it has to satisfy certain criteria of performance: criteria of

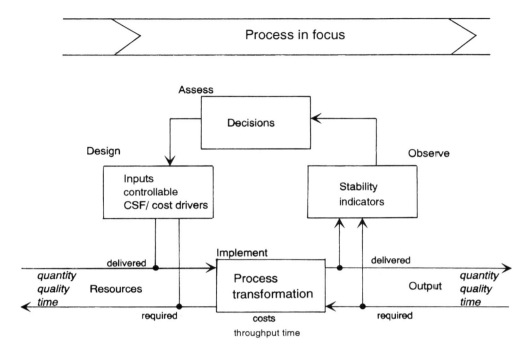

**Figure 9.1** Primary process control model

effectiveness (doing the right things) and of efficiency (doing things right). If the process is a customer order these criteria may include the following:

● Customer-specific criteria of effectiveness: Does the output meet the specified criteria in regard to quality, quantity, time and flexibility? These criteria are the outcome of negotiations between process owners and customers.
● Process-specific criteria of effectiveness: Even if the customer is satisfied, is the process socially acceptable? Is it comparable with similar processes? Are its emissions and environmental impact in line with stakeholders' expectations?
● Process-specific criteria of efficiency: Is the use of resources in line with the targets the process owners have set for themselves? Does the process require more resources (costs) in quantity, quality, or time than were reckoned with?

*Decisions, Corresponding To The 'Assessment' Phase*

It is necessary to 'assess' the outcomes of a controlled process. If these do not meet performance criteria, the controllable inputs of the process have to be changed. Deciding the nature of the necessary changes requires the assessment and interpretation of the results of the process, as measured by the stability indicators. A machine operator might slow down or stop a machine if the rate of defects is above a certain level, a marketing manager might raise the price of goods that show an extraordinary demand or corporate managers might change the company's portfolio of businesses to rectify continuing losses.

*Controllable Inputs—The 'Design' Phase*

Assessment leads to the 'design' of actions; this is based on models, tacit or explicit. Not all the process variables and inputs are under the control of the process owners; for control purposes one has to rely on variables that do critically influence the process and can, also, be controlled. These are the critical success factors for this process. Controllable variables are those under the discretion of the particular level of management that is in focus. They are the outcome of negotiations between different levels and, also, other factors such as technology and the time available to react. Reaction temperature and the purity of raw materials might be the critical variables in a chemical reaction. Temperature might be controlled by the process control system at, say, five-minute intervals. The purity of raw materials may depend on what the supplying refinery has put into the pipeline. This, in turn, may depend on the contracts that have been negotiated with the supplier and whether the supplier is able to stick to them. To change the quality of the refinery products may be a long-term process of multiple negotiations. Hence, the quality of raw materials may be considered uncontrollable in the short term but controllable in the long run.

*Process Or Transformation—Corresponding To The 'Implementation' Phase*

Most of the complexity involved in producing change lies, of course, in the process itself and not in its management. The process as such is recursively constituted by autonomous primary processes; these 'implement' the transformation that the process implies. The process produces a certain output, in a manner determined by the controllable and non-controllable variables governing its functioning. To achieve the transformation that produces this output, resources are consumed. The output is produced in order to satisfy agreements previously made with stakeholders.

The overall primary process is the result of the integration of a network of primary processes, in each of which are repeated the same learning and information loops as are found in the overall process. Similarly, each of these lower-level primary processes results from integrating a network of still lower-level primary processes, in each of which are again found the same learning and information loops, and so forth.

## Enhanced Process Control

In order to understand better the learning and information loops found in primary processes we need to supplement this model with certain additional components, shown in Figure 9.2. These components have the effect of enhancing the 'observing', 'assessing' and 'design' phases.

*Enhancing The 'Observing' Phase*

We have already made a distinction between input variables that are controllable by management and those that are non-controllable. Clearly, in order to react early enough in the case of disturbances resulting from non-controllable variables, a feed-

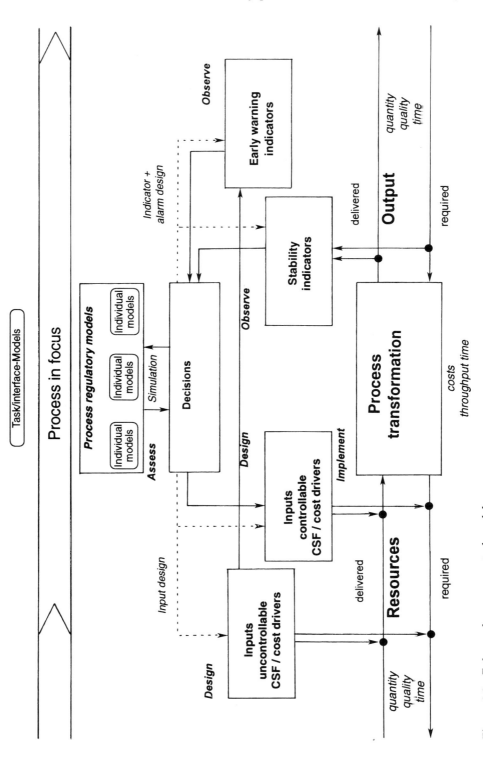

**Figure 9.2** Enhanced process control model

forward mechanism is necessary. Such a mechanism requires a good grasp of the dynamic complexity buffeting the process, i.e., of distant causes affecting its behaviour, as in Senge (1992). Understanding these is both a way of avoiding superstitious learning and a platform for designing early-warning information systems with which to anticipate disturbances.

Knowledge of upcoming disturbances can influence decisions, enabling the regulator to overcome their negative aspects and make use of the positive ones. For instance, motorists will adjust their speed when they see a sign warning of a traffic control operation in their area. Again, a refinery may issue a warning that a higher than usual rate of pollutants is to be expected for the next three hours. This enables the management of an adjacent chemical plant to change filters or put an additional distillation process into operation. The term 'early warning indicators' is used in the context of strategic management to denote indicators that detect long-range turbulence in the environment.

As stated, in order to have early warning signals a good understanding of causal loops, i.e., of dynamic complexity, may be necessary. Often models need to be developed from various standpoints and with the aid of different metaphors. Their use is the essence of 'systemic thinking'.

### Enhancing The 'Assessment' Phase

Our enhanced process control model ought also to help us understand how primary process performance is *assessed*.

Whether a primary process is judged to be performing well or not depends upon multiple interactions among the stakeholders. The ultimate criterion by which its performance is judged is that of stability in the interactions between process owners and other stakeholders. In the end, however, its criteria of performance must be defined within the process itself. For each primary process is or should be autonomous, able to define its own purposes. The process owners, in other words, are responsible for this definition; responsibility stops with them.

From the discussions in Part Two it is clear that any control system needs both an adequate model of the situation to be controlled—this is the Conant-Ashby theorem—and sufficient complexity for control purposes, as stated in Ashby's law of requisite variety. These requirements imply, in the case of primary processes, that the process owners should have or develop:

- a model of the process,
- a model of the control process,
- a model of the model of the control process ('is our approach to management good enough? What about the underlying assumptions?' etc.),
- capacity to take appropriate actions.

Autonomy requires self-referential models. To start with, a model of the process is necessary in order to control the process as already defined. Beyond this, appropriate control actions require process owners to use organizational resources to the best of their ability. For this, it is necessary to have a 'model of the control process'; such knowledge helps them to conduct the conversations that are necessary in order to make the control process more robust—in particular, to have effective mechanisms for adaptation and monitoring control.

Next, our discussions in Chapters 5 and 8 will have made it clear that viability implies organizational development; that is, a capacity to change identity and purpose. For this, people in the organization, particularly those concerned with the organization's development, need an appreciation of the models of the control process; that is, they need a 'model of the model of the control process'. Such self-awareness is necessary for learning. Only if a control system can adjust these models in the light of its own experience, and so adjust its own behaviour, is the system capable of double-loop learning.

Policy makers need to adapt their models of the organization as they learn about internal and external events in order to allocate resources appropriately. It is, however, people who control processes. The regulation of a primary process is in general the task of several, if not many people; all share the same 'object' of control. Making regulation more effective thus often requires team learning; that is, transforming individual mental models into shared mental models. Fragmented learning as well as organizational learning dilemmas have to be prevented.

This requires well-designed communications, but learning is also facilitated by the explicit modelling of the problem of shared regulation, using models that take account of different roles and functions and the interfaces between them. These are 'task-interface' models, i.e., models of the interface between tasks. Such models fulfil the role of conceptual models in the learning loop of the methodology explained in Chapter 7.

Simulation may also be used. In general, the object is to equip the control system with models and hardware and software tools of sufficient capacity to enable it to make as many decisions as possible as fast and appropriately as needed.

The processes of normative, strategic and operational management are deeply interlinked. Fragmented learning can occur by either ignoring or mixing different levels of recursion when implementing necessary changes or by failing to integrate the different types of change required, e.g., structural changes or changes in quality management, personnel, information systems, etc. As we have seen and will see again, for management the concept of pre-control has profound consequences: managing organizational development and viability, i.e., normative management, defines potentials in the long run; potentials, in turn, are the long-term regulators of profit and liquidity. This is seen in Figure 8.1, 'Objectives and control variables at different logical levels of management'.

*Enhancing The 'Design' Phase*

When thrown into action, managers use their tacit models and therefore do not get into any explicit design task. However, whenever they experience—or better, anticipate—process breaks they may see the need to re-assess their models. This is the task of *design*.

Conversations may change the definition and meaning of primary processes and therefore their design. That is to say, as a result of conversations people may change their assessments of:

1. which variables are to be regarded as input variables and, of these, which are regarded as controllable;

2. which of them may be used as early warning indicators,
3. which variables are regarded as output variables and require stability indicators,
4. whether, how, when, and where these are to be measured and evaluated.

Thus, the specification of these variables also forms part of the design of process control.

Of course, the specific models related to the management of these variables will or should depend on the recursive level of the primary process. For instance, the models used by corporate managers should focus on the management of core competencies and the portfolio of businesses. These are likely to be the relevant decision-taking aspects for the responsible managers.

Sometimes the explicit modelling of individual decision-taking may be necessary; in other words, the modelling of the individual regulatory models through which 'personal mastery' is maintained. We may then be talking about models to control production processes, ranging from simple temperature and pressure controllers to fuzzy controllers, expert systems or neural networks.

Such decision-support facilities may help to overcome superstitious and fragmented learning, while improved measurement systems, communication channels and storage capacity may prevent ambiguous and superficial learning. All such resources add capacity to the design and control of input variables.

*On Relevant Information*

The learning loop is facilitated by adequate storage capacity. This makes possible a shared database in which relevant inputs, outputs and decisions are documented. Documentation of decisions constitutes the 'process memory'.

In informational terms this requires:

- defining the controllable input variables, their control range and means of transmission;
- defining uncontrollable factors, their measurement and range of influence;
- defining the stability indicators, their measurement and method of transmission;
- defining the early warning indicators, their measurement and method of transmission.

# CO-ORDINATION SYSTEMS: INTERLINKING PRIMARY PROCESSES

Primary processes consist of networks of lower-level primary processes.

Within these networks, processes may be connected in parallel, in series, or in loops. However they are connected, consideration should be given to the shared management of these processes, or at least their co-ordination, with a view to developing and enhancing:

1. mutual dependencies in the process sequence, for example reciprocal customer–supplier relationships,
2. possible synergistic effects.

Co-ordination implies the sharing of mental models of the processes to be co-ordinated. These models need not contain all the details of the individual processes, just those issues that are important for co-ordination; this illustrates how task-interface modelling may overcome the organizational modelling dilemma and, also, fragmented learning, i.e., in this case, sub-optimization of the whole process by the non-integrated optimization of individual processes.

Figure 9.3 shows the integration of one process, the 'process in focus', with neigh-bouring processes. It also shows the reciprocal harmonization of the processes through communication and informational links to some form of co-ordination.

It is important to note that co-ordination crosses the boundaries of individual processes and therefore must occupy a 'higher' vantage point; it belongs, therefore, to the 'next higher' level of recursion. It is, indeed, a fundamental part of the monitoring control mechanism that helps to create the higher level primary process. For this reason it is shown in the diagram at a level above that of the process in focus.

By and large, co-ordination is an outcome of multiple decisions taken in each of the co-ordinated processes. To prevent fragmented learning, the task-interface mod-els related to each process have to be part of the regulatory model of that process. Otherwise, co-ordination will be interpreted as autocratic interference, limiting the autonomy of individual processes.

Co-ordination can be implemented in many different ways. Each way requires a communication and information system, but different levels of effort may be in-volved. Thus co-ordination may be implemented

- through informal communications aiming at mutual adjustment;
- with the aid of a common planning body;
- with the aid of planning systems, for example MRP2;
- with the aid of KANBAN.

KANBAN—which is a very simple way of handling materials supplies for a process—is an archetype of co-ordination by self-regulation. Though its main application has been to supplies, its use can be generalized. The key to KANBAN is that once it is installed, a very limited exchange of information is all that is necessary for co-ordination. The mutual provision of information is, as it were 'materialized' in the KANBANs.

To see how it works, assume that a process requires about 400–600 screws every week. A defined quantity A (for example, 500 pcs.) of screws is ordered from the supplier each time the stock is less than a defined quantity B (for example, 1000 pcs.). Assume that the supplier has a delivery time of one week. In the most elementary and elegant form of KANBAN, you have three boxes numbered 1, 2, 3. If box 1 is empty, you send it to the supplier, who, within one week, will return it to you filled with 500 screws. By the end of the week, box 2 will be emptied and returned to the supplier. At that time you will expect box 1 to arrive refilled. Should it be delayed, you will use the supplies in box 3.

So at any time there are three boxes—though many KANBAN systems work with boxes 1 and 3 only. These are in the following states:

- Box 1 is half empty; from this you take screws for the ongoing process;
- Box 2 is waiting completely filled with screws; it serves as a buffer;

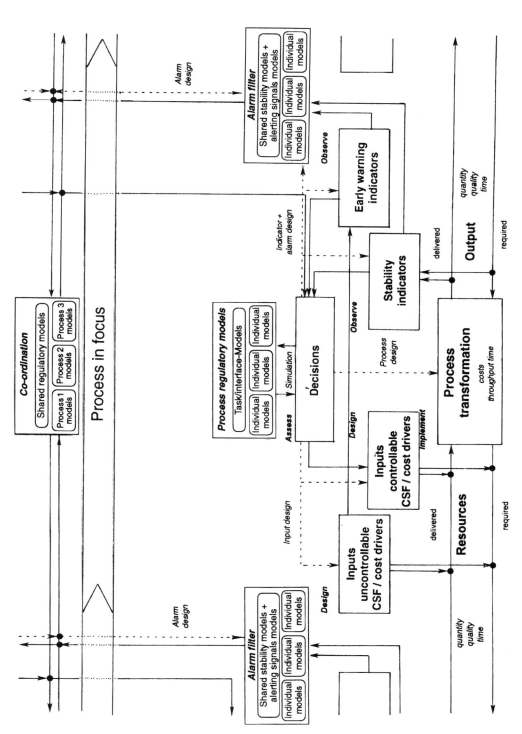

**Figure 9.3** Process co-ordination and control model

- Box 3 is on its way to the supplier to be refilled.

An order is thus communicated to the supplier by simply returning an empty screw box, to be exchanged for a refilled box as soon as possible. No additional order by paper or information system is required. Nor is there any need to plan how many screws you will need; just return the empty box!

Without KANBAN, co-ordination between these two processes would require the transmission of large amounts of data to the co-ordinating unit, including the status of the system and decisions by the various process controllers. The unit would then have to process this information and transmit co-ordination decisions back to the individual processes. In addition, information would be needed concerning the state of the interfaces between the two processes; and all this, for efficiency, would need to be in real time. Figure 9.4 illustrates. These information requirements are indeed large.

With KANBAN, reciprocal co-ordination takes the form of the exchange of KANBAN products or cards. The two processes involved co-ordinate each other as a result of mutual adjustment; this is an example of self-regulation. Any co-ordination going beyond this harmonization is necessary only in the event of deep-seated faults or changes in the procedure. For long-term changes, the nature and size of the KANBANS may be adjusted, as Figure 9.5 illustrates. The information requirements are much smaller.

Co-ordination is a fundamental aspect of primary process management. The trend is to move away from centralized systems. However, the need to articulate inter-recursive processes does make necessary the development of supervisory systems. Organizations do need co-ordination models; that is, they need management models based on a shared model of the individual primary processes that constitute the higher level primary process. The purpose of such models is optimization based on the performance criteria of higher levels of recursion.

The application of such optimization criteria, supported by large information systems, is common in large corporations. Among the co-ordination models used are, for instance, MRP (materials and resources planning) systems. We also find linear programming systems for the optimization of costs or marginal income and systems for the simulation of production lines to improve delivery date, costs or capacity utilization.

It is also commonly found that the design of these information systems does not take sufficient account of inter-recursive communication processes. In Chapter 5 we gave an example of this in a planning system to plan the allocation of orders to plants and machines.

## INFORMATION AND COMMUNICATION SYSTEMS FOR STRATEGIC MANAGEMENT

Each primary process should have its own strategic management.

Each primary process is the outcome of conversations between its 'here and now' management and its 'outside and then' management. The people who constitute a primary process share to a larger or lesser degree its identity and within this

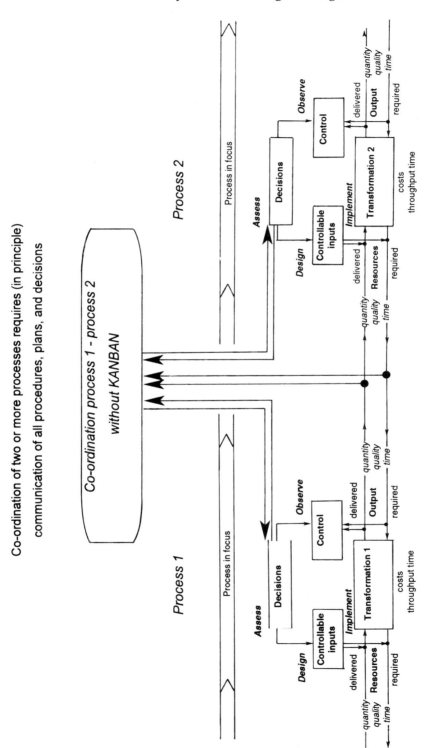

**Figure 9.4** Process co-ordination without KANBAN

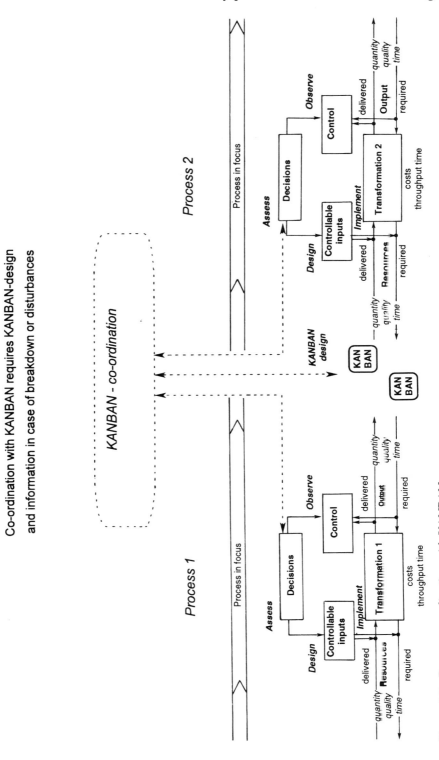

**Figure 9.5**  Process co-ordination with KANBAN

framework they share 'process regulatory models' and 'process innovation models' (see the related boxes in Figure 9.6 Strategic orientation in process control). Structurally, these aspects of strategic management are the policy, intelligence and control functions. It is up to the owners of each process to work out the information and communications necessary to enhance learning.

### On Relevant Information

Over the past 20 years new methods have emerged for strategic management. The corresponding information systems have consisted, for the most part, of strategic databases equipped with relevant information about products, markets and competitors. Also, a set of models have been used to give an appreciation of the business's competitive situation and to evaluate possible strategies. Among these models are:

- portfolio matrices in various forms
- the experience curve
- the substitution curve
- the product life-cycle
- the industry cost curve (ICC)
- models of the business process or value chain
- core competence matrices and profiles.

These models have been widely discussed in the literature and will not be further discussed here. The point, however, is that recursive logic suggests that strategic management needs to be based on much more than a product-market orientation. In fact, in Chapter 10 we will discuss how recent developments in strategic thinking are beginning to recognize the need to manage core competencies, beyond specific products and markets. What is becoming clear is the need to manage the corporation's primary process as much as the separate primary processes of the business units.

In any case, for every primary process there exist large opportunities to utilize information from outside the primary activity itself. There are a wide range of external databases to support individual or group learning. Informational links to be considered included those to external institutions such as industrial associations, research facilities, universities, and so on.

All primary processes need an organizational memory, i.e., a database for organizational experience, in order to prevent errors being repeated out of ignorance. This would answer such questions as: how did we behave during the last economic downturn? Why isn't this price increase working again?

To reduce duplication of effort, organizations need systems to relate people to 'problem solutions' and 'problem-solving specialists'. People need to be able to answer the question: 'who in the company has already worked on this solution method?' where the 'method' might be the use of an industrial cost curve, use of linear programming, short-time working, a business process re-engineering project, ABC analysis, optimization of a product range or shutting down of a plant. There is also a need for benchmarking, i.e., the exchange of experience going beyond the limits of one's own primary process regarding the solution of specific process design problems.

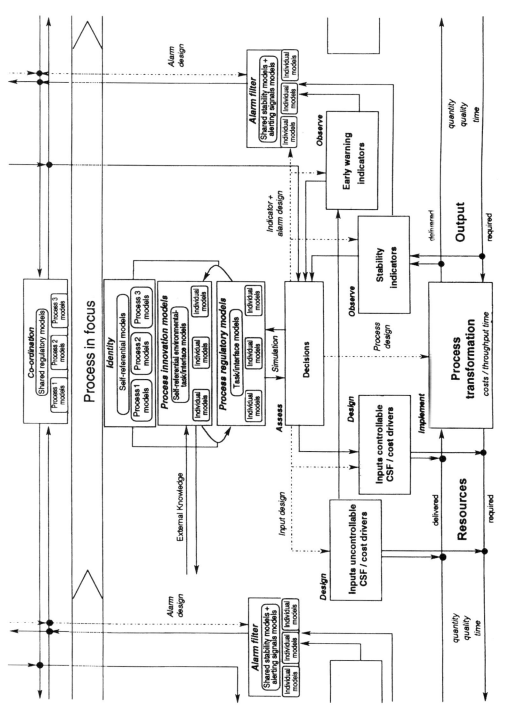

**Figure 9.6**  Strategic orientation in process control

To support the creation of shared mental models there is a reservoir of techniques and of facilitators able to apply them. There are, in particular, methodologies such as the cybernetic methodology and the organizational disciplines mentioned by Senge (1992). In terms of information systems support, there are simulation models that enable the limits of action in complex situations to be learned and understood in a game scenario, e.g. using 'business unit' simulators or 'region' simulators. There are also modelling systems and interaction models for analysing, planning, and influencing complex situations; examples of these are influence matrices and action structures such as those included in the sensitivity model of Vester (1988).

But organizational memory is much more than a matter of explicit knowledge crystallized in databases and standard operating procedures. We know much more than we can say. The decisive component of organizational memory and capability is the tacit knowledge residing in the individuals and teams that constitute a corporation. Tacit knowledge can be leveraged with information systems and other tools, but it can only be cultivated, grown and diffused through communication between people.

### On Necessary Communications

The strategic orientation of a process, as shown in Figure 9.6, takes the form of:

- the alignment of primary process objectives with those of the next higher level(s) of recursion and those of the embedded primary processes. For this purpose there are a range of inter-recursive resources for reaching bargaining agreements. An outcome of these negotiations are 'process regulatory models' that define the scope of action and responsibility for those responsible for each process, including their obligations to provide information and to report. Reaching these agreements should be neither a top-down nor a bottom-up process, but rather a self-referential, step-by-step process of building shared mental models in the organization about its desirable future—as described in Chapter 8;
- creation of the process environment through the intelligence function—meaning, in this context, the innovation function—that is inherent to the process. The objective, in the narrower sense, is to develop communications that identify future trends and orient the process towards the future by utilizing external knowledge; in the broader sense, it is to 'create the future' by creating a capacity to exchange information with the environment.

All these communications are articulated through an analysis conducted by a reciprocal exchange of information between the 'process innovation models' and the 'process regulatory models'. The latter are fed by experience in process control. The identity of the process provides the framework for this exchange; thus it includes discussion of both efficiency and effectiveness.

Additional information and communication processes that should be mentioned here are:

- decision-taking;
- explicit modelling of process-specific innovation and future-orientated concepts by making individual mental models explicit—thereby increasing personal mastery—so that they take into account the needs of strategy, the self-understanding of the next higher level of recursion and the unit's identity;

- analysis of these models from various standpoints and with the aid of different metaphors; that is, systems thinking;
- team learning; that is, the transformation of individual mental models into shared mental models;
- explicit modelling of a shared concept of the future of the process with a view to assessing its viability. Explicit modelling of shared mental models—e.g. simulation with the help of system dynamics models—taking into account their self-referential character and external orientation and, at the same time, the different roles and tasks to be performed, as revealed by task-interface models;
- simulation of the current process situation and possible future alternative process designs with reference to these shared mental models, leading to the building of process innovation models. For this, it is necessary to equip the intelligence function with appropriate tools for the analysis of the environment. It needs capacity for the measurement, transmission and storage of:
  ○ information flows from and to the environment;
  ○ information flows between process innovation models and process regulatory models.

# VALUE ORIENTATION

Vision and values provide critical orientation for an organization to be effective in the long run—as we will see in Chapter 10.

A vision must be experienced by people

1. as an expression of basic values the company stands for, which all its members share enthusiastically and are unconditionally committed to realizing,
2. as a fundamental mental model orientating all primary processes.

It provides a basis for organizational cohesion and a platform for the planning, management and control of primary processes. Processes and their information systems must be designed so that they produce these values.

In addition to the standard accounting systems for values like money, i.e. for accounting for costs and earnings, accounting systems for other values are necessary. This aspect of management is in its infancy.

Processes such as transformations, should be designed and managed so as to be oriented not just toward costs but toward other values, such as, for example:

- health and safety at work,
- employee satisfaction and motivation,
- customer satisfaction or benefit,
- the interests of shareholders and providers of capital,
- the interests of the region or the general public,
- ecological sustainability.

This has repercussions for the design of information systems and the use of information technology (IS/IT). In principle, systems would have to be designed and dimensioned for each 'value', as in Figure 9.7.

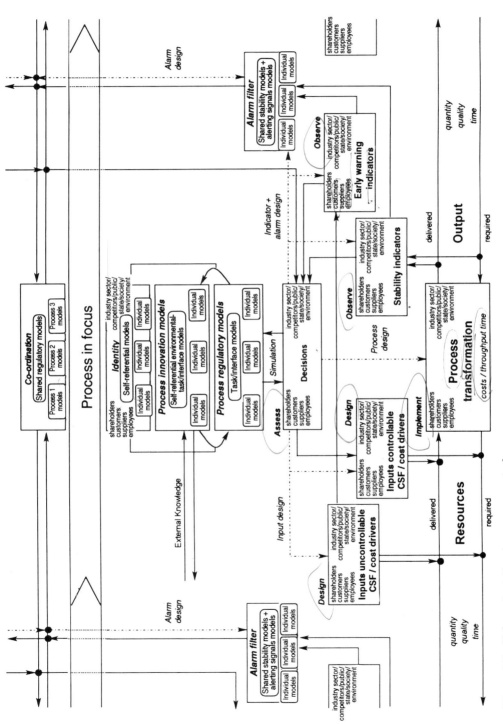

**Figure 9.7** Value orientation in process control

Today accounting and information systems are strongly dominated by process regulatory models. In the future we expect that these systems will provⅾe a balance between process regulation and process innovation, as people's conversations become more balanced between a broad, visionary outlook and a focused, 'here and now' approach.

Information systems will have to incorporate the values of stakeholders, using models for processes at different levels of recursion. Corporations today, at the highest level of recursion, recognize the need for sustainable primary processes. Business units have to reckon with the views of customers about their products. Manufacturing plants need to consider the effects of manufacturing on their local environments.

Information systems associated with 'stakeholder value' are of utmost relevance; that is often where information systems can be of most help to the business, either by creating value themselves or by enabling a form of process design and process management that will lead to competitive advantage. However, a lot of conceptual training will be necessary for people to install and use them for the benefit of their organization.

The following list summarizes the factors relevant to value management in a company belonging to our sample:

*With respect to shareholders and providers of capital:*
- Interest of stakeholder: an appropriate return for foreseeable risk—via, for example, share prices and dividends
- Relevant parameters: cash flow return on investment (CFROI)
  capital value
  stock exchange valuation
- Control variables: self-image
  core competencies
  core business
  participation policy
  financing policy
  group organization
  management personnel
  synergy of critical resources
- Level of recursion: group or division
- Functions involved: finance department, setting rules for measurement
  asset management

*With respect to customers and consumers:*
- Interest of stakeholder: TQM (total quality management)
  quality products at appropriate prices
  product quality, service, price level, level of
  innovation
- Relevant parameters: relative competitive position in terms of products,
  quality, service, costs, percentage of sales of new
  products
  price level, earnings
- Control variables: product market strategy
  quality management

development of new products
orientation of business processes
environmental management

- Levels of recursion: strategic business units
strategic markets and products

- Functions involved: quality department to evaluate the proper standards
marketing to assess customer needs
R&D to develop new products
logistics to administer the customer-supplier chain
for internal and external material and information
flow
finance to define calculations of cost and earnings

*With respect to suppliers:*
- Stakeholder's interest: a reliable customer, appropriate prices, innovations
- Relevant parameter: relative procurement costs, share of net product
- Control variables: procurement management
orientation of business processes
quality management

- Levels of recursion: group or division
strategic business units
strategic markets and products

- Functions involved: procurement department to co-ordinate requirements
and outline agreements
quality department to evaluate the proper standards
logistics to administer the customer–supplier chain for
internal and external material and information flow

*With respect to employees:*
- Stakeholder's interest: interesting work in a 'clean' company
job security, working conditions, working
environment, salary level, pension schemes,
employee participation

- Relevant parameter: turnover
- Control variables: personnel management
orientation of business processes
quality management
environmental management
safety management
personnel and social policy
relations with unions

- Levels of recursion: group or division
strategic business units

- Functions involved: personnel department to co-ordinate requirements
and outline agreements
personnel management for local motivation by responsible managers with personnel focus, e.g., foremen,
plant managers, departmental managers, works
managers, affiliated companies at home and abroad

*With respect to competing companies in the same sector:*
- Stakeholder's interest:      attractiveness of the sector
  co-operation in many conceivable forms e g., take-
  overs, joint ventures, participation, spin-offs
  development of industry standards i.e.,
  standardization
  development of new products and joint exploitation
  of purchasing power
  co-operation in logistics i.e., in building d_stribution
  channels, etc.
- Relevant parameters:      market turbulence, price changes
  friendly or unfriendly competitive actions
- Control variables:      participation policy
  strategic planning
  orientation of business processes
- Levels of recursion:      group or division in the case of capital participation
  strategic business units
  strategic markets and products

*With respect to the public and the state:*
- Stakeholder's interest:      sustainable development
  tax revenue, subsidies requirement, jobs,
  infrastructure
  health, safety, environment
- Relevant parameters:      approvals policy, objections
- Control variables:      regional management
  strategic planning
  safety management
  environment management
  personnel policy, social policy
- Levels of recursion:      group or division
  strategic business units
- Functions involved:      works management for regional orientation
  affiliated companies at home and abroad

*With respect to society and the environment:*
- Stakeholder's interest:      responsible care
  safety, use of resources, pollution balance
- Relevant parameters:      product eco-balances
  energy and pollutant balances at production sites
- Control variables:      strategic planning and product policy
  environmental management
  safety management
  quality management
- Levels of recursion:      group and division
  strategic business units
  strategic markets and products
- Functions:      works management for regional orientation
  affiliated companies at home and abroad

# CONCLUSIONS

In this chapter we have offered an architecture for the organization's information and communications system. It is intended to reflect the complexity of the organization. Starting from the basic primary processes, those of individuals on the shop floor, we have built up the total complexity of the large corporation.

The first aspect to highlight is what Kelly (1994, p. 41) calls the 'subsumed' nature of this architecture. New layers of control are built that subsume earlier ones: primary business processes are contained in primary business processes and the latter are contained in larger 'subsuming' primary processes. Each wider process adds new value to the processes subsumed. What is particular to social organizations is that all primary processes, starting from the basic ones, create their own identity, i.e., rely on their own autonomy to define what they are. This implies that process owners and actors may create as much complexity as the stability of their interactions with other stakeholders allows them to create. Whether we are talking about a plant or the corporation as a whole the scope of their management is determined by the viability of their primary activities.

In a non-hierarchical organization the complexity relevant to process owners does not necessarily increase as primary processes are enlarged. We may, of course, expect that total process complexity grows as it subsumes more processes. But all process owners are dealing with operational, strategic and normative management issues; these logical levels of management recur within all primary processes. This point was highlighted in the previous chapter but it is only in this chapter that we have explained the information and communications mechanisms entailed in its realization.

The management of each primary process involves the capacity to observe outcomes, assess possibilities and design actions in order to create and maintain a primary transformation process. Therefore each primary process is a learning process in its own right, for which learning obstacles need to be sorted out. In this chapter we have explained the information requirements for an efficient and effective performance of the process. However, no amount of information will be enough for effective performance if communications among the participants fail to produce both shared mental models focused on the relevant primary process and adequate actions. In the end, as the reader would expect, organizational effectiveness depends both on people's communicative competence and their chances of communicating through an effective structure.

# Chapter 10

# Management and Meta-management

## INTRODUCTION

Several schools of thought have evolved in recent years on the subject of 'strategic management'; they highlight the difficulties of understanding and improving this type of management. However, they offer a substantial reservoir of accumulated knowledge. In this chapter we will use the ideas of recursive management and complexity to integrate a number of the emerging concepts on strategic management.

Chapters 8 and 9 have emphasized the distribution of strategic issues between structural levels in the organization. At the end of Chapter 9, the idea of 'subsuming' emerged as a way of understanding the architecture of an organization's complexity. Primary activities at all levels of recursion have strategic concerns of their own; all of them need to have a long-term orientation in order to develop viability. In a large corporation, possible foci of strategic concern for the corporation as whole, for its divisions and for its strategic business units (SBUs) are, respectively, core competencies, product technology, and product or market. The problem is to articulate these strategies. For this, appropriate structures are required. Where do responsibilities begin and end with structurally interlinked strategies and problems?

Developing competencies and performing well in areas related to success factors are the requirements for competing successfully against other companies. Competence and potentials (for example, high market share for products or core activities, efficient technology protected by patents, personnel with high skills, a motivating working climate, capability for lean production and effective organizational structures) are the strategic pre-controls for cash flow and profit.

The Archimedean point for strategic management lies in current and future customer problems. Customer problems can in turn be broken down into various components—the factors influencing respective buying decisions. These are, for example, technical specifications, delivery time, keeping of dates or style of communications used in marketing. The engine that generates value between the enterprise and its customers is their effective and efficient strategic coupling. Figure 10.1 shows this coupling. Gomez (1993, p. 39) describes this loop as follows:

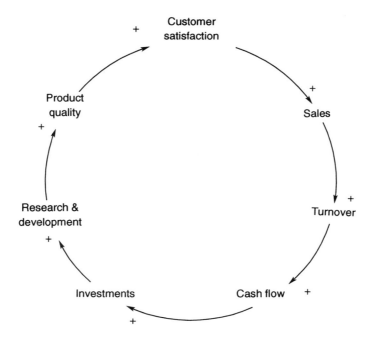

**Figure 10.1** Central loop, or 'motor', of the enterprise (Gomez, 1993)

> The better the quality of the product range the greater the customer benefit, the more sales, the higher the earnings, the more disposable resources for capital expenditures, the better the research and development, the more new products, the better the quality of the product range, etc.

This basic loop can be extended to include additional aspects of strategic management. Greater customer benefit creates competitive advantages; these in turn increase the prospect of a higher cash flow. As a result, opportunities improve for more intensive supervision and training of personnel, recruitment of qualified employees and the development of an attractive incentive system. Improved safety standards can be introduced, and research projects with a higher risk/opportunity profile can be initiated. Improved relations with neighbours at the enterprise's various sites become possible, and local authorities and central government receive higher taxes and levies; Gomez (1993, pp. 36f.) discusses various action frameworks of this kind.

The endeavour of strategic management, as developed primarily by business consultants, is to provide suitable methods to produce the interrelationships described in these action frameworks. The critical disadvantage of virtually all these approaches lies in the fact that the strategies are isolated from the structures producing them—or at least, this connection is not elaborated with sufficient precision. The recursive division of tasks and the simultaneous coupling of normative, strategic and operational management remain unclear. For many years, for example, scientific and practical debate in this area has been dominated by the relationships between the components of market attractiveness and relative competitive position at product group level, and by portfolio standard strategies; yet these debates have shown limited recognition of the structures producing these strategies. They have not gone much further than recognizing, according to current practice in large enterprises, that business units are responsible for product market strategies. A methodology that is often highly sophisticated results in confusion between strategic planning and real-life strategy—in other words, between the ritual of the rain-maker and the necessary rain.

The highly complex inter-recursive interactions that resolve the conflict between the necessary autonomy of the 'lower-level units' and the control responsibilities of 'higher management levels' are generally dealt with in as cursory a fashion as the design of strategic information systems. Yet, as Schuhmann (1991, pp. 50f) and Espejo (1993a) point out, these systems generally do not have the capacity to handle the control-autonomy dilemma.

In this chapter we first discuss the braiding of structure and strategy in general. Then, we explore the role of vision in the strategic process. Finally, we focus on 'head office', that is, on the management of the corporation as a whole and the meta-management of the subsumed primary processes. We discuss the company's primary process and how it adds value to the primary processes it subsumes. At the same time we illustrate the complexity of intra- and inter-recursive interactions.

## THE COMPLEMENTARITY OF STRATEGY, STRUCTURE AND CULTURE

A cybernetic theory of strategic management should make it possible to comprehend the dynamic complementarity of strategy, structure and culture.

The viable system model and the cybernetic methodology, described in Part Two, supply a logic and a semantic, a language and grammar for the interaction, i.e., the co-ordination of actions, of the people in an enterprise, people who generally are not geniuses nor desire to be cyborgs. (The word 'cyborg' is actually an abbreviation for 'cybernetic organism'—in a mechanistic sense.) Such a language can help with the identification of interrelationships, e.g., between structure, vision and strategy, and the decoding of meaning. They help us to order the chaos of possible events and their permanent interpretation in the actions of the participants.

In the organizational context of strategic management, the object is to discover how organizations learn and acquire, and then maintain and enhance, strategically relevant organizational properties. These properties are, for example:

- responsiveness—sensitivity to challenge, in other words to opportunity and risk;
- capacity for innovation—the finding, evaluation and implementation of new ideas;
- adaptiveness—adaptation to external change;
- flexibility—reaction to problems;
- communicative competence—scope of treatment, intensity of communication and rules for reaching a consensus on important and, especially, or controversial subjects.

In Chapter 8 we discussed in general terms the structural implications of strategic management. This section will focus on a deeper discussion of the interdependencies between these structural requirements.

With regard to strategies themselves, strategic management is concerned with the problem of 'what' is to be learnt; what individual technical skills, e.g., as a chemist, businessman or craftsman; and collective abilities such as competence in particular technologies or logistics are necessary in order for the enterprise to gain an edge over competitors? How does it know that it is doing the right things right?

Strategic management is, among other things, a continuous process of designing the future development of the company and making it happen at the same time. This is the view of Mintzberg (1976; 1994), who has pleaded for combining rational–analytic, synoptic and intuitive–synthetic, as well as incremental modes of strategy-making. Quinn (1980) and Schwaninger (1989) take similar views.

The organization must constantly draw conclusions from the signals (perturbations) arriving from the environment. Now, according to Hanna (1988, p. 180) 'All organizations are perfectly designed to get the results they get'. They are determined by the complexity of their processes and structures; they cannot do otherwise than as these allow them to. Bureaucratic structures generate bureaucratic solutions to problems. The strategic objective of 'competitive advantage through quality', for example, very often results in no more than irrelevant manuals produced in accordance with the international standard ISO 9000; it does not mean superior products.

Environmental changes, however, generally call for structural adjustments consistent with successful, long-term, viability. How is this need fulfilled?

Common interventions intended to trigger strategic change include decentralization, regrouping of business units to form new divisions, changed functions for co-operation between central departments, subsidiaries and divisions, and general announcements of new rules or yardsticks such as increased innovation, customer orientation or better communication. Often, because of people's reluctance to change, such interventions produce no more than 'single-loop learning', first-order change and new espoused structures within the enterprise that are not necessarily used. Deep-rooted shared mental models of the kind referred to in Part Two, Chapter 6 remain untouched; the structure of applied values and dominant rules of behaviour remain the same.

We know that single-loop learning does not create lasting competitive advantage; at most it may bring temporary advantages or offset disadvantages. If, however, every competitor consults the same advisors, uses the same tools and concepts, e.g., TQM, lean organization, often merely putting old wine in new bottles, and if all those in the theatre of competition stand on their chairs for a better view, none of them will be better off.

Strategic management, then, depends on processes that overcome superficial, fragmented and organization-constrained learning. It has to reach the deep structures of the enterprise; in order to be effective it has to change the rules of the game and trigger double-loop learning.

The cybernetic methodology offers a heuristic approach to the management of this difficult process. It helps to work out what structures are necessary to implement strategic processes and which strategic processes are enabled or inhibited by existing structures. It helps to make clear *how* the normative, strategic and operational tasks of management are interdependent. These tasks are neither top-down nor bottom-up but recursive: it is essential to break down the strategic management process in accordance with the organization's 'unfolding of complexity', right down to the basic primary processes. The people involved in the intra- and inter-recursive inter-actions of the policy, intelligence and control functions from one level of recursion to another must identify and interpret, via shared mental models, the external chal-lenges, i.e., the opportunities and risks, that face their primary processes; at which point we must recall the 'shared mental models dilemma' of Chapter 6 and the discussion of primary processes and information management in Chapter 9. They must then concentrate their capacities on appropriate actions, i.e., on strategies and their implementation. Those in the policy function need to support the sharing of mental models by providing a vision for people's interactions and by orchestrating these interactions; this is their responsibility for normative management. Those in the intelligence and control functions are responsible for the specific definition of the organization's primary process; working together, they are responsible for strategic management. Finally, those in the control function have to control strategy imple-mentation through a process of resources bargaining and objectives agreement with the embedded primary activities; they are responsible for operational management.

Managers within the enterprise see the strategic task from different perspectives. They normally view it from different units and disciplines. Strategic processes have to result in the dynamic integration of this diversity. Relevant cybernetic loops have to be closed. Learning processes have to be initiated and accelerated to exploit the total potential of the enterprise and its resources with a view to achieving competi-tive advantage and creating lasting values.

Let us use a simple example to illustrate the above interrelationships. The simultaneous improvement of customer service (effectiveness) and productivity (eff-iciency) will generally be the task of a business unit. This unit may solve the problem by, for example, improving the logistics between the various production steps or by narrowing the product range. In some simple cases the related problem solving may require only single-loop learning. But if, for example, the production department of this business unit (BU) shows little understanding of the need for improved cus-tomer service, or if sales is reluctant to accept a reduction in the breadth of the existing product range, then solving the problem within the BU may require double-loop learning: shared mental models may need changing. For instance, the members of the business unit may need to appreciate the importance of customer benefit as a strategic factor.

To take this example further, when it is recognized at divisional level that there are other BUs in the division in which customer satisfaction is being reduced in favour of more efficient production, or that a successful logistics project in a business unit could be used as an example to other units, then action also needs to be taken at the divisional level.

New values, e.g., customer benefit, need to be accepted, a dominant culture of technological efficiency needs to be reduced to its level of strategic significance, and new skills, such as logistics, need to be introduced. These changes require organiza-tional double-loop learning. Their steering, because they affect several BUs, should be the concern of meta-management, i.e., divisional management. In this case, a vision that strives toward becoming an 'effective division' would serve as a model for new strategies orientated toward customer benefit. Implementing the strategy might require overcoming learning obstacles by enhancing, via better communications and resources, i.e., via structural adjustments to improve the monitoring control mechanism, the existing agreements on objectives between the divisional manager and the concerned business unit managers.

This simple example is enough to illustrate the difficulties that strategic management has to overcome. This is confirmed by the widespread scientific and practical debate about the need for greater customer orientation and the requirement for a more rapid tempo of innovation. The difficulties are compounded by the breaking-down of a 'whole' task into functional, work-sharing steps. This makes it extraordinarily difficult in some cases to identify even simple interrelationships and to find solutions to relatively straightforward problems within organizations. Customer orientation means, first and foremost, determining the elements that make up customer benefit; it means materially and psychologically linking the departmentalized activities to form a process; for example, linking production and sales by the process of integrated logistics. It requires the development of new yardsticks for success, such as a customer satisfaction index, and the use of new methods. It involves asking questions such as: how can the quality of a business unit move in two years from 250 to 800 points in the Malcolm Baldridge Award measurement system?

It is important to understand that offering greater customer benefit than the competition not only offers the prospect of higher average returns—as the PIMS statistics confirm—but also facilitates access to strategically relevant information that is, in turn, necessary to sustain or expedite product innovations. As a rule, according to Sattelberger (1991, p. 37), 70% of innovative ideas come from customers; only 30% are autonomously generated inside the company. The strategic question, then, is: what makes a business unit more likely to access this information? The answer lies in routine operations: improved service and more reliable deliveries, which in turn depend on the quality of the production logistics and organizational systems. These are the means by which customer satisfaction is increased and confidence in the enterprise's capability as an innovative supplier is reinforced.

The example shows that strategy in a turbulent environment is generally linked to the need for double-loop learning. It is necessary to change the organization's genetic code, not just its lifestyle. The 'more of the same syndrome', i.e., treating the symptoms rather than the disease, creates a pathological circle of single-loop learning. Often it exacerbates the problem by putting it off until later or shifting it onto another department, e.g., from production to sales and back again. In such cases, strategic intervention may be worse than the disease.

Strategic management, then, is not so much concerned with 'optimum' partial solutions as with understanding and developing the communication processes that create competitive advantages and values. There is a fundamental barrier to overcome here, one which very often prevents all forms of learning, from increasing the effectiveness of sub-processes such as customer satisfaction to fundamental organizational transformations.

Before strategic change can take place and new skills be acquired, before the competitive position of products can be improved and additional values be created, fundamental hurdles have to be overcome. The gap between intention and action has to be narrowed; the obstacles to learning how to learn have to be removed—the very obstacles discussed in Chapters 4 and 6 of Part Two.

As noted previously, and stressed by Argyris (1994, p. 80), the 'theory in use' almost universally observed by organizations is one in which individuals, groups and organizations 'intelligently' protect themselves from solving problems by building up defensive routines. Values that steer the course of action—exercise unilateral control, maximize winning and minimize losing, suppress negative feelings and be as rational as possible—lead to a situation in which errors are ignored and problems are not discussed. The reinforcement of deception by camouflage can trigger a vicious circle of collective 'well-meant insincerity', going to the lengths of a fundamentalist terrorism of the *status quo*. Organizations of all kinds have to recognize this danger before they embark on changes that make double-loop learning possible. Organizational and individual learning obstacles created by defensive routines can only be overcome if the whole process of individual and organizational learning, with its closely linked single and double loops, is understood and made the subject of organizational debate.

Another essential is to foster a culture within the enterprise that tolerates blunt contradiction, encourages constructive criticism and, in the collective quest for truth, does not make hierarchical seniority a reason to put a one-sided weighting on technical competence. In a complex environment, the philosophical problem 'What is truth?' becomes 'Who decides what truth is?' Frank communication must be more than just a catch-phrase if strategic management is to have a chance; nowhere is the need to couple structure and strategy so clear as when there are defensive routines to be overcome, especially when solving a particular problem can bring personal discomfort or disadvantage.

In summary, the quality and relevance of strategies depends on the quality of the communication processes that produce the structures in place. Improving these structures is a way of improving the chances of defining and implementing effective strategies. The strategy process consists of people shaping cultural processes, thereby producing structures that lead to effective—or ineffective—strategies.

## VISIONS: TARGET MODEL FOR STRATEGIES

A vision is an outcome of normative management. It should reflect the values and ideals of stakeholders. It provides the logical basis for strategic management. Visions are not mystical or utopian images but combinations of entrepreneurial intuition and realistic analysis.

A vision is a map showing new roads to the goal, a compass for unknown territory, a sharp-edged machete in the jungle. Visions are guidelines for action; they rely on individual local competence, thereby making less necessary direct regulatory interventions. They help to co-ordinate action.

Elements of a vision deal with such questions as:

1. What does effective organization mean? What relationship exists between the autonomy of the parts and the cohesion of the whole and between self-organization and intervention?

2. What stakeholder interests have to be observed, and how will the weighting attached to various stakeholders change in the future? For example, what conclusions can be drawn from new societal requirements such as sustainable development or responsible care?

3. What competencies already exist, and what must be developed, in order to comply with obligations to stakeholders and to achieve competitive advantages? In which businesses will the enterprise preferably engage? Who will take what responsibility in the development of competencies and pre-market competition?

4. How can the enterprise create benefits, how can it achieve a dynamic surplus through its use of resources, and how can it assess and confirm which operating sectors and organizational levels have contributed to that surplus?

5. How should the company transmit a more effective vision so that defensive patterns are overcome and strategies become more successful?

Vision is the dynamic shared mental model of what Drucker (1994) calls the 'theory of the business'. It is subject to constant review. It encompasses statements relating to aims (what is to be achieved), the relevant environment, the organizational structure and strategy. The multitude of themes entailed by a vision, its role in giving a rough image of objectives and in defining broad fields of action, indicate that visions can only rarely be developed by one charismatic leader and entrepreneur of genius, in the Schumpeterian sense.

In large enterprises, visions—if they are not to be mere commonplaces but generators of strategic action—are generally the result of an effective sharing of mental models (SMM).

Individual or group-based models of possible futures for the enterprise are often tacit, interest-dictated, resistant to change and influenced by differences in technical background, e.g., that of a chemist or a marketing expert. Without a fundamental knowledge of the conditions under which organizational learning is successful, the SMM of the visions will lack the necessary energy potential to produce a permanent change in the strategic agenda—influencing, for example, which actions will have priority in future and which forms of interaction will be preferred. The lowest common denominator generally leads only to slogans and empty consensus.

Visions cannot be ordered or imposed by the power of the hierarchy; this is why their effectiveness is primarily dependent on how many people in the enterprise understand them, accept them, and interpret them in their own individual terms. In this process, too, people face the *shared mental models dilemma*. Detailed models adequate at the 'object level' are hard to convert into shared mental models. Only confidence and loyalty, disciplined regard for subsidiarity, defence of autonomy and avoidance of individual and organizational alienation can overcome this dilemma.

It is the responsibility of the enterprise's normative management, i.e., of its policy function, to promote this process of sharing mental models—the process we call 'vision'—through communication and insights. For example, in the event of a change from centrally controlled to decentralized management, it has to project its own understanding of the problems to be overcome. The command-and-control principle of hierarchical control down to detailed levels makes it simple for those involved to delegate responsibility. It also makes it easy for them to complain that this inefficient form of control is an organizational deprivation of rights.

Autonomy implies that people define their own objectives and tasks, albeit with the aid of guiding principles. Autonomy creates identification and motivation. Decentralization, on the other hand—defined as the combination of autonomy and self-sufficiency—is risky, reducing the scope for assigning blame to others. It calls for initiative and intrinsic motivation. Members of enterprises that are to be deprived of the bureaucratic regulation that may, over many years, have become a familiar and comforting straitjacket become insecure; they react with anxiety, frustration and uncertainty; they take flight into what they call routine. Employees in enterprises constantly call for greater decentralization, autonomy and the abolition of bureaucratic regulation. As soon, however, as organizational change is introduced, tending to reduce the intensity of command and control, the same employees adopt extraordinarily skilful defensive routines to avoid the clearer responsibility for success or failure and the higher personal or organizational risk.

Defensive patterns become stabilized or reinforced precisely when the intention is to eliminate them. In such cases, the leadership provided by senior management faces the challenge of changing the rules of the game and visibly applying that change to itself in a consistent and disciplined manner. A first requirement for this is acknowledgement of what Scott-Morgan (1994) calls 'the power of unwritten laws in the enterprise'. Leading change through a vision is, moreover, not only the concern of top management; it is a recursive process. Leadership, therefore, is a quality that has to be distributed within the enterprise if it is to be successful.

The content and task of visions can be summarized as follows.

In a turbulent environment it is scarcely possible to have rules laid down in the organization to deal with all eventualities; organizational effectiveness depends on many spontaneous actions and decisions. The purpose of a vision is to ensure the common orientation of these actions, thus acting as a powerful attenuator of environmental complexity; the foci for products, markets, customers, etc., are thus reduced to those to which the self-image applies. The vision acts also as a powerful amplifier of people's complexity within the company; people are free to discover their own and varied ways within that framework.

The vision thus defines the normative framework for strategic management; at the same time management gives the vision an operational form by generating from it a myriad of organizational activities. This generative mechanism is reinforced by the recursive nature of organizations. Typically, the overall company vision provides the framework for divisional visions, allowing these to define their own self-images; in turn these visions provide the framework for business units' visions and strategies, and these for visions at the next level of recursion, e.g., at the level of specific products or market segments.

Perhaps a reason why many organizational transformation projects fail in complex organizations—private and public enterprises, hospitals, universities etc., can be found in an inadequate understanding of the dynamic, recursive resolution of organizational vision in an SMM process. Hence the potential of the vision, its normative force, is insufficient to change, by means of strategies, the *status quo*.

## CORPORATE STRATEGY: THE TASKS OF CENTRAL CORPORATE MANAGEMENT

The quality of a vision is apparent when it is implemented through strategic action. Often we hear it said, as expressed by Ackoff (1992, p. 231): 'When you get rid of what you don't want, you do not necessarily get what you do want and moreover you often get something you want even less.'

Intending requires *being able*. Albert (1991, pp. 91f) reminds us that *ultra posse nemo obligatur*! i.e., nobody can be obliged beyond capability.

As implied by the cybernetic framework, learning demands:

1. a structure which promotes the target qualities of the enterprise e.g., being responsive and innovative;
2. the knowledge of necessary capabilities and related resources that can be intentionally bundled by means of strategies.

On the basis of industrial foresight, of present and future expected benefits to the stakeholders and of competitive patterns, strategies are necessary to:

1. build up and develop, at enterprise level, competencies which provide an edge over the competition;
2. create products with competitive advantages by sustaining and developing existing potentials and establishing new ones.

Vision and strategy are not to be separated, but constitute logical aspects of a systemic action framework: the connected elements of this framework are: vision, strategy, competitive advantage and lasting generation of values for stakeholders.

A consistent systemic development of vision and strategy throughout the organization requires:

1. knowledge of the current capabilities of the enterprise and its primary activities, and of the scope for further development, i.e., adequate mechanisms for monitoring control at all recursive levels;
2. a recursive architecture of the normative and strategic processes, i.e., adequate mechanisms of adaptation at all recursive levels;
3. a broad understanding of which additional competencies need to be developed;
4. availability of appropriate resources;
5. the efficient utilization of potentials and resources in order to achieve a lasting dynamic gain, i.e., value enhancement.

In what follows we will be describing various themes of strategic management in their systemic context. The emphasis will be on head office; in other words, on corporate strategy. We will illustrate the processes implied by the creation of value at the corporate level; that is, the processes implied in the creation of a corporate primary process.

The head office represents the management of the company and the meta-management of divisions. Divisional management provides the meta-management for business units. Business units have entrepreneurial and technical capacity and the resources for product market strategies.

The logic of viability means that for all these structural levels:

1. effective organizational structures are a fundamental requirement for long-term competitive advantage;
2. visions are models for and generators of strategic actions;

3. strategies are decisions on actions that are implemented and, if necessary, adopted in the operating business by a recursive process.

The head office as the management of the total enterprise has to perform tasks that cannot be undertaken by divisions BUs and so forth, but are of primary importance for the viability of the enterprise.

For these tasks, head office needs entrepreneurial and professional qualifications; that is, appropriate management capacity and the necessary resources. The success of the board of management is measured by the extent to which it increases the value of the enterprise over and above the sum of the values of the BUs.

Of course, in applying this statement we must be sure that we identify BUs correctly. This may need further clarification because of the often uneasy relation between divisions and BUs. Divisions are frequently not seen as businesses in their own right, merely as convenient umbrellas under which to cluster related business units. If this viewpoint is taken, divisions are not primary activities but mere amplifiers of the board's capacity to manage the business units (see Chapter 5). In general, we take the view that divisions are, or ought to be, viable businesses in their own right; we have therefore treated them as a recursion in the unfolding of the business. We accept, however, that often this is not the case. In what follows, therefore, 'business units' may refer to divisions or to strategic business units (SBUs), depending on the strategic status accorded to these.

In recent years, two important components have been developed for the strategic management of the head office:

1. the management of core competencies;
2. the shareholder value approach.

These two components, together with our theory for an effective learning organization, can provide the platform for a successful corporate strategy. The strategy concepts of the 1970s and 1980s—essentially developed for product market strategies and functional strategies—can be usefully classified by showing them to be applicable at certain levels of recursion of an effective organization. They are not generally applicable to the strategic management of the whole.

The essential tasks of head office, responsible for the management of the total enterprise, are twofold, involving three activities:

Firstly, the meta-management of the BUs, through *Activity A: the creation of synergy among them*. We discuss this in more detail in the next section.

Secondly, the management of the corporation, i.e., the task of reconfiguring it. For this purpose corporate management needs to get involved in: *Activity B: the management of the enterprise's portfolio* and *Activity C: the management of core competencies*. We deal with these two activities in the following sections.

### Activity A: Creating Synergy

In general, business units are relatively independent units within the enterprise, focused on product market strategies and their implementation.

Business units often interpret autonomy as isolation. The board of management of an enterprise may, however, create direct synergistic effects as a result of its synoptic knowledge of the critical success factors for its various BUs, e.g., by the transfer of skills or cloning of capabilities, and attenuate the effects of dysfunctional conflicts. The discovery and exploitation of synergistic effects cannot be imposed; it is an intentional SMM (shared mental models) process between the board of management and the units involved, working through the appropriate structures. Synergistic effects arise when the management takes its cue from 'Beer's Razor': 'Don't use the central command channel without necessity'. This is the axiom stated by Beer (1979, p. 218).

One example of a synergistic potential that has, also, a high degree of potential for conflict is the management of vertical production chains, such as are frequently encountered in chemical enterprises. A chain of this kind may begin, for example, with the production of chlorine and sodium hydroxide solution, which are linked products, continue through the vinyl chloride monomer to polyvinyl chloride and end up with production of film and its processing, again in an independent step. In each case, the downstream step not only acts as an internal supplier for the next step but, at the same time, sells its product in the market place to customers who, in turn, are often in competition with the internal customer. Each stage of production can thus be run as an independent business unit.

An example of how synergistic effects can arise in this case occurs when the film business unit finds itself able to translate its external customers' requirements into specific properties of the raw material and can pass this specification on to the appropriate business unit. This would mean that the latter's development department can create an improved product and so strengthen its competitive position. But will the film business gain? Efficiency advantages for the whole production chain can be achieved provided that specific rules governing quantity and price limits for buying in product from third parties are agreed—not imposed! The point is that centralized regulations are often perceived by certain BUs in a chain as being unfair, e.g., because transfer price mechanisms are based on costs and not on the purchasing power of the internal customer with third parties.

The effective management of internal technology, quality and cost combinations or the promotion of high-risk innovative projects in such a way that the enterprise as a whole gains, without giving individual BUs a sense of permanent unfair treatment through bureaucratic intervention, is an exceptionally difficult task. It can be facilitated by adequate inter-recursive management—especially through an adequate development of the control and co-ordination functions, discussed in Chapter 5.

## Activity B: The Management Of The Enterprise's Portfolio

The enterprise's board of management has to assume that business units often close their eyes to developments that do, in the long term, pose a threat to their existence or autonomy.

This is why BUs are often no more prepared to invest in innovative projects of their own, from which they cannot expect any short-term success, than they are to share existing competencies with other BUs when they see no advantage in it— thereby practising synergy avoidance. The board of management has, therefore, to take on the responsibility for promoting innovative projects whose risk is not accepted by BUs.

Frequently, the obvious is not innovative in the sense of competitive advantage. Good prospects of innovation often involve a corresponding risk. The central management of the enterprise therefore has to reduce, through its management style, i.e., by balancing praise and criticism, the effects of excessively short-sighted, short-term, insular, profit-centre thinking in the business units.

The portfolio of an enterprise shows, for the various business units:

1. how they relate to one another in terms of market attractiveness—measured, for example, in terms of growth or intensity of competition;
2. their relative competitive position, based on market share, on benchmarking important processes by comparison with leading enterprises or by position on the industrial cost curve;
3. their return on capital and other factors influencing their marketability;
4. their cash flow.

By appropriate configuration of its BUs, the management has the opportunity to increase the value of the enterprise beyond the sum of the values of the individual businesses and to exploit opportunities for growth and profit while minimizing capital costs. The portfolio provides information on the strengths of the individual BUs, which of them offer particularly good prospects for investments, and which do not. The financial yardstick for the value contributed by a business unit as a reward for its competence and position is the cash-flow return on investment (CFROI). Economic value is created only when the CFROI exceeds the capital costs of an enterprise. Cross-business unit restructuring is thus an important task of central management and another way of converting its vision, via a strategy, into actions that increase value. To do this, the board of management needs information on, for example:

1. sectoral and technological trends, e.g., in the pharmaceutical industry, the increasing importance of molecular biology and genetic engineering and the decreasing role of chemistry;
2. the life-cycle positions of products, from which a corresponding financial requirement or surplus can be derived;
3. regional changes of focus in various markets or in the global flows of goods, e.g., changes in relative competitive position within the regions of the USA, Western Europe and Asia.

The board needs all these kinds of information in order to involve itself in the ongoing process of reconfiguring the company.

The criteria for weighting individual BUs within the enterprise's portfolio are their corresponding contributions to the core competencies and to the enterprise's value enhancement potential, based on lasting competitive advantage. As a result of the analysis, core and marginal businesses are identified and appropriate objectives developed for each of these categories—in terms, for example, of the generation of cash or returns, yardsticks for competitive advantages (benchmarking) and incentive systems.

Analysis of the enterprise's portfolio of product/market combinations can make it possible to derive not only criteria for the allocation of resources, e.g., personnel, capital, management capacity, but also competence portfolios, which can be further developed by specific actions on the part of head office; actions to be discussed further in the next section. The recognition of particular clusters of competencies may lead management to create new structural levels, e.g., to form operating divisions in which particular skills can be better exploited and developed than in the former structures.

Restructuring is thus also an important way in which head office can increase the competitiveness of the enterprise—positioning it by focusing it better—and exploit it for long-term increases in value. For this purpose, the management of the enterprise has to have the necessary qualifications and capacity to develop a differentiated strategy. Decisions to diversify solely in pursuit of growth have become considerably less favoured in recent years as a way of increasing the value of the enterprise. Scale benefits, i.e., economies of scale and of scope, are often more than offset by the costs of uncontrolled complexity or increasing inflexibility; that is, by the insufficient ability of the enterprise to adapt to problems. Synergistic effects, often only vaguely defined, have proved impossible to achieve in the case of many acquisitions. In large enterprises, the unplanned costs of diversification and restructuring often amount to billions of dollars in welfare requirements, special write-downs, the dismantling of installations or buildings and residual costs. According to Hamel and Prahalad (1994, p. 12), these burdens may be 'simply the penalty that a company must pay for not having anticipated the future'. Often, however, capital costs increase with the intensity of diversification, indicating a lack of confidence on the part of the capital market in the ability of the head office to create synergistic effects and run a wide corporate portfolio successfully. Therefore, in some cases, according to Porter (1987, p. 52), the capital market, i.e., the network of shareholders, investment funds, pension funds, banks and insurance companies, 'rewards companies that follow the portfolio-management-model with a conglomerate discount; the value of the whole is less than its parts'.

## Activity C: The Management Of Core Competencies

Traditional organization and management concepts result in a paradox. Increased division of labour accelerates the growth of knowledge; it is further accelerated by its continuous realization through technology and organization, which creates the potential for further growth. With the rising tempo of innovation, however, its products, often gained with much labour and at great expense, become devalued increasingly quickly: innovation devours its young!

The average product development time, according to Metzger and Gründler (1994, p. 139) is between 60% and 80% longer than the average product life. This means that development of a new product has to start before its predecessor has even been launched on the market. Thus, while the research expense for innovative solutions increases, the potential payback period for invested funds becomes shorter and shorter.

Another consequence of the progressive increase in knowledge is a steady reduction in the proportion of traditional shop-floor work and materials to the final cost of the product. In the case of microchips, for example, materials now account for only 3% of production costs; by contrast, the costs for developing and applying the necessary knowledge amount to 70%. The difference relates to other costs. Proportions are similar, according to Otte (1994, p. 1) in pharmaceuticals.

Although knowledge is becoming the most important resource of the future, its half-life is constantly reduced. The future is, as it were, drawing ever closer to the present. Even so, it becomes increasingly difficult to identify and predict as a pattern.

The future is what management can imagine in the present. Their imagination is used to create shared future visions and to derive action decisions from them. Sensitivity to external signals, the characteristics, developed in Chapter 8 of Part Three, of an intelligent organization and the speed of its learning processes are, therefore, decisive competitive advantages. In discussions of international competitiveness, often the main question is how technological edges enjoyed by other countries, e.g., in microelectronics or genetic engineering, can be caught up with: 'We need more innovation, more intelligent products and, above all, increased government funding.'

However, the deeper problem of choosing organizational structures that expedite innovation cannot be solved by increasing expenditure on technological projects alone. The 'cybernetics of innovation', i.e., the structural and processual mechanisms that support innovation, are little discussed, receive no government assistance and are too little noted by science and business.

Discussion of international technological competition is another good example of how the 'more of the same syndrome' leads primarily to single-loop learning and to the expensive treatment of symptoms—not to lasting competitive advantage. The innovative tortoise of the familiar fairy tale is faster than the subsidized hare. Management that aims to achieve competitive advantages with specific innovation, e.g., with information technology, needs:

1. a changed view of organization—the view we have developed in Part Two;
2. a deeper and wider understanding of strategy.

The strategic debate was for too long dominated by the 'structure-conduct-performance' paradigm. This meant, as advocated, for example, by Porter (1991), that analysis of effect of the market dynamics of a particular business and of the relative competitive positions of an enterprise's BUs, achieved by benchmarking elements of the value-creation chain, determined a selection of strategies, e.g., cost leadership, differentiation, and strategic behaviour, i.e., 'conduct', through which desired success 'performance' seemed achievable.

The reality is rather different. Within the enterprise, the task of developing, for each product, a competitive market strategy so as to gain advantage from its relative position—measured, for example, in terms of market share—is the responsibility of relatively autonomous BUs or operating divisions. If, however, development times become longer and longer and product cycles shorter and shorter, then the question that becomes most important is: what stocks of knowledge exist in the various BUs, in other corporate units and even outside the company—even within competitors—which, via strategic alliances and interorganizational networks, may have a reciprocal reinforcing effect of the kind described in Part One, so that

1. they can be aggregated at enterprise level (alternatively, via alliances, networks or joint ventures) so as to create specific competencies;
2. new products can be derived from these competencies;
3. new competencies can be developed;

4. new competitive arenas can be entered.

To put it another way: what skills and potentials for success exist in the various BUs, that may be separated from each other by the guarantee of autonomy or by the insular behaviour of these units, and may therefore be at risk from rationalization or restructuring, but that, if appropriately combined, could have a major positive effect on the competitiveness and earning power of the enterprise?

The competence concept, as developed by Hamel and Prahalad (1994) and Hamel and Aimé (1994), tries to provide answers to these questions. We have discussed the essential characteristics of core competencies in Chapter 8.

The tempo of change in the corporate environment shifts the causes of long-term success more onto core competencies than onto products. These changes affect the identity of the enterprise. The enterprise's development, i.e., its reconfiguration as needed, becomes paramount for viability. Core competencies, as already emphasized, can find their outlet in products for different BUs or specific businesses. The core competencies of Canon in the fields of optics, image processing and microprocessor control have enabled it to develop such apparently heterogeneous markets as copiers, laser printers, cameras and image scanners; Sony's miniaturization skills have led to the Walkman, the portable CD player and the pocket TV. Examples of functional core competencies can be found at Toyota, with its talent for lean management or lean enterprise. Another functional core competence is the outstanding logistical ability of Wal-Mart, which, according to Stalk, Evans and Shulman (1992), has enabled this enterprise within less than 15 years to achieve a position as the largest and highest-earning retail business in the world.

According to the vivid diagram produced by Prahalad and Hamel (1990), the entire undertaking grows from the roots that embody the core competencies. These 'nourish' core products, which are marketed in the various business units. Figure 10.2 illustrates this.

This image provides an impressionistic idea of the interactions that take place within the recursive cybernetic structure of the enterprise in the production of knowledge and skills, whereby competitive advantage accrues to it by way of organizational learning.

Core competencies have a much longer development and utilization time than products. Toyota's competence of 'lean production', meaning production that combines high quality with economy, has developed over a period of about 40 years; it took JVC more than 20 years to develop wide-ranging competence in various applications of video technology—according to Hamel and Prahalad (1994, pp. 12, 200). Just as important as the problem of the temporal dimension of core competencies, however, is the question: why was the ability to combine quality and cost leadership with competence in leisure electronics developed in Japan and not, for example, in the USA or Germany?

Core competencies create new potentials; they create the space for new products and services. This is facilitated by effective cybernetic structures that foster the generation of knowledge and skills, bringing competitive advantage as an outcome of organizational learning.

The identification of potential customers is an essential factor in the evaluation and development of core competencies, as it is in the development of new products.

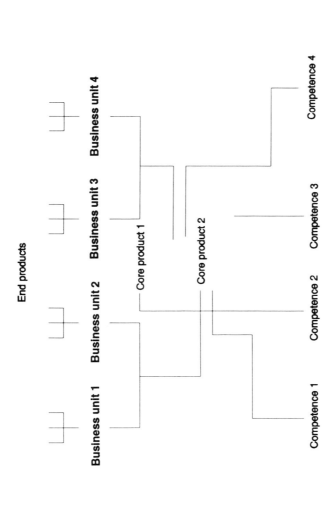

Like a tree, the whole enterprise grows from its roots. Its competences nourish core products, and these give rise to business units whose ultimate fruits are finished products.

Figure 10.2  Like a tree

However, here the stakeholder aspect becomes even more significant because of the long periods needed for competencies to arise in a form in which they can be utilized. The interests of stakeholders determine the enterprise's vector of effectiveness, i.e., the extent to which it does the right things. A strategy based on core competencies may imply wider target groups and different strategy assessment criteria than one based on products; the enterprise may therefore need a broader profile of skills.

The management board will have to take account of the target groups' different interests in its strategy and in its strategic criteria. Conversely, of course, stakeholders have to take heed of the enterprise's interests, especially its viability: a government that imposes an unfavourable economic framework through its monetary or social policy, unions that make excessive use of their powers, local authorities that inflate minor operational problems, customers with no understanding of the enterprise's problems, ideology-driven requirements that obstruct technological development, all must share responsibility for the consequences: the collapse of enterprises, loss of jobs, reduced tax revenue and general loss of competitiveness. The fact that any enterprise has a limited capacity to react to the influence exerted by stakeholders or to take them actively into account is, again, something that follows from our discussion of the management of complexity in Part Two.

The enterprise can be connected to its stakeholders by means of various strategies; examples are:

- Value management that is orientated toward the expectations of shareholders or other providers of capital that they will obtain a long-term and appropriate return on capital invested;
- Quality management, or 'total quality', that designs and orientates internal and external processes and their interfaces in such a way as to resolve conflicts between the changing needs of customers and suppliers and the capabilities of the company;
- Sector or industry management that is orientated—to the extent that such orientation is recognized in the competitive environment—toward building up, increasing or maintaining the attractiveness or competitiveness of the sector and its position in the overall economy;
- Human resources management that increases and sustains the motivation and learning capacity of individual employees and the capacity of employees to work together in teams or project groups, i.e., that supports the organizational disciplines of systems thinking, personal mastery and team-learning described in Chapter 6, Part Two;
- Safety management, or 'responsible care', that preserves the health of employees, neighbours and others and avoids accidents of all kinds that could damage the company's property, that of other people, or natural resources;
- Regional management that, in developing the economic and social structure and infrastructure of company sites, is orientated toward the needs of government bodies—whether local authorities, cities, regions, countries or states—and their neighbours. This includes consideration of subsidies and taxes imposed on different activities;

- Environment-friendly management, or 'sustainable development', that is orientated toward the preservation or most economical use of natural resources and existential needs, both in the use of the various company sites and through the processes of raw material selection, procurement, product design production, distribution and ultimate product disposal.

The interests of different groups of stakeholders, weighted by the vision of the company, are given a targeted orientation by strategic management.

A stakeholder-orientated description of core competencies is essential if management wants to undertake its integrative strategic task on a global basis. Prompt identification and adequate weighting of stakeholders' requirements can lead to new business opportunities that bring competitive advantage; for example, the requirement for sustainable development has led to the development of environment-friendly technologies that can be licensed, or of recycling methods that can also be licensed or sold. Indeed, according to the Welt am Sonntag of May 1995 there are in Germany 700 000 jobs in environmental protection.

Ultimately, however, we repeat what was said at the beginning of this chapter: from the standpoint of economics of corporate management, the decisive yardstick for evaluating a strategy remains its influence on the value of the enterprise. This is because only an economically successful enterprise can meet the requirements of a wide variety of interested groups.

Management of the competence portfolio is a necessary supplement to the strategic perspective of corporate management, going beyond the previously dominant focus on product/market combinations. Core competencies concentrate management capacity on the internal network of strategically relevant knowledge and its utilization and development. Knowledge, skills and appropriate resources are distributed within the enterprise, in its existing units; because of this, they may be fixed in their location by traditional structural criteria based on markets, products and technologies. Knowledge, skills and resources are therefore often isolated from one another. Combining them to produce effective competencies—consisting of people, intangible assets and resources—requires effective structural design; it needs an external 'radar' to pick up weak signals and link them to internal selection, weighting and communication procedures.

Core competencies are much more than knowledge libraries or expert systems. They are the results of the 'brain of the firm', the intangible output of a successful strategy by central corporate management and its interaction with the downstream units of the enterprise. The core competence concept underlines the value of redundancy; that is, the need for duplication of resources and free-floating intelligence directed toward achieving viability. For instance, experts in the process control of machinery on the basis of fuzzy logic might be able to co-operate fruitfully with production logistics experts from various business units and with computer experts from central departments. However, they would be unable to form a network to create 'improved customer service' that would, at the same time, form the nucleus for a future core competence if they were fully loaded in their respective departments or see no career prospects in such a project.

Rigid hierarchical structures, in which skills and resources are regarded virtually as 'local property', the synergistic transfer of existing skills is considered to be an unnecessary cost burden and any larger-than-locally-required expert capacity is dismantled as superfluous, may not allow the creation or development of enterprise-specific core competencies.

Heterarchies, of the kind described in Part One, with fluctuating relationships and loose yet conceptually fixed information links—such as would be found in projects with a structure based on the viable system model (VSM)—are necessary for developing core competencies. So is the overcoming of primitive command-and-control principles. The development and integration of skills can never be imposed.

It is necessary to design a communications network through which there will be a sharing of the technical expertise used both to develop, produce and market products and to provide internal services, such as logistics, to several business units. The purpose of such a network is the 'production and utilization of specific knowledge'. It must, of course, have a recursive structure. It must also have spare personnel available to it, if those who should supply the relevant knowledge are not to neglect other important tasks, e.g., the development of new types of products for their own business units.

Central management must be responsible for the recursive development and propagation of core competencies in the enterprise. By undertaking this it creates a potential that is more comprehensive in content and of longer-term value than the potential for competing with a focus on products and markets as recommended by structure–conduct–performance approach. Corporate strategies then go beyond market segmentation, market share, cumulative volume, cost-cutting potential based on the experience curve and cash flow. Corporate strategy should be more, too, than the high-quality management of existing BUs in accordance with financial criteria. Otherwise, as Hamel and Prahalad (1994) point out, the enterprise's BUs could report directly 'to Wall Street', allowing shareholders to make their investment and diversification decisions by managing their individual portfolios in accordance with their personal profit and risk preferences.

In addition, corporate strategy must be a collective strategy, because it is only through strategic dialogue with other units in the enterprise that centralized expertise is utilized, motivation is obtained and the sense of being a necessary part of a large unit is nurtured and reinforced.

Core competencies put the emphasis on competition between firms for talented staff, for long-term links with universities and reliable, lasting soft integration with strategic customers and suppliers. They also put the emphasis on the selective synthesis of a large number of internal skills and technologies and the integrative design of knowledge communication for higher-quality competence. They point toward competition for core product share or core activities share, as in Quinn (1980), which is not necessarily identical with product market share. Canon, for example, according to Hamel and Prahalad (1994), is in competition with Apple and Hewlett Packard in the field of laser printers; at the same time, it provides the key component of these units—the printer engines—to its competitors. Thus its share of the laser printer market is much smaller than its share of the market in this vital component.

The management of core competencies is perhaps critical to the viability of any enterprise, but particularly to that of large, global companies; as such it should be the concern of such a company's general management. For this purpose it needs appropriate functional capacity. The task is not one to be delegated to lower levels of recursion; if the erosion of existing competencies is to be preventec, or at least attenuated and compensated for by new competencies, the centre must take charge. In the same way as business units get their strategic meaning from product market strategies, the enterprise as a whole gets its meaning from nurturing and utilizing existing core competencies and developing new ones. In Hamel and Prahalad's chart (1994, p. 227), reproduced in Figure 10.3, this task is clearly illustrated.

|  | Existing | New |
|---|---|---|
| **New** | What new core competences will we need to build to protect, and to extend our franchise in current market? | What new core competences will we need to build to participate in the most exciting markets of the future? |
| **Existing** | What is the opportunity to improve our position in existing markets by better leveraging our existing core competences? | What new products or services could we create by creatively redeploying or recombining our current core competences? |

**Core competence** (vertical axis: New / Existing)

**Market** (horizontal axis: Existing / New)

**Figure 10.3**  Establishing the core competence agenda (Hamel and Prahalad, 1994)

Like any other management level in the enterprise, corporate management needs the essential system functions of policy, intelligence, control and co-ordination. Normative management embodied in the policy function, is responsible for vision and corporate values. For this it needs a strong interface with stakeholders. This is provided by the enterprise's intelligence function as it identifies the strategies being pursued by itself and other parties and communicates the requirements for what Hamel and Prahalad (1994, p. 295) call 'premarket competition'; that is, the competitive management of core competencies. The control and co-ordination functions are necessary to establish, nurture and utilize existing core competencies. A task that may emerge for the enterprise's control function is, for example, the integration of the core competence contributions of various BUs.

The concept of core competencies thus provides a focus for the attention of corporate management; it takes strategic analysis and strategic action to the head office management level. The two questions it poses are: what factors influence competitive advantages at product market level? How are these factors managed within the enterprise?

The problem is a systemic one: corporate strategy should be more than the sum of product and market strategies. There must be a realization that other causes, again, lie behind the portfolio of core competencies; what is needed is a learning organization supported by a recursive structure. Creating this structure for the corporation is the task of corporate management. This is where its experience, foresight and entrepreneurial courage and ability to think in terms of relationships are needed.

Most of its capacity must be devoted to this task, and not to bureaucratic supervision and details such as the product market strategy of business units.

The concept of core competence is a paragon of the intertwined nature of structure and strategy, made apparent by the cybernetic methodology and the use of the viable system model as a heuristic method for the design of structures. Appropriate structures help to create and distil core competencies from business unit skills.

The strategic logic of what we have said can be summarized as follows: recursive structures improve individual learning and individual skills. Thereby they encourage organizational learning and the creation of core competencies that can stabilize competitive advantage in the long term and can, via competitive products, be transformed into values that make viability beyond survival more probable.

### The Evaluation Of Strategies By Value Management: The Shareholder Value Approach

We now want to discuss another component of the strategic task of head office: the shareholder value approach.

Strategies should be designed to show ways in which an enterprise can generate value. They should make the enterprise more attractive to its stakeholders than its competitors.

The preferences of various groups are different. Benefits and benefit expectations are subjective and, from the standpoint of the enterprise, frequently contradictory. The enterprise's interest groups also base their decisions on different alternative options: shareholders, for example, base them on expected share prices for enterprises in the same or different industries, while customers and employees base them on other firms' offers.

It is not our intention to elaborate the details of the shareholder value approach (cf. Lewis, 1994; Lehmann, 1994; Gomez, 1993 and Rappaport, 1986). However we want to point out its systemic relevance and work out the conditions for making it a valuable tool for corporate management.

The shareholder value approach provides a good example of relating an enterprise's viability to its economic environment. Enterprises offer to their environment some kind of vector of effectiveness and naturally they try to achieve it as efficiently as possible. Yet the answer to this offer is in the hands of the stakeholders; for instance answers are customer orders, stock prices or bank ratings. It is vital for companies to develop a good appreciation of these responses. For a business enterprise it is essential to measure its viability and the development of its organizational intelligence in economic terms. In order to be honoured with credit-worthiness it has to be seen as able to generate positive cashflows in spite of the risks involved. This external judgement of economic viability will confirm (or not) management's actions as they pursue viability (cf. logical levels of management in Chapter 8).

Thus, the intelligence functions of primary activities at all recursion levels have to look out for these vital signals from their environments. For business units these signals may be derived from benchmarking activities or by watching their marketshare. For the corporation as a whole these signals are given, among others, by the evolution of their stock prices. It may not matter if these stock prices oscillate or are difficult to predict in the short term. Also, it is not necessary to 'enter this black box' in order to understand the function it performs. Of course, it would be of interest to disentangle the various influences, and their interrelations forming the stock prices. However the main interest of management is the 'observer-dependent' nature of these signals of economic viability. These signals have a global range from New York to London and from Frankfurt to Tokyo.

Corporate management has to interpret the implications of the evolution of stock prices for its primary activities (divisions, business units, ...) and take actions accordingly. To be effective these actions should be consistent with the actions of primary activities. We can visualize the CyberSyn approach, as described earlier supporting this process.

Enterprises can influence the purchasing decisions of investors, and hence the stock price, by providing additional information. This, however, requires instruments to link internal measures to their expected contributions to added value (see Figures 10.4 and 10.5). The value of the enterprise thus becomes a practicable parameter for entrepreneurial decisions, one which is intended to ensure the growth of the enterprise and, at the same time, to provide a guide to whether economic resources are being used effectively. The value of the enterprise—in other words, the capitalized cash flows—is not, of course, sufficient in itself to say anything about how these cash flows are being used—whether as additional incentives for the workforce, as dividends for shareholders or as investments for the future viability of the enterprise.

| Company/Group | Value contribution of group/company = Total value of company - $\Sigma$ Values of individual BUs (if isolated) - Cost of group management |
|---|---|
| Division/Business Unit | Value contribution of division/business unit = Total value of division/business unit - $\Sigma$ Values of individual plants (if isolated) - Cost of division/business unit management |
| Plant | Value contribution of plant = Total value of plant - $\Sigma$ Values of individual production units (if isolated) - Cost of plant management |
| (Semi-) Autonomous Production Units | Value contribution of production unit Total value of production unit - $\Sigma$ Values of individual production lines (if isolated) - Cost of production unit management |
| | Value of the group/company = $\Sigma\Sigma$ Values of individual units (if isolated) + $\Sigma\Sigma$ Value contributions of management |

**Figure 10.4**   Value contribution at several levels of an organization

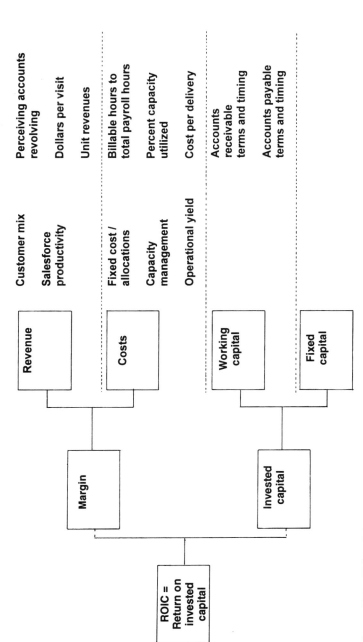

Figure 10.5   Value drivers

A quantitative yardstick for evaluating strategies needs to have the following properties:

1. The effects of alternative strategies on the value of the enterprise have to be shown.
2. It should be possible to decompose it in accordance with the recursive breakdown of the organization's tasks, that is, from the enterprise as a whole to its operating divisions and BUs, important individual acquisitions or investment projects, down to the various 'value drivers', e.g., productivity of production processes, individual plants, rate of capital turnover, etc. Figure 10.5 illustrates.

It is only in this way that the evaluation of business units and strategies becomes comparable, the value contributed by various levels within the enterprise becomes capable of allocation, the importance of certain areas of business, e.g., whether they are core or fringe businesses, and their classification by level of performance becomes transparent and the use of resources becomes controllable on a value-oriented basis.

3. A high degree of correlation between the internal method of evaluation and the external price valuation is needed. The method developed by the Boston Consulting Group already meets this requirement to a high degree, as described by Lewis (1994, pp. 46f.)

Profit, as the difference between income and expenditure, fails to meet these requirements. This is because among other factors, there is a wide variety of valuation options for costs, earnings, balance-sheet assets and liabilities; there are differing legal regulations in various countries governing multinational enterprises; and finally, there are distortions caused by the periodization of expenditures, the disregarding of regional inflation differences and failure to take into account the different times at which the various yearly profits are accrued. Thus profit offers no basis for an adequately comparable and concise yardstick for strategy evaluation.

A practicable theory that links strategic corporate control to the conditions of international capital markets exists only in embryo, as Lehmann (1994) points out. However, it is clear that with the increasing decentralization of large enterprises and the global responsibility of operating divisions or BUs for their results, the finance function, which in the past was largely centralized, is being shifted into these units.

The shareholder value concept is also a step towards integration of business area strategies and financial strategy. However, no uniform method is yet available. As a rule, the DCF (discounted cash flow) method is applied, but differences of opinion exist as regards, for example, the definition of cash flows (before or after capital expenditures or taxes), the assessment of risks for investment alternatives, the taking into account of residual book values of capital expenditures and, in particular, the assumed durability of competitive advantages. Lewis (1994, pp. 23f.) discusses the various methods of calculation and gives detailed examples.

Empirical studies by the Boston Consulting Group—discussed by Lewis (1994, p. 257)—have shown that above-average cash flows resulting from competitive advantages tend to converge toward the industry average after a certain time. The factors that influence the rate of convergence are the components that make up the dynamics of the market and the intensity of their interaction; for example, the life cycle of the product and barriers to market entry and exit. Management must struggle against this convergence; it does so by stabilizing its competitive advantage according to the logic of the learning organization, establishing the enterprise's core competencies, improving the competitive position of its product/market combinations and the selective control of its value drivers. The notorious hockey stick of many plans shows that this strategic logic is not complied with. Unrealistic forward book-keeping is used instead of strategic management. Incremental changes in critical success factors—slightly higher market share, slightly higher productivity, minor savings on the budgets each year—do not create a decisive competitive success, nor bring about a lasting increase in the value of the enterprise or in the price listed on the stock exchange.

The evaluation of strategies by the shareholder approach integrates the strategic success patterns for competitive advantages with financial evaluation criteria, with the aim of internal and external comparability. Above-average performance also has to be reflected in above-average returns or increases in value for the shareholders. An integrated strategy concept constantly forces the management to ask and answer a number of important questions:

1. To what extent is the meaning of strategy understood within enterprises and converted into a recursive process of shared mental models?
2. What value contributions are being generated by the various management levels? How intensive is the strategic dialogue concerning success and failure, and is the cause-effect link between the various levels being taken into account?
3. Is ambitious benchmarking (stretch) being practised as a performance yardstick?
4. Which strategic measures, at what strategy levels, can compensate possible erosion of core competencies or a deterioration in the competitive position of products?
5. Are the strategic classification of business units and their performance criteria consistently being taken into account in investment decisions?
6. How is the paradox of innovation being managed—how to do what is urgent without neglecting what is necessary?
7. How is communication with the stakeholders, e.g., shareholders, structured?

The answers to these questions have to be an integral constituent of routine corporate management at all levels. In order to influence the stock market, in other words to achieve an above-average valuation from the external viewpoint, the corporate management and the heads of operating divisions and business units must constantly endeavour to create competitive advantages by continuous improvements in core competence, by restructuring the portfolio, by obtaining a stronger position in the various lines of business and by selective management of value drivers. The long-term price of the shares is a relentless yardstick for the intelligence of the organization, i.e., 'viability beyond survival'. Its compatible components—the cash values of the enterprise and its BUs or important major projects—are, if calculated appropriately, an equally robust yardstick for the various strategic activities. Such an action concept can probably only become firmly established internally as a result of changed measurements in the information systems and linking to the reimbursement system used in management.

**The Management Of Divisions And Business Units: A Hallmark Of Leadership**

Often the board of management of an enterprise, which ultimately bears responsibility for the overall viability of the organization, uses a divisional structure to manage the BUs. This makes it necessary to manage the next level of the enterprise, i.e., the operating divisions, in accordance with guiding principles that are compatible with the organizational model of its vision. There is no other 'boundary' in the enterprise where the gap between 'espoused theory' and 'theory in use' is so apparent and so disadvantageous for the progress of the enterprise. The board of management has to clarify, in an SMM process, the question of what leadership means in an effective organization, and has to ensure that its actions reflect its answers to that question in a careful, disciplined manner. It is essential for its exemplary function that the standards it intends to set, and must set, are also applied to its own tasks:

1. The management of the company has to show how the performance of its direct task—such as the restructuring of the product portfolio—has increased the value of the enterprise over and above the costs of the central administration. This will enable those affected to understand decisions by the board of management and legitimize authority through achievement.

2. Co-operation within the board of management must be based on compliance with rules of effective teamwork. Consensus, for example, regarding vision and the necessary strategies derived from it cannot be demonstrated by official pronouncements but becomes apparent as a result of consistency in everyday activities. Employees within the enterprise observe very closely whether a distinction is made between variety of opinion and difference of opinion and whether, at least, H.A. Simon's 'procedural rationality' is being practised—in other words whether consensus-controlled rules for dissent exist in the event of conflict. Opinions will always differ regarding the causes of problems and ways of solving them; but they require the visible setting of behavioural examples based on trust, loyalty, entrepreneurial courage, frankness and modesty. The 'boss' should concede that success is very often attributable to 'the others'; he should also concede that these 'others' frequently include a favourable business trend or cycle.

3. This logic can be replicated through the different levels of recursion—the divisions, the BUs, etc.—right down to the level of the individual team or even workplace. Higher levels of recursion can only be justified if their managements add value in such a way that 'the whole is more than the sum of its parts'. Figure 10.4 illustrates this.

# SUMMARY

We may now say that strategic management is the planning, control and development of effective organizations through recursively articulated or emergent strategies with the aim of long-term, successful existence. Competitive advantage is a multivariate, constantly moving target. More important than current products, therefore, are the organizational properties that produce new products and skills or generate new competencies. The speed with which internal structures identify external and internal signals and shape them into strategies on the basis of technical expertise determines the permanence of competitive advantage and value production.

In this chapter we have illustrated the management of the corporation and the meta-management of its primary activities. Meta-management is concerned with the allocation of resources to primary activities, i.e., with resource bargaining, and the creation of corporate synergies through these activities. Management is concerned with the reconfiguration of primary activities, i.e., of business units, within the framework of a shared vision. For the corporate level to develop its own identity and add value to the business units it needs to manage its own affairs, not theirs. Managing the business portfolio and the organization's core competencies are two possible strategies for corporate management.

Structurally, meta-management depends on enabling inter-recursive links, which provide the context within which visions can be shared and capabilities assessed. These links take the form of the mechanism for monitoring control.

Structurally, management depends on enabling intra-recursive links between those with a view of the 'outside and then'—the intelligence function—and those with a view of the 'inside and now'—the control function—in the context of a leadership with a strong vision. These links take the form of the mechanism for adaptation.

Perhaps the most critical aspect of corporate management is its ability to reconfigure the total business by creating, developing and maintaining core competencies. The effectiveness of the intra-recursive mechanisms for effecting this depends upon:

- the *intelligence function*'s effective interaction with the organization's milieu; this is necessary in order to recognize new possibilities.
- the *control function*'s effective interaction with the organization's internal resources; this is necessary in order to recognize capabilities.

The mechanism for adaptation defines new value potentials.

We have, therefore, recognized two fundamental directions for strategy. On the one hand, it is essential to manage internal synergies by adding value to existing organizational resources. On the other, it is essential to reconfigure the organization's products and services jointly, in co-operation with customers, as new possibilities and competencies are invented. This is a key mechanism by which to add value to the total business. Pursuing these strategic directions requires structures with the capacity to produce and reproduce the corresponding strategies.

In this chapter we have illustrated these ideas with reference to the functions of head office. However, it should by now be clear that strategic management is a recursive function. Head office strategic management subsumes divisional strategic management, which subsumes the strategic management of business units and so forth.

# Chapter 11

# Conclusion

## INTRODUCTION

We have now reached the end of our journey. In this chapter we bring together the different parts of this book.

In Part One we introduced a handful of issues of concern to managers today. From the discussion of these we distilled a set of postulates for effective organization and management.

Part Two was conceptual in nature. First we offered a language for understanding people's action in organizations. Then the viable system model was developed as a framework within which to locate people in an organizational context. This was followed by the OADI-SMM model as a means of diagnosing individual and organizational learning problems. Finally, we offered the cybernetic methodology as a framework within which to relate these learning processes to the organization's structure.

Part Three focused on the strategic processes of an organization, using the conceptual support provided by Part Two. The emphasis was on the recursive nature of these processes; we showed not only that thinking and doing had to be closely intertwined, but also how to design this braiding through the design of the organization structure.

An intelligent organization must be able to produce itself so as to remain well adjusted to its medium, now and in the future. This requires its managers to develop a deep appreciation of the control-autonomy complementarity. Autonomy implies seeing organizations from within, and this can only be done, recursively, by those within it. Control is concerned with the cohesion of the whole and this, in democratic organizations, can only be achieved by respecting the autonomy of the parts and the alignment of their interests. In this sense Part Three was an attempt to redress today's emphasis on control from the outside. A key idea of this part was the architecture of organizational complexity based upon the idea of 'subsuming'; basic primary processes are subsumed in more global primary processes. In order to justify this embedment, the latter should be more than the addition of subsumed processes; they must add value to them. This idea was illustrated with reference to a global corporation in Chapter 10.

In this final chapter we will revisit the postulates of management offered in Part One, now supported by the concepts of recursion, autonomy and complexity that we have developed. We want to reinforce the manner in which systemic thinking, in particular cybernetics and system theory, serves as a framework for the design of comprehensive organizational fitness.

The postulates were grouped in four domains: those related to the performance of organizations, those related to their structural basis, those related to the relationships transforming structure into process and vice versa, and those related to the individuals embodying these relationships. In the conclusions we are now drawing we will use the same postulates but relate them somewhat differently.

Our discussion is organized around the following argument:

• First, we will consider *structure* to be the embodiment of organizational relationships.
• We will then emphasize that structure and process are two sides of the same coin; thereby we will make it clear that *process orientation* is natural in organizations.
• Simultaneously we will make it clear that structure and process are the outcome of interpersonal *communications*; this is the third theme of the conclusions.
• However, as we develop a deeper awareness of the organization as a whole we necessarily have to increase our appreciation of the *environment*. In effect this is no more than developing sensitivity to all those resources—human and other—that provide an ecological niche for the organization's long term viability.
• As we develop a deeper understanding of the organization's relationship with its environment, issues such as *strategy and performance* become meaningful. We are now concerned with the processes that create self-awareness in the organization: What business are we in? What is excellent performance in this business? This is the fifth theme of our conclusions.
• Change, however, happens all the time. People and organizations as they adjust to each other and to the wider environment need to constantly redefine and improve their performance; they depend for this on *individual and organizational learning*.
• Finally, as people and organizations learn they transform themselves. This transformation relates not only to conceptual, but also to operational learning; our final theme is the full-fledged *process of change*.

## STRUCTURE AND COMPLEXITY

The structure of an organization is defined by the people and other resources embodying its relationships.

The same relationship may have different embodiments; in this sense, a given structure makes possible a variety of relationships. At the same time, the distribution of available resources defines what relationships cannot exist. For instance, despite good intentions, participative relationships cannot emerge in an organization with an allocation of resources skewed to the top levels of management. Failure to recognize this means that managements often espouse particular relationships that stakeholders on the receiving end never experience.

The fact that structures are embodied in people's relationships means that:

I 1. Organizations are created and shaped by their people. They do not have an existence independent of them.

Now effective structures are those that manage complexity effectively. These are the ones that support viability beyond survival.

In order to have an effective management of complexity we have argued for recursive structures; that is, for structures that support the emergence of auto-nomous units within autonomous units. The viable system model (VSM), developed in Chapter 5, offers a paradigm for this type of structure.

Implementing a recursive structure is not easy. Creating this kind of structure requires a fundamental organizational transformation; it is necessary to see the cohesion of organizations as the outcome of people's alignment of interests and not as the outcome of their submission to the interests of the hierarchy. Metaphorically, organizations should resemble grapes in a cluster rather than single large fruits. This view implies that people at all structural levels may possess, show, use and develop similar individual complexity. The 'worker' on the shop floor and the 'senior man-ager' in the headquarters need not have different time horizons. Our view implies a sophisticated worker, responsible for a full task and possessing autonomy.

The recipe for developing an effective organization is to create the structural conditions for such complexity to emerge; that is, to create a generator of organiza-tional complexity. But many organizations are far from this model. Not only is there a lack of clarity about primary processes, i.e., full tasks, but there are cultural barriers and resource constraints that reduce the chances of such a transformation.

S 1. Effective structures are a fundamental requirement for the management of complexity. They allow organizations to create opportunities for themselves as well as to respond to disturbances and change.

S 2. Organizations need structures that foster autonomy and local problem solving capacity.

Lack of clarity about primary tasks makes it common for senior managers to develop relationships that inhibit the autonomy of lower structural levels. This is common within plants, where management have difficulties in seeing workers as being themselves managers. But it also occurs in units at higher structural levels; a common case, discussed in Chapter 5, concerns the responsibilities of divisions in large corporations. Despite companies recognizing the need for operational divi-sions and creating divisions that are clusters of business units roughly correspond-ing to holistic primary processes, i.e., to some kind of recursive organization, their management is, by and large, hierarchical and not recursive.

The question is: are operational divisions primary processes or not? At this point, the gap between VSM criteria of effectiveness and the 'theory in use' is often apparent and potentially dangerous for the progress of the enterprise. The board of manage-ment has to clarify, in a 'shared mental models' (SMM) process, the question as to what leadership means in an effective organization. It then has to ensure that its actions reflect its answers to that question in a careful, disciplined manner. Instead, as described in Chapter 5, the board often gets directly involved in policy issues confront-ing business units (BUs); the divisions are bypassed. This reflects a lack of appreciation of the need for autonomous divisions, responsible for primary processes.

In relational terms divisional managers are placed in a hierarchical relationship with board members; they are not managing their divisions as autonomous units but as resources of the board. Organizationally, the approach reduces the chances of divisions creating 'fresh' complexity to enhance the organization's performance; the board's views dominate the management of business units.

Systemically, the essential objective of control is to give direction and enable movement, not to supervise every aspect of the lower level's work. Control, therefore, should concentrate primarily on constructing and developing the conditions for successful self-organization.

To assert this principle of control in a recursive organization is not to reduce the actual, effective powers of senior management. It is, however, to cause them to abandon the illusion of omnipotence in favour of releasing the large-scale organizational potential that is brought into existence in all organizations based on recursive structures. Management is more than intuition, more than charisma, more than outstanding technical expertise. Management, however, does not need any new formulas or techniques!

Are we proposing detached management? No: management, in the sense of the structuring, controlling and developing complex organizations, needs the scientific basis of a heuristic for dealing with the core of its integrative task. This takes the form of a wealth of different activities, each of them dealing with complexity. The practical embodiment of a guidance architecture, with the VSM as a reference model, was illustrated in Chapter 5.

S 5. Organizations need to develop control mechanisms that foster both autonomy and cohesion.

# PROCESS ORIENTATION

The structure of an organization is not its skeleton; that metaphor has a static overtone. The structure is defined by people's patterns of interaction. We produce the structure as we interact with others, enabled by resources of one kind or another; interactive processes produce the structure and the structure produces the processes, i.e., allows us to engage in some interactions and not others. Structure and process are two sides of the same coin.

This is the case whether we are considering a functional or a recursive organization. Functional structures, those organized around functions rather than businesses, are also recursive. There is no way for a group of people, however good they are, to mastermind a large complex task from the centre; in one form or another they depend on autonomous units within autonomous units to function.

The distinction between 'functional' and 'business-unit' structuring is, therefore, a matter of degree rather than of alternatives. The perception in functional structures is that it is difficult to integrate the organization's corporate functions; management is seen as 'fractional' rather than holistic. The structure is 'too centralized'. However, autonomous teams or business units also have a functional structure. Division of labour is the rule in all organizational units. The difference is that an autonomous team will produce a natural integration of these functions. We espouse the view that, because of small numbers and perhaps of co-location, teams have a natural capacity to integrate separate functions.

Functional structures require a high degree of resource centralization in order to work. This is likely to be the case in small teams even more than in large organizations. As functions are centralized more and more central capacity is required in order to take into account functional interdependencies; that is, to see the organizational task as a whole. If this capacity is not adequate the quality of functional integration will be poor, creating a fractional organization.

The advantage of the 'subsuming' recursive structure is its progressive matching of integrative resources to primary processes as demanded by the complexity of the task. As operational teams develop the capacity to integrate basic primary processes and manage them by themselves, they take away from more general management the responsibility for these processes, thereby increasing the capacity for functional integration at the general level. Of course, today new information technology is making changes in the capacity for functional integration. Increasingly, it is making possible to centralize resources without losing functional flexibility; resource centralization becomes possible at the same time as functional decentralization. This is at the core of 'business process re-engineering'.

We conclude that effective recursive structures are likely to reduce the resources required to achieve the functional integration implied by complex tasks. Chapter 10 was all about corporate management integrating business units into a complex total business, i.e. the corporation, subsuming under it everything except the company's core competencies and business portfolio. For this purpose, corporate management had to succeed in integrating a number of human and technological resources in order to achieve a business with a higher value than the addition of the business units' values. We made the point that this is not easy; we often find businesses whose value is less than the aggregated value of the parts, i.e., the business units.

> S 3. Organizational effectiveness depends on managing interdependencies so as to move from a functional to a process orientation; from a Tayloristic to a systemic paradigm.
>
> R 3. To cope with change, organization and business process redesign are essential for many corporations. For this, the multilevel logic of management—operational, strategic and normative—must be understood.
>
> R 6. An effective organization is built on ongoing communications, which can be enabled by powerful technology.

In Chapter 9 we made it clear that primary processes, at all levels of recursion, are focused on the customer. Interactions with customers happen as people in the organization produce, jointly with them, new problem solutions; as they design new products and services, sort out the logistics of orders or produce these orders. In a recursive structure everyone, through the primary processes they are concerned with, is interacting with the customer. At the same time, in the recursive organization all primary activities, as they define and redefine the purpose of their activities, are inventing and re-inventing their markets. This invention is supported by the strategic processes of meta-management; that is, by the creation of new value potentials and the realization of existing ones. Effective organization requires consistency between market and customer orientation; it makes no sense to develop markets if the organization has no operational capacity to service them.

R 1. **People in organizations need to develop an appreciation of the meaning of customer and market orientation.**

The operational capacity we are concerned with here is the capacity to satisfy customers. It involves a dynamic interaction. As people in the organization's many primary processes develop an awareness of their customers and of their customers' needs they see the need for continuous improvement.

P 5. **Organizations need to foster quality ('fitness for purpose') and continual improvement in all their activities, that is, they need to do better what they already do.**

# COMMUNICATIONS

A theme throughout this book has been communications. We have tried to direct attention to the need for communication rather than mere information.

Often managers are obsessed by information; they believe that more and better information will improve their performance. In this book we have pointed out that information is irrelevant if supporting communications are inadequate. Performance is far more related to the quality of communications than to information.

This is reflected in the emphasis we have given to conversations, the sharing of mental models (SMM) and SMM dilemma. It is also reflected in the stress we have placed on the relevance of structure.

Communications between management at successive structural levels is fraught with problems. Interactions need to conform to the criteria of effective organization. Intervention by 'higher' management must take into account that its supervisory power is limited by its supervisory knowledge and communication skills. Power may demonstrate strength but, as a result, frequently fails to achieve the desired effect and merely results in a loss of necessary authority. Control must therefore be distributed in 'the architecture of the system'. An essential aim of decentralization is to increase within the organization the capacity to receive external signals and to transform them into information and action. Interventions should, in principle, be limited to the cases where autonomy vitally compromises the cohesion of the whole. It is essential to improve the communicative competence of managers.

Decentralization implies autonomy for primary activities, supported by the necessary resources. As a result, responsibility becomes fairly accountable. Unfortunately, the advantages of decentralization are often not achieved. Overcoming the control dilemma discussed in Chapter 5 presents practical difficulties. Inter-recursive communications are particularly difficult; autonomy and cohesion—which are the needs of the two parties involved in such communication—depend on the communications being effective. We have frequently referred to individual and organizational defensive patterns, by which important problems are often bypassed and the bypass covered up. This means that even if communication channels exist, the requirement that communication must be open and oriented so far as its content is concerned by the logic of vision, strategy and implementation, is not sufficient to overcome defensive patterns. Putting a sparrow in a bigger cage does not make it a nightingale.

The solution to the shared mental models dilemma shows how the entrepreneurial autonomy of the business unit can harmonize with the responsibility link between different management levels. Information relationships are structured in such a manner that the higher level can fulfil its responsibility and, on the lower levels, understanding is activated by motivation and not destroyed by permanent intervention. Shared mental models can only relate, and only need to relate, to the essential variables of a business unit.

These communication problems are not, however, exclusive to interactions within the organization; they occur in interactions with all stakeholders. Creating a win-win culture in all these interactions is above all a communicational challenge.

R 7. Organizations need to develop a capacity for cultural transformation towards more open and participative structures.

R 4. Organizations need to develop a co-operative culture, breaking boundaries and developing synergistic alliances with suppliers, customers, competitors and other external stakeholders.

R 5. Relationships with stakeholders require effective communications, creating overlapping domains of interest and common responsibility.

## ENVIRONMENT

Based on the ideas developed in Part Two, it is possible to make a distinction between 'an organization in its environment' and 'an organization in its medium'.

A common meaning attached to 'environment' is, simply, the external circumstances affecting the enterprise. On the other hand a connotation of 'medium' is that of the substrata, or surroundings, in which an organization exists.

Accordingly, 'the organization in its environment' is normally understood as a strategic concept. Its focus is on planning response strategies, based on intelligence information gathered by those in the organization whose concern is the 'outside and then'. In a hierarchical organization these are likely to be the planners, marketeers and others working mostly at the corporate level. They develop models and strategic plans to respond to environmental challenges and opportunities. The rest are concerned with the organization's 'doing'.

Recursive structures do not follow this logic; everyone in the organization should be concerned with the outside. Everyone interacts with the organization's environment.

On the other hand, to refer to 'the organization in its medium' is to focus on the autonomy of the total organization and its parts. It is a relationship concept. Its focus is on everyone's instant-by-instant communications with this environment—the organization's medium. The emissions of the plant, the local interactions with the rest of the community, the day-to-day interactions with suppliers and customers, the ethics of managers as they define their own rewards—all of these and more are aspects of this interaction with the medium.

An emphasis on 'environment' rather than on 'medium' is an emphasis on planning and strategy rather than on communications. Of course knowledge about the environment is necessary, and people at all levels need to develop a deeper grasp of the cause-effect loops relating the organization to other environmental actors. Such models of the environment are necessary to develop a sense of connectivity with the actions of these other actors; they are necessary to anticipate the likely outcomes of our decisions and to develop a sense of the longer term. However, if these models are decoupled from the operational capacity of the organization or reflect a poor understanding of the environment, they may not only be irrelevant but positively dangerous to the long-term viability of the organization.

The idea that only a few individuals are concerned with the environment, namely those responsible for working out the strategy and producing responses at the corporate level, is replaced by the idea that everyone is responsible for the organization's balance with its medium. Every single person should develop an appreciation of how his or her actions, as members of the organization, affect the medium. These actions define the fit of the organization with its medium; it is only if corporate-level strategies and plans are consistent with this fit that they will be useful.

In an organization that is well adjusted to its medium, corporate plans and strategies are catalysts of people's coordination of actions. If, however, this is not the case, no amount of information and planning is of any help. Corporate plans and strategies are merely the tip of the communicational iceberg.

To deal with the outside world based on information and plans produced by a corporate group that is oblivious to the capabilities of all other organizational members will not allow an organization to achieve effective stability with its environment. Everybody needs to learn how to communicate with their part of the environment; that is, needs to learn how to manage the 'environmental' impact of his or her actions. This seems to be the intuitive underpinning of movements like total quality management, ecological management and others. A 'responsive' organization, then, is one that is sensitive to its 'medium' rather than focused on its 'environment'. It is, therefore, aware of far more complexity than the 'strategic' organization. The latter is over-centralized and on the whole liable to mishandle the human resources involved in its constitution.

I 5. People and teams in organizations need to develop an awareness of the systemic implications of their actions.

R 2. People in organizations need to develop an appreciation of ecological issues and the capacity to deal with them responsibly.

P 9. Organizations need to develop a sustainable ecological balance with their milieu.

## STRATEGY AND PERFORMANCE

Strategy is a concern of all autonomous units. It consists of reflection about themselves and their environment.

Normative, strategic and operational management are relevant management levels in all autonomous units. Normative management is responsible for the organization's vision, identity and values and is, therefore responsible for the organization's development over time. It defines criteria for strategic processes; that is, for the processes responsible for creating new value potentials. As explained in Chapter 8, these processes also depend on a good grasp of the organization's extant value potentials. Operational management is concerned with the use of these potentials.

> P 3. Organizations have to adhere steadfastly to their core values in realizing their visions. This implies going beyond mere efficiency and profit orientation.

Criteria for both effectiveness (doing the right things) and efficiency (doing things right) need, therefore, to be defined by each autonomous unit. In defining these criteria, it should be noted that effectiveness, i.e., flexibility in the face of problems, requires redundancy within the system. Redundancy, therefore, is a necessary property and its costs need to be borne. Efficiency paranoia, confusing 'lean' in the sense of anorexic with 'lean' in the sense of fit, is a frequently encountered pathological guidance syndrome, involving 'rationalization' without rationality.

Criteria should be quantified whenever possible, a point often neglected in regard to criteria of effectiveness. Surveys confirm, for example, that customer orientation, i.e., concentration on product innovation, quality and service, ranks first among the business objectives pursued by managers. This makes it all the more extraordinary that most information systems include virtually no variables for measuring effectiveness. When measurements are not made, essential parameters of the commercial success of business units cannot be selectively improved or actions quantified in terms of the planned success. Vague concepts—such as a flexible pricing policy, a range of specialities, good service, cost-conscious production, committed research—favour the *status quo* and supply patterns of immunization against innovation. Suggestions for improvement are easily seen as personal criticism; management capacity becomes tied up in controversy. Insofar, then, as the extent to which objectives are achieved is to be monitored from outside to inside—meaning, for example, oriented towards the customer and measured against the competition—the customary efficiency criteria have to be supplemented by measures and yardsticks for the development of effectiveness. This calls for organizational learning processes, to which a few simple rules apply, including this one. If you are looking for quick ways to change an organization's behaviour, change the measurement system; what gets measured, gets done. Moreover, as Ackoff (1986, p. 37) points out, 'It's better to use imprecise measures of what is wanted than precise measures of what is not'.

Control variables should not, however, consist of quantifiable factors alone. Soft factors, e.g. trust, loyalty, identification with tasks and with the enterprise, entrepreneurial courage, team spirit, creativeness, sense of responsibility, intrinsic motivation, are often the ones that move the measurable parameters.

Effectiveness and efficiency measurements need to reflect the perceptions of stakeholders and be benchmarked against leading enterprises. The corporate management must have an eye to an appropriate 'fit' between objectives and resource requirements. The frequent remark 'earn some money before you develop a strategy' contradicts this rule and prevents the 'stretch' that is necessary to achieve taxing objectives with emotional energy and analytical understanding. Where possible, success factors should be divided into the components that can be influenced and those that cannot. Otherwise, an element of external arbitrariness enters into agreements made. For example, the strategic position of an operating sector—as a result of management's planning of the control function—can hardly be isolated from the current cyclical economic situation in the industry. Nor can a fair distinction easily be made between qualified and less qualified management.

While it is apparent that there are a number of critical factors beyond an enterprise's control, it is also clear that its performance must be sensitive to the requirements, needs and concerns not only of its customers, but also of its suppliers, employees, owners, local community and the more 'distant' environment. Today it is becoming increasingly clear that such sensitivity is not only an ethical imperative but also the source of better economic performance. Using clean technologies is cheaper than cleaning up the environment; training and developing people creates more value for the company than ever more sophisticated information systems to control them; making suppliers' contracts more stable and responsive to their interests is likely to increase their commitment to the company, and so forth.

> P 1. Excellent organizational performance requires delivering high value to all stakeholders.

Now to enhance an organization's performance it is necessary to create enabling structures; that is, structures that produce win-win relationships. This is a point of particular significance for those working in the organization. The recursive structure is one that does not assume monolithic objectives and goals. On the contrary, effective performance requires the creative, unpredictable and enhancing contribution of all autonomous teams and individuals. They have to add new insights and perspectives to the vision and objectives of those with an overview of the organization's activities. In this process, the organization's products and services are created by all these people, not only by those with an overview. As implied above, the problem is to create structures with the channel capacity to support the alignment of objectives, interests and purposes. This theme was developed and illustrated in Part Two, in particular in Chapters 4 and 5.

> P 4. Effective organization is required to channel a variety of viewpoints into joint action. This is achieved through the alignment of goals and intent.

The same theme was developed further in Part Three, where we discussed the management processes that lead to the discovery of new value potentials. These are the drivers for performance. The power of the recursive organization as a construct is in its capacity not only to make apparent the need for distributed processes but, most significantly, in its capacity to say something about how to produce this distribution. Its value is as a design heuristic. In Chapter 8 we made this fundamental connection between strategy and structure.

Systemic thinking sees management as a recursively interlinked network of control processes. The control of individual processes and process-chains was described in Chapter 9. We emphasized the value added by each level of management through primary processes. The complexity relevant to each management level was related to the critical success factors at that level.

Chapters 8, 9 and 10 discussed the managerial tasks necessary to interlink value management within and between levels of recursion. To maximize the value of the company, each primary activity has to fulfil generic tasks; these are, for example, portfolio management and core competencies management at the company level and, at the level of divisions and business units, technology management and market segment management. Each primary activity has to produce a generic contribution to the value of the company, which has to be compared to the costs it generates. Only if there is a positive differential does the activity justify its existence.

To know that each activity is justified, we need to develop an adequate information system for management. Such a system should be a facsimile of the organization structure. It should succeed in combining the information used for the control of individual primary processes into a system for the whole organization; that is the concept that underlies CyberSyn/Cyberfilter—the system that we offered as a methodology for relating strategy, structure and information systems.

> P 2. Organizations must develop vision and a strategic management in order to create value potentials. This applies to all structural levels.
>
> P 7. Organizations have to discover, articulate and realize potentials all the time and at all structural levels.

## LEARNING

Another theme of this book has been that of individual and organizational learning.

We are constantly dealing with a wide range of threatening and challenging situations. At the same time, we are inventing the organizations we work for and, also, inventing in these organizations.

We do all this through interactions. As we interact, we create structures for ourselves to learn. The quality of our interactions depends partly on our interactive abilities and partly on the structural conditions within which they take place. It is not possible to have effective structures and processes if the quality of our interactions is poor. The content of our conversations—the skills we have in creating positive emotions, motivating others, getting valid information from them, getting their commitment and so forth—creates the structures and processes we experience.

As we learn these skills we become more effective operators. We develop the ability to modify structures and processes as operational conditions change. This is the hallmark of learning. We learn as we solve problems. The organization learns as we share our mental models and develop common maps to support organizational action. We have argued the need to develop effective interactions and to operate within enabling structures in order for this learning to take place.

Learning requires the minimization of organizational defence routines and the removal of learning obstacles. These learning problems were discussed in Chapters 6 and 7. The OADI-SMM model is an effective heuristic to understand how to bring about a synergetic interlinking of individual and shared mental models. By helping to identify possible learning barriers this model provides a blueprint for avoiding learning pathologies.

The cybernetic methodology was offered as a means by which to solve problems in an organizational context. It shows how to support learning processes by focusing simultaneously on specific conversations and on the organizational processes that support them. The aim of this methodology is to create conditions for effective problem solving; that is, structural conditions for learning. Learning loops cannot be effective without an underlying effective cybernetic loop, and vice versa. Both loops need to be considered at the same time.

> P 8. The capacity for learning must be created structurally and fostered culturally.
> R 5. Relationships with stakeholders require effective communications, creating over-lapping domains of interest and common responsibility.

Our background and history, the groups we have worked with, the training we have received and so forth all influence the way we experience our interactions and the ways in which we relate to the organizational context of our work. We describe this as our *Weltanschauung* or worldview. Unless we develop as individuals the capacity to become aware of such 'blinkers', we will have learning difficulties. In Chapter 4 we discussed the challenge of being observers of our own action. Such observational capabilities are necessary to make possible recursive structures. The stronger are our mental constraints, the less adequate is likely to be our learning and the smaller the chance that we will truly realize innovative autonomous units within autonomous units. It is in this dynamics that we see the interplay between culture, learning and structure.

Individual learning traits have an influence on the organization's ability to reconfigure itself, i.e., on its ability to reassess its history as a result of seeing new possibilities and thereafter to define a new identity for itself. As discussed in Chapter 8, this kind of organizational learning is fundamental to the achievement of viability beyond survival; that is, to the achievement of organizational development. Such a reconfiguring capacity will depend on the quality of the learning processes that produce shared organizational maps.

> I 4. Proper understanding of an organization requires reflection by unorthodox, open minds and team learning.
> I 3. Individuals and teams need to develop the capacity to learn new modes of operation and thinking, as well as to learn to do better what they already do.
> P 6. Organizations need to develop the capacity to learn new modes of operation; that is, they need to learn to reconfigure themselves.

The ability to orchestrate these learning processes is critical in today's organization. Such processes are the platform for 'development' and therefore are responsible for the pre-controls of effective organizational performance. In today's organization the crucial skills for a manager are communicational and conceptual.

> I 6. Effective leadership is increasingly based on conceptual and interpersonal rather than technical competencies.

## TRANSFORMATION

Organizational transformation encompasses all the issues we have discussed; it is concerned with structure, processes, communications, environment, performance and learning. It begins with individual transformation.

This book has offered a range of concepts that challenge established practices. It is true that over the past few years, we have seen the emergence of a number of new managerial and organizational approaches that have been whole-heartedly espoused by people in organizations: flat structures, participative management, total quality management, process orientation—all are accepted terms in organizations today. The problem is not lack of new insights but lack of the means to produce the related organizational change. It is only by learning how to produce this change that a genuine organizational transformation will take place.

We judge that the impact of these new ideas has been mostly at the level of conceptual, rather than operational learning. For the latter, we still seem to lack a good grasp of complexity—meaning the complexity of detail that is associated with autonomy and recursive structures, rather than the dynamic complexity associated with a better intellectual understanding of cause-and-effect relationships. We can improve our models of these relationships as much as we like; if they are not expressed or embodied in our interactions, i.e., in our capacity to produce change, they will remain artificial models, unconnected to our practice.

Recognizing the difference between the distinctions we make about our moment-to-moment interactions and the distinctions we make about others' actions, as observers, is of crucial importance. Our complexity is nothing more than the distinctions we are able to make when in action. That is our reality. On the other hand, the distinctions we ascribe to others, (including ourselves while in self-reflection) say more about us as observers, than about the observed. The observer mode is, however, crucial to effective communications.

What must be realized is that the distinctions, i.e., the complexity of detail, that we make through our actions are orders of magnitude larger than the distinctions we make as observers. It is the first complexity, that emerging from our moment-to-moment actions, that we need to take into account for effective participation in change processes. In this book we have shown, in Chapters 4 and 5, how this individual complexity relates to the complexity of the organization; indeed, our actions depend on a wider operational domain, that of the organizations in which our actions are embedded.

Organizations are constituted as closed networks of people's interactions. The implication of the term 'closure', as used here, is that organizations are structure-determined. Change in them is the outcome of a closed network of multiple adjustments taking place among the participants as they adjust to each other's position in response to external perturbations. Change is determined by the internal coherence of the structure and not by information about external events. Change may be triggered by information; it is not determined by it. This was the point we made earlier when we made the distinction between environment and medium.

It becomes clear, therefore, that the concept of information belongs to the domain of observation, i.e. the domain in which we talk about interactions, and not to our operational domain. The concept of information is not, therefore, enough to enable us to understand the complexity of change processes; what organizations receive from their environment are perturbations that are absorbed in different ways by different structures. To a large degree it is not the content of a message that determines the response but the structure that absorbs the message; that is, it is the structural capacity of the organization. We are constantly receiving information, i.e., messages, on matters for which we have no structure to be 'informed'. However valuable these messages might have been for the organization's viability, they are not 'heard' i.e. known. They are simply dissipated in the complexity of the organization. The same message received by a different structure would have produced a very different response.

S 6. Creativity must be leveraged by structures that support individual and organizational transformation.

Individual transformation takes place as we anchor our actions in new distinctions. In this sense we think that this book provides the platform for individual transformation.

I 2. Individuals and teams need to develop the ability to realize their potentials.

Organizational transformation, however, depends on organizational learning; that is, on the sharing of newly-made distinctions. But such learning is itself structure-determined. In hierarchical, coercive structures the anchoring of distinctions is related to the power of the people involved in sharing interactions. In the extreme, those wielding greater power have more flexibility to invent the organization than those in powerless positions. The latter operate in situations defined for them—a fact that propels them into a fixed, 'objective' world that they have no option but to construe as implied by the distinctions made by those in power. In other words, while those in positions of power are actively inventing their world, those in power-less positions operate in a predefined world.

This explains, to some degree, the difficulties we encounter in producing genuine organizational transformation. Managers, in spite of espousing participative theories of organization and in spite of their good intentions, behave and relate to the rest in ways which reinforce the enacting of their own distinctions. Even the most genuine participative distinctions are often not the outcome of people's autonomy; they are defined from above. It is this relationship that people experience, i.e., its paternalistic nature; they soon forget the nice words coming with it.

S 4. Organizations need to provide the conditions for people to develop themselves, i.e. to find and create new possibilities.

Power is to a large degree enacted by the dominant distinctions; that is, by those distinctions that are considered valid and legitimate in a given context. In other words, we are saying that while our individual complexity is defined by our distinctions, organizational complexity is defined by shared distinctions. In this context, empowerment makes sense only when people, whatever their role or wherever they operate in the organization, have the chance to invent and ground their distinctions in organizational work. If the organization structure only allows those at the corporate level to enact organizational distinctions—by, for instance, unfairly restricting workers' autonomy—then, clearly, not only does the organization as a whole lose (by creating conditions for less organizational complexity) but individuals are likely to feel less committed to the organization. Their own purposes are less likely to be aligned with those of corporate managers. Empowerment, i.e., the capacity to enact distinctions, requires from us a better understanding of the organization structures that provide the context for our action.

R 8. Organizations need to be effective in implementing change. Conflict and stress have to be used constructively.

It is natural and necessary—if everyone is to participate in the organization's invention—to develop structures that create the conditions for autonomy and effective participation. The viable system model is a tool for this purpose.

R 7. Organizations need to develop a capacity for cultural transformation towards more open and participative structures.

The VSM is a useful and powerful model with which to study communication and control processes particularly for situations where it makes no sense to assume people's shared agreement about the organization's objectives. Indeed it is necessary to accept the fundamental disagreements inherent to the variety of viewpoints in an organization, or the often coercive nature of organizational relationships; we hope that our views about complexity have helped the readers to see the relevance of the VSM in conflicting and coercive situations.

Complexity, conflict and coercion are not independent categories. Indeed, to suggest that a situation can be complex and void of conflict and coercion is to suggest that situational complexity is independent of the people involved in the situation; it would give to complexity an objective connotation. It would imply reducing the situation to its technical diversity, thereby transforming the organization into a highly complex technical artefact. In this book we have, on the contrary, emphasized human diversity.

I 6. Effective leadership is increasingly based on conceptual and interpersonal rather than technical competences.

Complexity has been perhaps the core concept of this book. We have stressed, in particular, the need to pay attention to *detail* complexity, i.e., the complexity that consists in a situation having many variables. Detail complexity, however, entails dynamic complexity, i.e., as Espejo (1994) points out, it tends to bring about a situation in which cause and effect are subtle and the effects over time of interventions are not obvious. Thus it is necessary to pay attention also to dynamic complexity. We made it clear in Part Two that organizations, in order to perform well, must have the capacity to absorb every single disturbance that may take their behaviour out of their target set.

There is no way around devising increasingly complex solutions to increasingly complex problems. We have pointed out in this book that it is wrong to infer from this that the problem solver's inherent complexity has to be as large as that of the situation being controlled! Good systemic thinking requires an understanding of self-organizing and self-regulating principles and the ability to use them to one's advantage.

If our epistemology were one in which we made distinctions without paying attention to time and connectivity, i.e., without closing loops, we would experience all kinds of situational breakdowns, being blind to many connections that produce unexpected behaviours. This, however, is not the case. The general proposition stands: experiencing breaks for which we do not have response capacity will in all cases produce instability in our interactions and hinder our performance. Our response capacity may of course be impaired by a poor understanding of the dynamic nature of the world, as it may be impaired by other conceptual shortcomings. If as a result of this, we emphasize the understanding of the organization's connectivity with its environment at the expense of creating effective structures capable of producing an ecological fit for the organization in its medium, the chances are that we will overlook the real issues of organizational transformation.

# Bibliography

Ackoff, R. L. (1978). *The Art of Problem Solving. Accompanied by Ackoff's Fables.* New York: Wiley.

Ackoff, R. L. (1981). *Creating the Corporate Future.* New York: Wiley.

Ackoff, R. L. (1986). *Management in Small Doses.* New York: Wiley.

Ackoff, R. L. (1992). Some notes on a working visit to South Africa. *Systems Practice*, Vol. 5.

Ackoff, R. L. (1994). *The Democratic Corporation.* New York and Oxford: Oxford University Press.

Adams, D. (1985). *The Hitchhikers Guide to the Galaxy.* London: BBC Press.

Albert, H. (1991). *Traktat über kritische Vernunft.* Tübingen: J.C.B. Mohr.

Argyris, C. and Schön, D. A. (1978). *Organizational Learning: A Theory of Action Perspective.* Reading, MA: Addison-Wesley.

Argyris, C. (1990). *Overcoming Organizational Defenses. Facilitating Organizational Learning.* Boston: Allyn and Bacon.

Argyris, C. (1993). *On Organizational Learning.* Cambridge, MA: Blackwell.

Argyris, C. (1994). Good communication that blocks learning. *Harvard Business Review*, July–August, p. 80.

Ashby, W. R. (1964). *An Introduction to Cybernetics.* London: Methuen.

Bateson, G. (1972). *Steps Towards an Ecology of Mind.* London: Intertex Books.

Beer, S. (1966). *Decision and Control.* Chichester: Wiley.

Beer, S. (1975). *Platform for Change.* Chichester: Wiley.

Beer, S. (1979). *The Heart of Enterprise.* Chichester: Wiley.

Beer, S. (1981). *Brain of the Firm.* (2nd ed.) Chichester: Wiley.

Beer, S. (1985). *Diagnosing the System for Organisations.* Chichester: Wiley.

Beer, S. (1994). *Beyond Dispute: The Invention of Team Syntegrity.* Chichester: Wiley.

Berger, S., Dertouzoss, M. L., Lester, R. K., Solow, R. M. and Thurow, L. C. (1989). Toward a New Industrial America. *Scientific American*, Vol. 260, June, pp. 21–29.

Bleicher, K. (1992). *Das Konzept. Integriertes Management, St. Galler Management-Konzept,* (2nd ed.) Frankfurt and New York: Campus Verlag.

Bolman, L. G. and Deal, T. E. (1991). *Modern Approaches to Understanding and Managing Organizations,* (2nd ed.) San Francisco, London: Jossey-Bass.

Bowersox, D. J., *et al.* (1992). *Logistical Excellence.* Burlington, MA: Digital Press.

Boynton, A. C. (1993). Achieving dynamic stability through information technology. *California Management Review*, Vol. 35 and 2, Winter, pp. 58–77.

Boynton, A. C. and Victor, B. (1991). Beyond flexibility: the dynamically stable organization. *California Management Review*, Vol. 34 and 1, Fall, pp. 53–66.

Buaron (1981). New game strategies. *The McKinsey Quarterly*, Spring pp. 24–40.

Burke, T. (1989). Industry and environment: towards a common agenda. In: *European Integration and Global Competitiveness*, 19. Internationales Managementgespräch an der Hochschule St. Gallen.

Buzzell, R. D. and Gale, B. T. (1987). *The PIMS Principles.* New York, London: Free Press, Collier.

Cameron, K. S., and Whetton, D. A. (eds) (1983). *Organizational Effectiveness: A Comparison of Multiple Models.* New York: Academic Press.

Checkland, P. (1981). *Systems Thinking, Systems Practice*. Chichester: Wiley.

Checkland, P. and Scholes, J. (1990). *Soft Systems Methodology in Action*. Chichester: Wiley.

Ciba-Geigy (1991). *Our Vision*. Basel: Ciba-Geigy Corporation.

Clarkson, M. B. E. (1995). A stakeholder framework for analyzing and evaluating corporate social performance. *Academy of Management Review*, Vol. 20, No. 1, pp. 92–117

Clifford, D. K. and Cavanagh, R. E. (1985). *The Winning Performance. How America's High-Growth Midsize Companies Succeed*. New York: Bantam Books.

Collins, J. C. and Porras, J. I. (1994). *Built to Last. Successful Habits of Visionary Companies*. New York: Harper & Row.

Conant, R. C. and Ashby, W. R. (1970). Every good regulator of a system must be a model of that system. *International Journal of System Science*. Vol. 1, No. 2, pp. 89–97.

Copeland, T. E., Koller, T. and Murrin, J. (1994). *Valuation: Measuring and Managing the Value of Companies*, (2nd ed.) New York: Wiley.

Crosby, P. B. (1984). *Quality Without Tears*. New York: McGraw-Hill.

Crosby, P. B. (1992). *Completeness: Quality For The 21st Century*. New York: Dutton.

Csikszentmihalyi, M. (1992). *FLOW. Das Geheimnis des Glücks*. Stuttgart: Klett-Cotta.

Csikszentmihalyi, M. (1993). *Beyond Boredom and Anxiety—The Experience of Play in Work and Games*. San Francisco: Jossey-Bass.

Davidow, W. H. and Malone, M. S. (1992). *The Virtual Corporation*. New York: Burlingame Books.

Davies, C., Demb, A. and Espejo, R. (1979). *Organization for Program Management*. Chichester: Wiley.

Deal, T. E. and Kennedy, A. A. (1982). *Corporate Cultures. The Rites and Rituals of Corporate Life*. Reading, MA: Addison-Wesley.

Deming, W. E. (1986). *Out of The Crisis: Quality, Productivity and Competitive Position*. Cambridge: Cambridge University Press.

Deutsch, C. (1993). Bitter nötig. *Wirtschaftswoche*, No. 46, November, pp. 65–69.

Donaldson, T. and Preston, L. E. (1995). The stakeholder theory of the corporation: concepts, evidence, and implications. *Academy of Management Review*, Vol. 20, No. 1, pp. 65–91.

Drucker, P. F. (1980). *Managing in Turbulent Times*. London: Heinemann.

Drucker, P. F. (1992). *Managing for the Future: The 1990s and beyond*. New York: Dutton.

Drucker, P. F. (1993). The post-capitalist executive: an interview with Peter F. Drucker (interviewer: T. George Harris). *Harvard Business Review*, May–June, pp. 115–122.

Drucker, P. F. (1994). The theory of the business. *Harvard Business Review*, Sept–Oct, pp. 95f.

Eden, C. (1989). Managing the environment as a means to managing complexity. In: *Rational Analysis in a Problematic World*, ed. J. Rosehead, Chichester: Wiley.

Espejo, R. (1982). *Management and Information: The Complementarity Control-Autonomy*. The University of Aston Management Centre, Working Paper Series No. 238, June.

Espejo, R. (1987). From machines to people and organizations: a cybernetic insight of management. In: *New Directions in Management Science* (M. Jackson and P. Keys, eds). Aldershot: Gower.

Espejo, R. (1989a). The viable system model revisited. In: *The Viable System Model: Interpretations and Applications of Stafford Beer's VSM* (R. Espejo and R. Harnden, eds). Chichester: Wiley.

Espejo, R. (1989b). A method to study organizations. In: *The Viable System Model: Interpretations and Applications of Stafford Beer's VSM* (R. Espejo and R. Harnden, eds). Chichester: Wiley.

Espejo, R. (1990). Complexity and change. *Systems Practice*, Vol. 3, No. 3.

Espejo, R. (1993a). Giving requisite variety to strategy and information systems. In: *Systems Science: Addressing Global Issues*, Proceedings of UK Systems Society Annual Meeting, Paisley, July 1993. (F. Stowell, D. West and J. Howell, eds) New York: Plenum.

Espejo, R. (1993b). Management of complexity in problem solving. In: *Organizational Fitness. Corporate Effectiveness Through Management Cybernetics* (R. Espejo and M. Schwaninger, eds). Frankfurt and New York: Campus Verlag.

Espejo, R. (1993c). Strategy, structure and information management. *Journal of Information Systems*, No. 3, pp. 17–31.

Espejo, R. (1994). What is systems thinking? *System Dynamics Review*, Vol. 10, Nos. 2–3 (Summer–Fall), pp. 199–212.

Espejo, R. and Garcia, O. (1984). A tool for distributed planning. Proceedings—*Orwellian Symposium and International Conference on Systems Research, Information and Cybernetics.* Baden Baden.

Espejo, R. and Harnden, R., eds (1989). *The Viable System Model. Interpretations and Applications of Stafford Beer's VSM.* Chichester: Wiley.

Espejo, R. and Schwaninger, M., eds (1993). *Organizational Fitness. Corporate Effectiveness Through Management Cybernetics.* Frankfurt and New York: Campus Verlag.

Espejo, R. and Watt, J. (1979). Management information systems: a system for design. *Journal of Cybernetics.* Vol. 9, No. 3.

Espejo, R. and Watt, J. (1988). Information management, organization and managerial effectiveness. *Journal of the Operational Research Society,* Vol. 39, No. 1, pp. 7–14.

Etzioni, A. (1968). *The Active Society: A Theory of Societal and Political Processes.* London, New York: Collier, MacMillan.

Fitzgerald, G. (1992). *Executive Information Systems and Their Development: A Research Study.* Oxford Institute of Information Management, Templeton College, Oxford. Unpublished paper.

Flood, R. L. (1993). What quality management really lacks. In: *Organizational Fitness. Corporate Effectiveness Through Management Cybernetics* (R. Espejo and M. Schwaninger, eds). Frankfurt and New York: Campus Verlag.

Flores, F. (1982). *Management and Communication in the Office of the Future.* Doctoral Thesis, Stanford University, California.

Foerster, H. v. (1977). The curious behaviour of complex systems: lessons from biology. In: *Futures Research, New Directions* (H. A. Linstone and W.H. C. Simmonds, eds). Reading, MA: Addison-Wesley.

Foerster, H.v. (1984). *Observing Systems,* 2nd edition. Seaside, CA: Intersystems Publications.

Forrester, T. W. (1968). *Principles of Systems* (2nd ed.), Portland, OR: Productivity Press.

Gälweiler, A. (1979). Die strategische Führung der Unternehmung. In: Haberland, G., Hrsg. *Der Kaufmännische Geschäftsführer,* Kap. 3.1, München: Moderne Industrie.

Gälweiler, A. (1990). *Strategische Unternehmensführung,* zusammengestellt, bearbeitet and ergänzt von M. Schwaninger, 2nd edition, Frankfurt, New York: Campus Verlag.

Giddens, A. (1984). *The Constitution of Society.* Cambridge: Polity Press.

Gomez, P. (1993). *Werte-Management* (Value management). Düsseldorf: Econ-Verlag.

Goodman, P. S., Pennings, J. M. and Associates (1977). *New Perspectives on Organizational Effectiveness.* San Francisco: Jossey-Bass.

Hagedorn, J. and Schakenrad, J. (1994). The effect of strategic technology alliances on company performance. *Strategic Management Journal,* Vol. 15, pp. 291–309.

Hamel, G. and Aimé, H., eds (1994). *Competence-based Competition.* New York: Wiley.

Hamel, G. and Prahalad, C. K. (1994). *Competing For The Future.* Boston, MA: Harvard Business School Press.

Hammer, M. and Champy, J. (1993). *Reengineering the Corporation.* London: Brealey.

Hanna, D. (1988). *Designing Organizations for High Performance.* Reading, MA: Addison-Wesley.

Hansen, G. S. and Wernerfelt, B. (1989). Determination of firm performance: the relative importance of economic and organizational factors. *Strategic Management Journal,* Vol. 10, pp. 399–411.

Harrison, P. J. and Stevens, C. F. (1971). A Bayesian approach to short-term forecasting. *Operational Res. Qu.,* Vol. 22, p. 4.

Hedlund, G. (1993). Assumptions of hierarchy and heterarchy, with applications to management in the multinational corporation. In: *Organization Theory and the Multinational Corporation,* (S. Ghoshal and E. Westney, eds). London: Macmillan.

Herzberg, F. (1987). One more time: how do you motivate employees? *Harvard Business Review,* September–October, pp. 109–120.

ISO (International Standards Organization) (1988). *Norm 8402.* Zürich: SNV (Schweizerische Normen Vereinigung).

Jackson, M. C. (1989). Evaluating the managerial significance of the VSM. In: *The Viable System Model. Interpretations and Applications of Stafford Beer's VSM.* (R. Espejo and R. Harnden, eds). Chichester: Wiley.

Jantsch, E. and Waddington, C. H., eds (1976). *Evolution and Consciousness: Human Systems in Transition*. Reading, MA: Addison-Wesley.

Jaques, E. (1990). In praise of hierarchy. *Harvard Business Review*, January–February, pp. 127–133.

Jarillo, J. C. (1988). On strategic networks. *Strategic Management Journal*, Vol. 9, pp. 831–81.

Juran, J. M. (1989). *Juran on Leadership for Quality. An Executive Handbook*. New York: Free Press.

Keen, P. (1991). *Shaping the Future*. Cambridge, MA: Harvard Business School Press.

Kelly, K. (1994). *Out of Control: The New Biology of Machines*. London: Fourth Estate Ltd.

Kim, D. (1993). The link between individual and organizational learning. *Sloan Management Review*, Fall, pp. 37–50.

Kleindorfer, P. R. and Schoemaker, P. J. H. (1993). *Decision Sciences: An Integrative Perspective*. Cambridge: Cambridge University Press.

Kofman, F. (1992). Lecture Slides, Cambridge Massachusetts: MIT Sloan School of Management. Quoted in D. Kim's paper. *Sloan Management Review*, Fall, p. 39.

Kotler, P. (1994). *Marketing Management: Analysis, Planning, Implementation, and Control* (8th ed.). Englewood Cliffs: Prentice-Hall.

Kotter, J. and Heskett, J. (1992). *Corporate Culture and Performance*. New York: Free Press.

Krieg, W. (1985). Management- und Unternehmungsentwicklung—Bausteine eines integrierten Ansatzes. In: *Integriertes Management* (G. J. B. Probst and H. Siegwart, eds). Bern, Stuttgart: Haupt.

Krippendorff, K. (1986). *A Dictionary of Cybernetics*. Philadelphia, PA: University of Pennsylvania.

Lehmann, S. (1994). *Neue Wege in der Bewertung börsennotierter Aktiengesellschaften* (New ways of evaluating the public limited companies listed on the Stock Exchange). Darmstadt: Deutscher Universitätsverlag.

Lewis, T. G. (1994). *Steigerung des Unternehmenswertes* (Total Value Management). Landsberg/Lech: Verlag Moderne Industrie.

Linstone, H. A. and Simmonds, W. H. C., eds (1977). *Futures Research. New Directions*. Reading, MA: Addison-Wesley.

Luhmann, N. (1985). *A Sociology Theory of Law*. London: Routledge & Kegan Paul.

Malik, F. (1987). Messbare Erfolgspotentiale. *GDI (Gottlieb Duttweiler Institut)—Impuls*, Vol. 3, pp. 53–60.

March, J. G. and Olson, J. P. (1975). The uncertainty of the past; organizational ambiguous learning. *European Journal of Political Research*, Vol. 3, pp. 147–171.

Markides, C. C. (1995). Diversification, restructuring and economic performance. *Strategic Management Journal*, Vol. 16, pp. 101–118.

Maslow, A. N. (1970) *Motivation and Personality*, (2nd ed.). New York: Harper & Row.

Maturana, H. (1987). Everything is said by an observer. In *Gaia: A Way of Knowing* (W. Thompson, ed.). California: Lindisfarne Press.

Maturana, H. and Varela, F. (1980). *Autopoiesis and Cognition: The Realization of the Living*. Boston: Reidel.

Maturana, H. and Varela, F. (1987). *The Tree of Knowledge: The Biological Roots of Human Understanding*. Boston: New Library Science.

Metzger, R. and Gründler, H.-C. (1994). *Zurück auf Spitzenniveau* (Back to the top). Frankfurt: Campus Verlag.

Miles, R. H. (1980). *Macro Organizational Behaviour*. Santa Monica, CA: Goodyear.

Mintzberg, H. (1976). Planning on the left and managing on the right. *Harvard Business Review*, July–Aug, pp. 49–58.

Mintzberg, H. (1994). *The Rise and Fall of Strategic Planning: Reconceiving Roles for Planning Plans and Planners*. New York: Free Press.

Morecroft, J. D. W. and Sterman, J. D. eds (1994). *Modeling for Learning Organizations*. Portland OR: Productivity Press.

Morgan, G. (1986). *Images of Organization*. Beverly Hills: SAGE.

Morgan, G. (1993). *Imaginization: the Art of Creative Management*. Newbury Park: SAGE.

Nanus, B. (1992). *Visionary Leadership: Creating a Compelling Sense of Direction for Your Organization*. San Francisco: Jossey-Bass.

Nonka, I. and Takeuchi, H. (1995). *The Knowledge-Creating Company*. New York: Oxford University Press..

Otte, R. (1994). Arbeit, Eigentum und Wissen (Work, property and knowledge). *Blick durch die Wirtschaft*. November 10.

Peters, T. J. and Waterman, R. H. (1982). *In Search of Excellence*. New York: Harper & Row.

Peters, T. J. (1988). *Thriving on Chaos: Handbook for a Managerial Revolution*. New York: Random House.

Peters, T. J. (1992) *Liberation Management: Necessary Disorganization for the Nanosecond Nineties*. London: Macmillan.

Pine, J. B. (1993). *Mass Customization: The New Frontier in Business Competition*. Boston, MA: Harvard Business School Press.

Porter, M. E. (1980). *Competitive Strategy: Techniques for Analyzing Industries and Competitors*. New York: Free Press.

Porter, M. E. (1985). *Competitive Advantage*. New York: Free Press.

Porter, M. E. (1987). From competitive advantage to corporate strategy. *Harvard Business Review*. May–June, pp. 43–59.

Porter, M. E. (1991). Towards a dynamic theory of strategy. *Strategic Management Journal*, Special issue, Vol. 12, Winter, pp. 95–117.

Prahalad, C. K. and Hamel, G. (1990). The core competence of the corporation. *Harvard Business Review*, May–June, pp. 79–91.

Prigogine, J. (1989). The philosophy of instability. *Futures*, Vol. 21, No. 4, pp. 396–400.

Probst, G. J. B. and Siegwart, H., eds (1985). *Integriertes Management*. Bern, Stuttgart: Haupt.

Pümpin, C. (1989). *Das Dynamik-Prinzip*, Düsseldorf: Econ.

Pümpin, C. (1991). *Corporate Dynamism*. Aldershot: Gower.

Quinn, J. B. (1980). *Strategies for Change. Logical Incrementalism*. Homewood, IL: Irwin.

Quinn, J. B. (1992). *Intelligent Enterprise*. New York: Free Press.

Ramanujam, V., Camillus, J. C. and Ventrakatraman, N. (1986). Trends in strategic planning. In: *Strategic Management Handbook* (W. R. King and D. I. Cleland, eds). New York: Van Nostrand Reinhold, pp. 611–628.

Rappaport, A. (1986). *Creating Shareholder Value: The New Standard for Business Performance*. New York: Free Press.

Richardson, E. and Pugh, A. (1981). *Introduction to System Dynamics Modelling with DYNAMO*, Portland, OR: Productivity Press.

Roberts, E. (1978). *Managerial Applications of System Dynamics*. Cambridge, MA: MIT Press.

Rockart, J. F. (1979). Chief executives define their own data needs. *Harvard Business Review*, Vol. 57, No. 2, pp. 81–93.

Ruskin, J. (1865, first publication). *Sesame and Lilies*, 1907 edition. London: George Allen.

Sattelberger, T. (1991). *Die lernende Organisation*. Wiesbaden: Gabler.

Savage, C. (1990). *Fifth Generation Management*. Burlington, MA: Digital Press.

Schein, E. H. (1985). *Organizational Culture and Leadership*. San Francisco: Jossey Bass.

Schoemaker, P. J. H. (1992). How to link strategic vision to core capabilities. *Sloan Management Review*, Fall, pp. 67–81.

Schuhmann, W. (1990). Strategy for information systems in the film division of Hoechst AG. *Systems Practice*, Vol. 3, No. 3.

Schuhmann, W. (1991). *Informationsmanagement*. Frankfurt and New York: Campus Verlag.

Schwaninger, M. (1984). Zur Architektur integraler Planungssysteme. *Harvard Manager*. I. Quartal., pp. 102–110.

Schwaninger, M. (1988). *Anwendung der integralen Unternehmungsentwicklung*. Bern, Stuttgart: Haupt.

Schwaninger, M. (1989). *Integrale Unternehmungsplanung*. Frankfurt and New York: Campus Verlag.

Schwaninger, M. (1990a). Embodiments of organizational fitness. *Systems Practice*, Vol. 3, No. 3.

Schwaninger, M. (1990b). Umweltverantwortung: Manager sind herausgefordert. *Management Zeitschrift IO*, 59, Jg., 1, pp. 89–94.

Schwaninger, M. (1993). A concept of organizational fitness. In: *Organizational Fitness. Corporate Effectiveness Through Management Cybernetics* (R. Espejo and M. Schwaninger, eds). Frankfurt and New York: Campus Verlag.

Schwaninger, M. (1994a). *Management-Systeme*. Frankfurt, New York: Campus Verlag.

Schwaninger, M. (1994b). *Die intelligente Organisation als lebensfähige Heterarchie*. Diskussionsbeiträge des Instituts für Betriebswirtschaft an der Hochschule St. Gallen.

Scott-Morton, M. ed., (1991). *The Corporation of the Future*. New York and Oxford: Oxford University Press.

Scott-Morgan, P. (1994). *Die heimlichen Spielregeln* (Unwritten Rules of the Game). Frankfurt: Campus Verlag.

Senge, P. M. (1992). *The Fifth Discipline. The Art and Practice of the Learning Organization*. London: Century Business.

Stalk, G., Evans, P. and Shulman, L. E. (1992). Competing on capabilities: the new rules of corporate strategy. *Harvard Business Review*, March–April, pp. 57–69.

Steger, U. (1988). *Umwelt-Management*. Wiesbaden: Gabler.

Syncho Ltd. (1990). *CyberFilter Manual*. Birmingham, UK: Aston Science Park.

Thomas, L., Harri-Augstein, F. and Sheila, E. (1985). *Self-Organized Learning. Foundations of a Conversational Science for Psychology*. London: Routledge & Kegan Paul.

Tjosvold, D. (1991). *Conflict-positive Organization: Stimulate Diversity and Create Unity*. Reading, MA: Addison-Wesley.

Tjosvold, D. (1993). *Learning to Manage Conflict: Getting People to Work together Productively*. Lexington, MA: Lexington Books.

Tully, S. (1993). The modular corporation. *Fortune*, February 8, pp. 52–56.

Ulrich, H. and Krieg, W., eds (1974). *St. Galler Management-Modell*. 3rd edn. Bern: Haupt.

Ulrich, H. (1984). *Management*. Bern, Stuttgart: Haupt.

Underwood, L. (1994). *Intelligent Manufacturing*. Wokingham: Addison-Wesley.

Utterback, J. M. (1994). *Mastering the Dynamics of Innovation*. Boston, MA: Harvard Business School Press.

Vester, F. (1988). The biocybernetic approach as a basis for planning our environment. *Systems Practice*, Vol. 1, pp. 399–414.

Vickers, G. (1965). *The Art of Judgement*. London: Chapman & Hall.

Whittaker, R. (1992). *Venues for Contexture. Research Reports in Information Processing and Computer Science*; NR UMADP-RRIPCS 15.92, Sweden: University of Umea.

Wight, O. (1984). *Manufacturing Resource Planning: MRP II. Unlocking America's Productivity Potential*, 2nd edn. New York: Oliver Wight Limited Publications Inc.

Winograd, T. and Flores, F. (1986). *Understanding Computers and Cognition*. Norwood, New Jersey: Ablex Publ. Co.

Wunderer, R. and Kuhn, T. (1992). *Zukunftstrends in der Personal-arbeit: Schweizerisches Personalmanagement und Personalwesen 2000*. Bern: Haupt.

Zammuto, R. F. (1982). *Assessing Organizational Effectiveness*. Albany, NY: State University of New York Press.

Zeeuw, G. de (1986). Social change and the design of enquiry. In: *Sociocybernetic Paradoxes* (F. Geyer and J. van der Zouwen, eds). London: Sage.

# Index